Development Management

Despite significant financial investments, the rate of development and pace of poverty reduction in developing and transitional countries has not always matched expectations. Development management typically involves complex interactions between governmental and non-governmental organisations, donors and members of the public, and can be difficult to navigate.

This volume brings together a group of international contributors to explore the theoretical and empirical underpinnings of development management, and to consider the prospects and challenges associated with it in the context of both developing and transitional countries. Referring to dominant norms and values in public and developmental organisations, development management is tied up with the attitudes and perceptions of various stakeholders including: government officials, public sector managers, aid workers, donors and members of the public. Attempting to make sense of complex interactions between these actors is highly problematic and calls for new approaches, models and insights. Based on cutting-edge research, the chapters challenge much of the previous discourse on the subject and evaluate the challenges and opportunities that it presents.

Development Management offers academics, researchers and practitioners of public administration, business and management, international development and political science a comprehensive and state-of-the-art review of current research on development management in the context of developing and transitional countries.

Justice Nyigmah Bawole is a Senior Lecturer and Head of Department of the Department of Public Administration and Health Services Management, University of Ghana Business School, Ghana.

Farhad Hossain is a Senior Lecturer at the Global Development Institute (GDI), School of Environment, Education and Development at the University of Manchester, UK.

Asad K. Ghalib is Lecturer in Management Sciences at Liverpool Hope University, UK.

Christopher J. Rees is a Senior Lecturer in Organisational Change and Development at the Institute of Development Policy and Management, University of Manchester, UK.

Aminu Mamman is a Reader at the Global Development Institute at the University of Manchester, UK.

Routledge Studies in Development Economics

For a complete list of titles in this series, please visit www.routledge.com/
series/SE0266

Development Management
Theory and practice

Edited by Justice Nyigmah Bawole,
Farhad Hossain, Asad K. Ghalib,
Christopher J. Rees and
Aminu Mamman

LONDON AND NEW YORK

First published 2017 by Routledge

2 Park Square, Milton Park, Abingdon, Oxfordshire OX14 4RN
52 Vanderbilt Avenue, New York, NY 10017

Routledge is an imprint of the Taylor & Francis Group, an informa business

First issued in paperback 2019

British Library Cataloguing in Publication Data
A catalogue record for this book is available from the British Library

Library of Congress Cataloging in Publication Data
Names: Bawole, Justice Nyigmah, editor.
Title: Development management in developing and transitional countries : theory and practice / edited by Justice Nyigmah Bawole, Farhad Hossain, Asad K. Ghalib, Christopher J. Rees and Aminu Mamman.
Description: Abingdon, Oxon ; New York, NY : Routledge, 2017.
Identifiers: LCCN 2016020494| ISBN 9781138646414 (hardback) | ISBN 9781315627564 (ebook)
Subjects: LCSH: Economic development—Developing countries. | Economic assistance—Developing countries. | Social planning—Developing countries. | Developing countries—Economic policy.
Classification: LCC HC59.7 .D3748 2017 | DDC 338.9109172/4—dc23
LC record available at https://lccn.loc.gov/2016020494

ISBN: 978-1-138-64641-4 (hbk)
ISBN: 978-0-367-87735-4 (pbk)

Typeset in Bembo
by diacriTech, Chennai

Contents

Figures

Tables

Contributors

Motolani A. Agbebi is a doctoral candidate at the University of Tampere, Finland. Her PhD topic focuses on China's economic engagement in Africa. The research is examining the human capital development implications of Chinese economic engagement in Africa with a particular focus on Nigeria. Motolani holds a Master's degree in Human Resource Management (International Development) from the Institute for Development Policy and Management (IDPM), University of Manchester, United Kingdom. Motolani has carried out research and published in areas relating to human capital in Africa, strategic international human resource management in multinational corporations, management in Africa, and Chinese economic engagement in Africa. Her primary areas of research interest are: human capacity building in the SME sector, Sino-Africa relations and its implications for Africa's development, and human resource management in multinational corporations.

Patricia Agupusi is currently a postdoctoral Fellow at Watson Institute for International and Public Affairs, RI, USA. She is a political economy scholar with background in philosophy, international law and economics. Her research interests are in the intersection between state/market institutions and development. Her work has appeared in peer-reviewed journals. Her first published book of which she is a principal author is titled *Homegrown Development in Africa: Illusion or Reality?* (Routledge, 2015). She has contributed commentary on the Nigeria political landscape in the Global Post and Global Observatory. Patricia is currently conducting a major research project on the challenges of non-state terrorism in transition states with special focus on the Boko Haram insurgency in West Africa.

Albert Ahenkan graduated with a BA Honours in Social Science from the Kwame Nkrumah University of Science and Technology (KNUST), Kumasi, Ghana, in 1998. He obtained his Master's and PhD from the Vrije Universiteit Brussel (VUB), Brussels, Belgium, in 2006 and 2011, respectively. He is currently a senior lecturer in the department of Public Administration and Health Services Management of the University of Ghana Business School. His areas of expertise include sustainable development, environment and development, climate change, public policy, project management and environmental management. Dr. Ahenkan has consulted for many organizations including Ministry of Lands and Natural Resources, Ministry of Environment, Science, Technology and Innovation (MESTI), UNDP, Ministry of Finance, NEPAD, GIZ, etc. Dr. Ahenkan has published over 20 articles in international peer-reviewed journals. He has also initiated and managed a good number of development projects on sustainable development, environmental management and forest resources creation in Ghana.

La'aleh Al-Aali graduated from the American University of Sharjah, United Arab Emirates, with a BSc in Business Administration majoring in Management Information systems in 2004. Dr. Al-Aali was awarded a Chevening Scholarship for a Master's degree in Human Resource Management and graduated with Distinction in 2007 from the University of Manchester, UK. She holds ten years of solid experience in Human Resource Management and Development, in industries ranging from telecom and petroleum in the areas of HRD strategies, performance management and career planning. She recently completed a PhD at the University of Manchester in the area of Development Policy and Management with a thesis titled "Nationalization: A case from the Middle East". The research focus on was on nationalization strategies in the Gulf Cooperation Council Countries analysing nationalization issues and building a Human Resource Development framework to build capacities in the GCC region. Currently, Dr. Al-Aali is involved in consulting projects for the private sector in Bahrain and is a part-time trainer conducting HR and soft skills training of HR.

Bejan David Analoui is a Senior Lecturer in Leadership within the People, Management and Organisations department, at The Business School, University of Huddersfield, UK. Prior to this he was based at Bangor University in North Wales, where he worked as a Research Officer and facilitator for the LEAD Wales leadership development programme. Bejan holds a BA (Hons) in Philosophy from the University of Manchester, UK and an MBA and PhD (management studies) from Bangor University, UK. His research interests include leadership, knowledge management, and teaching and learning. He has published in the *Journal of Management Development* and the *International Journal of Management Education*.

Farhad Analoui holds the position of Professor of International Development and Human Resource Management at the Bradford Centre for International Development, University of Bradford, UK. He has worked in the fields of management development, public sector reform, human resource development and capacity building for SMEs for over 28 years. His main focus of investigation has been in India, Romania, Ghana, and the Middle East, where he has focussed particularly on Palestinian SMEs. Farhad worked as a consultant and researcher with the Croatian public sector where he focussed on building and developing middle and senior management leadership capacity (2008–2011). He has also published several volumes on strategic management for SMEs within the UK (Thomson, 2003) and Palestine (Ashgate, 2006), and has written a volume on strategic HRM (Thomson Learning, 2007). He is currently working on a volume examining the World Bank and UNDP Capacity Building for Development programme (Palgrave, 2016).

Justice Nyigmah Bawole is a Senior Lecturer and Head of Department of the Department of Public Administration and Health Services Management, University of Ghana Business School, Accra, Ghana. He obtained a PhD in Development Policy and Management from IDPM, University of Manchester, UK. His research interests include ethics in public administration, public sector performance management, sustainable development, particularly environment–poverty relationships, poverty reduction, NGO management and state–third sector relationships. Dr. Bawole has published widely in reputable journals such as *International Journal of Public Administration*, *Journal of Public Affairs*, *Voluntas*, *International Review of Administrative Sciences*, *Community Development*, *Public Organisation Review*, and *Environmental Management*.

Carol Brunt is an Assistant Professor in the College of Business and Economics (CoBE) at the University of Wisconsin-Whitewater, WI, USA. She holds a PhD from the University of Manchester, UK and a Master's degree from Queen's University, Kingston, ON, Canada. She is also a development practitioner. Prior to joining academia, Carol held multiple management positions within the development sector in countries throughout Sub-Saharan Africa. Carol has published in peer-reviewed journals including the International Journal of Human Resource Management and presented at management conferences including the African Academy of Management, the Academy of Management (AOM), and the International Research Society for Public Management (IRSPM). She is active in the Public and Nonprofit Division of the Academy of Management (AOM).

Derek Eldridge is an Honorary Fellow in the Institute for Development Policy and Management, University of Manchester, UK, and is currently responsible for teaching human resource development and aspects of organisational change. He has had a long connection with the University of Manchester and was formerly Capacity Building Director for the Centre on Regulation and Competition for which he instituted change projects for regulatory bodies in South Africa, Malaysia, Jordan and the Philippines. Additionally, he has designed and participated in a number of capacity building projects for public service reform including the professionalization of human resource management and development in

Malawi and Tanzania. Also, he led the Evaluation of the UK's Higher Education Links Scheme which involved the analysis of four hundred globally distributed projects and was a lead consultant for the evaluation of training for the UN Secretariat. He co-authored the book *Global Human Resource Management*.

Asad K. Ghalib has been associated with a number of institutes and organisations around the world in the academic, development, research, not-for-profit, financial and banking services industry. He is currently a Lecturer in Management Sciences at the Liverpool Hope Business School at Liverpool Hope University, UK. He previously held positions with The Royal Bank of Scotland, National Westminster Bank and HSBC in Manchester and also with Grameen Bank, UNDP's International Policy Centre for Inclusive Growth, Brasilia, United Nations World Institute for Development Economics Research, Helsinki, Centre for Policy Studies (CPS), Central European University, Budapest, Research and Expertise Centre for Survey Methodology, Barcelona and Kiel Institute for the World Economy, Germany. He has also held voluntary positions with Human Appeal International, Barnardo's children's charity and Oxfam. Asad has researched and written extensively on areas relating to international development encompassing topics such as corporate social responsibility, social business enterprises, access to financial services, micro-leasing and poverty alleviation, knowledge management for development, international management and social and economic assessment of microfinance programmes. His expertise lies in various models and techniques related to household index-based poverty ranking and gauging the socio-economic impact of microfinance and allied social protection models. He earned a Doctorate in Development Policy and Management from the Institute for Development Policy and Management (IDPM), School of Environment, Education and Development, University of Manchester, UK. He was elected to the Fellowship of the Royal Society of Arts (FRSA) for his services and commitment towards the field of international development. He holds a Fellowship of the Higher Education Academy (FHEA) and is a member of the European Survey Research Association (ESRA), Human Development and Capability Association (HDCA), and the Development Studies Association (DSA).

Farhad Hossain is a Senior Lecturer at the Global Development Institute (GDI), School of Environment, Education and Development at the University of Manchester, UK, where he directs the MSc Programme in Human Resource Management (International Development). He has carried out research in a number of countries in Africa, Asia, Europe and North America. From 2009 to 2012 he worked as Executive Editor of the *International Journal of Public Administration*. His current research interests include public policy and management, development administration, local governance and decentralization, organizational behaviour, and institutional and policy aspects of development NGOs and microfinance institutions (MFIs).

Mohammed Ibrahim teaches Public Administration and Academic Writing at the School of Continuing and Distance Education, University of Ghana. He has also held several other positions such as Adjunct Lecturer at Methodist University College, Ghana, and Teaching & Research Assistant at the University of Ghana Business School. He has close to a decade of experience as Assistant Director in the Ghana Civil Service and Local Government Service. Mohammed was at one time a district business development officer during which period he led the implementation of the Rural Enterprises Programme, an SME intervention by the Government of Ghana, AfDB, and IFAD. He serves as an ad hoc reviewer for several international peer-reviewed academic journals. His current research interests include policy analysis, local governance and poverty reduction, social protection, and organizational development.

Iram A. Khan is a civil servant who is currently working as Joint Secretary, Cabinet Division, Government of Pakistan. Dr. Khan obtained his MA (Econ) in Public Policy & Management on the Chevening scholarship from the University of Manchester, UK, in 1998. He also received his PhD from the same university in 2003. In 2007, he visited the Public Utility Research Center, University of Florida, USA, as a Fulbright scholar. Dr. Khan has published a number of papers in local and international journals. His research interests are in the areas of public policy, public sector management, knowledge management and regulatory governance.

Anthony Sumnaya Kumasey is a Lecturer at the University of Professional Studies, Accra, Ghana, and a PhD Candidate with the Global Development Institute (GDI), School of Environment, Education and Development, University of Manchester, UK. Anthony has both administrative and academic experience in Ghanaian universities. His current research interests include administrative ethics, CSR, development administration, organizational behaviour and organizational change and development.

Shaoheng Li is a PhD candidate at the Institute for Development Policy and Management (IDPM), School of Environment, Education and Development (SEED), University of Manchester, UK. Her dissertation focuses on human resource management (HRM) in privately owned small and medium-sized enterprises (SMEs) in China. She holds a Master's degree in Human Resource Management from the University of Manchester. Prior to coming to Manchester, Shaoheng worked in the private sector in China for four years. Her research interests include HRM, IHRM, SME development, and cross-cultural organisational behaviour.

Aminu Mamman is a Reader at the Global Development Institute (formerly, Institute of Development Policy and Management), University of Manchester, UK. He obtained a PhD degree from Cardiff Business School,

Cardiff University, UK. Aminu has published widely in reputable journals such as *Organization Studies*, *British Journal of Management*, *International Business Review* and *International Journal of Human Resource Management*. His research interests include managerial cognition especially with reference to globalization; managing SMEs in developing countries; developing African institutions and leaders; and diffusion and modification of management innovation. His recent book (*SMEs and Poverty Reduction: Strategic Management Perspective*) addresses the critical question of how the small business sector can contribute to poverty reduction in Africa.

James Kwame Mensah is Lecturer at the Department of Business Administration, University of Professional Studies, Accra, Ghana. Mensah holds a PhD in Development Administration from the Graduate School of Public Administration, National Institute of Development Administration (Thailand), and an MPhil in Public Administration and Bachelor of Arts in Sociology with Political Science from the University of Ghana, Legon. His research interests include talent management, public sector human resource management, development management and local economic development. He has published in peer-reviewed and reputable academic journals.

Nana Yaw Oppong is Senior Lecturer in Human Resource Management at the School of Business of the University of Cape Coast, Ghana. He has a PhD in Talent Management and Development (Leeds); MBA in International Business (London); and BA (Hons) in Secretaryship & Diploma in Education (Cape Coast). He has taught at the Leeds Business School, UK, and has also worked in human resource managerial roles and currently serves on the board of a successful rural bank. Nana's research interests include cross-cultural HRM; talent management and development; indigenous research methodologies; and human resource policy evaluation with a special interest in the Ghanaian mining industry. He has many publications covering these areas and has presented papers at conferences in Ghana, Greece, the UK, Germany, Australia and Hong Kong. He is also a consultant in human resource management and development.

Christopher J. Rees is a Senior Lecturer in Organisational Change and Development at the Global Development Institute (GDI), University of Manchester, UK. He is a Chartered Psychologist and holds two Master's degrees and a PhD from the University of Manchester. Prior to commencing full-time academic work, he held senior positions in the public and financial services sectors in the UK. Chris has published widely in a wide range of international journals including the *Journal of Business Ethics*, *International Journal of Human Resource Management*, *International Journal of Public Administration*, and the *Journal of Organisational Change Management*. He has is on various editorial journal boards and is a Visiting Honorary Chair at Beijing University of Technology, China.

Piyawadee Rohitarachoon is a lecturer in Public Administration and Public Personnel Management. She is currently based at the School of Political and Social Science, University of Phayao, Thailand. Her main areas of research are human resource practices, public personnel management, and central–local relations. She has worked on various projects in Ghana, Tanzania, Vietnam, Lao PDR and Thailand. She is currently lecturing in public human resource management, public administration systems and organisation and management.

Francis Nangbeviel Sanyare is a Lecturer at the Department of Social, Political and Historical Studies, University for Development Studies, Wa Campus, Ghana. He is also a Recognised Teacher of the University of Liverpool Online management programs. He obtained a PhD in Development Policy and Management from the Global Development Institute (GDI), School of Environment, Education and Development, University of Manchester, UK. His research interests include elites and local government administration, public governance and administration, development policy, gender and local governance, and NGO and third-sector management.

Nicha Sathornkich is a Public Sector Development Officer (senior professional level) at the Office of the Public Sector Development Commission, Thailand. She is currently the Director of provincial performance monitoring and the evaluation standard group in the Public Sector Performance Evaluation Directorate. Her research and professional works fall into an umbrella of public administration, evaluation and monitoring, and effectiveness standards. She has carried out research on the development and implementation of a performance management system in the Thai public sector.

Manisha Verma is a civil servant in India. She holds a Bachelor's degree in Electrical Engineering and a Master's degree in Public Policy and Management. She also has a PhD in Public Policy and Development from the University of Manchester, UK. She is interested in issues of governance, new forms of governing structures such as partnerships with the private sector and non-state actors, issues of public service delivery, systemic reforms in governance, and enhancing public sector capacities. She has published in peer-reviewed journals, contributed chapters to edited books, reviewed articles for international journals and presented papers at international conferences.

Hamza Bukari Zakaria is a Lecturer at the School of Public Service and Governance, Ghana Institute of Management and Public Administration (GIMPA), where he teaches at the graduate level. His research focuses on decentralization and local government administration, performance management, leadership, public administration and spirituality in organizational contexts. Hamza has published in *Public Administration and Development*, *Public Organisation Review*, *International Journal of Public Administration* and the *Journal of Management, Spirituality & Religion*.

Part I

Development management

Concepts and theories

1 Development management

A conceptual and theoretical overview

Justice Nyigmah Bawole, Farhad Hossain,
Asad K. Ghalib, Christopher J. Rees and
Aminu Mamman

Introduction

In many parts of the developing world, the failure of development interventions rather than the absence of resources have been the bane of progress. It is almost taken for granted that once development interventions are fashioned and implemented, 'development' should follow. However, it is important to recognize that, the management aspect of development, which was arguably hitherto taken for granted, is as vital as development itself. The concept of development should therefore, be discussed along – but not at the expense of – management. This significant observation in modern development thought and practice has necessitated a process of critical reflection upon the meaning, administration, institutions and practices through which diverse forms of development are conceived and delivered (Dar and Cooke, 2008). This has also led to the application of management principles in the achievement of development objectives. Thus, development is not a one-way street: in one direction, valuable insights from concepts, assumptions and critical analysis of development theories is pertinent for an informed decision on the choices and courses of action to development. On the other hand, the conception and analysis of development can be broadened and deepened by incorporating the diverse theories and principles of management.

It is perceived that the challenges of society such as poverty, malnutrition, unemployment, inequality and illiteracy, among others, can be properly addressed when interventions are implemented within the context and broader umbrella of management. Thus, management should occupy an important nucleus and be invoked as a critical element in the development agenda. Development management therefore involves a radical rethinking and identification of some management imperatives in ways that ensure better outcomes and consequently address the concerns and priorities of the recipients of development interventions. Development management is of strategic importance in economic and social development especially in developing countries. It has the potential to influence the success or failure of developmental activities and plans. The concept has been widely discussed and debated because of its important ramifications. Much has been written about the concept by both practitioners and scholars in terms of its meaning, theories, processes and influences. Generally, development management is a deliberate attempt to cause development by actively steering institutional and organizational changes towards greater levels of efficiency and effectiveness.

This chapter explores the concepts and theories of development management. The chapter is organized as follows: the next section discusses the concept of development followed by an examination of development as a multinational concept. The third section concentrates on explaining the term development management while the fourth part highlights some notable development theories. A chapter summary and conclusion is then provided in the next section. The final section provides a summary and outline of the book.

What is development?

The term development has dominated discussions at the local, national and international levels. Viewed from a common-sense perspective to describe what needs to happen if the poor are to be raised out of poverty, the term development appears unproblematic. On the other hand, the objectives of development and how they should be pursued have remained highly debated in the international political arena. Thus, the meaning of development is amorphous, elusive and highly contested theoretically and politically making it one of the slippery concepts of our time. This characteristic of development often affects the approach that observers, analysts and practitioners prescribe and adopt to deal with developmental issues and societal problems (Zafarullah and Huque, 2012). It has been equated to several terms such as economic growth, industrialization, progress, modernization, expansion and advancement, among others. The breadth and scope of development keeps changing as we understand it better and as previous suggested solutions to the challenges of development fail. The disagreements and divergence in defining the term development makes it easier to criticize and contest suggested definitions than providing an alternative definition of development.

Indeed, definitions of development go beyond academic debates to its conception among international development agencies, leading to different political and policy implications. For instance, there is disagreement on the measure of development between the World Bank and the United Nations Development Programme (UNDP). Whereas the UNDP uses its Human Development Index (HDI) to measure development based on a range of factors such as educational attainment, health purchasing power and human rights, among others, the World Bank in its annual World Development Reports mainly uses economic criteria as a measure of development. This has policy implications to the extent that there are disagreements as to which policy to pursue to attack poverty and what to do to achieve development (Thomas, 1996). At the national and local levels there is also disagreement on the definition of poverty and what can be done to reduce it as part of the means of ensuring development. Whereas NGOs who work directly with the local people emphasize the immediate needs of the people, a government's attention is on economic growth and industrialization, leading to differences in development policies.

Thomas (1992: 7) distinguishes two major ways in which the term development can be used: first, we could define development as an historical process of social change in which societies are transformed over long periods; and second, development could be defined as consisting of deliberate efforts aimed at progress on the part of various agencies, including governments, all kinds of organizations and social movements. Dwivedi, Khator and Nef (2007: 2) looked at development in terms of the spread and consolidation of the material, natural and spiritual well-being of people and nations. For them, well-being goes beyond aggregation of indexes and parameters to include being able to live in a safe and sustainable environment; sharing in the material benefits of their labour in an equitable and persistent way; nurturing networks of social support and solidarity; empowerment and living freely without discrimination, violence, fear and abuse; and lastly, a set of values, practices and cognitions that permit people to take charge of their own future. Development therefore implies a process of moving from unsatisfactory social, economic and political conditions towards a desired situation through medium- to long-term intervention and processes.

In the discussion of development, Seers (1979) is concerned about what is happening to poverty, unemployment and inequality – implying that the reduction in these could be termed as development. On the other hand, if there is a high increase in them, it would be strange for development to occur in spite of the increase in per capita income. Similarly, Sen (1999) christened development as freedom. To him 'development requires the removal of major sources of un-freedom: poverty as well as tyranny, poor economic opportunities as well as systematic social deprivation, neglect of public facilities as well as intolerance or over activity of repressive states' (p. 1). However, both Seers and Sen did not totally neglect the importance of the economic aspect of development; they only argued that it is not sufficient for total development. In other words, economic development cannot explain all the factors of development in that the concept goes beyond changes in economic indicators.

Taking a broader perspective, Todaro and Smith (2012: 5) defined the concept as the process of improving the quality of all human lives and capabilities by raising people's levels of living, self-esteem and freedom. This definition appears to broaden the scope to cover Sen's capability approach which will enable each individual to enjoy their freedom. A major factor that has been introduced into the meaning of development is happiness. Todaro and Smith (2012: 19) explained that happiness is part of human well-being because it helps to expand individuals' capability to function. In fact, Bhutan has adopted gross national happiness instead of gross national income as a measure of development progress. Thus, while the economic definition of development is by no means inconsequential, it does not provide adequate and reliable distribution of wealth. Therefore, to get a better understanding of development, it should be best described as the interaction of both economic and non-economic factors. Therefore, it is preferable to describe development as multidimensional.

Development as a multidimensional concept

The struggle for development in all its forms is probably one of the most challenging tasks facing most governments globally, especially in developing countries. Thus, unless one pretends, development challenges can be seen everywhere, although the form and nature of them vary from region to region and country to country. Thus, since World War II, developing countries continue to strive for development in order to improve upon the living conditions of the poor who are mostly in the majority (Turner, Hulme and McCourt, 2015). The term development has therefore assumed significance, having been prefixed with many terms, such as administration (development administration) and management (development management), and due to its involvement in the work of many agencies at the international level (World Bank, UNDP), national level and local level as well as in non-governmental organizations.

One of the ways of dealing with the ambiguities associated with defining the concept of development is to tackle it from a multidimensional perspective. This ranges from economic to social, political, environmental and cultural perspectives, among others. Earlier definitions of development have taken an economic focus measured in terms of GNP per capita, economic growth industrialization and modernization (Thomas, 1996). The World Bank for instance defines development in terms of GNP per capita especially in categorizing countries as developed and developing. Therefore, GNP per capita is a wealth-based indicator of measuring development. According to Willis (2005) the use of a wealth indicator is deemed appropriate because it is assumed that greater wealth comes with other benefits such as improved health, education and quality of life. Therefore, policies normally embarked on to ensure development include improving growth rates, industrialization, employing import substitution measures, promoting savings and investment, raising income levels, creating employment, distributing income, agricultural modernization, setting up export-oriented ventures, building infrastructures, technological progress, utilizing external aid, and so on (Zafarullah and Huque, 2012). The view was that economic growth will have a trickle-down effect to reduce poverty and improve societal well-being (Todaro and Smith, 2003).

However, this position lost its merit as a lot of social problems became obvious such as inequality, environmental issues, political issues, unemployment and poverty. Thus, in spite of the impressive economic growth figures experienced by many countries, especially developing ones, they have not experienced much change in the standard of living of the masses (Seers, 1979; Sen, 1999). Sen (1999) argued that economic measures may not be an accurate measure of development in that it is possible to rapidly grow economically but with bad literacy rate, health, life expectancy and nutrition. It has then become apparent that defining development in terms of economic growth is insufficient and probably socially damaging. Indeed, economic development has not been able to solve society's problems and experiences show that this indicator of development is naive. Social, political and environmental problems have been rising in both developed and developing countries.

In other words, while per capita income is important to development, other objectives such as reducing poverty, expanding access to health services, and education, among others, are equally important. It is therefore clear that this single yardstick of economic development has lost its value with the view that development is not entirely economic but rather a multidimensional process involving the reorientation and reorganization of the entire economic and social system.

Today, the unilateral definition of development has been replaced and the concept now enjoys multidimensional characteristics. It is generally agreed that economic development is necessary but not sufficient to improve human well-being and poverty reduction. Instead, development efforts must be directed at all aspects of well-being including social development. The shift to multidimensionality was advocated and spearheaded by scholars such as Seers, Sen and Goulet, and organizations such as the UNDP, IGOs and NGOs. In this way, development assumes several characteristics such as freedom, capability, sustainability and happiness. There are several dimensions but common among them are economic, social, cultural, political, participatory and ecological. It is argued that the combination of these dimensions is aimed at achieving the total well-being of a society and its people. This dimension of social development has been articulated in the Millennium Development Goals (MDGs) which emphasize freedom, equality, solidarity and tolerance. The Copenhagen Social Summit of 1995 defines social development around three basic issues: poverty eradication, employment generation and social harmony. Even though the concept of social development is used differently in various disciplines such as sociology, social work, psychology and social policy, in development management, it is generally about government policies and programmes emphasizing the 'social aspect' of development such as increasing literacy, reducing poverty, combating malnutrition and improving access to health and education (Midgley, 2013).

Zafarullah and Huque (2012) made the point that the economic aspect of development has been complemented by the social dimension to enhance the total well-being of a society and its people. Therefore, expanding social choices has become important to increase opportunities for social actions. Extending this into the realm of public policy and development management, the social dimension of development requires the state, international organizations and other development agencies to consciously intervene in the provision of social services such as education, housing and health to address the problems of inequality and poverty. This dimension echoes Seers's (1979) definition of development as poverty alleviation, raising employment, decreasing inequality, wider educational opportunities, political participation, reduced dependency on foreign assistance and self-reliance.

The discussion of development also has a political dimension. This aspect is seen as promoting and nurturing liberties and freedom, empowering people, and giving them the voice they deserve. This also includes participation by creating opportunities for individuals and allowing civil society to play a creative role in poverty alleviation, creating networks, engendering social roles and building social capital (Zafarullah and Huque, 2012). This may also make citizens feel included in society's divergent pursuits, and value their worth and capabilities, believing in themselves as well as earning recognition and respect.

As pointed out earlier in this chapter, given that there is no agreed definition of what constitutes development, the term is accepted as multidimensional, which thereby influences the design and implementation of interventions aimed at development. Indeed, the focus and effectiveness of development interventions are mostly unclear at birth since they are often grounded in conceptual ambiguity. As a result, the debate regarding the most effective way of administering development interventions continues. Generally, development is multidimensional and must encompass every aspect of society and interventions that make individuals comfortable and able to live dignified lives and pursue their dreams.

What is development management?

Development remains one of the most daunting challenges for the developing countries of Africa, Latin America, Asia and the Pacific. Governments as well as international development organizations are struggling to find an appropriate and long-lasting solution to the problem of underdevelopment. However, it has become clear that economic and social challenges and inequality cannot solely be removed by only development intervention; it has to be complemented by systematic management principles that would seek the realization of developmental goals. That is, the context of managing development has changed with new strategies, ideas and institutions and governments and international development agencies need to adopt proactive management strategies in the design and implementation of development interventions. Development management is a crucial concept as it provides the understanding of the drivers for economic and social development. Development management has its root in development administration and this has been confirmed in the extant literature. For instance Brinkerhoff and Coston (1999) in their assessment of development management trace its history from the 1950s and acknowledge that it is actually a continuation of development administration. Esman (1991) for instance contends that it is difficult to pinpoint what informed the transition from development administration to development management.

Thomas (1992: 105) distinguishes between development management as the management of any type of task in the context of development and development management as the management of development efforts (management of interventions, with conflict of goals). In his subsequent paper, Thomas (1999) added a third dimension, development management as a style of management. In defining development management Thomas (1996) argued that the nature of the task at hand determines the appropriate version of management. Hence, if development is considered to be a long-term historical change process, then development management may be viewed as the management of any type of task in the context of development. On the other hand, if development is viewed as deliberate efforts at progress, then development management would be characterized as the management of deliberate efforts at progress on the part of one of a number of agencies, the management of intervention in the process of social change in the context of conflicts of goals, values and interests (Thomas, 1996: 106). Therefore, the two conceptions of development influence the meaning of development management which Thomas (1996) summed up as management in development and management of development. From a radical participative perspective, Thomas (1996) contends that development management may be viewed as the management of interventions on behalf of the relatively powerless.

However, in another study, Thomas (1999) redefined development management as 'management undertaken with a development orientation, rather than management in the context of the development process or the management of development interventions or tasks' (p. 10). He is very cautious in making a distinction between the 'management of development' – managing deliberately designed development interventions by the best means available, and 'management for development' – where development management is seen as a style of management designed deliberately for development intervention or to enhance development. Even though elsewhere Thomas (2000) agreed that development management is the progressive management of development, he is certainly not sure about how this progressive orientation is put in practice due to ambiguity with values, disagreements over the definition of development as well as power struggles. Development management will often therefore remain an idealistic concept, rather than a description of what takes place (Thomas, 2000). Brinkerhoff and Coston (1999) provided a similar view on development management which they defined as 'managing the processes and building the capacity necessary to achieve improvements in people's lives and communities' well-being, including understanding and dealing with the array of constraints that impinge upon their achievement: political, institutional, social, cultural and so on' (p. 347).

Very often, some students and researchers use development management and development assistance interchangeably. This is perhaps based on an intervenist perspective to the extent that it is about international development assistance and the programs that look to ensure development in developing countries. From this perspective, Brinkerhoff and Coston (1999) argued that development management is a broadly diverse concept which focuses on four facets. First, development management is a means of improving efficiency and effectiveness of foreign assistance and expansion of the policy agenda of international agencies; second, development management is a toolkit for the application of a range of management and analytical tools which are basically adopted from a variety of social science disciplines; third, development management integrates a value dimension with an emphasis on self-determination, empowerment and fair distribution of development benefits; and finally, development management is a process intervention that self-consciously addresses political and value issues. While these facets together constitute development management as a field of theory and practice, there are bound to be intrinsic tensions among them (Brinkerhoff and Coston, 1999).

Zafarullah and Huque (2012: 411) argued that development management as a field is interdisciplinary and utilizes the wealth of knowledge from different fields such as sociology, political science, economics and management for societal well-being and progress. The multifaceted nature of development management is what

Brinkerhoff and Coston (1999: 350) called development management as a toolkit. This is basically about 'the application of a range of management and analytical tools adapted from a variety of disciplines, including strategic management, public policy, public administration, psychology, anthropology and political science' (p. 350). Again, it is relevant to economic growth, poverty alleviation and overall national development in both developed and developing worlds (Brinkerhoff and Coston, 1999). Development management has progressively stretched to include bureaucratic reorientation and restructuring, the integration of politics and culture into management improvement, participatory and performance-based service delivery and program management, community and NGO capacity building, and policy reform and implementation (Brinkerhoff and Coston, 1999: 348–9). Thomas (1996) catalogued a number of conceptual and skill areas demonstrating the uniqueness of development management as a new field distinct from traditional development administration. He argued that his list is not an exhaustive one and even that integration of them is problematic, and it is not at all easy to take each separately.

Both Thomas (1996) and Brinkerhoff and Coston (1999) appear to agree that development management incorporates more conventional management for getting the job done by the best means possible. In terms of its focus, development management, in the opinion of Brinkerhoff (2008: 989), initially focused on public sector efficiency and effectiveness in fulfilling basic core functions and on the performance agenda introduced by New Public Management (NPM) as well as politics and process. Brinkerhoff added that, when good governance came into the metric of development, the focus of development management expanded to include the relationship between public sector and non-state partners as well as their functions. Thus, as time goes by, development management expands to include all actors – public sector, private sector, international groups, IGOs, NGOs, and all agencies that should take part in development. Hence, Brinkerhoff (2002) intimates that networks and partnership has entered the vocabulary of development management. This role is even broader in a failed or fragile state and includes rebuilding the state, issues of legitimacy and security of citizens (Brinkerhoff, 2008). Development organizations undertake many activities – some are not specifically part of development interventions, to the extent that some values are called into question by unpredicted changes in conditions or by the actions of other organizations. It is therefore the way a development agency responds to such prospects and unanticipated challenges that demonstrates the extent to which its management can be termed *development* management in the sense of management which is always *for* development (Thomas, 1999: 13).

While other scholars (McCourt, 2001; Parker, 2002; Fine and Jomo, 2006; Cooke and Dar, 2008) share similar views with Thomas' assumption that a pro-poor orientation to development management is possible as well as desirable; they, however, submit that this may inevitably be distorted by the very means used to promote it. Influenced by post-colonial, post-development and critical management studies, these scholars heavily critique and even seek to reject the possibility of progressive development management. Their contention is that development management, just like all management forms, appears to emphasize a 'managerialist' perspective to the extent that the means of management will inescapably displace the ends of policy (McCourt, 2001; Parker, 2002) because managers will be aligned to their political and economic considerations which is likely to be different from the interests of poor people (Fine and Jomo, 2006). For instance, the study by Brinkerhoff and Brinkerhoff (2010) of development managers in the United States articulated a normative commitment to their work but they were dismayed by the fact that a pro-poor orientation has so often been lacking from development management practice. Empirical research by Abouassi (2010) involving Lebanese development managers confirmed that development managers in Lebanon were in their way also struggling to apply pro-poor values in their everyday practice

Development management can be described as an informed, conscious and deliberate attempt to ensure that institutions and organizations bring about efficiency and effectiveness to economic growth, equity, poverty reduction and freedom in the lives of citizens in a way which is faster than their natural rate of progressive change. Development management also requires the adoption of alternative development thinking and practice such as social inclusion, community development and empowerment as a way of comprehensively addressing the issue of development. Managers of development are therefore seen as change agents who must continuously and deliberately seek to enact and implement development policies aimed at economic growth, reducing poverty, ensuring equity and sustainable distribution of benefits and most importantly empowering citizens. Hence, development management requires that experts, scholars and public managers should engage in critical dialogue with international development agencies, development partners, national government and their agencies, local level agencies, and all citizens.

This situation however makes development management value-laden, which is often worsened by the incorporation of politics into donors' policies and agendas, thereby deranging the local agenda in the recipient country which is either absent or fragmented (Abouassi, 2010). As a result of this situation, development management needs to clear about which policies to engage with. Critical issues of accountability, power relations and international relations are significant in development management dialogue (Brinkerhoff and Brinkerhoff, 2010). In conclusion, development management generally means managing development interventions in ways that improve the existing condition of society for better humanity. Arriving at this feat requires paying attention to how tasks are specified, how data are collected and monitored, how decisions are made, and how collaboration is enacted among the broad array of both public sector and non-state actors that characterize state–society relations (Brinkerhoff and Coston, 1999). It is also about getting potential beneficiaries involved from the design of development intervention to their implementation.

Theories of development

From the agrarian society to the industrial society and the current global technological world, society has been developing and progressing as the goals of society keep changing based on its needs and aspirations. From the assumptions of efficient management of resources, exportation of raw materials to the industrialized world, and the building of infrastructure, the direction of development policy has changed to industrialization and the importation of ideas from the developed world to the underdeveloped one as the theory of development. Therefore, the emphasis on development in the past was on the transmission of social, economic and political structures to the less developed countries to reflect Western ideals (Zafarullah and Huque, 2012). Later this assumption was considered as fallacious as economic progress led to unanticipated social consequences.

The challenges of development and the causes of underdevelopment were later attributed to the role of the Western world in manipulating the less developed countries. Thus, dependency theory argued that the causes of underdevelopment are to be found outside the arena of third-world countries. Similarly, geographical explanations have been used to explain the causes of underdevelopment in poor countries. Many other theories and approaches have been used to explain the conditions and the reasons for the underdevelopment of poor countries. Whereas a number of theories have been discussed in relation to development over the years, this section will mainly concentrate on a few development theories: modernization theory, dependency theory, economic theories of development, geographical explanations and institutional theories. Second, this section is not seeking to give a broad history of the theories of development but rather a brief summary to establish their relevance in understanding modern development thinking and approaches. It important to note that the extant literature gives an indication of how the theoretical foundations of development interventions continue to change over the years as the term becomes well understood and what are believed to be the causes of underdevelopment as well as which types and kinds of intervention are deemed to be appropriate.

Modernization theory

Whereas some modernization theorists attributed the problem of the third world to lack of capital for growth (Rostow, 1966), others attributed it to the lack of value systems such as profit motives (Apter, 1966). Thus, modernization theory takes a behavioural view of the development process. The main thrust of this theory is to identify the conditions that gave rise to development in developed countries. The argument is that by identifying the factors that gave rise to development in the first-world countries, such factors can be replicated in third-world countries to achieve development. As noted by Black (1991: 16), with the non-existent or primitive basic infrastructure in third-world countries, the solution seemed obvious: the transplantation of superior technologies, institutions, habits and values from the West to the non-West. According to Rapley (2007), whatever be their stand, modernization theorists generally approved that underdevelopment is an initial stage of the development process and that developed countries have gone past that stage. For instance, in his book, *The Stages of Economic Growth*, Rostow argued that societies progress in the same linear fashion towards development. Thus, modernization theory postulates that development is a transition and transformation that societies had to undergo in order to become developed.

Modernization implies a transition from primitive economies to high-intensive technology economies. Thus, development is a linear progression from traditional society through to the age of mass consumption (Rostow, 1960); developed countries such as Europe and North America had gone past that stage and hence third-world countries had to follow in the footsteps of successful countries. Therefore, countries of Africa, Asia and Latin America are undeveloped because of their outmoded social, economic and political structures. In order for developing countries to advance on the path of development, therefore, modernization theorists recommended the Westernizing of elites, training, proper administrative and bureaucratic structure, and imbibing entrepreneurial spirit into the citizenry of the third-world countries (Rapley, 2007). Therefore, technology and socio-political practices of the developed world must be transferred to underdeveloped societies (Servaes and Malikhao, 2009: 159). This had implications for development management to the extent that development interventions and development managers in underdeveloped countries have to embark on industrialization and shift from traditional outdated economic, cultural, social and political structures. Applying the modernization theory to development management simply means development managers have to carefully study and ply the path of development as well as replicate various interventions that have been adopted by developed countries to reach their present. Developed countries also have a role to play to the development of those countries that lagged behind by providing capital and technical support to accelerate their pace of development. Indeed, through aid, capital and technical assistance, developed countries and international development agencies have contributed to addressing the development challenges in the third world.

In the 1950s modernization theory held great promise, and developing or newly independent countries happily embraced it. However, later events exposed the flaws in this modernist conception of development as the late 1960s was characterized by 'increased poverty, growing indebtedness, political repression, economic stagnation and a host of other ills' (Turner, Hulme and McCourt, 2015: 6). The theory has also been heavily criticized. Modernization theorists have approached the concept of development from a Eurocentric position, thinking that what worked in Europe and North America may work in Asia, Africa and Latin America (Zafarullah and Huque, 2012: 59). The theory has also been criticized as being deterministic by positing that every society must pass through the same stages to development. Modernization theory assumes rather wrongly that development is unidirectional as change cannot always be straight and orderly or continuous. Indeed there are many paths to development to the extent that there can be reversal (Zafarullah and Huque, 2012).

Dependency theory

The discontentment with modernization theory suddenly brought in a new line of thinking about development theory which highlighted the element of dependency. Dependency may be described as a situation in which the economies of one group of countries are conditioned by the development and expansion of others. The crux of dependency theory is that the world is interconnected, making some countries winners and others losers. According to this theory, the world economy is divided into the core and periphery areas. The centre benefits from and exploits the periphery (Black, 1991: 29). Dependency theorists argued that the relationship between Western and underdeveloped countries is that of exploitative, dependency and economic relationship which is inconsistent with the ideals of development. The most distinguished feature of dependency theory is its insistence that it is not the internal characteristics of undeveloped countries so much but the structure of the international system, especially its economic aspects, that is the significant variable to be examined to understand underdevelopment of third-world countries (Smith, 1979: 248; Black, 1991: 28). In other words, dependency theory submits that external factors are responsible for the underdevelopment of poor countries in that the deprivation of surplus at the periphery promotes the continuous development of the centre and this ensures the underdevelopment of the periphery (Uche, 1994). Indeed, Black (1991: 28) argued that the dominant foreign power benefits at the expense of its client states, while the clientele class benefits at the expense of other classes. The structure of international development has been manipulated in a way that the less developed countries have to depend on the West for technology, finance, markets and imports to the extent that they cannot exist without depending on them.

Servaes and Malikhao (2009: 161) argued cogently that 'the main interest of Western monopoly capitalism was to prevent, or, if that was impossible, to slow down and to control the economic development of underdeveloped countries'. Therefore, the most significant hindrance to the development of poor countries is not the shortage of capital or management, but the present international system. Black (1991: 28–29) emphatically stated that foreign assistance and aid are a means of extracting capital from third-world countries; and even if it brings economic growth, it may distort the pattern of growth by creating inequalities among classes and regions within client states. To change the fortunes of the underdeveloped countries, dependency theorists recommend that the less developed countries must dissociate themselves from the world market and strive for self-reliance (Servaes and Malikhao, 2009: 162). Applying this theory to development management means that development managers seeking to boost and sustain visible development in developing countries should introduce interventions that will make them self-reliant, breaking free from the existing economic order perpetuated by the centre. These assumptions have influenced development management for some time now by introducing self-help projects, the participation and involvement of beneficiaries in the conception, design and implementation of development interventions, and adoption of indigenous and local knowledge in the development effort.

It is obvious that most underdeveloped countries are economically weak and too indebted to operate autonomously (Servaes and Malikhao, 2009: 163). The theory underestimated the power and influence that underdeveloped countries have over their own development issues, but rather attributed their woes to Western developed countries (Smith, 1979), and avoided considerations of internal constraints and struggles. Another criticism of the theory is that it lengthily addressed the causes of underdevelopment of poor countries, but never provided practical ways and means of addressing the problem of underdevelopment.

Economic theories of development

In the post-World War II period, a number of economic theories influenced by major leading thinkers such as Adam Smith, David Ricardo and Karl Marx, among others, were propounded to explain how nations could develop. Smith's work on *The Wealth of Nations* emphasizes the accumulation of capital, specialization and division of labour, saving and investment in all sectors as key to economic growth. Smith argued that government regulations are detrimental to economic growth and that the system should be regulated by the 'invisible hands' of the market (Willis, 2005). The 'invisible hand' is a more powerful tool than government regulation of production in that individuals act rationally based on the principles of demand and supply. The work of Smith is still influential today as the market is currently controlled by the principles of demand and supply. David Ricardo on his part proposed the theory of comparative advantage and argued that countries should specialize in products that they produce better and therefore engage in international trade that would be mutually beneficial to them. In other words, countries should utilize and specialize, and export products and commodities that they best produce at relatively low costs. Specialization makes countries efficient with greater capacity for growth than trying to produce everything (Willis, 2005).

Karl Marx's view of development was that it was a process that all societies pass through. Put differently, Marx argued that society moves from one stage to the other. Thus, in the primitive society, land, tools and other basic economic resources were communally owned. In feudal societies, which were mainly found in the Western world, they were organized based on agricultural production where land was owned by the few where tenants rented for farming. The third stage of society is the capitalist society where it is divided into those who own the means of production and those who do not. The have-nots have to earn a living by selling their labour to those who own the means of production. In the analysis of Marx, the capitalist society will be toppled and communism will triumph and in this kind of society the means of production will be owned by the state or the people (Willis, 2005). In the final analysis, the present state of capitalism is just one of the stages in transition and this will be usurped by socialism. Private ownership of property will fade away and everything will be communal ownership but individuals will contribute according to their abilities and receive according to their needs.

After the Great Economic Depression in the USA in the 1930s, John Maynard Keynes argued that the government had a role to play in economic growth in contradiction to the views of Smith. Keynes advocated real investments as the key to economic growth with the view that these could have a multiplier effect by creating jobs and further generation of growth. Government should intervene in the economy to bring about economic growth through either monetary policies or government expenditure. Government expenditure can produce a multiplier effect in that when the government spends on road construction it will generate jobs for both the workers and suppliers: workers spend their money supporting other people's jobs, companies invest, and the cycle continues (Willis, 2005). In other words, Keynes believed that government expenditure will lead to a trickle-down process to benefit society at large. Economic theories of development that emphasize the invisible hands of the market greatly influenced development management. With this in mind, development interventions in developed countries shifted to the assumption that development outcomes could be determined by the free interplay of demand and supply, leading to the adoption of NPM, privatization and liberalization. Such policies as structural adjustment programmes had their root in economic theories of development. But as others have argued in Chapter 2 of this book and elsewhere, later events in history have questioned the wisdom in allowing the market a free rein.

Geographical theories of development

Differences in geographical conditions have been invoked by scholars to explain variations in levels of development. According to the geography hypothesis of development, natural resources, climate and other geographical factors provide the ultimate explanation for development. A key proponent of this theory is Jeffrey D. Sachs. He argued that the role of geography and resource endowments in development should not be underestimated (Sachs, 2008: 86). It is argued that sub-Saharan Africa and other regions are struggling today for improved economic development as a result of diseases, geographical isolation, low technological productivity and resource limitations. Sachs (2008: 87) intimates that Africa, for instance, was characterized by the most adverse malaria in the world because it had a climate conducive to year round transmission of malaria from person to person. Chang (2012) added that being too close to the equator, African countries suffer from tropical diseases (e.g. malaria), which reduce worker productivity and raise healthcare costs. The argument continued that tropical regions lagged far behind temperate regions in economic development because of the former's unfavourable climate, soils and topography (Bloom and Sachs, 1998).

Therefore, the reason for the prevalence of poverty in countries in Africa and Asia can be attributed to the continent's extraordinarily disadvantageous geography (Sachs, 2008). The landlocked nature of many poor countries makes it difficult for them to integrate into the global economy, and therefore affects their ability to benefit sufficiently from the process of economic integration and globalization (Sachs, 2008). Furthermore, poor countries suffer from the bad neighbourhood effect. Thus, they are surrounded by other poor countries with small markets and frequently characterized by violence and conflicts. To ensure development, development managers should emphasize and embark on interventions that seek to tackle geographical and environmental challenges such as drought and malaria, among others. The adoption of this approach to ensuring development in developing countries has been witnessed in a number of development agencies contributing their quota to dealing with tropical diseases, climate change interventions and irrigation facilities, among other approaches. However, this explanation has been criticized because even though there may be a correlation between geography and development, correlation is not causation. Also, looking at institutions as an important factor has been omitted from the explanation of the causes of development (Acemoglu, 2008). For instance, Switzerland and Austria are two of the richest economies in the world, but they are landlocked (Chang, 2012). Similarly, Botswana, a completely landlocked country, is one of Africa's most developed countries.

Institutional theories of development

Institutional theory has been used as a candidate to explain the fundamental causes of the differences between developed and developing countries. Proponents here include Dani Rodrik, Daron Acemoglu and Simon Johnson, among others. They attributed the high income levels in Western countries to superior institutions such as democracy, freedom and property rights, among others. Acemoglu (2008: 73) made the point that societies with good institutions encourage investment in machinery, human capital and better technologies and consequently these countries have achieved economic prosperity. Good institutions have three characteristics: first, enforcement of property rights, second, constraints on the actions of the elites, politicians and other powerful groups, and third, equality of opportunity. All these encourage investment and provide equal platforms for development. Therefore, during the latter part of the 1980s and in the 1990s the means to ensure development has been on institutions, governance, democracy, rule of law and human rights. The assumption is that once the right institutions are in place development will follow and this was the focus of development management in that period.

Sachs (2008: 86) opposed this argument and explained that the barriers to economic development in poor countries are far more complex than institutional shortcomings. He espoused that institutions matter but they don't matter exclusively and that instead of focusing on institutions, it would be wise to devote more effort to fighting AIDS, tuberculosis and malaria in African and Asian countries. It is also worth the effort to address the depletion of soil nutrients and build more roads to connect remote populations to regional markets as these are the main causes of underdevelopment (Sachs, 2008).

It appears scholars are now coming to terms with the fact that in view of the numerous points raised above, none of the theories can escape criticisms. However, it is useful to acknowledge that various strands of the theories could be useful in varied circumstances. In approaching development management, therefore, it appears one cannot fully analyze outcomes without ascertaining the theoretical orientations behind the interventions.

Summary and conclusion

The term development management is comprised of two words – development and management – with both having implications on the definition of the term. Development is a complex term. In the 1950s, the term development was primarily linked to economic development in developing countries, leading to the pursuit of industrialization and the use of GNP per capita as the yardstick for measuring development. However, the economic definition encountered many challenges and therefore the term has been broadened and is now perceived as a multifaceted one that comprises social, political and cultural as well as environmental dimensions. It is, therefore, easier to criticize definitions of development than to offer one. In simple terms, development is a process of change, growth, progress and people reaching an acceptable standard of living, especially with regard to the basic things they need to live. However, development is a never-ending process as people will always strive to improve the quality of their lives. The quest and thirst for development led to disciplines of studying and administering development such as development administration, development studies and development management, among others. From development to development administration, development management has currently become the dominant discipline of study to understand the nuances of carrying out development interventions.

However, confusion abounds in both academic and donor circles about what development management actually means. While variations are noticeable, there appears to be some consensus that development management implies a conscious and deliberate attempt to ensure progress from an undesirable situation to a tolerable one. While development management appears to mean the application of managerial principles in the administration of development interventions, it may have unfortunate consequences where development managers may displace the objective of development with their political and economic interest rather than the interest of the citizens. Managing development therefore appears to be a daunting task not only because of the challenges surrounding what the appropriate way to achieve development is but also the varied interests of the actors. Development managers are also sometimes influenced by many theories that have been advanced and experimented with over the years. Indeed, no one theory is complete enough to serve as the most compelling tool in achieving the goals of total development. Instead, at any point in time development managers tease out the best elements of each theory and complement them with practical lessons to cautiously apply them.

There has been growing interest in development management research as part of the efforts to provide more insight into what works for developing countries especially. The strands of research that make up this volume reflect the wide array of interests among scholars and the extent to which some of the fundamental assumptions underlying the development management discourse have been put to test both in terms of theoretical grounding and practical application. There is no denying that the topics covered in this volume are by no means exhaustive, given the cornucopia of development management studies produced in the last several years. However, the varied array of topics and different contexts within which the studies were conducted largely reflect the generality of the current discourse and practice in the field.

Book overview

Related to the above point, one of the major strengths of this collection is its international character; it contains studies conducted in Ghana, Thailand, Croatia, China, South Africa, Kenya, India, Pakistan and the Middle East. The book is divided into three main parts. The first part contains three chapters, including this one, which attempt to traverse the definitional maze surrounding the concepts and theories of development. The three chapters also set the context for the various discussions in the other chapters by providing some insight into the extent to which the definitional and conceptual issues in development have influenced development management in theory and practice.

In this chapter, we saw Bawole, Hossain, Ghalib, Rees and Mamman point out that the concept of development and the theories that undergird it have been variously contested. Whilst calling for a more holistic definition of development, they also point out the weaknesses and strengths of popular theories. To them, even though the objectives of and approaches to development remain highly debated, there is some promise in improving development outcomes through the application of development management. In the second chapter, Bawole, Ibrahim, Hossain and Mensah attempt to trace the past pathways and future trajectories of development management in the developing world. To them the persistence of underdevelopment in the face of numerous lofty interventions in the developing world could be explained by the unsettled misunderstandings that characterize the concept of development itself and the extent to which this confusion influences the design and implementation of interventions. They envisage that the effectiveness of future development management interventions could be largely based on according the state more significant roles, recognizing and moderating the effects of competitive clientelist political realities and leveraging on developing country ethical values. In the third chapter, Kumasey, Bawole, Hossain and Ibrahim explore the critical role of ethics and values in development management. To them, development management interventions have been largely frustrated as a result of the ethical vacuum that surrounds their implementation in developing countries. This is especially so when tried and tested traditional ethical values have been supplanted by so-called best practice from the developed world. Whilst underscoring the primacy of ethics and values in ensuring better development outcomes, the authors call for a clear and reliable climate within which public officials, NGOs and development partners operate.

The second part of the book considers the role of capacity building and performance management in ensuring the successful implementation of development management programmes in the developing world. Here, through their study on the Gulf Co-operation Council Countries, Aaali and Rees explore the implementation of nationalization policies in the Middle East and the extent to which such policies have enhanced employment opportunities for citizens in the countries studied. They conclude by underscoring the centrality of human resource development to the effective implementation of nationalization policies. In the next chapter, Oppong offers a comparative study on management development, focusing on Ghana's mining sector. While highlighting the overwhelming but taken-for-granted importance of indigenous Ghanaian learning methods in management development, he advocates the localization of Western methods for holistic development of national managers.

In Chapter 5, Sathornkich, Rohitarachoon, Eldridge and Hossain examine the role of performance management in ensuring effective provincial administration in Thailand. Based on their findings, they call for the need to build the capacity of personnel in order to enhance their knowledge in and ability to contribute to the realization of the objectives of the performance management regime. The authors further recommend more attention in budget coordination and setting realistic performance measures. In another chapter, Analoui and Analoui focus on the capacity development needs of middle managers in Croatia's civil services. They conclude that the introduction of management development programmes has increased the awareness of middle managers on the importance of learning and personal development. More importantly, civil servants now see themselves as operating in a service organization which is accountable to its clients. In the last chapter of this section, Mamman, Zakaria and Agbebi investigate the significance of spirituality in the pursuit poverty reduction in Africa. They argue that previous 'neutral' approaches to developing policy makers and SME operators were not based on a collaborative long-term sustainability perspective. The authors, therefore, conclude that sensitizing policy makers and SME operators using ideas they understand and believe in holds greater prospects in changing undesirable behaviour.

The last section of the book discusses actors in development management as well as practices and lessons. In the first of the series of chapters, Bawole and Hossain seek to examine actor pluralism in the context of development management in Africa. They find that in the continuous search for development, many ambiguities exist in actor interfaces; and, there are strategic manoeuvres utilized by various actors in their struggles to reassert or redefine their priorities, interests and network configurations in development management. On their part, Sanyare, Hossain and Rees reflect on the capacity of local governments in managing development in Africa. Based on evidence from northern Ghana, the authors conclude that there is little chance of enhancing local administrative performance especially where there are scarce resources, and basic administrative procedures are deliberately undermined. In the next chapter, Li and Rees discuss the complex nature of SME operations in China and the adoption of current HRM practices in that context. They conclude their study by providing a theoretical framework to shed light on the relationship between some identified determinates and HRM practices in China's SMEs.

In the following chapter, Agupusi assesses the role of the Small, Medium and Micro-sized Enterprises (SMMEs) in poverty reduction in South Africa. Using Alexandra as a case study, the author also examines the contributions of both government and the private sector initiatives in supporting SMME development. The study finds that whilst there is great promise in harnessing SMMEs for poverty alleviation, it appears visible gains are lacking because there are no specific policies and concerted interventions to support the development of SMMEs. This section is further enriched by some focus on the contribution of NGOs to broader development outcomes. Brunt, for instance, examines the governance structure of INGOs in Kenya and finds that there is a unidirectional information flow and hierarchical structures that restrict middle management participation in decision making. In the opinion of the author, therefore, there is the need to increase participation and production capacity of middle management as potential change agents in ensuring organizational stability and continuity. Elsewhere in another chapter, Ahenkan investigates the implementation of the Millennium Development Goals (MDGs) in Ghana's local government settings. He found out that although some positive gains have accrued to local communities through the MDGs, the results were generally mixed. To him, therefore, scaling-up efforts by local governments, communities and other stakeholders was crucial in managing development at the grassroots level.

In an era when many developing countries have resorted to public–private partnerships (PPPs) as alternative means of service delivery, Verma provides some useful lessons in the chapter on PPPs in India's highways. Contrary to the widely held view that PPPs provide better services, the Indian experience points to multiple problems that detract from potential gains. Specifically, public partners are found to be responsible for many administrative hurdles that frustrate the implementation of PPPs. Within the same region, Khan and Ghalib also offer some appraisal of Pakistan's project implementation failures. They identified unreliable financial inflows, lack of top management support, incompetence of project team members and frequent transfers of project staff as some of the factors leading to project implementation failures in that country.

Finally, in the concluding chapter, Bawole, Hossain, Ghalib, Rees and Mamman re-emphasize the importance of development management as an instrument for development effectiveness in third-world countries. Here, they assemble some useful lessons in development management practice as highlighted in the preceding chapters.

Acknowledgments

We are very grateful to the contributors of the chapters for making this book project possible. We are also indebted to the numerous scholars who served as reviewers in the review process. Special appreciation also goes to the Routledge team for the immense support and cooperation throughout various stages of the book project.

References

Abouassi, K. (2010). International development management through a southern lens. *Public Administration and Development*, 30(2), 116–123.

Acemoglu, D. (2008). Root causes: a historical approach to assessing the role of institutions in economic development. In Secondi, G. (ed.), *The Development Economics Reader* (pp. 36–43). New York: Routledge.

Apter, D. E. (1965). *The Politics of Modernization*. Chicago: University of Chicago Press.

Black, J. K. (1991). *Development in Theory and Practice: Bridging the Gap*. San Francisco: Westview Press.

Bloom, D. E. and Sachs, J. D. (1998). Geography, demography, and economic growth in Africa. (Revised), October 1998. Available at www.cid.harvard.edu/archive/malaria/docs/brookafr.pdf. Accessed on 18 January 2016.

Brinkerhoff, D. W. (2008). The state and international development management: shifting tides, changing boundaries, and future directions. *Public Administration Review*, 68(6), 985–1001.

Brinkerhoff, D. W. and Coston, J. M. (1999). International development management in a globalized world. *Public Administration Review*, 59(4), 346–361.

Brinkerhoff, J. (2002). *Partnership for International Development: Rhetoric or Results?* Boulder, CO: Lynne Rienner.

Brinkerhoff, J. M. and Brinkerhoff D. W. (2010). International development management: a northern perspective. *Public Administration and Development*, 30(2), 102–115.

Chang, H. (2012). Industrial policy: can Africa do it? Paper presented at IEA/World Bank Roundtable on Industrial Policy in Africa Pretoria, South Africa, 3–4 July 2012.

Cooke, B. and Dar, S. (2008). Introduction: the new development management. In Cooke and Dar (eds.), *The New Development Management: Critiquing the Dual Modernization* (pp. 1–17). London: Zed Books.

Dar, S. and Cooke, B. (eds.) (2008). *The New Development Management: Critiquing the Dual Modernization*. London and New York: Zed Books.

Dwivedi, O. P., Khator, R. and Nef, J. (2007). *Managing Development in a Global Context*. London: Palgrave Macmillan.

Esman, M. (1991). *Managerial Dimensions of Development, Perspectives and Strategies*. West Hartford: Kumarian Press.

Fine, B. and Jomo, K. S. (2006). *The New Development Economics: After the Washington Consensus*. London: Zed Books.

McCourt, W. (2001). Moving the public management debate forward: a contingency approach. In McCourt, W. and Minogue, M. (eds.), *The Internationalization of Public Management: Reinventing the Third World State* (pp. 220–253). Cheltenham: Edward Elgar.

Midgley, J. (2013). *Social Development: Theory and Practice*. Thousand Oaks: Sage.

Parker, M. (2002). *Against Management: Organization in the Age of Managerialism*. Cambridge: Polity.

Rapley, J. (2007). *Understanding Development: Theory and Practice in the Third World*. London: Lynne Reinner.

Rostow, W. W. (1960). *The Stages of Growth: A Non-Communist Manifesto*. London: Cambridge University Press.

Rostow, W. W. (1966). *The Stages of Economic Growth*. Cambridge: Cambridge University Press.

Sachs, J. D. (2008). Institutions matter, but not for everything. In Secondi, G. (ed.), *The Development Economics Reader* (pp. 86–91). New York: Routledge.

Seers, D. (1979). The meaning of development. In Lehmann, D. (ed.), *Development Theory: Four Critical Studies* (pp. 9–30). London: Frank Cass.

Sen, A. (1999). *Development as Freedom*. New York: Knopf.

Servaes, J. and Malikhao, P. (2009). Development communication approaches in an international perspective. In Servaes, J. (ed.), *Communication for Development and Social Change* (pp. 158–179). Thousand Oaks: California, USA.

Smith, T. (1979). The underdevelopment of development literature: the case of dependency theory. *World Politics*, 31(2), 247–288.

Thomas, A. (1992). Introduction. In Thomas, A. and Allen, T. (eds.), *Poverty and Development in the 1990s* (pp. 1–9). Oxford: Oxford University Press.

Thomas, A. (1996). What is development management? *Journal of International Development*, 8(1), 95–110.

Thomas, A. (1999). What makes good development management? *Development in Practice*. 9(1–2), 9–17.

Thomas, A. (2000). What makes good development management? In Eade, D. (ed.), *Development and Management* (pp. 40–52). Oxford: Oxfam.

Todaro, M. P. and Smith, S. C. (2003). *Economic Development* (8th edition). Addison Wesley: New York.

Todaro, M. P. and Smith, S. C. (2012). *Economic Development* (11th edition). Addison Wesley: New York.

Turner, M., Hulme, D. and McCourt, W. (2015). *Governance, Management and Development: Making the State Work*. London: Palgrave Macmillan.

Uche, L. U. (1994). Some reflections on the dependency theory. *Africa Media Review*, 8(2), 39–55.

Willis, K. (2005). *Theories and Practices of Development*. New York: Routledge.

Zafarullah, H. and Huque, A. S. (2012). *Managing Development in a Globalised World: Concepts, Processes and Institutions*. New York: CRC Press.

2 Development management in the developing world

Past pathways and future trajectories

Justice Nyigmah Bawole, Mohammed Ibrahim, Farhad Hossain and James Kwame Mensah

Introduction

Development continues to elude many nations across the world. Even the so-called developed countries have yet to reach the ideal destination since they have to contend with pockets of poverty, inequality and other symptoms of underdevelopment. In relative terms, however, the pangs of poverty and underdevelopment are not only more overwhelming in the developing world but also present a desperate situation in need of urgent solution. The significance of this point is further highlighted in the widespread even if mistaken assumption that only developing countries qualify as ideal candidates for development prescriptions or interventions proffered by multinationals and development experts, at least in the last several decades. Following World War II, there have been increasing and varied attempts by various countries, mostly the so-called developing or third-world countries, to ensure improved socio-economic development (Turner, Hulme and McCourt, 2015). Despite these attempts, few success stories have been reported, implying that many countries continue to grapple with finding the right formula or panacea to the hydra-headed problems of poverty, social exclusion, food insecurity, macro-economic instability, inequality and unemployment, among other issues, that make life extremely difficult in the developing world.

Many scholars, practitioners and multilateral agencies have attempted to explain the persistence of underdevelopment in the face of numerous seemingly lofty interventions (Acemoglu and Robinson, 2012; Frankel, 2005; Dwivedi, Khator and Nef, 2007). Among other reasons, the public sector stands accused. In their influential work *Governance, Management and Development*, Turner, Hulme and McCourt (2015) sum up these observations when they contend that rather than being the catalysts for development, public sector organizations have ended up frustrating development processes in developing countries. The public sectors in developing countries have been accused of having failed to shape development outcomes through the provision of tailored and workable policies to politicians. They have also been cited for their ineptitude, corruption and general lack of efficiency and effectiveness in delivering services. Whilst these arguments and observations hold some promise in explaining the lack of development effectiveness in third-world countries, we contend that a more viable approach to understanding the problem should have regard to the confusion that surrounds the concept of development itself. It is evident, even superfluous, to point out that the unsettled misunderstanding that characterizes the definition of development among scholars and practitioners alike, as has been rightly pointed out in Chapter 1 of this book, influences the design and implementation of interventions aimed at addressing development problems. Thus, the focus and efficacy of development interventions are mostly suspect at birth since they are often grounded in conceptual ambivalence or ambiguity. Drawing from his almost four decades of involvement in development interventions across all continents, Frankel (2005: 4) breaks from conventional wisdom when he argues that 'development economic theories' which informed such interventions 'were sometimes … unrealistic, outdated, inapplicable or too idealistic …'. More importantly, although it is highly surprising that 'personal greed, corruption, political, cultural, religious, historic, and environmental differences or constraints' were hardly considered in the design of strategies or policies, some paradigms were recommended, if not imposed, on countries and organizations for implementation 'as if one solution were to fit all development requirements' (Frankel, 2005: 1).

The above insights by no means discredit the relevance or suitability of all development initiatives or processes in the developing world. However, they lay the ground for a rethink of such interventions as developing nations attempt to refine, or replace, them for better outcomes. Recently, for instance, development management (DM) has become the fad in the transition towards development. Whilst DM holds some signs of promise, it has also been critiqued on numerous counts (Turner, Hulme and McCourt, 2015; Hirschmann, 1999; Thomas, 1996). Although several studies have attempted to settle the definitional problems of development management, little attention has been paid to the relevance of the confusion inherent in the concept of development itself and the ripple effect it has on DM. Similarly, studies on DM are often preoccupied with distinguishing between the new concept and other development paradigms and in so doing fail to realize the transitional linkages or complementary power of those paradigms. Thus, as developing countries explore viable conceptual and practical bases for redefining development approaches, there is the need for studies that analyze the earlier pathways of development management as a starting point for predicting and shaping future trajectories. To the extent that such studies are arguably limited in the literature, this chapter attempts to contribute towards filling the gap in the development management discourse.

But such a discussion cannot proceed without revisiting the idea and theories of development, even if briefly. Our approach is premised on the need to escape the temptation to discuss development management in a vacuum. The rest of the chapter is structured as follows: the first section discusses the concept of development, noting its confusions and meeting points as well as the theoretical underpinnings of modern development strategies. Here, even though various theories of development have been discussed in the literature especially following World War II, our focus is limited to a few of those theories that have been dominant in shaping development interventions or designs. The second section delves into development administration with particular emphasis on its inseparability from development management and hence the need to appropriately regard it as the incipient stage of DM. The birth, or re-birth, of development management is then discussed, followed by some critique of DM as a viable paradigm. What follows is an attempt to explore the changing character of DM. The chapter then concludes with some recommendations.

Development: in search of a universal definition

Discussions on the concept of development are more convergent on the diversity of its definition than what the meaning of the concept is. In other words, the only thing that is universal about definitions of the concept of development is that it means different things to different groups in different contexts. Whilst many have thought of development as the socio-economic and political changes that continue to take place in Africa, Asia, Latin America, the Caribbean and the South Pacific (Turner, Hulme and McCourt, 2015), others see it as essentially the transition from poor or undesired state to a desired condition that provides room for the pursuit of societal or individual needs. The different conceptions of and approaches to development between multilaterals such as the World Bank and the United Nations Development Programme (UNDP) have been variously cited in the literature to highlight the contested meaning of the concept. Whilst the former leads the camp of economic enthusiasts to view development as improved gains in gross national product and industrialization, among others, the UNDP and its supporters see development through a cornucopia of indicators including improvement in access to health, food, clothing, education and security. Although the economic definition is by no means insignificant, it has often been cited as narrow because behind the reported figures could be wide disparities in terms of concentration of wealth. For instance, whilst the GNI per capita of Saudi Arabia and other oil-rich countries could look appealing on paper, the wealth of such countries is concentrated in a few hands. Hence, using such indicators to measure development could miss the point. More holistic definitions have therefore been advocated.

In an earlier study, Seers (1979) and other scholars drew attention to addressing issues of poverty, employment and inequality as well as expansion in access to social services as constituting development. In later years, scholars such as Sen (2001) and Todaro and Smith (2014) have emphasized access to freedom and enhanced dignity as well as opportunities to break away from poverty, among others, as constituting the required ingredients for meaningful development. In his seminal work *Development as Freedom*, Sen (2001: 2) for instance defines development as 'the removal of major sources of un-freedom: poverty as well as tyranny, poor economic opportunities as well as systematic social deprivation, neglect of public facilities as well as intolerance or over activity of repressive states'.

Suffice to argue at this stage, however, that differences in approaches to understanding development have implications for the kind and quality of strategies that are designed to address development or underdevelopment concerns. Does history or current development thinking and practice provide any modicum of information on the kind of philosophical orientations that shape development interventions in the developing world? If so, in what form(s) have such interventions taken, and what are the implications for future development efforts?

Approaches to development: dominant theories

The theoretical foundations of development interventions continue to change over the years. For the purposes of this study, the 1950s and beyond are considered. It needs to be emphasized that whilst particular theories are often cited as characteristic of some development era, it is possible that other theories or approaches would have co-existed at the time (Willis, 2005). It has been contended that between 1950 and 1960, modernization theory was the dominant approach to promoting or managing development in the third world (Willis, 2005). This approach viewed development as a linear path in which a country progresses from one state of development to another, usually desired, stage (Rostow, 1960). Proponents of this theory posited that countries that aspired to development needed to follow the example of the already developed European countries or the United States. Thus, through conscious planning, developing countries could avoid the traps of development uncertainties by importing best practices in the form of technology, institutions and values from the developed world (Willis, 2005). The approach held great promise, and developing or newly independent countries happily embraced it. However, later events exposed the flaws in this modernist conception of development as the late 1960s was characterized by 'increased poverty, growing indebtedness, political repression, economic stagnation and a host of other ills' (Turner, Hulme and McCourt, 2015: 6).

Vociferous in their critique of the modernization theory, some neo-Marxists proffered alternative explanations to the underdevelopment of the third world. Through what they termed dependency theory, these scholars contended that developing countries were poor because the developed world had perpetuated an exploitative order which makes the latter benefit from the underdevelopment of the former (Frank, 1971). Thus, contrary to previous notions by modernization theorists, the problems of the developing world were externally imposed rather than internal. In other words, far from being partners in development or concerned well-wishers, it is in the interest of the developed world to ensure that the developing world (referred to as the periphery) lagged behind in a manner that entrenches their subservient role or dependency on the center. To these theorists, the only way to ensure visible and sustained development was for the developing countries to be self-reliant, breaking free from the existing economic order perpetuated by the center. The weakness of such a proposition was that it was of course as utopian as it was impractical. Indeed, in an increasingly globalized world, no country could afford to live in a state of autarky as dependency theorists appeared to propose. It is needless to emphasize that such an approach would end up worsening development gains, even if those gains may have been negligible.

Following the above, neo-liberalists argued that the key to development was for government to retreat, allowing development outcomes to be determined by the free interplay of demand and supply (Turner, Hulme and McCourt, 2015). But economic fallouts such as the global financial crises provided ample justification that the market alone cannot hold the balance of development without moderating or enabling interventions by government (Dwivedi, Khator and Nef, 2007; Frankel, 2005). There is therefore, a surge in advocacy to bring the government back as the leading player in the theater of development. It is worth mentioning that several other theories have been advanced to explain spatial differences in development; these include arguments about poor geography and more recently, (in)effective institutions (Acemoglu and Robinson, 2012). Although these theories also have their shortcomings, it is widely recognized that the lack of conceptual clarity that surrounds development strategies and implementation cannot be detached from 'severe losses, misguided interventions and poor results in development practice' (Turner, Hulme and McCourt, 2015: 13). Elsewhere, Frankel (2005: 6) submits that 'the very process of development is under attack now and radical changes must be introduced if the advance of development is to continue'. It appears the solution lies in appreciating the impracticability of arriving at definitional consensus whilst renewing our knowledge in and resolve to ensuring better outcomes. One way would be, perhaps, to employ management principles in guiding the pursuit of development goals whilst minimizing waste.

Whilst the concept of management has evolved since the last century, it is important to note that context-specific situations are necessary in determining which approach would be appropriate to realizing sound development outcomes. Thus, although the distinction drawn by Paton (1991) is useful, its applicability is better viewed in the following quotation from Thomas (1996: 6):

> The nature of the task in hand, and its context, will determine which is more appropriate. For example, to achieve quick and effective promotion of humanitarian relief in an emergency it may be essential to think of management in terms of 'command and control', while the management of a successful agency giving advice and assistance to small businesses may be better thought of in terms of 'empowerment and enabling'. This seems to unite the two views into the simple idea of management as *getting the work done by the best means available*.

Development administration: the incipient stage in development management

Much of the literature does not distinguish between development administration (DA) and development management (Thomas, 1996; Esman, 1991). Indeed, Esman (1991) sums up this position when he argues that the rebranding of development administration as development management was rather cosmetic as it was not informed by any change in substance or methodology. In short he believes that scholars could hardly point to any reason for the change in name. Others view DA as a precursor to DM (Dwivedi, Khator and Nef, 2007; Brinkerhoff and Coston, 1999). This chapter supports the widely held view that although some differences may exist upon close scrutiny, the introduction of development management in no way meant the end of development administration. In fact, the former is a refinement of the latter, even if this improvement is negligible at best. Therefore, we treat development administration in this section as the initial stage of development management.

The conventional wisdom which surrounded the crave for urgent development initiatives in the third world following World War II was the primacy of the state as the 'engine of development'. It was believed that the problem of the developing world was administrative in nature (Stone, 1965), hence the need to equip public sector bureaucrats who could lead a conscious planning process aimed at development (Riggs, 1970). This acquisition of 'a new lustre' by the bureaucracies (Siffin, 1966) resulted in the birth of development administration. According to Riggs (1970: 6–7), regarded as the earliest proponent of DA:

> Development administration refers to the administration of development pro-grammes, to the methods used by large scale organizations, notably government, to implement policies and plans designed to meet development challenges.

Another definition put forward by Schaffer (1973: 245) viewed DA as being in respect of:

> development programmes, policies and projects in those conditions in which there are unusually wide and new demands and in which there are peculiarly low capacities and severe obstacles to meeting them.

In reality, the emergence of development administration was a re-introduction of the principles of modernization theory since it was based on a 'Western model of rational administrative authority' (McCourt and Gilrajani, 2010: 2). Put differently, development administration 'was a form of administrative engineering imported from the West and embodying faith in the application of rational scientific principles and the efficacy of Keynesian welfare economics' (Turner, Hulme and McCourt, 2015: 15).

The approach to development in this era followed the path of 'external inducements, the transfer of technology, and training by foreign experts' (Dwivedi, Khator and Nef, 2007) as the surest way of transforming the third-world public services from the moribund traditional state to the ideal modern bureaucracy. Elsewhere, Turner, Hulme and McCourt (2015) have identified similar pathways taken by development administration. They point out that development administration proceeded on the notion of 'big government' highlighting its similarity with bureaucracy. Two, development administration relied on the so-called elite comprising politicians, planners and other technical experts who would engineer a trickle down of development from the urban to the rural centers through bureaucratic machineries. The idea was for such a minority group to constitute the critical mass of people who could provide direction and focus in planning aimed at 'transforming their societies into replicas of the modern Western nation-state' (Turner, Hulme and McCourt, 2015). The third approach to development administration was to ensure that where the requisite tools of plan and programme implementation were lacking, transfer of administrative skills and competence was done to fill the gap. Fourth, the transfer of the tool bags or 'administrative capability' was deemed as possible through aid from the West to the developing countries. The fifth approach to realizing development outcomes through development administration was to moderate, if not supplant, the effects of traditional culture which was deemed to be inimical to development.

The emphasis on bureaucracy as the engine for administering development was not based on mere obsession to expand the involvement of the state in development. Rather, the motivation seemed to have been influenced by the absence of or distrust in an effective private sector in the fledgling independent developing countries (Hirschmann, 1999). Thus, 'development placed its hopes on bureaucracy' because it provided 'the prime location of skills, education, organization and initiative, provider of public equity, and generator of development' (Hirschmann, 1999: 3).

In their bid to ensure 'high efficiency and effectiveness' through 'the entrenchment of bureaucratic standards' (Dwivedi, Khator and Nef, 2007), therefore, developing countries embraced the new model. Consequently, various strategies were adopted. Earlier attempts looked to de-bureaucratize the public sectors in a way that made them more innovative and less risk-averse. However, the third-world bureaucrats still clung to their old process; nor were they given the requisite support by politicians for the reform processes despite the rhetoric of the latter (Hirschmann, 1999). It turned out that third-world bureaucrats, rather than being the engines of reforms aimed at development, were rather concerned with serving their personal interests. As Hirschmann (1999) has pointed out, the bureaucrats would seize every opportunity to call for localization, training and professionalization at the expense of refining or reconceptualizing their roles and responsibilities in the new development agenda. Attempts at circumventions, re-orientation, and decentralization did very little to transform the bureaucracy for effective administration of development as had been envisaged.

Following from the above, many studies have concluded that the development administration paradigm began to 'crumble' since the belief that developing countries could champion their own development had been dashed. This was particularly so in the period immediately following the UN Second Development Decade. Here, the spread of immense political, socio-economic (the oil price shocks), as well as cultural and ideological crises (Dwivedi, Khator and Nef, 2007) stagnated economic growth. As scholars began to appreciate the 'deadlock' in development administration (Schaffer, 1969), it became apparent that a bureaucracy full of 'patronage and rent-seeking' could hardly serve as the *vanguard elite* in addressing underdevelopment in the third world. The search for a new or better paradigm was therefore imperative (McCourt and Gulrajani, 2010).

The next section discusses the new character of development administration in the garb of development management. The section will also point to some emerging critiques of development management and how these could influence possible future trajectories as developing countries attempt to negotiate their ways out of underdevelopment.

The transition from development administration to development management

The growing discontent with development administration necessitated the introduction of, or transition into, another approach to development known as development management. Although some scholars believe the change is only in name and not content, Cooke (2001: 11) has noted that there is little dispute about the 'continuity' between development administration and development management. Despite this transition and skepticism of some scholars, development management lays claim to some distinctiveness in approach. Brinkerhoff and Coston (1999: 348–349) point to some of the distinctions when they observe that development management attempts to break away from 'technocratic, universalist, public sector administration model' which was characteristic of the earlier development administration, to a more holistic 'bureaucratic re-orientation and restructuring, the integration of politics and culture into management ... participatory and performance-based service delivery ...'. According to Thomas (1996), the concept of development management could be analyzed based on two views of development, namely, development as a historical process and as a conscious or deliberate attempt at progress. The former leads to a conceptualization of development management as management in the context of the development process whereas the latter relates to management of the development effort. To these was added the concept of development management as management in the quest to shape development outcomes (Thomas, 1999). In another study, Brinkerhoff and Coston (1999) point to development management as representing four related aspects as follows: a means to foreign assistance agendas, a toolkit, values and process. The foregoing implies that the meaning of development management includes, but is not limited to, applying best practice to achieve better development outcomes mostly through interventions from and collaborative efforts by development partners.

Development management was largely influenced by a new set of doctrines which constituted New Public Management. Here, the pathway to development was to borrow so-called best practice from the private sector and bring it into the public sector. Given that earlier assumptions or experiences viewed the public sector largely as more of a 'problem than a solution' (Dwivedi, Khator and Nef, 2007: 120), developing countries aimed at development through 'privatization, downsizing, localizing, and outsourcing ...' (Dwivedi, Khator and Nef, 2007: 119). The pathway to development was to ensure effectiveness and efficiency in the provision of public services. On the one hand the public sector re-oriented itself, at least on the face of it, through market-centred managerialism in the performance of its mandate. In reducing the cost of project and programme implementation, for instance, government business was largely decentralized internally and externally. More importantly, the public sector attempted to create the enabling environment for the private sector to thrive.

Another characteristic pathway of development management was the expansion of the space for non-state actors such as civil society organizations (CSOs) or NGOs to operate. Whilst serving as a complementary force to addressing the development gaps, the NGOs also provided expertise to and watchdog roles in the implementation of development projects and programmes. The emergence of the NGOs was particularly important as they were seen as the best provider of 'welfare services and micro-enterprise initiatives' (Hirschmann, 1999: 17). Till date, evidence of the emergence of local and international NGOs can be found in almost all developing countries across the world. From their contribution to healthcare provision in Bangladesh to leading the advocacy for better livelihoods of default custodians of oil-rich Niger Delta in Nigeria or mining areas in Ghana's Western Region, the contributions of NGOs have been so ubiquitous or overwhelming that developing countries can no more imagine how they could have survived without NGOs. This by no means suggests that the record of NGOs in developing countries is without some blemished spots. They have often been blamed for viewing their interventions as favours, hence discounting or failing to incorporate the contributions of potential beneficiaries during planning. Others have been cited for their lack of accountability and transparency even though they are quick to cast the fast stone when public sector entities are involved.

As the development management movement continues to explore ways of becoming more relevant in the twenty-first century, it has embraced the concept of participation as a means of enhancing development effectiveness. It has been contended that previous approaches took it for granted that beneficiaries of development programmes would remain passive recipients of such interventions. However, such assumptions, influenced by so-called best practice experience from the developed world, were challenged by practical realities in the developing world which called for the need to plan with, rather than plan for, beneficiaries. Thus, recent development interventions emphasize the significance of getting members of potential beneficiary populations involved from the design stage to the implementation stage. This approach is also believed to provide such a form of empowerment to beneficiaries as to ensure that there is accountability, transparency and value for money in project implementation. Notwithstanding, evidence abounds in most developing countries that the requirement for participation is usually adhered to by project and programme designers in their quest to satisfy donor requirements. The result is that such requirements are hardly implemented.

The balance sheet of development management: implications for future trajectories

Despite its claim to being the new panacea to the development challenges of the third world, development management has been criticized as being replete with 'policy failures and operational mishaps' (Dwivedi, Khator and Nef, 2007: 2).

It has been suggested that whilst development management had some prospects, it appeared part of the reasons for its failures was the reluctance of public sector bureaucrats to relinquish their hold on the development machinery. After all, as Dwivedi, Khator and Nef (2007) have argued, bureaucrats were often threatened because the call to development management was an invitation to preside over their own doom. Thus the ingenuity expected from bureaucrats to enhance development management was rather employed to frustrate it. Other scholars believe that the context of developing countries made it almost impracticable to imbibe the doctrines of New Public Management on the basis of which donors conditioned their aid and other interventions. But as developing countries explore new approaches to and future trajectories for managing development (Frankel, 2005), several overlapping and sometimes cyclical recommendations have been proffered. Some of these recommendations are also informed by the changing character of managing development in the developing world.

One, some scholars believe that attempts at reforms have often been an invitation to bring back more of the same approaches that created the problems they seek to address (Dwivedi, Khator and Nef, 2007). For instance, it is obvious that the public sector cannot afford to stand aloof from the development front. And in order to enhance its role, it has been recommended that the bureaucracy needs to be brought back as a strong driving agent for future development interventions (Hirschmann, 1999). In this regard, ways are being sought to make the state an effective entity is pushing inclusive development. Thus, future development management approaches will include a re-look at earlier reforms that regarded the public sector as a hydra-headed monster which is not only disinclined to change but also seizes every opportunity to muddy the waters of development.

Another suggestion for future direction is for development management to be receptive to practical realities accumulated by third-world development practitioners instead of the straitjacket, restrictive approaches. Citing Gulrajani (2010) for instance, Turner, Hulme and McCourt (2015) have called for a pluralistic and political approach that helps practitioners to identify, and possibly assert, their roles in the theatre of development. Perhaps one way of practicalizing this approach is to also emphasize the relevance of third-world values and ethics as enablers of development rather than the previous antagonism to their incorporation into development strategies.

Turner, Hulme and McCourt (2015) further draw attention to the increasingly fashionable emphasis by Acemoglu and Robinson (2012) on the primacy of effective institutions. Whilst there is a call for strong institutions, instead of strong men, as US President Obama pointed out in his first official visit to Africa, the current discourse led by Acemoglu, Robinson and others rather bemoans the transfer of inappropriate institutions to developing countries. Put differently, future efforts would require a departure from importing and mimicking Western institutions in the hope that they could achieve for the developing world what they did for their developed counterparts. However, the call for stronger, context-specific institutions needs further caution and commentary. Turner, Hulme and McCourt (2015), for instance, argue that such processes could, in all probability, fall in the trap of elite capture, hence the danger of repeating the very problems which were the subject of criticism of the bureaucratic approach to the incipient stage in development management (otherwise called development administration). Development experiences in the developing world are full of examples that give grounding to this caution. Abdulai and Hulme (2014) have noted, for instance, that in Ghana, powerful elites and ruling coalitions are able to capture the institutional design in order to shape resource allocations to satisfy clientelistic considerations. Thus, whilst the call for a redefinition of the development management approach through effective and locally engineered institutions holds good promise, it would require more diligence to avoid likely traps.

The increasing influence of the political settlements (Khan, 2010) framework to understanding third-world development policies and outcomes will, or has to, have implications for the trajectories to be adopted by development management. It is becoming significantly evident that the assumption that the application of managerial principles alone could yield significant results independent of the political environment is flawed. Indeed, in developing democracies, the design and implementation of development policies are not necessarily based on scientific or equity logic. Rather, they are influenced by considerations that are deemed to hold greater electoral promise for the political elite (Hirvi and Whitfield, 2015; Abdulai and Hulme, 2014; Whitfield, 2010). So, as donor agencies and development scholars attempt to reform the development management agenda for better outcomes, they would have to contend with the daunting task of either courting the elusive logic of objectivity of politicians or seek to clip their feathers. Whilst developing country politicians are adept at circumventing attempts to loosen their grip, relative gains are possible. For example, the success of the implementation of the First Compact of the Millennium Challenge Account and transition to the second phase in Ghana is explained largely by the ability of the US government to resist attempts by Ghanaian political elites to change the players of the game.

Conclusion

Approaches to the development management and the theories that undergird them have evolved in the last three decades or so. Whilst some confusion abounds in academic and donor circles about what development management actually means, various definitions revolve around *management in the context of a development process* as well as *management of the development efforts* (Thomas, 1996). Another strand of definitions also considers development management as a deliberate attempt to achieve development outcomes through effective and efficient means. In its infant stage, development management assumed the nomenclature of development administration, placing its hopes in the third-world bureaucracies as the engines of development effectiveness. However, the hopes of advocates of the development administration paradigm, and developing countries in particular, were dashed as the bureaucrats ended up frustrating, rather than aiding development. There was thus a craving for a new approach resulting in the re-packaging of the concept in the form of development management; this time, the role of the public sector was de-emphasized, with increasing focus on the private sector and a call on public sector organizations to adopt best practice from the private sector. This approach, which was largely influenced by the New Public Management paradigm, was later to be reformed to include elements of participation and empowerment. Despite these pathways, development management was seen as having hit a 'deadlock'. Others also saw the approach as being littered with 'lucklustre' records, with the result that new trajectories are not only predictable but also necessary. The new trajectory incidentally includes bringing back the state as a prime player in the development equation whilst highlighting the significance of developing context-specific institutions and strategies. It is also envisaged that development management advocates would rethink the rather erroneous assumption that development could necessarily be effective by a mere application of managerial principles without regard to partisan, clientelistic political realities. However, whilst the new trajectories promise the twin benefits of building on the strength of the earlier pathways and avoiding their associated mistakes, the growing evidence of the role of partisan, competitive political considerations in shaping development outcomes calls for more vigilance in preventing possible elite capture. There is also a lot to be said for re-negotiating the role of developing country ethical values in the development process in order to address the vacuum created by earlier antagonistic approaches which erroneously viewed traditional institutions as inimical to development.

References

Abdulai, A.-G. and Hulme, D. (2014). The politics of regional inequality in Ghana: state elites, donors and PRSPS. *Development Policy Review*, 33(5), 529–553.

Acemoglu, D. and Robinson, J.A. (2012). *Why Nations Fail: The Origins of Power, Prosperity and Poverty*. New York: Crown Business.

Brinkerhoff, D. W. and Coston, J. M. (1999). International development management in a globalized world. *Public Administration Review*, 59(4), 346–361.

Cooke, B. (2001). *From Colonial Administration to Development Management*. University of Manchester, UK. Institute for Development Policy and Management (IDPM).

Dwivedi, O. P., Khator, R. and Nef, J. (2007). *Managing Development in a Global Context*. London: Palgrave Macmillan.

Esman, M. J. (1991). *Management Dimensions of Development: Perspectives and Strategies*. West Hartford: Kumarian Press.

Frank, A. (1971). *Capitalism and Underdevelopment in Latin America*. Harmondsworth: Penguin.

Frankel, E. G. (2005). *Managing Development: Measures of Success and Failure in Development*. London: Palgrave Macmillan.

Gulrajani, N. (2010). New vistas for development management: examining radical–reformist possibilities and potential. *Public Administration and Development*, 30(2), 136–148.

Hirschmann, D. (1999). Development management versus third world bureaucracies: a brief history of conflicting interests. *Development and Change*, 30(2), 287–305.

Hirvi, M. and Whitfield, L. (2015). Public-service provision in clientelist political settlements: lessons from Ghana's urban water sector. *Development Policy Review*, 33(2), 135–158.

Khan, M. (2010). *Political Settlements and the Governance of Growth-Enhancing Institutions*. London: SOAS.

McCourt, W. and Gulrajani, N. (2010). The future of development management: introduction to the special issue. *Public Administration and Development*, 30(2), 81–90.

Paton, R. (1991). *Managing with a Purpose*. Milton Keynes: The Open University.

Riggs, F. W. (1970). *Introduction*. In Riggs, F. (ed.), *Frontiers of Development Administration* (pp. 3–37). Durham: Duke University Press.

Rostow, W. W. (1960). *The Stages of Growth: A Non-Communist Manifesto*. Cambridge: Cambridge University Press.

Schaffer, B. B. (1969). The deadlock in development administration. In Leys, C. (ed.), *Politics and Change in Developing Countries* (pp. 177–212). Cambridge: Cambridge University Press.

Schaffer, B. B. (1973). *The Administrative Factor: Papers in Organization, Politics and Development*. London: Frank Cass.

Seers, D. (1979). The meaning of development. In Lehmann, D. (ed.), *Development Theory: Four Critical Studies* (pp. 9–30). London: Frank Cass.

Sen, A. (2001). *Development as Freedom*. Oxford: Oxford University Press.

Siffin, W. J. (1966). *Thai Bureaucracy: Institutional Change and Development*. Honolulu: East-West Center.

Stone, D. C. (1965). Government machinery necessary for development. In Kriesberg, M. (ed.), *Public Administration in Developing Countries* (pp. 49–67). Washington, D.C.: The Brookings Institution (Proceedings from a 1963 conference in Bogota).

Thomas, A. (1996). What is development management? *Journal of International Development*, 8(1), 95–110.

Thomas, A. (1999). What makes good development management? *Development in Practice*, 9(1–2), 9–17.

Todaro, M. P. and Smith, S. C. (2014). *Economic Development* (12th ed.). New York: Trans-Atlantic Publications.

Turner, M., Hulme, D. and McCourt, W. (2015). *Governance, Management and Development: Making the State Work*. London: Palgrave Macmillan.

Whitfield, L. (2010). The state elite, PRSPS and policy implementation in aid-dependent Ghana. *Third World Quarterly*, 31(5), 721–737.

Willis, K. (2005). *Theories and Practice of Development*. London: Routledge.

3 Ethics, values and development management

Anthony Sumnaya Kumasey, Justice Nyigmah Bawole, Farhad Hossain and Mohammed Ibrahim

Introduction

In contemporary times, there has been a rise in unethical practices including absconding with public funds, fraud, conflicts of interest, blatant waste, sexual harassment (Benavides et al., 2012), bribery and corruption (Ryvkin and Serra, 2012), and other illegal conducts in public, private and non-governmental organizations (NGOs). Indeed, ethical misconduct among politicians, public and private administrators is so pervasive that it is difficult to point to any country that 'seems immune to the global ethical breakdown' that has stifled development processes and outcomes (Dwivedi et al., 2007: 198). Consequently, several scholars, including Turner et al. (2015: 1) have opined that the public sector in developing countries is largely corrupt and inefficient, resulting in its failure to provide sound policy advise to government and build synergies with NGOs and other development partners. This point was reiterated by the World Bank as far back as 1997 in its World Development Report when it alluded to the presence of unethical behaviours including patronage and has deplored these tendencies as a 'disease of government' (Turner et al., 2015; World Bank, 1997). These behaviours have harmful effects on individuals, organizations, as well as countries, both developed and developing. For instance, it has been estimated that about 5 per cent of global annual revenues (approximately 2.9 trillion dollars) is lost due to various forms of corruption or unethical behaviours (Association of Certified Fraud Examiners, 2010).

These unethical behaviours threaten the reputation (Van Riel and Fombrun, 2007), financial performance (Orlitzky et al., 2003), continuity of organizations (Grant and Visconti, 2006) and the eventual development of developing countries (United Nations, 2001). Clearly, the wanton relegation and exposure of the 'protective layer of public morality' to the 'onslaught of dishonesty, sleaziness, deception, and possessive individualism' as well as mis-performance, ineptitude and unpredictability are a disincentive to development efforts in third-world countries. A re-awakening of the ethical consciousness of developing countries is therefore not only promising but also a sine qua non for ensuring development effectiveness. This realization has resulted in the resurgence of interest in ethics and values in many countries around the world (Childs, 2012; Williams, 2011), a phenomenon which Kernaghan (2003: 712) describes succinctly as the 'ethics era', i.e. a period within which there has been increased focus on public service ethics and values.

The major concern of governments especially in developing countries is to improve the standard of living of the citizenry by showing commitment through progressive policies and practices. This improvement can only be successfully achieved if public and private sector employees imbibe and exhibit a high sense of ethics and values in the field of development management. Scholars have thus called for, among others, the promotion of values in development management (Brinkerhoff and Brinkerhoff, 2010). Despite this recognition and call to action, it appears there is a dearth of studies that explicitly explore the role of values, ethics and morality in development management (Fischer and Kothari, 2011; Wood et al., 2010). The priority therefore for researchers, practitioners and students of development management is to inculcate the 'value agenda' (McCourt, 2007: 430) into the developmental arena of developing countries. Public service providers are expected to have higher ethical standards because they are seen as the guardians or custodians of contemporary administrative state (Rosenbloom et al., 2009) and are therefore supposed to serve in the interest of the general public.

Closely related to the above is the issue of trust between citizens and public officials, which is seen as the bedrock of governance (Rose and Lawton, 1999). Public officials are expected to act in the best interest of the citizenry in order to gain their trust. Further, another need for high ethical standards in the public service is to mitigate the incidence of corruption and other unethical activities (Davis, 2003). Additionally, in this 'ethics era' society expects all and sundry to be ethical. Strict adherence to ethics and values will ensure that all actors in development will behave ethically and thereby curing the 'disease of government'. We will be looking at the topic from the perspectives of ethics, values and development management.

Ethics

The term 'ethics' according to Davis (2003) originated from the Greek word 'ethos' meaning habitual or customary conduct and exists in every society. Ethics has been defined variedly. Freakley and Burgh (2000: 97) opined that ethics can simply be understood as 'what we ought to do', that is to say, it requires judgment and reasoning in decision making that raise questions regarding what is right, wrong, good or bad conduct, fair or just. Others have defined ethics as the science or study of the morality of human behaviour (Albanese, 2008; Banks, 2004). Trevino and Nelson (2013) have elucidated that ethics are the principles, norms and standards of conduct governing an individual or groups. Ethics therefore seeks to examine the moral philosophy of human conduct, the goodness and badness, or rightness and wrongness of human behaviour, drawing on complex philosophies, such as teleology and deontology (Pollock, 2007; Souryal, 2007). Ethics begins with care, that is, caring about human and natural life, the welfare of others, honest and trustworthy communication, and fundamental individual and group freedom (Bowman and West, 2014). From the above definitions, ethics can be classified based on two forms of behaviours: ethical and unethical behaviours. Ethical behaviours are the behaviours that are consistent with the principles, norms and standards of business practice that have been agreed upon by society (Trevino and Nelson, 2013) and such norms according to Mbatha (2005) include humaneness, honesty, justice, reasonableness, freedom, truth, decency, integrity, order, fairness and openness.

On the other hand, unethical behaviours are conceptualized as behaviours that violate social norms regarding what is right and wrong (Noe and Rebello, 1994). Other authors have implied that unethical behaviours are those that violate one's deeply held beliefs concerning what is right and wrong (May et al., 2003; Dubinsky and Jolson, 1991). More broadly, Victor and Cullen (1988) have described unethical behaviour as that which is inappropriate when facing a decision that has implications for other people. Examples of unethical practices amongst others include bribery and corruption, absconding with public funds, fraud, conflict of interest, blatant waste, misuse of confidential information and falsification of records (Trevino and Nelson, 2013; Benavides et al., 2012; Ryvkin and Serra, 2012).

Public values

According to de Graaf and van der Wal (2008: 84), 'values are hard to define and hard to locate; they are neither here nor there … values never come just by themselves; they never appear unaccompanied. Values are always attached to a value manifestation and express a quality'. The word 'values' in the narrower sense is used to refer to 'what is considered good, desirable or worthwhile', while in a broader sense it refers to 'all kinds of lightness, obligation, virtue, beauty, truth and holiness' (Frankena, 1967: 229–230). Williams (1968) defines values as the criteria people use to select and justify actions and to evaluate people, including the self, and events. Values can also be understood as 'ideas about what is good, right, and desirable in a society' or as 'conceptions of the desirable that guide the way social actors (organizational leaders, policy-makers and individuals) select actions, evaluate people and events, and explain their actions and evaluations' (Schwartz, 1999: 24). Thus, values are societal principles, goals and standards that members within a group or organization believe to be intrinsically worthy (Thomas, 2013; Hatch and Cunliffe, 2006). Linking it to the public sector, a public value is associated with a principle that must be followed or a standard that must be met by public organizations while they regulate or produce their service (Jørgensen, 2007) and can become manifest through codes, ethics, norms or principles (Jørgensen and Vrangbæk, 2011). Bozeman (2007: 13) defined public values as 'the rights, benefits, and prerogatives to which citizens should (and should not) be entitled; the obligations of citizens to society, the state and one another; and the principles on which governments and policies should be based'. Therefore, public values help members of an organization to understand how they should act in that organization (Moorhead and Griffin, 1989: 494–497) and also serve as the link between the daily work of public servants and the broad aims of democratic governance (Kernaghan, 2003).

Values are not only relevant to organizations, but to individuals and societies as well (Bowman and West, 2014; Thomas, 2013), and they impact individuals' attitudes, approach to life situations, relationships, interactions with people and within organizational settings, and the meaning they assign to situations and the behaviours of others. Thus, values are seen as the 'prime drivers of personal, social, and professional choices' (Suar and Khuntia, 2010: 443). Individuals therefore bring to the organization their personal beliefs, perceptions, goals, choices and actions and they rely on these to judge people and situations and also to make decisions (Thomas, 2013; Rohan, 2000; Schwartz, 1994). However, these values vary from person to person, and therefore become more complex to identify for larger groups, likewise societies within a particular nation have developed their respective social values and these values dictate societal behaviour in terms of the importance they attach to each value (Garcia-Zamor, 2015). To make values impact workplace behaviours and practices, they need to be developed, endorsed and implemented properly (Atchison, 2007; Thomas, 2013).

Difference between values and ethics

The terms 'values' and 'ethics' are often used synonymously but they do not mean the same thing. Values can be defined as 'enduring beliefs that influence the choices we make among available means or ends' (Rokeach, 1973: 5). Ethics in most times relate with issues of right or wrong, good or evil (Kakabadse et al., 2003: 478; Kernaghan, 2003; Kernaghan, 2000). Values in themselves do not actually do anything but it is the application of ethical codes to values that leads to particular behaviour. In effect, ethics are the rules that translate values into everyday life (OECD, 1996: 12). Ethics is about determining what is 'wrong', 'good', 'bad' or 'right', and ethical choices are informed by values which help actors decide on what option to take when faced with an ethical dilemma (Kakabadse et al., 2003: 479). Van Wart (1998: 163) argues that ethics are a subset of values, and that values form our broad, socially derived ethical standards for how the world should operate. Ethics, he proposes, is doing the right thing, that is, acting on values. This is buttressed by Henry (1998: xiv) when he argued that 'values can be ethical, unethical or simply non-ethical'. 'Ethical values' are increasingly regarded as a subset of public service values in general (Kernaghan, 2003: 711–712) because ethics translates values into action (Bowman and West, 2014). It could be inferred from the above that there is a close relationship between ethics and values which suggests a formalization of this relationship. In this direction, Kernaghan (2003) has observed that some countries have merged their ethics and values documents together and a few have provided a value foundation that underpins a superstructure of ethics and other rules. This study will therefore treat ethics and values as similar since they complement one another (Jørgensen and Vrangbæk, 2011; Thomas, 2013) and adopts Suar and Khuntia's (2010: 443) definition as the 'shared concepts of what individuals believe to be good, desirable, and righteous' for both ethics and values because they both determine how one ought to or ought not to behave or act.

The existence of socially sanctioned modes of conduct, expressed in ethical values, ensures some element of predictability which shapes the reciprocal relationships between the citizenry (often regarded as principals) and their agents tasked with the responsibility of ensuring that societal needs are met. From the foregoing discussion on ethics and values therefore, it could be seen that the citizenry expect public officials, NGOs and other developmental partners to behave or act ethically in the fulfilment of their duties (Mbatha, 2005). This viewpoint is based on the assumption that public service organizations including development partners exist to serve the interest of the public and therefore their actions should be determined by their specific codes of conduct which impinge on accountability, equality, justice, legality, impartiality, integrity, responsibility and transparency. However, some of these public servants and development partners have reportedly engaged in unethical behaviours by siphoning aid meant for development through outright embezzlement or by diverting it disproportionately to government employees and/or the well-connected elite (Garcia-Zamor, 2015). This leads to ineffective and unsatisfactory service provided by the government and other development partners.

Development management (DM)

The expectation of every citizen in a developed or developing country is that the government provides all the necessary developmental amenities. But in situations where the government is unable to meet these needs, she enters into a kind of partnership with NGOs and multilateral and bilateral donors amongst others to meet these needs. The process of these developmental partners coming together to improve the living conditions of the citizenry falls under development management (DM). Even though it had been practiced under various names in the past, the field of DM became very popular in the 1980s and 1990s and played a leading role in development thinking, as it applied mainstream management concepts like strategic choice, strategic management, leadership and organisational culture to the problems of development (McCourt and Gulrajani, 2010). Earlier definitions of DM have underscored the need to improve national administrative capabilities as well as donor and foundation-sponsored development programmes (Riggs, 1970). For instance, Brinkerhoff and Coston (1999: 347) view DM as 'managing the processes and building the capacity necessary to achieve improvements in people's lives and communities' well-being, including understanding and dealing with the array of constraints that impinge upon their achievement'. Thomas (1996: 106) defined development management as 'the management of deliberate efforts at progress on the part of one of a number of agencies, the management of intervention in the process of social change in the context of conflicts of goals, values and interests'.

Later on, Thomas (1999: 10) refined his definition to refer to 'what is needed to carry out development tasks successfully'. Brinkerhoff and Brinkerhoff (2006) defined DM to include four dimensions, namely values, a process, tools and means to institutional agendas. They explained these dimensions as follows:

a) **Values:** DM incorporates a value dimension that emphasizes self-determination, empowerment, and an equitable distribution of development benefits. Accordingly, it emphasizes the clinical mode of client- or beneficiary-driven processes, making responsiveness, respect and feasibility primary over technical correctness and expediency. This dimension also recognizes the inherent political nature of development, acknowledging that it creates winners and losers, and works with, rather than assumes away, the political aspects of development.

b) **Process**: DM is a process intervention, where the application of tools in pursuit of objectives is undertaken in ways that self-consciously address political and value issues. As such, managing development is a transformational process for all concerned, including the intervention agent.

c) **Tools**: DM promotes the application of a range of management and analytical tools adapted from a variety of social science disciplines, including strategic management, organization development, psychology and political science. These tools roughly represent the science of the profession (the competencies most easily acquired through graduate study and book learning) though their application is artful, in accordance with the values and process dimensions noted above.

d) **Means to institutional agendas**: DM is most commonly pursued in the context of organizations and other institutions participating in what can be viewed as the international development industry. As such, DM is a means to improving the efficiency and effectiveness of these assistance programs in accordance with corresponding policy agendas, organizational missions and project objectives. (Brinkerhoff and Brinkerhoff, 2006; Brinkerhoff and Brinkerhoff, 2010)

From the foregoing, development management is aimed at social goals or 'institutional agendas' that are external to any one organization. It involves intervention or influence rather than direct use of resources to meet goals, and it is process rather than only task oriented, and involves values and clashes between goals (Thomas, 2007). Further, development management is seen as being able to deliberately steer social progress via the application of certain kinds of practices, including as means to foreign aid and development policy agendas, as toolkits to achieve progressive social change by linking intentions to actions, as positive values that address both the style and goal of management in political and normative terms, and as processes that operate at the individual, organisational and sectoral levels (Brinkerhoff, 2008), and is focused on enhancing performance through efficacy and efficiency (Guess and Gabriellyan, 2007; Heady et al., 2007).

In contemporary times, the major actors of DM including non-profit organizations, non-governmental organizations, multinational organizations, bilateral organizations, contracted corporations, and even the fracturing of government into state or local governments (Garcia-Zamor, 2015) have all teamed up to bring about change through activities related to poverty reduction, equitable and sustainable distribution of benefits, and empowerment and it is believed that this can only be achieved through good governance. States that are unresponsive, corrupt and incompetent have difficulty mobilizing resources and delivering services to their citizens (World Bank, 1997; Kaufmann et al., 2006; Leonard, 2010). This therefore prevents them from achieving their main goals of poverty reduction, empowerment and equitable and sustainable distribution of resources.

One of the major challenges facing DM is maintaining a consistent position on values while acting to fulfil the institutional agendas of development actors in the process (Abouassi, 2010). DM understands the state in the context of its relationships to non-state actors, including the private sector, nongovernmental organizations and hybrid organizations such as social enterprises (Brinkerhoff, 2008; Guess and Gabrielyan 2007: 571). In entering into partnership for development, their respective values tend to clash (leading to values contestations) and this raises ethical issues (Garcia-Zamor, 2015) as values impact on how individuals feel about themselves, their work, and organizations (Posner and Schmidt, 1994). If these impacts are negative, egocentric and self-rewarding, then naturally, unethical behaviours would be the norm. In light of these, public officials and other development partners, especially some NGOs, have been labelled as corrupt because of the growing suspicion, accompanied by increased evidence, that these organizations have been tolerating corrupt practices, nepotism, favouritism and embezzlement of donor funds (Ebrahim, 2003; Garcia-Zamor, 2015; Harsh et al., 2010; Kimemia, 2015; Smith, 2010; Transparency International [TI], 2005; Werker and Ahmed, 2008). Developing countries are believed to be the worst affected by the clash of values, or rather the displacement of values. This is because their timely tested cultural arrangements, which served as a policing force in discouraging or punishing anti-social behaviour, such as bribery and corruption, were supplanted by a 'Western style of management, consumerism, and individualism' (Dwivedi et al., 2007: 198). This seeming rush to throw away traditional cultural values and the subsequent failure of the so-called modern 'values to take root' meant that 'no specific standards were left against which the conduct of public officials (as well as business people) could be measured' (Dwivedi et al., 2007: 198). In effect, public institutional frameworks guiding the conduct of development actors in developing countries were either lacking or fragile at best. The next sections examine some unethical behaviours and their impact on development management.

Corruption

Corruption is a world-wide phenomenon and no country is immune from its associated dangers (TI, 2010). Though difficult to measure, the overall impression is that the level of corruption is increasing (Gebel, 2012; TI, 2010). For instance, Transparency International (TI, 2010) has acknowledged that the world is witnessing a rise in corruption and the World Bank (2007: 40) also opines that 'while some progress has been made in strengthening state capacity and accountability worldwide, there is little evidence that this has had a significant aggregate impact on reducing corruption'. The Global Corruption Barometer 2010 has indicated that corruption has increased over the last three years, as six out of ten people around the world are perceived to be corrupt and more than 20 countries have reported significant increases in petty bribery since 2006 (TI, 2010). It is easy to talk about corruption, but like other complex social phenomena, it is difficult to define it as the meaning shifts with the speaker (Rose-Ackermann, 2004).

According to Khan (1996), corruption is a behaviour that deviates from the formal rules of conduct governing the actions of someone in a position of public authority because of private motives such as wealth, power or status. The World Bank and Transparency International also define corruption as 'the abuse of power for private benefits' (World Bank, 1997; TI, 2004), either by an individual or institution in the public or private sector. Nye (1967: 418) views corruption as an official misuse, abuse or unsanctioned or unscheduled use of public office, entrusted power or public resources for personal gains. From the above, corruption could be said to be any wrongdoing on the part of an authority or powerful party through means that are illegitimate, immoral or incompatible with ethical standards in order to satisfy his or her private gains. 'Private gain' is used here to mean direct or indirect forms of benefit that would accrue to any economic actor or his family, associates or group.

Corruption may exist in various scales or levels and permeates virtually every facet of organizational life. Corruption or corrupt behaviours include abuse of power, bribery, fraud and theft, extortion, conflict of interest, embezzlement of funds, financial mismanagement, waste and misappropriation of state property, nepotism and granting of favours to personal acquaintances, acceptance of improper gifts, kickbacks, manipulation of information, discrimination and sexual harassment, perversion of justice, non-performance of duties, election tampering, tax evasion, illegal surveillance, misuse of office seals and stationery, and public officials condoning and conniving with criminal actors (Bowman and West, 2014; Agbiboa, 2013; Lasthuizen et al., 2011; Vargas-Hernández, 2011; Huberts, 2008; TI, 2000). Corruption is therefore used as an umbrella term to cover all the integrity violations including unethical and unprofessional behaviours (Gray, 2013; Lessig, 2011; Huberts, 2008). The negative impacts of corruption have been highlighted in the literature.

Corruption constitutes a major problem in the world because it hampers investment and economic growth (Burke et al., 2011; Sekkat and Me´on, 2005; Barro, 2000), aggravates problems of underground economies (Bjørnskov, 2011; Dreher et al., 2009), discourages foreign aid as donor nations grapple with how to ensure that aid money does not end up in private pockets (Nwabuzor, 2005), and widens the gap between the rich and the poor (Uslaner, 2008; Gupta et al., 2002). Corruption also creates obstacles to economic and political reform (Hellman et al., 2003), imposes considerable human welfare losses (Kaufmann et al., 2005), incurs the loss of legitimacy and effectiveness and adds to the taxpayers burden, and increases openings for organized crime (Bowman and West, 2014). In addition to these, corruption leads to price distortion, subversion of democratic processes, increased financial and commercial risks and a general decline in the ethics and morality of the society (Senior, 2006). Further, corruption leads to the loss of government revenue (Burke et al., 2011; Fjeldstad and Tungodden, 2003), high cost of doing business, promotes the illegal export of resources, encourages conspicuous consumption, and creates general distrust (Caiden et al., 2001). Moreover, corruption also leads to greater political instability and lowers direct foreign investment (Burke et al., 2011: 16). Corruption is therefore seen as an impediment to economic growth and sustainable development especially in emerging economies (Nguemegne, 2011; Balogun, 2003; Nwabuzor, 2005) because it rewards indolence and penalizes hard work, undermines morale and esprit de corps, and compromises the nation's security (Balogun, 2003).

Conflict of interest

This is another unethical behaviour that is closely related to corruption. A conflict of interest results when one's private interests cloud one's judgement in a manner that compromises the objective performance of official duties (MacDonald et al., 2002). In the case of a public official, it could be said that there is conflict of interest when 'personal interests of a public official conflict with those of their obligation to act in the best interest of the state' (UNODC, 2004). Some of the categories of conflict of interest include self-dealing, accepting benefits, influence peddling, using employers' property for private advantage, using confidential information for personal gain, outside employment and post-retirement employment (Kernaghan and Langford, 1990). It is important to point out that conflict of interest situations need not necessarily be cases where there is actual performance of a duty in a manner that gives one unfair advantage by virtue of one's position or one's connections. It can also arise when there is some justifiable perception, on the balance of probability, that given one's perceived interest (either now or in future) in a transaction or the results of an action, one could be influenced to act unfairly. In line with the above, Genckaya (2009: 6) identifies three types of conflict of interest, namely actual (*a public official is in a position to be influenced*), perceived (*a public official is in a position to appear to be influenced*) and potential (*where a public official may be influenced in the future*). All these types ought to be avoided in order to ensure trust and prevent the possibility of eroding or frustrating competition. Conflict of interest, even the appearance of it, can severely harm the reputation of an organization (OECD, 2005) and therefore has to be avoided. More specifically, it can result in 'corrupt conduct, abuse of public office, misconduct, breach of trust, or unlawful action' (OECD, 2005: 8). These could be detrimental to development management efforts as they stand to engender inefficient use of resources and the lack of cooperation or support from development actors who may feel that the machinery of public sector decision making and resource allocation is designed to satisfy the needs of a privileged few at the expense of others.

Moonlighting

Moonlighting is considered as a situation where an individual maintains his/her primary employment and also engages in additional work for pay (Shishko and Rostker, 1976). This practice is becoming common in the developing world where most office holders or duty bearers often complain about a wide disconnect between their earnings and financial responsibilities or societal expectations. Whilst the effects of moonlighting on development management may, on the face of it, appear rather remote, a closer inspection reveals otherwise. This is because the identified adverse effects on organizations have implications for development outcomes. This is especially so when it is generally recognized that moonlighting can result in placing the employee in competition with the employer. Also, as a result of moonlighting, the employee's work performance is affected; there is gross abuse of the employer's resources and potential breach of confidentiality; the employee is likely to use his/her position to solicit business, thus diverting business from his/her employer; and there is the potential danger of employers suffering reputational problems when employees misapply the work procedure to discredit the employer (Kernaghan and Langford, 1990; Langford, 1991).

It is sometimes argued that moonlighting may not always be negative since it could lead to the acquisition of more skills and optimization of unused man-hours. Others also argue that there are instances where there is no conflicting commitment in the jobs one engages in (Kernaghan, 1991). However, given the adverse effects cited earlier, it is not surprising that the practice is frowned upon especially in countries where its effects have substantially detracted from overall development.

Other ethical issues

Apart from the above-named ethical issues, scholars have identified other unethical issues confronting individuals and organizations. For instance, Butts (2012: 127) and Boyle et al. (2001: 19–20) identified greed, engaging in covert operations, producing misleading services, reneging or cheating on negotiated terms, and creating unclear and/or inappropriate policies that can cause others to lie to get the job done. Other forms include lying for the sake of business, obstructing or stalling actions and processes and obeying authority in a mindless routine (Boyle et al., 2001: 19–20; Butts, 2012: 127).

Inculcating ethics and values in development management

From the foregoing, the need to inculcate ethics and values in DM cannot be over-emphasized. The first step is the establishment of a code of ethics/conduct for all development actors. Codes of ethics have been found to be an important activator of employee commitment including affective, normative and continuance commitments in organizations. Affective commitment springs from a sense of emotional attachment to the organization. Here, the urge to remain part of the organization, possibly sharing in its failures and successes, influences one's commitment to organizational goals and ideals (Meyer and Allen, 1984). Continuance commitment, on the other hand, is generated by the fear of the unknown, that is, the costs one is likely to incur if one were to leave the organization. With regard to normative commitment, the organizational participant feels obligated to stay or presumes quitting is simply not the right thing to do (Allen and Meyer, 1990). In this case therefore, even when the person has some compelling reasons to leave, he would regard staying as the lesser of two evils.

The extant literature has identified several ways in which code of ethics can assist in shaping the behaviour of organizational participants for the effective and efficient realization of desired outcomes. Given the relevance of ethical values to development management therefore, this study contends that a clear and people-centred code of ethics could lessen the likelihood of ethical misconducts which often frustrate development effectiveness. This is strengthened by earlier findings that suggest that a code of ethics can positively affect the existing organizational climate leading to the exhibition of positive workplace behaviours (Singhapakdi et al., 2010). As we sought to point out earlier, the quality and mode of dissemination of a code of ethics to organizational actors involved in a development process, including public officials, project managers and development partners, has implications for its effectiveness. Here, organizations need to communicate their code of ethics in clear terms to all organizational members, and ensure members understand the codes and live them. Further, the codes must be accompanied by strict compliance measures and other ethics initiatives including rewards and punitive sanctions. It is also important that employees are socialized into the value system of the organization. Top management commitment and ethical leadership are also necessary ingredients for the holistic acceptance of the codes leading to employee commitment in the organization. Externally, organizations must show their adherence to ethics and values by portraying it in their mission statement and also displaying it at vantage points of the organization including the organization's website.

Another means by which ethics and values could be harnessed for effective development management is for developing countries especially to re-examine the current ethical regime that governs the pursuit of the development aspirations. As societies evolve, members fashion their behaviour in conformity with some social expectations. These expectations are rooted in centuries of direct and indirect interactions or exchanges. Even though the values that define some of these expectations must submit to changes or refinement in the face of globalization, it is utopian at best to assume that traditional values that have evolved over time could be replaced entirely in revolutionary fashion as development management enthusiasts often suggest. As stated elsewhere in this paper, the relegation of developing country culturally suited ethical values and the subsequent almost uncompromising projection of foreign best practice has implications for the extent to which development management actors would submit to or imbibe those ethical values.

Put differently, we argue for a rethink of earlier positions in development management and modern thought that viewed developing country ethical values as inherently inimical, thus making the transfer of foreign ethical values (in the garb of best practice) a prerequisite for better development management outcomes. Thus, whilst inculcating ethical values is essential, such values must be receptive to if not emphasize local ethical values to prevent a possible alienation of development actors.

Conclusion

Developing countries continue to explore various strategies in their quest to empower the citizenry and consequently break free from the shackles of poverty and underdevelopment. Some of these strategies are mostly attempts to replicate so-called best practices from the developed world. The adoption of development management as the new way of negotiating the maze of development is one of several attempts adopted by the developing world in the immediate post-colonial days. Whilst development management has evolved, it is often contended that its effects have been largely neutralized or frustrated as a result of the ethical vacuum that surrounds its application in developing countries. The primacy of ethics and values in ensuring positive development outcomes has therefore gained increasing recognition in recent times. As we have sought to argue in this chapter, developing countries that aspire to better development management outcomes must of necessity ensure that the ethical and moral climate within which public officials, NGOs and other development partners operate, are clear, reliable and present at all times. In doing this however, it is instructive to note that harnessing the potential of the 'ethics era' must not lead to the total abandonment or collapse of the prevailing cultural values which have taken centuries to evolve. Instead, a negotiation and refinement process which blends modern best practices and progressive cultural values is recommended.

References

AbouAssi, K. (2010). International development management through a Southern lens. *Public Administration and Development*, 30(2), 116–123.

Agbiboa, D. E. (2013). Corruption and economic crime in Nigeria. *African Security Review*, 22(1), 47–66.

Albanese, J. S. (2008). *Professional Ethics in Criminal Justice: Being Ethical When No One Is Looking*. Boston, MA: Pearson Allyn & Bacon.

Allen, N. J., and Meyer, J. P. (1990). The measurement and antecedents of affective, continuance and normative commitment to the organization. *Journal of Occupational Psychology*, 63(1), 1–18.

Association of Certified Fraud Examiners (2010). Report to the nations: on occupational fraud and abuse. 2010 global fraud study.

Atchison, G. M. (2007). Values congruency: a qualitative investigation into how first level managers view congruence between personal values and corporate values (unpublished doctoral dissertation). Capella University, Minneapolis, MN.

Balogun, M. J. (2003). Causative and enabling factors in public integrity: a focus on leadership, institutions, and character formation. *Public Integrity*, 5, 127–147.

Banks, C. (2004). *Criminal Justice Ethics: Theory and Practice*. Thousand Oaks, CA: Sage.

Barro, R. (2000). Rule of law, democracy and economic performance. In O'Driscoll, G., Holmes, K. and Kirkpatrick, M. (eds.), *2000 Index of Economic Freedom* (pp. 31–51). Washington, DC: The Heritage Foundation/Dow Jones Company Inc.

Benavides, A., Dicke, L. A. and Maleckaite, V. (2012). Creating public sector pedestals and examining falls from grace: examining ICMA ethical sanctions. *International Journal of Public Administration*, 35(11), 749–759.

Bjørnskov, C. (2011). Combating corruption: on the interplay between institutional quality and social trust. *Journal of Law and Economics*, 54(1), 135–159.

Bowman, J. S. and West, J. P. (2014). *Public Service Ethics: Individual and Institutional Responsibilities*. Washington, DC: Sage Publication.

Boyle, P. J., DuBose, E. R., Ellingson, S. J., Guinn, D. E. and McCurdy, D. B. (2001). *Organizational Ethics in Health Care: Principles, Cases, and Practical Solutions*. San Francisco: John Wiley and Sons.

Bozeman, B. (2007). *Public Values and Public Interest: Counterbalancing Economic Individualism*. Washington, DC: Georgetown University Press.

Brinkerhoff, D. W. (2008). The state and international development management: shifting tides, changing boundaries, and future directions. *Public Administration Review*, 68(6), 985–1001.

Brinkerhoff, D. W. and Brinkerhoff, J. M. (2006). International development management in a globalized world. In Otenyo, E., Lind, N. (eds.), *Comparative Public Administration: The Essential Readings* (pp. 831–862). Amsterdam and Oxford: Elsevier Press.

Brinkerhoff, D. W. and Coston, J. M. (1999). International development management in a globalized world. *Public Administration Review*, 59(4), 346–361.

Brinkerhoff, J. M. and Brinkerhoff, D. W. (2010). International development management: a northern perspective. *Public Administration and Development*, 30, 102–115.

Burke, E., Tomlinson, C. and Cooper, C. L. (2011). *Crime and Corruption in Organizations: Why It Occurs and What to Do About It*. Surrey, England: Gower Publishing Ltd.

Butts, J. B. (2012). *Ethics in Organizations and Leadership*. Boston: Jones & Bartlett Publishers.

Caiden, G. E., Dwivedi, O. P. and Jabbra, J. (2001). Corruption and governance. In Caiden, G. E., Dwivedi, O. P. and Jabbra, J. (eds.), *Where Corruption Lives*. Bloomfield, CT: Kumar.

Childs, J. (2012). Demonstrating the need for effective business ethics: an alternative approach. *Business and Society Review*, 117(2), 221–232.

Davis, H. (2003). Ethics and standards of conduct. In Bovaird, T. and Loffler, E. (eds.), *Public Management and Governance*. London: Routledge.

de Graaf, G. and van der Wal, Z. (2008). On value differences experienced by sector switchers. *Administration and Society*, 40(1), 79–103.

Dreher, A., Kotsogiannis, C. and McCorriston, S. (2009). How do institutions affect corruption and the shadow economy? *International Tax and Public Finance*, 16(6), 773–796.

Dubinsky, A. J. and Jolson, M. A. (1991). A cross-national investigation of industrial salespeople's ethical perceptions. *Journal of International Business Studies*, 22(4), 651–670.

Dwivedi, O. P., Khator, R. and Nef, J. (2007). *Managing Development in a Global Context*. Basingstoke: Palgrave Macmillan.

Ebrahim, A. (2003). Making sense of accountability: conceptual perspectives for northern and southern nonprofits. *Nonprofit Management and Leadership*, 14(2), 191–212.

Fischer, M. and Kothari, U. (2011). Development paths: values, ethics and morality. *Journal of International Development*, 23, 767–770.

Fjeldstad, O.-H. and Tungodden, B. (2003). Fiscal corruption: a vice or a virtue? *World Development*, 31(8), 1459–1467.

Frankena, W. (1967). Values and valuation. In Edwards, P. (ed.), *Encyclopaedia of Philosophy*. New York: Macmillan.

Freakley, M. and Burgh, G. (2000). *Engaging with Ethics: Ethical Inquiry for Teachers*. Australia: Social Science Press.

Garcia-Zamor, J. -C. (2015). Quality of governance and ethical public service delivery (PSD) in developing countries. *Journal of Management and Strategy*, 6(3), 28–37.

Gebel, A. C. (2012). Human nature and morality in the anti-corruption discourse of transparency international. *Public Administration and Development*, 32(1), 109–128.

Genckaya, O. F. (2009). Conflict of interest in Turkish public administration. In Council of Ethics for the Public Service, *Ethics for the Prevention of Corruption in Turkey*. European Commission and Council of Europe publication. Available at https://www.coe.int/t/dghl/cooperation/economiccrime/corruption/projects/tyec/1062-TYEC%20Research%20-%20Conflict%20of%20Interest. Accessed 16 February 2016.

Grant, R. M. and Visconti, M. (2006). The strategic background to corporate accounting scandals. *Long Range Planning*, 39(4), 361–383.

Gray, G. C. (2013). Insider accounts of institutional corruption: examining the social organization of unethical behaviour. *British Journal of Criminology*, 53(4), 533–551.

Guess, G. and Gabriellyan, V. (2007). Comparative and international administration. In Rabin, J., Hildreth, W. and Miller, G. (eds.), *Handbook of Public Administration* (3rd ed.) (pp. 585–605). Boca Raton: Taylor and Francis.

Gupta, S., Davoodi, H. and Alonso-Terme, R. (2002). Does corruption affect income inequality and poverty? *Economics of Governance*, 3(1), 23–45.

Harsh, M., Mbatia, P. and Shrum, W. (2010). Accountability and inaction: NGOs and resource lodging in development. *Development and Change*, 41(2), 253–278.

Hatch, M. J. and Cunliffe, A. L. (2006). *Organizational Theory: Modern, Symbolic, and Post-Modern Perspectives*. New York: Oxford University Press.

Heady, F., Perlman, B. and Rivera, M. (2007). Issues in comparative and international administration. In Rabin, J., Hildreth, W. and Miller, G. (eds.), *Handbook of Public Administration*. Boca Raton: Taylor and Francis.

Hellman, J. S., Jones, G. and Kaufmann, D. (2003). Seize the state, seize the day: state capture and influence in transition economies. *Journal of Comparative Economics*, 31(4), 751–773.

Henry, N. (1998). Foreword. In Van Wart, M. (ed.), *Changing Public Sector Values*. New York: Garland.

Huberts, L. W. J. C. (2008). Global ethics and corruption. In Berman, E. M. and Rabin, J. (eds.), *Encyclopedia of Public Administration and Public Policy* (2nd ed.). New York: Taylor & Francis.

Jørgensen, T. B. (2007). Public values, their nature, stability and change. The case of Denmark. *Public Administration Quarterly*, 30(4), 365–398.

Jørgensen, T. B. and Vrangbæk, K. (2011). Value dynamics: towards a framework for analyzing public value changes. *International Journal of Public Administration*, 34(8), 486–496.

Kakabadse, A., Korac-Kakabadse, N. and Kouzmin, A. (2003). Ethics, values and behaviours: comparison of three case studies examining the paucity of leadership in government. *Public Administration*, 81(3), 477–508.

Kaufmann, D., Kraay, A. and Mastruzzi, M. (2005). *Governance Matters IV: Governance Indicators for 1996–2004*. Policy research working paper no. 3630. Washington, DC: The World Bank.

Kaufmann, D. Kraay, A. and Mastruzzi, M. (2006). *Governance Matters V: Governance Indicators for 1996–2005*. The World Bank: Washington, DC.

Kernaghan, K. (1991). *Do Unto Others: Proceedings of a Conference on Ethics in Government and Business* (Vol. 34, No. 1). Institute of Public Administration of Canada.

Kernaghan, K. (2000). The post-bureaucratic organization and public service values. *International Review of Administrative Sciences*, 66, 91–104.

Kernaghan, K. (2003). Integrating values into public service: the values statement as center-piece. *Public Administration Review*, 63(6), 711–719.

Kernaghan, K. and Langford, J. (1990). *The Responsible Public Servant*. Halifax, NS: Institute for Research on Public Policy.

Khan, M. H. (1996). A typology of corrupt transactions in developing countries. IDS bulletin. *Liberalization and the New Corruption*, 27(2), 12–21.

Kimemia, D. (2015). Non-governmental organizations and corruption: the case of Kenya. In Mudacumura, G. M. and Morçöl, G. (eds.), *Challenges to Democratic Governance in Developing Countries*. London: Springer.

Langford, J. W. (1991). Moonlighting and mobility. *Canadian Public Administration*, 34(1), 62–72.

Lasthuizen, K., Huberts, L. and Heres, L. (2011). How to measure integrity violations. *Public Management Review*, 13(3), 383–408.

Leonard, D. K. (2010). 'Pockets' of effective agencies in weak governance states: where are they likely and why does it matter? *Public Administration and Development*, 30(2), 91–101.

Lessig, L. (2011). *Republic Lost: How Money Corrupts Congress—and a Plan to Stop It*. New York: Twelve Hachette Book Group.

MacDonald, C., McDonald, M. and Norman, W. (2002). Charitable conflicts of interest. *Journal of Business Ethics*, 39(1-2), 67–74.

May, D. R., Chan, A. Y. L., Hodges, T. D. and Avolio, B. J. (2003). Developing the moral component of authentic leadership. *Organizational Dynamics*, 32(3), 247–260.

Mbatha, J. S. (2005). *The Ethical Dilemmas of Whistle-Blowing and Corruption in the South African Public Sector*. Award of the degree of PhD, University Of Zululand, South Africa.

McCourt, W. (2007). Impartiality through bureaucracy? A Sri Lankan approach to managing values. *Journal of International Development*, 19, 429–442.

McCourt, W. and Gulrajani, N. (2010). The future of development management: introduction to the special issue. *Public Administration and Development*, 30(2), 81–90.

Meyer, J. P. and Allen, N. J. (1984). Testing the 'side-bet theory' of organizational commitment: some methodological considerations. *Journal of Applied Psychology*, 69(3), 372.

Moorhead, G. and Griffin, R. W. (1989). *Organizational Behaviour*. Boston: Houghton Mifflin.

Nguemegne, J. P. (2011). Fighting corruption in Africa: the anticorruption system in Cameroon. *International Journal of Organization Theory and Behavior*, 14(1), 83–121.

Noe, T. H. and Rebello, M. J. (1994). Dynamics of business ethics and economic activity. *American Economic Review*, 84(3), 531.

Nwabuzor, A. (2005). Corruption and development: new initiatives in economic openness and strengthened rule of law. *Journal of Business Ethics*, 59, 121–138.

Nye, J. S. (1967). Corruption and political development: a cost-benefit analysis. *The American Political Science Review*, 61(2), 417–427.

OECD (1996). *Ethics in the Public Service: Current Issues and Practices*. Paris: Organization for Economic Cooperation and Development.

OECD (2005). Managing conflict of interest in the public sector: a toolkit. Available at www.oecd.org/governance/ethics/49107986. Accessed 5 March 2016.

Orlitzky, M., Schmidt, F. L. and Rynes, S. L. (2003). Corporate social and financial performance: a meta-analysis. *Organization Studies*, 24(3), 403–441.

Pollock, J. (2007). *Ethical Dilemmas and Decision Making in Criminal Justice*. Belmont: Wadsworth.

Posner, B. Z. and Schmidt, W. H. (1994). An updated look at the values and expectations of federal government executives. *Public Administration Review*, 54(1), 20.

Riggs, F. W. (1970). The idea of development administration. In Weidner, E. (ed.), *Development Administration in Asia* (pp. 25–72). Durham, NC: Duke University Pres.

Rohan, M. J. (2000). A rose by any name? The values construct. *Personality & Social Psychology Review (Lawrence Erlbaum Associates)*, 4(3), 255–277.

Rokeach, M. (1973). *The Human Side of Values*. New York: Free Press.

Rose, A. and Lawton, A. (eds.) (1999). *Public Services Management*. Harlow: Pearson Education Ltd.

Rose-Ackermann, S. (2004). The challenge of poor governance and corruption. Copenhagen Consensus Challenge Paper, p. 62.

Rosenbloom, D. H., Kravchuk, R. S. and Clerkin, R. (2009). *Public Administration: Understanding Management, Politics, and Law in the Public Sector*. Boston: McGraw-Hill.

Ryvkin, D. and Serra, D. (2012). How corruptible are you? Bribery under uncertainty. *Journal of Economic Behavior & Organization*, 81(2), 466–477.

Schwartz, S. H. (1994). Are there universal aspects in the structure and contents of human values? *Journal of Social Issues*, 50(4), 19–45.

Schwartz, S. H. (1999). A theory of cultural values and some implications for work. *Applied Psychology: An International Review*, 48(1), 23–47.

Sekkat, K. and Me´on, P. -G. (2005). Does corruption grease or sand the wheels of growth? *Public Choice*, 122, 69–97.

Senior, I. (2006). *Corruption – the World's Big C: Cases, Causes, Consequences, and Cures*. Great Britain: Institute of Economic Affairs.

Shishko, R. and Rostker, B. (1976). The economics of multiple job holding. *American Economic Review*, 66(3), 298–308.

Singhapakdi, A., Sirgy, M. J., Lee, D. L. and Vitell, J. S. (2010). The effects of ethics institutionalization on marketing managers: the mediating role of implicit institutionalization and the moderating role of socialization. *Journal of Macro Marketing*, 30(1), 77–92.

Smith, D. J. (2010). Corruption, NGOs, and development in Nigeria. *Third World Quarterly*, 31(2), 243–258.

Souryal, S. S. (2007). *Ethics in Criminal Justice: In Search of the Truth* (4th ed.). Cincinnati, OH: Anderson Publication.

Suar, D. and Khuntia, R. (2010). Influence of personal values and value congruence on unethical practices and work behavior. *Journal of Business Ethics*, 97(3), 443–460.

Thomas, A. (1996). What is development management? *Journal of International Development*, (8)1, 95–110.

Thomas, A. (1999). What makes good development management? *Development in Practice* 9(1–2), 9–17.

Thomas, A. (2007). Development management—values and partnerships. *Journal of International Development*, 19(3), 383–388.

Thomas, T. P. (2013). *The Effect of Personal Values, Organizational Values, and Person-Organization Fit on Ethical Behaviors and Organizational Commitment Outcomes among Substance Abuse Counselors: A Preliminary Investigation*. PhD thesis, University of Iowa.

TI. (2000). *Corruption Perceptions Index 2000*. Berlin: Transparency International.

TI. (2004). *Transparency International 2004 Annual Report*. Berlin: Transparency International.

TI. (2005). *Global Corruption Report 2005*. Available at www.trasparency.org. Accessed 12 December 2015.

TI. (2010). *Corruption Perceptions Index 2010*. Berlin: Transparency International.

Trevino, L. A. and Nelson, K. A. (2013). *Managing Business Ethics: Straight Talk about How to Do It Right (6th ed.)*. Danvers, MA: Wiley and Sons.

Turner, M., Hulme, D. and McCourt, W. (2015). *Governance, Management and Development: Making the State Work* (2nd ed.). London: Palgrave.

United Nations (2001). *Public Service Ethics in Africa*. New York: United Nations Department of Economic and Social Affairs, Division for Public Economics and Public Administration.

UNODC. (2004). *UN Anti-Corruption Toolkit* (3rd ed.). Vienna: UN.

Uslaner, E. M. (2008). *Corruption, Inequality, and the Rule of Law: The Bulging Pocket*. Cambridge: Cambridge University Press.

Van Riel, C. B. and Fombrun, C. J. (2007). *Essentials of Corporate Communication*. Oxford, UK: Routledge.

Van Wart, M. (1998). *Changing Public Sector Values*. New York: Garland Publishing.

Vargas-Hernández, J. G. (2011). The multiple faces of corruption: typology, forms and levels. *Contemporary Legal and Economic Issues*, 3, 269–290.

Victor, B. and Cullen, J. B. (1988). The organizational bases of ethical work climates. *Administrative Science Quarterly*, 33(1), 101–125.

Werker, E. and Ahmed, F. Z. (2008). What do nongovernmental organizations do? *Journal of Economic Perspectives*, 22(2): 73–92.

Williams, R. M. (1968). Values. In Sills, D. L. (ed.) *International Encyclopedia of the Social Sciences*. New York: Macmillan.

Williams, S. L. (2011). Engaging values in international business practice. *Business Horizons*, 54(4), 315–324.

Wood, G., Kothari, U. and Fischer, A. (eds.) (2010). *Development Paths: Values, Ethics and Morality, Virtual Issue of the Journal of International Development*, August. Available at http://onlinelibrary.wiley.com/journal/10.1002. Accessed 20 January 2016.

World Bank (1997). *World Development Report 1997: The Changing Role of the State*. New York: Oxford University Press.

World Bank (2007). Strengthening World Bank group engagement on governance and anticorruption. Main Report. Washington DC, World Bank Group. Available at http://documents.worldbank.org/curated/en/2007/03/7478369/strengthening-world-bank-group-engagement-governance-anticorruption-vol-1-2-main-report. Accessed 17 December 2015.

Part II

Development management

Capacity building and performance management

4 Nationalization strategies in the Gulf Co-operation Council (GCC) countries

A human resource development (HRD) perspective

La'aleh Al-Aaali and Christopher J. Rees

Introduction

Over recent decades, the governments of Gulf Co-operation Council (GCC) countries in the Middle East have exerted considerable efforts to formulate labour market strategies designed to improve their economic development through the improvement of employment opportunities for GCC nationals. These nationalization strategies, variously labelled using terms such as Saudization, Omanization, Emiratization and Bahrainization, are primarily intended to create employment opportunities for nationals in the private sector and, further, to limit the dependence of those countries on expatriate labour. Although formulated independently by the various GCC governments, these nationalization strategies tend to share common elements including imposed quotas for the employment of nationals, education and training systems to improve the employability of nationals, and attractive incentive schemes for companies which adhere to nationalization policies.

Despite the implementation of these strategies across many GCC labour markets, nationalization levels in the private sector remain relatively low particularly when compared to the levels of employment of nationals in the public sector of the GCC countries. In terms of causal factors which may explain this situation, there is emerging evidence to indicate that nationals across the GCC still see the private sector as an unattractive employment arena associated with relatively low salaries, unfavourable working hours and poor working conditions, while being demeaning in terms of social status. In addition, further evidence suggests that the impact of these perceptions is compounded by the actions of local business leaders who often hold stereotypes of nationals as being less productive than expatriate workers; thus there has been strong resistance in the business community to nationalization initiatives which are seen by private sector employers as exerting adverse effects on the productivity and profitability of their firms.

Given the difficulties that have been encountered in implementing nationalization strategies across the GCC, the main aim of this chapter is to consider the potential contribution of human resource development (HRD) in supporting nationalization processes. That is, the chapter seeks to explore the potential for HRD frameworks to impact positively on the employment-related knowledge, skills and perceptions of nationals in the GCC. In order to address this aim, the chapter has two complementary objectives. The first objective is to provide an analysis of GCC-related nationalization literature which has emerged in recent years with a view to identifying key features of nationalization initiatives and also some of the factors which have hindered nationalization initiatives in this region. The second objective is to identify specific components of HRD which may contribute to effective nationalization programmes. Thus, the chapter proceeds to consider the nature of nationalization initiatives in the GCC region. Subsequent sections of the chapter explore reasons why nationalization programmes have been resisted by key stakeholders and also the role that can be played by HRD in overcoming this resistance.

The nature of nationalization initiatives in the GCC

In order to underpin their booming oil economies, GCC countries in the Middle East have, over recent decades, made extensive use of expatriate labour. For the GCC region as a whole, Forstenlechner and Rutledge (2011) report that, in 2010, nationals represented only 38 per cent of the workforce. This externally oriented approach to meeting labour demands has not been confined to the oil and gas sector; in fact, expatriates have also played an important role in the diversification of the production base and development of the service sector (Fasano and Iqbal, 2003). In essence, the employment of large numbers of foreigners has been a structural necessity in these resource rich economies. As a consequence, unlike in Western Europe, where foreign workers have tended to complement the national workforce, expatriates have become the established and dominant labour force in revenue-generating private sectors of the GCC's national economies (Kapiszewski, 2001); foreign workers have, in the main, been employed in the private sector while the majority of the national labour force has been employed in the well-remunerated and undemanding public sector, thus resulting in a segmented market labour market (Winckler, 2009; Forstenlechner and Rutledge, 2010).

In their analysis of employment in the GCC, Mellahi and Wood (2002) indicate that governments initially adopted a fairly laissez-faire approach to this large scale employment of expatriates but soon came to realize the serious long-term political, economic and social consequences of dependence on a large expatriate workforce (Al-Lamki, 1998; Rees et al., 2007). These consequences included, for example, remittance outflows (Pakkiasamy, 2004); relatively high wage costs as a proportion of gross domestic product (Fasano and Goyal, 2004); issues of negative organizational commitment (Yaghi and Aljaidi, 2014); and unemployment among well-qualified nationals with high salary expectations (Fasano and Goyal, 2004; Toledo, 2006; Al-Kibsi et al., 2007; Harry, 2007). In response to these challenges, GCC states have worked relatively independently on nationalization (sometimes referred to as localization) labour market strategies collectively labelled as 'gulfization' (Al-Lamki, 2005). At the level of the individual state, these strategies are now referred to as Bahrainization, Saudization, Omanization, Emiratization, Kuwaitization and Qatarization (Rees et al., 2007).

One of the main features of nationalization in the GCC region surrounds its quantitative nature, that is, the literature review reveals that nationalization programs in the GCC rely heavily on setting quotas. Measures to curb the growth of foreign workers typically include mandated targets for nationalization in different employment sectors, permit requirements and levy fees for foreign workers, attractive incentives and preferential treatment for companies adhering to nationalization policies (Maloney, 1998; Ruppert, 1998). For example, Godwin (2006) describes Emiratization as an affirmative action quota-driven employment policy that ensures UAE nationals are given employment opportunities in the private sector through selected industries considered suitable for national men and women (Rees et al., 2007). In 1995, Saudi Arabia passed legislation requiring every employer of twenty or more workers to employ a minimum of 5 per cent Saudi nationals, which was increased to 25 per cent in 2000, 30 per cent in 2002 and 75 per cent in 2005 (Al-Kibsi et al., 2007). In the United Arab Emirates, certain jobs such as human resource managers, secretaries and public relations officers were limited to Emiratis only (Forstenlechner, 2008). Similarly in Oman, different Omanization percentages are set for local companies, assisting services, engineers and draughtsman in the oil and gas sector (Al-Lamki, 2005). In the Kingdom of Saudi Arabia, the government has set percentages for different positions and industries (Madhi and Barrientos, 2003). Another restriction aimed at discouraging expatriates was that non-nationals were barred from entering into a commercial venture without a national partner to involve nationals in the new projects that were being undertaken in various economic fields. Instead, the appearance of 'silent partners' appeared by merely signing contracts and completing formalities and receiving 51 per cent of the revenues (Winckler, 2009).

When examining nationalization programmes in the GCC, it becomes clear that they focus on reducing the reliance on expatriates by replacing them with local workers; thus, the underlying rationale of these programmes is to introduce a form of 'positive discrimination' which is intended to work in favour of GCC nationals in employment contexts (Harry, 2007) and, as a result, reduce a country's reliance on expatriate labour. Forstenlechner (2008) highlights that these approaches to nationalization may be presented in terms of image and marketing campaigns based on tangible success stories. He also notes the potential use of combined measures which include the length of the average service of nationals on the payroll, the promotional track record of nationals and the number and quality of on-the-job training and support provided to national employees. Further, it has been pointed out that quantitative measures alone cannot gauge the success of nationalization initiatives; there is also a need for qualitative methods that show attitudinal and motivational states towards nationalization in order to inform effective change management strategies (Rees et al., 2007).

As noted above, the primary aim of nationalization strategies is to create employment opportunities for nationals in the private sector and, further, to limit state dependence on expatriate labour. Despite the introduction of these policies by state governments across the GCC, there is evidence that they have faced wide-scale resistance from both employers and nationals (Rees et al., 2007; Hodgson and Hanson, 2014). In the next sections of the chapter, this resistance is explored from the perspectives of both nationals and employers.

Nationals' resistance to nationalization

The literature indicates that there is a tendency among nationals in the GCC to seek actively public sector white-collar jobs in managerial roles as opposed to jobs in private sector organizations. This tendency may be linked partly, but certainly not exclusively, to remuneration packages; in the GCC region, a government job, as well as coming with tenure and a generous pension, often provides a salary several times higher than the equivalent private sector position (Abdalla et al., 2010). Further, working in the private sector is sometimes perceived as debasing a national's social standing. In addition, cultural barriers and pressures tend to discourage, if not exclude, nationals from many service jobs in the private sector. That is, jobs such as taxi drivers, food service clerks and all forms of household work are considered by many nationals to be the domain of foreigners. There is also some evidence that tribal influence may discourage nationals from engaging in highly competitive environments that are often associated with private sector contexts (Hasan, 2015). Hence, although in some areas of the private sector, such as banking, nationalization initiatives appear to have been received relatively positively by nationals, private sector organizations have, in overall terms, struggled to reach the employment quotas for nationals set by national governments. The technical and manual jobs that were created by the drive to diversify the economy in private sector retail and service organizations have tended to be seen by nationals as incompatible to their aspirations, resulting in major challenges for nationalization initiatives (Wilkins, 2002).

Many nationals have traditionally seen high-paying, low-stress government positions as a 'birthright'. This perception has, in turn, led many nationals to stay out of the workforce and wait for jobs to become available in either government and/or organizations recommended by family members. This mindset has also, at times, been indirectly reinforced at the highest level of government in countries such as Saudi Arabia which, prior to 1984, required nationals to work for the government in return for receiving educational sponsorship (Al-Dosary and Rahman, 2005). Similarly, Kuwait failed to implement its Kuwaitization policy owing to the government's determination to provide employment to Kuwaiti newcomers to the labour market; this resulted in a situation where more than 95 per cent of the national labour force was employed by the government in 1994 (Winckler, 2009).

In essence, the literature provides ample evidence that GCC nationals find unacceptable the private sector's working conditions of long and irregular hours, restrictions on time spent on cultural and religious observances, short periods of leave, and a disciplined approach to employee performance (Al-Enezi, 2002; Al-Lamki, 1998; Kapiszewski, 2003; Madhi and Barrientos, 2003). In contrast, the public sector is perceived to offer higher salaries (Godwin, 2006; Nelson, 2004) and better non-monetary benefits (Nelson, 2004). The remuneration package in the government sector for unskilled and semi-skilled work is twice that of the private sector (Al-Lamki, 1998; Eickelman, 1991). The public sector's attractions include a traditional working environment, Arabic as the preferred language and an opportunity to practise 'wasta' (using connections) (Freek, 2004). For example, Al-Lamki (1998) explains how the government sector seems to be the 'employer of choice' among Omanis who see it as offering life-long employment, further educational opportunities, high wages, benefits, good working conditions, attractive working hours, and retirement benefits. In contrast, Al-Ali (2008) states that nationals see the private sector as offering limited career development, training and promotion prospects. Freek (2004) suggested that higher labour turnover in the private sector was partly due to employers' general lack of career development strategies due to the transient nature of the majority of the workforce. This suggests the need to re-evaluate human resource strategies and a need for increased consideration of cultural sensitivity in terms of workplace conditions, performance-related remuneration and rewards, fast-track career development programmes and career counselling (Farrell, 2008).

Employers' resistance to nationalization

Another source of resistance to nationalization in GCC countries has emanated from private sector employers (Goby, 2015). Various studies have reported that these employers tend to view nationals negatively in terms of their suitability for employment. Thus, nationals tend to be seen as 'less productive' (Nelson, 2004) and also stereotyped as being under skilled and unmotivated. Further, as the salary expectations of nationals tend to be higher than those of expatriate workers, the cost of expatriate labour is seen by employers to be considerably less than that of national labour (Morris, 2005). Again, these perceptions have, at times, been reinforced by national governments through nationalization initiatives. For example, the United Arab Emirates introduced minimum wage provisions that applied only to nationals and also mandatory pension contributions to the State for each of their Emirati employees (Forestenlechner et al., 2012).

Various studies have sought to explore specific reasons why private sector employers have tended to resist employing nationals. For example, Al-Ali (2008) highlights low fluency in English and low levels of trust as barriers to workforce participation. Similarly, Al-Lakmi (1998) found that the private sector in Oman discourages and disqualifies Omanis from applying because of the requirements for work experience and English language skills. Al-Dosary (2004) describes seventeen factors which are believed to be accounting for the low participation rates of Saudi workers in the private sector. These factors include language skills, lower wages and benefits, inflexibility of relocation in the Kingdom, and long working hours. In addition, the formal and informal rights of the nationals compared to expatriates may contribute to employers' apparent reluctance to recruit nationals within the GCC (Harry, 2007). These rights may disrupt aspects of the 'hire and fire' culture that some private sector employers routinely practice when dealing with expatriates (Mellahi, 2006).

The impact of these negative perceptions of private sector employers towards nationals has led some of them to see nationalization employment quota systems as potentially harmful interventions which are adversely affecting the productivity and profitability of private sector organizations in the GCC; indeed, some private sector employers view nationalization initiatives as a form of indirect taxation. This view has resulted in some private sector employers practising what has been termed a 'window dressing operation', that is, hiring the bare minimum of nationals that the given quota stipulates and then placing some or all of these 'ghost workers' in non-strategic positions with no career development opportunities. Similar practices have been reported in Saudi Arabia where national workers have been used primarily to show the firm's commitment to the Saudization strategy (Mellahi, 2006).

Overcoming resistance to nationalization using human resource development

The above analysis reflects that mandates and taxes are unlikely to meet nationalization targets given the wide-scale resistance to these interventions among key groups of stakeholders. Rather, there is a need for a long-term change management process within nationalization. For nationalization strategies to succeed, it is essential to consider the perspectives of both the young educated Emirati nationals and the employment-related demands of private sector employers. Both sides are crucial to meeting development needs at an individual and organizational level and thus to address the human resource development challenge in the GCC region. In effect, there is a need to manage, retain and develop nationals while, at the same time, acknowledging the profit-driven objectives of private sector employers (Achoui, 2009). Change management processes need to embed human resource development activities into nationalization strategies through the integration of HRD activities and nationalization issues and, by doing so, address the well-documented resistance of nationals and employers to government-driven nationalization strategies.

Using a literature-based analysis, essential aspects of nationalization strategies and HRD concepts and activities were identified and then mapped against one another in order highlight the commonalities and differences between these subject areas (see Table 4.1). By comparing nationalization issues with HRD activities, common themes become evident; these themes point to the centrality of addressing nationalization issues through learning, development, education, career development, organizational culture, performance improvement and human capital development investments rather than through taxes and mandates that have a short-term effect and do not address issues of resistance.

The mapping exercise presented in Table 4.1 highlights the vital role that HRD-related activities should play when implementing nationalization strategies in the GCC region. HRD places a central focus upon issues such as development of human capacity, culture change, learning, education, skill development and career development. These issues are directly relevant to concerns held by both nationals

Table 4.1 HRD activities derived from HRD definitions in relation to nationalization

HRD definition	Derived HRD activity	Nationalization issues derived from resistance between nationals and private sector employers	Common theme between HRD and nationalization area of focus
'In economic terms, it could be described as the accumulation of human capital and its effective investment in the development of an economy. In short, the processes of human resource development unlock the door to modernization' (Harbison and Myers, 1964: 2).	Investment of human capital development	Utilization of national human resources Strategic approach	Human capital development
'The process of increasing the knowledge, the skills, and the capacities of all the people in a society' (Harbison and Myers, 1964: 2).	Increasing the knowledge, skills and capacities of all the people	Training and development	Learning and development
'Series of organized activities conducted within a specific time and designed to produce behavioural change' (Nadler, 1970: 3).	Produce behavioural change through a series of organized activities	Training and development	Learning and development
'Organized learning experiences provided by employers within a specific period of time to bring about the possibility of performance improvement and or personal growth' (Nadler and Nadler, 1989: 6).	Performance improvement and or personal growth through organized learning experiences	Retention through career development and performance management	Career development

(*continued*)

HRD definition	Derived HRD activity	Nationalization issues derived from resistance between nationals and private sector employers	Common theme between HRD and nationalization area of focus
'The integrated use of training and development, organization development, and career development to improve individual, group, and organizational effectiveness' (McLagan, 1989: 52).	Training and development, organization development, and career development	Training and development Retention through career development and performance management	Learning and development Career development
'The field of study and practice responsible for the fostering of a long-term, work-related learning capacity at the individual, group, and organizational level of organizations … by enhancing individuals' capacity to learn, to help groups overcome barriers to learning, and to help organizations create a culture which promotes continuous learning' (Watkins, 1995: 2).	Long-term, work-related learning capacity at the individual, group and organizational level of organizations Enhances individuals' capacity to learn Create a culture which promotes continuous learning	Training and development Learning culture	Organizational culture Learning and development
'A process of developing and/or unleashing human expertise through organization development and personnel training and development for the purpose of improving performance' (Swanson, 1995: 208).	Organization development and personnel training and development Improving performance	Training and development Education and learning Performance management	Learning and development Education Performance improvement

HRD definition	Derived HRD activity	Nationalization issues derived from resistance between nationals and private sector employers	Common theme between HRD and nationalization area of focus
'Activities and processes which are intended to have an impact on organizational and individual learning … constituted by planned interventions in organizational and individual learning processes' (Stewart and McGoldrick, 1996: 1).	Planned interventions in organizational and individual learning processes	Training and development	Learning and development
'Developing their capacity for performance and for making meaning of their experience in the context of the organization's strategic needs and the requirements of their jobs' (Yorks, 2005: 11).	Develops capacity for performance Development within the organization's strategic needs and the requirements of jobs	Performance management	Performance improvement
'Human resource development is any process or activity that, either initially or over the long term, has the potential to develop adults' work-based knowledge, expertise, productivity, and satisfaction, whether for personal or group/team gain, or for the benefit of an organization, community, nation or, ultimately, the whole of humanity' (McLean and McLean, 2001:322).	Develops work-based knowledge, expertise, productivity, and satisfaction	Training and development Strategic approach Developing local talent for international exposure and integration	Learning and development Human capital development

(continued)

HRD definition	Derived HRD activity	Nationalization issues derived from resistance between nationals and private sector employers	Common theme between HRD and nationalization area of focus
'The interplay of global, national, organizational, and individual needs' (Walton, 1999: 54).	Interplay of global, national, organizational and individual needs	Strategic approach	Human capital development
'Processes of organized capability and competence-based learning experiences undertaken within a specified period of time to bring about individual and organizational growth and performance improvement, and to enhance national, economic, cultural and social development' (Lynham and Cunningham, 2004: 319).	Individual and organizational growth and performance improvement Enhances national, economic, cultural and social development	Education and learning Retention through career development and performance management Training and development	Learning and development Career development Performance improvement Learning and development
'IHRD is a broad term that concerns process that addresses the formulation and practice of HRD systems, practices, and policies at the global, societal, and organizational level. It can concern itself with how governments and international organizations develop and nurture international managers and how	Develop international managers	Developing local talent for international exposure and integration	Human capital development

HRD definition	Derived HRD activity	Nationalization issues derived from resistance between nationals and private sector employers	Common theme between HRD and nationalization area of focus
they develop global HRD systems; it can incorporate comparative analyses of HRD approaches across nations and also how societies develop national HRD policies' (Metcalfe and Rees, 2005: 455).			

and private sector employers. It is necessary to move towards a softer strategic approach by embedding HRD activities at a national level to ensure the practice of development that can reduce issues of resistance as reflected in the findings.

Conclusion

One of the main conclusions that can be drawn from the chapter is the extent to which nationalization strategies are intertwined with key elements of HRD frameworks and activities; as such, an effective nationalization programme is likely to draw from the field of HRD both in the development planning processes at the national level and at the level of organizational capacity building. In essence, having examined the general objectives of nationalization strategies, it is concluded that HRD should form an integral component of nationalization initiatives. Yet the findings also demonstrate the lack of overt engagement with HRD frameworks in nationalization activities at both the national and local levels. In reporting this finding, the chapter reflects that concepts of development, training, career planning, and retention are tangible yet often unspecified management-related activities which need to be embedded more firmly in nationalization policies in order to overcome the resistance to nationalization interventions which has featured prominently throughout the GCC region. Through a mapping exercise, the chapter has identified the extent to which HRD frameworks may be integrated into nationalization strategies.

References

Abdalla, I., Al Waqfi, M., Harb, N., Hijazi, R. and Zoubeidi, T. (2010). Labour policy and determinants of employment and income in a small, developing economy with labour shortage. *Review of Labour Economics and Industrial Relations*, 24(2), 163–177.

Achoui, M. (2009). Human resource development in Gulf countries: an analysis of the trends and challenges facing Saudi Arabia. *Human Resource Development International*, 12(1), 35–46.

Al-Ali, J. (2008). Emiratisation: drawing UAE nationals into their surging economy. *International Journal of Sociology and Social Policy*, 28(9–10), 365–379.

Al-Dosary, A. S. (2004). HRD or manpower policy? Options for government intervention in the local labour market that depends upon a foreign labour force: The Saudi Arabian perspective. *Human Resource Development International*, 7(1), 123–35.

Al-Dosary, A. and Rahman, S. (2005). Saudization (localization): a critical review. *Human Resource Development International*, 8(4), 495–502.

Al-Enezi, K. (2002). Kuwait's employment policy: its formulation, implications, and challenges. *International Journal of Public Administration*, 25(7), 885–900.

Al-Kibsi, G., Benkert, C. and Schubert, J. (2007). Getting labour policy to work in the Gulf. *The McKinsey Quarterly* Special Edition: Reappraising the Gulf States, February 1–29.

Al-Lamki, S. (1998). Barriers to Omanization in the private sector: the perceptions of Omani graduates. *International Journal of Human Resource Management*, 9(2), 377–400.

Al-Lamki, S. (2005). The role of the private sector in Omanization: the case of the banking industry in the sultanate of Oman. *International Journal of Management*, 22(2), 176–188.

Eickelman, D. (1991). *Counting and Surveying an Inner Oman Community*. Wisbech, England: Menas Press.

Farrell, F. (2008). Voices on Emiratization: the impact of Emirati culture on the workforce participation of national women in the UAE private banking sector. *Journal of Islamic Law and Culture*, 10(2), 107–168.

Fasano, G. and Goyal, R. (2004). *Emerging Strains in GCC Labour Markets*. Washington, DC: International Monetary Fund.

Fasano, U. and Iqbal, Z. (2003). *GCC Countries: From Oil Dependence to Diversification*. Washington, DC: International Monetary Fund.

Forstenlechner, I. (2008). Workforce nationalization in the UAE: image versus integration. *Education, Business and Society: Contemporary Middle Eastern Issues*, 1(2), 82–91.

Forstenlechner, I. and Rutledge, E. J. (2010). Growing levels of national unemployment in the Arab Gulf: time to update the 'social contract'. *Middle East Policy*, 17(2), 38–51.

Forstenlechner, I. and Rutledge, E. J. (2011). The GCC's 'demographic imbalance': perceptions, realities and policy options. *Middle East Policy Council*, 18(4), 25–43.

Freek, S. (2004). *Voices from the Shop Floor: The Impact of the Multicultural Work Environment on the UAE*. Dubai: TANMIA

Goby, V. (2015). Financialization and outsourcing in a different guise: the ethical chaos of workforce localization in the United Arab Emirates. *Journal of Business Ethics*, 31(2), 415–421.

Godwin, S. (2006). Globalization, education and Emiratisation: a study of the United Arab Emirates. *The Electronic Journal on Information Systems in Developing Countries*, 27(1), 1–14.

Harbison, F. and Myers, C. A. (1964). *Education, Manpower, and Economic Growth: Strategies of Human Resource Development*. New York: McGraw-Hill.

Harry, W. (2007). Employment creation and localization: the crucial human resource issue for the GCC. *International Journal of Human Resource Management*, 18(1), 132–146.

Hasan, S. (2015). Workforce localization in the GCC countries: policies, practices, and the labour exporting countries' responses. *Philippine Political Science Journal*, 36(2), 147–166.

Hodgson, S. and Hanson, D. (2014). Enforcing nationalisation in the GCC: private sector progress, strategy, and policy for sustainable nationalization. *Middle East Journal of Business*, 9(2), 17–24.

Kapiszewski, A. (2001). *Nationals and Expatriates: Population and Labour Dilemmas of the Gulf Cooperation Council States*. Reading: Ithaca Press.

Kapiszewski, A. (2003). The changing status of Arab migrant workers in the GCC. *Journal of Social Affairs*, 20(78), 33–60.

Lynham, S. A. and Cunningham, P. W. (2004). Human resource development: the South African case. In G. McLean, A. Osman-Gani and E. Cho (eds.), *Human Resource Development as National Policy* (pp. 315–325). Thousand Oaks, CA: Sage.

Madhi, S. T. and Barrientos, A. (2003). Saudisation and employment in Saudi Arabia. *Career Development International*, 8(2), 70–77.

Maloney, W. (1998). *The Structure of Labour markets in Developing Countries: Time Series Evidence on Competing Views*. Washington, DC: World Bank.

McLagan, P. (1989). Models for HRD practice (Human resource development). *Training and Development Journal*, 43(9), 49–60.

McLean, G. and McLean, L. (2001). If we can't define HRD in one country, how can we define it in an international context? *Human Resource Development International*, 4(3), 313–326.

Mellahi, K. (2006). Human resource development through vocational education in Gulf Cooperation Countries: the case of Saudi Arabia. *Journal of Vocational Education and Training*, 52(2), 329–344.

Mellahi, K. and Wood, G. (2002). Desperately seeking stability: the making and remaking of the Saudi Arabian petroleum growth regime. *Competition and Change*, 6(4), 345–362.

Metcalfe, B. and Rees, C. J. (2005). Theorizing advances in international human resource development. *Human Resource Development International*, 8(4), 449–465.

Morris, M. (2005). Organisation, social change and the United Arab Emirates. Paper presented to the Social Change in the 21st Century Conference, Centre for Social Change Research, Queensland University of Technology, 28 October 2005.

Nadler, L. (1970). *Developing Human Resources*. Houston: Gulf Publishing.

Nadler, L. and Nadler, Z. (1989). *Developing Human Resources*. San Francisco: Jossey Bass.

Nelson, C. (2004). UAE national women at work in the private sector: conditions and constraints. *Labour Market Study No. 20*, Dubai: Tanmia.

Pakkiasamy, D. (2004). *Saudi Arabia's Plan for Changing Its Workforce*. Washington, DC: Migration Policy Institute.

Rees, C. J., Mamman, A. and Bin Braik, A. (2007). Emiratization as a strategic HRM change initiative: case study evidence from UAE petroleum company. *International Journal of Human Resource Management*, 18(1), 33–53.

Ruppert, E. (1998). *Managing Foreign Labour in Singapore and Malaysia: Are There Lessons for GCC Countries?* Washington, DC: World Bank.

Stewart, J. and McGoldrick, J. (1996). *Human Resource Development: Perspectives, Strategies and Practice*. London: Pitman.

Swanson, R. A. (1995). Human resource development: performance is the key. *Human Resource Development Quarterly*, 6(2), 207–213.

Toledo, H. (2006). *The Problems and Prospects of Emiratization: Immigration in an Imperfect Labour Market*. Dubai: Dubai Economic Research Council.

Walton, J. (1999). *Strategic Human Resource Development*. Harlow: Pearson Education Limited.

Watkins, K. E. (1995). Many voices: defining human resource development from different disciplines. *Adult Education Quarterly*, 41(4), 241–255.

Wilkins, S. (2002). Human resource development through vocational education in the United Arab Emirates: the case of Dubai polytechnic. *Journal of Vocational Education and Training*, 54(1), 5–26.

Winckler, O. (2009). *Arab Political Demography* (2nd ed.). Brighton: Sussex Academic Press.

Yaghi, A. and Aljaidi, N. (2014). Examining organizational commitment among national and expatriate employees in the private and public sectors in United Arab Emirates. *International Journal of Public Administration*, 37(12), 801–811.

Yorks, L. (2005). *Strategic Human Resource Development*. Mason, OH: South-Western.

5 National managerial talent development in the Ghanaian mining industry

Comparative assessment of Western and indigenous approaches

Nana Yaw Oppong

Introduction

Managerial talent development (MTD) in improving productivity has become a powerful tool for management effectiveness (Grzeda and Assogbavi, 1999). Highlighting its importance in development management, Mumford (1998) calls for special attention to development of managers because they are major contributors to survival and growth of businesses, and therefore require investment in their development. This position presupposes that to ensure the provision of suitable development opportunities for the whole organization, managers must champion the formulation and implementation of strategy. It follows that they must acquire the relevant skills and incentives in order to be effective in executing their mandate. Mumford's call is more relevant to the African context. As observed by Schellekens (2007), in Africa there is often a 'management gap' between the demand for and supply of indigenous management talent at almost all levels and this is a major setback for economic development on the continent. Realizing the issue of the management gap and the need to address it for sustainable development, the government of Ghana made national managerial development a legal requirement for multinational companies entering the mining industry. This is not just a legal requirement but a pre-condition for the granting of a mining lease to these multinational companies as enshrined in the Minerals and Mining Law, 2006 (Act 703). Two significant provisions are worth noting: the *localization plan* (details of expatriate positions, and nationals to understudy these expatriates for eventual takeover) and *expatriates quota* (allowable number of expatriates in any company at any given time).

This initiative shows the seriousness the government of Ghana attaches to addressing the national management gap, which it is believed could be addressed through foreign multinational firms (MNCs) in industry. Here, national managers means indigenous Ghanaian managers in multinational mining subsidiaries in Ghana, as distinguished from expatriate managers. The extent of compliance with these provisions by the Western multinationals is, however, beyond the scope of this chapter. It is, however, important to point out the MNCs' argument that local managers lack the experience and expertise that expatriates have to drive efficiency in industry (Eshun and Jellicoe, 2011). The situation in the Ghanaian mining industry shows a wide management gap as demonstrated by the expatriate percentage in management, which is as high as 70 per cent in some companies. For instance, a study by Eshun and Jellicoe (2011) reveals that the percentages of expatriates in four major Ghanaian gold mining companies are 56 per cent, 60 per cent, 70 per cent and 70 per cent. A common reason assigned to this over-reliance on expatriate managers is their competence as compared to national managers.

Successful development of national managers equipped with the relevant expertise will therefore be a pivotal part of the mining industry's development as local managerial skills and expertise are essential resources and capabilities to industry (Amankwah-Amoah and Debrah, 2011). More importantly, skills and expertise are crucial in unlocking the potential of managers and thus make them capable of efficiently implementing strategic goals of their respective firms (Walumbwa, Aviola and Aryee, 2011). This justifies the many management development institutes and programmes in Africa (Kiggundu, 1991; Schellekens, 2007). However, these programmes follow Western concepts and curricula which, in most situations, do not suit the African context. On how the situation could be made better, Grzeda and Assogbavi (1999) write that critical consideration should be given to cultural roots when developing managers. They believe that Western values, objectives, contents, approaches and outcomes inherent in the Western MTD process cannot be implemented in sub-Saharan Africa without considering the host culture. This chapter therefore attempts to indigenize/localize the western managerial talent development process, as given by national managers in the Ghanaian mining industry, to suit the Ghanaian context.

National managers demonstrate strong Ghanaian identity and cultural practices at the workplace but still portray Western ideas in their people management practices including their own development. If national managers adhere to local cultural practices and at the same time follow Western development concepts, can they also be developed based on traditional methods to prepare them to work in Western multinational companies? This is the primary motivator for the chapter – to explore the effectiveness of indigenous methods vis-à-vis the Western approach as a step towards developing national managers in business organizations in Ghana. The approach has the potential of developing the mining industry since the way national managers work is influenced by their cultural and social values rather than work practices that are alien to them. Emphasis on indigenous knowledge here is to foster a renewed interest in the application of indigenous knowledge due to its important role for sustainable socio-economic development (Lwoga et al., 2010). This approach moves towards finding solution to the problem of indigenous knowledge, which is marginalized, neglected and suppressed due to ignorance and the dominant ideology of a particular historical period (Ocholla and Onyancha, 2005). The comparative assessment is therefore conducted from an indigenous perspective through the application of techniques and methods drawn from the traditions of the (indigenous) people being studied. This has the potential of producing an appropriate means of assessing the problem as well as devising solutions suitable to the people rather than non-indigenous people framing indigenous worldviews from a distance.

In this chapter, the concept of managerial talent development (Oppong, 2015) is adopted instead of traditional management development. This is to suit the purpose of the chapter, which focuses on development of people who are already managers but whose talents (skills directed towards a given managerial contribution) need to be developed for eventual takeover from expatriates. Management development in this context is therefore 'tailored' and departs from the traditional term. Additionally, it is appropriate to label it managerial talent instead of managerial skills. This is because in the light of employee development concern for skills means concern for all, but concern for talent means concern for a select few. The focus is on the development of those potential local managers for top senior management roles to run the industry. Also, whereas 'talent management' is usually used to describe the whole talent process, 'talent development' pertains to the training and development aspect, which is the major concern of the government of Ghana.

The rest of the chapter is organized as follows. The next section considers management talent development and explanation of the key terms used. This will be followed by the two cultural contexts within which the MTD issues are situated, followed by industry definition of talent development (as provided by national managers). Comparison of Western and indigenous approaches of developing people is presented next to ascertain how they match or contrast, with the conclusion occupying the final section of the chapter.

Management talent development

The issue of identifying and preparing the next generation of leadership talent in today's increasingly complex business environment is consistently cited by executives and boards as one of their most critical business priorities (Busine and Watt, 2005) due to its potential in development management. A talent – especially managerial talent – shortage is looming (Michaels, Handfield-Jones and Axelrod, 2001), and this will adversely impact every organization without regard to the type of industry in which an organization finds itself. It has been posited that this stems from the fact that the skill set possessed by available managers may not match the advanced, more complex skills required by businesses. It is therefore advised that organizations should take specific initiatives now to better position themselves to meet the challenge of the management talent shortage (Buhler, 2008). As observed by Dalton (2010), the growing awareness of the managerial role is because management has become essential to business success, a suggestion that MTD should be accorded the needed seriousness in businesses.

Charan (2010), emphasizing the need for management talent, says that in the fast-changing global marketplace, where familiar competitive advantages such as market shares and brands and patents are constantly at risk, talent has become the differentiator between companies that succeed and those that do not. According to him, 'if businesses managed their finances as loosely as they manage their talent development, most would go bankrupt' (Charan, 2010: 24). This gives weight to Ashton and Morton's (2005) view that getting the right people in pivotal roles at the right time should be nothing new to HR professionals. However, approached differently, talent management in general can create long-term organizational success and this is very important – creating a talent mindset in organizations. Considering it as simply a matter of anticipating the need for human capital and then setting out a plan to meet it, Cappelli (2008) believes that MTD exists to support the organization's overall objectives.

With specific reference to Ghana and Zimbabwe, Premoli (1998) notes that African countries have exceptional gold potential but success depends on acquisition of some talent from within the continent. This is because gold exploration techniques can easily be transferred from one continent to another, but people cannot easily relocate. It is therefore justified that 'most major explorers in Africa feel that their greatest problem is lack of suitable personnel, particularly at a senior level' (Premoli, 1998: 82). This complements Cullum and Turnbull's (2005) 'management gap', which suggests managerial training and development through learning in industry. Schellekens (2007) has, however, observed that training in management (in Africa) is a complex process; this is because knowledge and skill acquisition is not structured to suit contextual realities and demands. With regard to contextualization, although Africa south of the Sahara has similar cultural characteristics that could suit common training and development programmes, the presence of various foreign countries in African industries gives different dimensions to contextual needs of managerial talent development.

In this regard, and as pointed out by Myloni, Harzing and Mirza (2004), the wider culture and values of society within which the organization is embedded influence the operating culture of the organization. This demonstrates how society dominates organization in Africa. It will not be of much help, therefore, for one to talk about MTD in business organizations in Africa without working knowledge of the dominant environmental factors which managers being developed much interact with (Kiggundu, 1991). Kiggundu traces the administrative systems of pre-colonial Africa and blames the marginalization of the organizational forms, leadership styles, management processes, and managerial development programmes on the colonial masters. There is available evidence (Kiggundu, 1991) suggesting that the pre-colonial administrative systems, though relatively small in size, were homogenous in terms of membership, co-existed in relative harmony with the environment and used local technology and indigenous knowledge systems that worked well in Africa for Africans. Formal development of managers in Africa was however destroyed by the West and they planted their own colonial administrative systems. The phenomenon was on the premise that the colonialists were convinced of their cultural, biological and technological superiority vis-à-vis what they considered to be the utmost inferiority of African administrative systems. As a result, it appears Africa, at the time of independence, was without any capacity to manage, on a sustainable basis, the business institutions left behind by the colonialists (Israel, 1989). It is worth emphasizing that the situation was a result of the narrow and uninformed view of management and administration held by Africans due to their being deliberately denied MTD programmes. This is because they were not expected to assume managerial responsibilities in the foreseeable future (Israel, 1989).

Against this background, Schellekens (2007) concludes that training managers from developing countries requires reconceptualization of management training, expanding the concept to include an array of learning activities but not based on only formal classroom activities. Kiggundu (1991), on his part, emphasizes two reasons for re-engaging with indigenous knowledge and practices. The first reason is to draw attention to the neglected long and rich history of the continent, noting that present-day Africa is deeply rooted in its past. Therefore, one cannot attempt to develop a critical resource like local managers without first understanding the continent's distant past, which has a close link with its present and future. Second, it is important to raise a development question of how Africa can learn better from its past (before colonization destroyed the indigenous administrative system). This can assist in the design, implementation and evaluation of effective MTD programmes for the continent. To address these, one cannot limit oneself to books on management and administration, which are rather recent and mostly Western approaches that do not cover and appreciate the diverse and complex African continent, its people and social organizations (Kiggundu, 1991).

More generally in Africa, managing talent of the indigenous population tends to focus on low skills and low income economy. This is supported by the outcome of the study by Debrah and Ofori (2006) who, assessing the human resource development needs of Tanzania, revealed that funding for national human resource training programmes focused on low-level skills training as means of reducing unemployment of the grassroots because professionals and other higher level employees were considered privileged and therefore able to develop themselves in their careers. This does not only stifle the relevant managerial and technical skills needed to develop the economies of Africa but also puts the development of this aspect of skills development on employers. However, the government of Ghana has departed from this norm and has initiated efforts to develop local managers in the mining industry, which is the number two foreign exchange earner of the country.

The two contrasting cultures

This section looks at two cultures as relate to Ghana (the host culture) and the home countries of the MNCs (outgroup and the guest culture, collectively). While MTD has generally been considered from a US and Western Europe perspective, the author's interest is in Western Africa, specifically the mining industry of Ghana. As has been indicated, this industry has been dominated by western MNCs, who believe that expatriate managers are more efficient than national managers to achieve organizational goals; this has resulted in higher management positions allocated to expatriates. This suggests that the individualist focus inherent in most MTD practices is likely to continue, but this also comes at a price. From her study of ethnicity and human resource management practices in sub-Saharan Africa, Nyambegera (2002) revealed that MTD was a necessary tool for MNCs operating in Africa and explained that 'the ethnic diversity found in African organizations has played a role in excluding talented and capable people' (p. 1078). The argument reveals the need for Africa to move away from approaches of 'exclusion' and embrace those of 'inclusion'.

However, Western MNCs in Ghana individualize the MTD process around expatriate managers and this compounds the exclusion of not only local managers but also the suppression of their potential to become senior managers for eventual takeover of industry. Further, and this is crucial, it is culturally oppressive for local managers and the workforce as a whole. For example, if we make use of the work by Hofstede (1980) on the influence of national cultural values in the workplace, it can be shown that Ghana's scores contrast sharply with Western countries (see Table 5.1).

Hofstede developed his cultural dimensions using data from about 116,000 surveys by 88,000 IBM employees speaking 20 different languages from 72 countries. By this work, Hofstede created 'a new paradigm for the study of cultural difference: a four dimensional model of national culture' (Minkov and Hofstede, 2011: 10). The model was later expanded to five (Table 5.1) and updated based on his analysis of a wide range of other cross-cultural data. The study itself being cross-cultural in nature, its influence on subsequent understanding of cultures is hard to underestimate (Taras, Kirkman and Steel, 2010), as virtually all later models of culture include Hofstede's dimensions or have conformed to his approach. Although there is a competing model (see Trompenaars, 1993), Trompenaars acknowledged Hofstede for opening the eyes of management to the importance of cross-cultural dimensions of the subject. Blodgett, Bakir and Rose (2008) commend Hofstede for his pioneering

Table 5.1 Scores of cultural dimensions

	Individualism (IDV)	*Power Distance Index (PDI)*	*Masculinity (MAS)*	*Uncertainty Avoidance Index (UAI)*	*Long-Term Orientation (LTO)*
Cultural Dimensions	Degree to which personal needs are valued over the needs of the group	Amount of perceived power differential between authority figures and subordinates	Tough values such as competition and achievement, versus tender values such as interpersonal relationships and care for others	Degree of comfort one has with ambiguous or risky situations versus situations in which the outcome is assured	Orientation toward savings, thrift, and future plans versus a need for immediate gratification
USA	91	40	62	46	29
UK	89	35	66	35	25
Australia	90	36	61	51	31
World Average	43	55	50	64	45
Ghana	16	76	42	55	12

Source: The Hofstede Centre, n.d.

work in bringing the concept of culture to the forefront of the various behavioural science disciplines. McSweeney (2002) however criticizes Hofstede's cultural dimensions and wonders about the basis for the claim that influential national cultures exist, and emphasizes that nations are not the best units for studying cultures. Hofstede in his reply to McSweeney (refer to Hofstede, 2002) explains that nations are usually the only kind of units available for comparison and better than nothing. Hofstede's accession is supported by Williamson (2002) who warns that 'to reject Hofstede's ... models of national culture, before more satisfactory models have been developed, would be to throw away valuable insight' (p. 1391). Chapman (1997) also hails Hofstede's cultural dimensions and says that although they draw criticisms, there is no other contemporary framework in the general field of business and culture that is so general, so broad, so alluring, and so inviting as Hofstede's. Using this framework to differentiate between the two cultures in this chapter on the basis of countries is therefore more suitable than using any other framework.

The three countries (USA, UK and Australia) are chosen primarily because they are the three dominant Western countries in the Ghanaian mining industry. As could be seen from the table, their scores are similar and together contrast those of Ghana. The importance of these differences is how national cultural dimensions have translated into work values which have resulted in western MTD and HRM practices generally dominating in the Ghanaian mining industry. This dominance tendency has created a neglect of Ghanaian cultural values and practices that shape the behaviour of the indigenous people and have significant influence on MTD practices. As a result, Ghanaian workers tend not to mobilize their full strength and potential because they are not fully connected to the business. This is in part because Ghanaian cultures have not been integrated into the workplace and existing corporate cultures are foreign to most Ghanaian workers. There is therefore isolation and exclusiveness of the Ghanaian traditional values in industry (Mthembu, 1996). Employing Ghanaian cultural practices and social values in analyzing this important human resource practice therefore attempts to rekindle the relevance of Ghanaian national culture in work practices and most significantly, as it contributes to the employment relationship in foreign MNC subsidiaries in Ghana.

Industry definition of talent development

Earlier interview data collected and presented by Oppong and Gold (2013) produced the following description by national managers of their talent development, which is the way their development process becomes enacted.

> Identifying potentials and harnessing their (raw) talent towards the achievement of organisational goals. The harnessing process involves training and developing potentials; retaining and utilising them; deploying them within the organisation; and rewarding their contribution.

This definition is of two main parts – identification of potentials, which has to do with sourcing and selecting individuals for the MTD programme, and harnessing their talent. The harnessing processes include training and development;

retention and utilization; deployment; and rewarding contribution. These processes form components of the MTD programmes (as prevails in industry) and applied for the comparative assessment. This definition is however a reproduction of the Western idea of MTD, which focuses on modern technology and more formal written records, which is clearly in contrast to cultural practices and social values of indigenous managers. This shows how the Ghanaian manager responds to the overpowering foreign influences. This phenomenon is linked to African managers and management trainees attending schools in Western countries and experts from Western countries acting as management consultants in Africa. It is therefore not difficult to understand why African managers today cloak themselves with Western management concepts. Kwame Gyakye, a Ghanaian philosopher (see Gyekye, 1994), believes that this unquestioned acceptance of conformity with Western ideology and institutions is partly traced to preeminent African leaders, including Dr. Kwame Nkrumah of Ghana (the country's first President), who incorrectly regarded Western socialism to be compatible with traditional African communism, the result being Western socialist ideology as a framework for nation building in Africa, including people management. This has developed, according to Lassiter (2000), into a personal strategy for survival within the African community, and the individual is conditioned not to challenge that which he depends on and from which he cannot escape. These hegemonic dynamics of the West in their mining subsidiaries in Ghana are termed by Oppong and Gold (2013) as a new form of colonization. As argued by Oppong (2015), this tends to remove the government and businesses from ownership and management of the national resources which translates into displacement of development priorities.

Despite this strong Western influence, national managers deeply portray their Ghanaian identity and cultural practices at their workplaces. For instance, the author's encounter with some national managers revealed their willingness to conduct interviews in Ghanaian languages, while others were seen dressed in their traditional clothes (*fugu, kaba, batakari*). Others were also seen taking *koko na maasa* for breakfast and ushered the author into their offices with the traditional *akwaaba* (welcome), *wohotesen?* (how are you?), and *maakye/maaha* (good morning/good afternoon) greetings. One manager received a phone call in the local *Akan* language and told me after the call that the one at the other end of the line was the company lawyer giving feedback on an issue he was attending to in Accra (the national capital). One manager invited the author for lunch after an interview and preferred the local *fufu* meal so we had to go to a local restaurant. All these indicate how the managers preferred their traditions and customs, and how comfortable they were practising them. This contrast has been the main motivator for the study.

Comparison of Western concept of MTD to indigenous concept

Considering their strong cultural awareness and commitment, can the national managers in Western MNCs be developed applying the traditional Ghanaian methods of learning? Dr. Alan Mumford, an expert in managerial learning, condemns

MTD for being far too prone to picking the latest 'flavours of the month' and calls for the need to reflect on and consolidate what we have (see Mumford, 1998). Mumford goes further to encourage the academic world to pursue a positive fundamental but practical approach to learning. The MTD programme may be run by experts who will be conversant with the traditional Ghanaian method of learning and the MNCs should accept this method of development and its locally-relevant knowledge generation. Table 5.2 compares the Western concepts of talent development as produced by national managers with indigenous Ghanaian versions of developing people. This comparative assessment is based on the definition of managerial talent development produced by national managers.

Table 5.2 Western and indigenous Ghanaian approaches to managerial development

Western concept	*Indigenous view*
Identification	
Reliable database including performance review records; documented individual development plan; potential to excel as criteria to select individuals for the talent process. Manager's readiness level is important and determines who among the two to three managers selected should be given priority.	Identification of managers would be based on wisdom and memory of the master or trainer who is regarded as knowledgeable and trusted to orally provide information on potential to the selectors. This is based on respect for the aged, whose decisions are seldom challenged.
Training and development	
Trainee managers on the job given acting responsibilities; coaching; mentoring; job rotation. Also undergo structured courses in higher education institutions in Ghana and abroad, as well as international assignments in other subsidiaries or headquarters.	Traditional method of passing on elder's wisdom and trade to the young, who usually spends a number of years in the *kyerekyereni*, the teacher's compound. This goes with respect, determined by age as the Ghanaian traditional education is an age grade system. Trainees usually work in groups to highlight the shared values which are fundamental characteristics of Ghanaian identity and culture.
Retention and utilization	
Retention tools include light vehicles; accommodation, shares, production and end-of-year bonuses, as well as retention bonuses for talent. Retention also depends on senior management's support, letting trainee managers know that the organization nurtures and keeps talent.	Ghanaian traditional education promotes life-long learning. In Ghanaian traditional apprenticeship, end of training does not mean end of staying on the *kyerekyereni*, the teacher's compound and serving him. Learning continues through observation, self-determination and search for wisdom as it is only through the master that this is possible. Learning becomes a continuous process – young adults after their training continue to learn from the trainers.

Western concept	*Indigenous view*
Deploying talent	
Managers favour a person perspective, where individuals become the focus of talent development. The motive is multi-use of talent – not to focus on given role but to develop skills and knowledge of the individual (the manager) and make him useful to other roles in the organization so that they can be deployed to occupy other roles as and when required.	Traditionally, Ghanaians specialize in various professions which usually belong to families, e.g. *akuafo* represents a family of farmers. People are willing to be deployed into roles they believe to be the specialist roles that they are most fit to perform. They see deployment into roles as not just means of economic survival but as an integral part of their lives and the lives of their families and, in the spirit of *ubuntuism,* of the larger community (Oppong, 2013).
Rewarding contributions	
Managers are rewarded for their potential which translates into contributions to the company – rewards such as promotions and increases in pay. Rewards are based on an individual's performance record and individual reward packages are offered.	Rewards are usually in the form of titles, raising one's status in the community. Any such reward is identified prior to one's contribution which usually results from context among community members in pursuit of community projects. This encourages competitiveness among community members.

Identification

The identification stage, which forms a part of the two-tier definition, involves what to look for in an individual to be considered for a development programme. Three peculiar questions arise here. These questions are perceived to reveal the uncertainty and lack of clarity in talent identification. These include 'What makes someone a talent?'; 'Should the identification be based on position or the person being prepared to assume the position?' and 'Should the selection be based on attributes of the person being developed?' Analysing these questions and the varied views expressed by authors and business executives, these are viewed as a puzzle that needs to be overcome to pave the way for successful identification of individuals with the potential of offering good returns on investment in developing managers. This becomes a challenge mostly because of overreliance on a documented and structured approach to identifying potential for the development process. This hurdle, which reflects dominant Western methods, could be cleared through the traditional Ghanaian method. This brings to the fore the relevance of indigenous knowledge which is defined as a cumulative body of knowledge created over several decades, representing generations of creative thought and actions, within particular communities in an ecosystem of continuous residence in an effort to cope with an ever-changing socio-economic environment (Lwoga et al., 2010). This definition buttresses Mumford's (1998) call on the need to reflect on and consolidate what we have during the MTD process.

The traditional Ghanaian believes identification is the responsibility of the *kyerekyereni* (the teacher), who is elder, wise and respected in the community (Fasokun, 2005). It is the traditional Ghanaian's belief that knowledge is deposited in the mind of the elder and any decision given is accepted and trusted – his selection is therefore accepted and respected. The readiness level identified by managers as a criterion for selecting potential can be likened to the Ghanaian societal hierarchy, which can be transferred to industry. Managers being developed will respect who is first in line without any conflicts when this is made clear. Tasks and responsibilities should therefore be made clear and this will encourage participation because challenging the hierarchy could lead to sanctions. The learner will therefore not challenge the trainer or the training procedure. Readiness level could be likened to *gyinabre*, where one is meant to be (as demanded by elders or deities) and this is highly respected. Clear hierarchy, therefore, empowers managers through the managerial talent development process. Considering this benefit of indigenous talent identification, the Western approach has drawn criticism from Lwoga and Ngulube (2008), who believe that very little indigenous knowledge has been captured and recorded for preservation, therefore limiting access to an immensely valuable database. This chapter highlights this important aspect of indigenous knowledge, therefore departing from the Western form of knowledge management which, contrary to indigenous form, is based on written records.

Training and development

The training and development phase of the MTD process also has its traditional Ghanaian version. For instance, the coach–coached relationship in the Western context coincides with the *kyerekyereni–adesuani* (teacher–learner) relationship in the traditional Ghanaian context that brings about obedience and adherence to rules. Perceived as a wise expert with experience in the trade, instruction is taken from him or her without question or challenge, another attribute of Ghanaian indigenous education. Good discipline is part and parcel of the Ghanaian traditional education as learners respect the master and senior apprentices because the learner is taught about respect and is made to pay dearly for non-conformity. Sanctions are established through culture and taboos and each member appreciates the danger of failing to conform (Omolewa, 2007). Sanctions are not only from the master but also from the gods who are omnipresent and omniscient. This induces strict discipline since there is no wrongdoing that goes unpunished, either committed in the open or in secret, unlike the Western approach where wrongdoing needs to be proved or one has to be seen committing the act before he can be sanctioned. Applying coaching as part of the MTD process based on the traditional system will therefore bring about discipline, compliance and commitment to work.

Retention and utilization

With regard to retention and utilization, managers mentioned tools such as shares, end-of-year bonus, etc. to motivate employees to stay. The traditional Ghanaian method of education has its retention mechanism. There is life-long learning associated with the education – elders including grandparents, parents, uncles and aunts continue to teach younger adults essential knowledge, skills, attitudes and values (Nafukho, 2006), a continuous process even when those trained are married and are full adults. Apprentices after their training often continue to live on the trainer's compound to serve and tap their wisdom. This is because it is believed that once one is elder he continuous to be wiser and respected. So in Ghanaian society once we continue to live and grow, learning and development continue. This is a retention strategy that can be exploited by the mining industry to reap returns on investment in MTD. Once the organization is portrayed as a community within which there are people with wisdom that can be imparted, national managers will be prepared to continue to learn and will be committed to the organization in order to continue to learn. This will require an inclusiveness approach where the companies involve the national managers in activities such as decision making and scheduling of work to let them (community members) feel part of the business (a community).

Deployment

Another stage of the process is deploying developed managers to increase returns on investment as it reduces the tendency of one becoming redundant if developed for only one job and the job ceases to exist. The process involves assigning talented employees to other roles within the company; to another site of the subsidiary within Ghana; or to a subsidiary abroad (including headquarters). Guided by the basic value of pursuit of excellence (Omolewa, 2007) in his inherited profession and concern for the family or the wider society, the traditional Ghanaian would be motivated to devote him or herself to the role he is deployed into. This is the spirit of *ubuntu* (Bangura, 2005) which inspires the manager to view the business organization as a community to which he belongs, not just as a person with a fixed legal contract but as a member by choice (Choudhury, 1986), a mindset that could be created by senior managers of the individual mining companies.

Rewarding contributions

Rewarding contribution leads to retention but the main purpose is to ensure that one's contribution (after development) is commensurate with one's reward. The Ghanaian traditional approach reinforces this. The Ghanaian context however adds that any such reward is identified prior to one's contribution which usually results from a contest among men in pursuit of community projects such as who kills a wild animal threatening the community or who retrieves the body of a drowned community member from the riverbed. This has encouraged the indigenous Ghanaian to be competitive and improve performance. During the talent process, therefore, any reward should be predetermined and something that is seen as commensurate with one's contribution. As some national managers suggested, a national who eventually takes over from an expatriate manager should be given the package offered the predecessor (at least, less the expatriate elements). This, they believe, is the value of the national manager's contribution, and this has its roots in the traditional Ghanaian reward system which improves commitment during the development process (Owoyemi et al., 2011).

Conclusions

The process of development of local managers in foreign multinational mining subsidiaries in Ghana has been reviewed through the lens of Western and Ghanaian cultures. A comparative assessment of elements of the managerial talent development process has also been conducted employing the dominant Western approach and suggested traditional Ghanaian version. As the comparative assessment has revealed, the traditional Ghanaian education has its strong and enduring versions of the elements of the Western approach to managerial talent development, most of which the author speculates are stronger in driving the development process than the Western versions.

Senior managers of MNCs understanding or uncovering the invisible ideas behind the local managers' attitudes and practices is a way forward, because the companies are nested within societies (Hofstede and Peterson, 2000). Therefore, the surrounding Ghanaian culture is an important external influence on the organizational culture. There is therefore the need for mining companies to gain a minimal level of approval from the Ghanaian society (in the form of cultural practices) to function effectively (Sagiv and Schwartz, 2007). Such approval is necessary in order to develop managers through the way they learn and perform. This is because the Ghanaian will always be guided by his personal values, which are desirable goals that direct the way he selects actions, evaluates people and events, and explains such actions and evaluations (Rohan, 2000). As emerged from Nzelibe's (1986) research, most management problems in Africa are attributed to conflicting principles that underline Western and African management thoughts.

As a result, senior expatriate managers are to understand and appreciate local knowledge by identifying and supporting the themes which can provide a direct link to trainee managers in the talent process. This can allow managers to integrate their 'locally relevant experience' (Omolewa, 2007: 607) into the managerial talent development programme since these are knowledge and experiences that have meaning to them. As Duit (1991) opines, learning achieves the desired outcome when there is construction of similarities between the new and the already known because learning is an active construction process that can only take place based on previously acquired knowledge. This justifies the author's reflection on and consolidation of the traditional Ghanaian methods of learning and development in this chapter. Even in today's Ghana where Western education is revered, the indigenous Ghanaian does not see it as superior to traditional Ghanaian education. For instance, it is common to come across a situation where one with a defect in traditional knowledge and wisdom is often insulted as *yantetew' wo fie* (one without home training), and a stranger in his own society. The indigenous approach could help defuse this tension and reposition the mining companies in providing relevant contents in their national managerial development programmes.

References

Amankwah-Amoah, J. and Debrah, Y. A. (2011). Competing for scarce talent in a liberalized environment: evidence from the aviation industry in Africa. *International Journal of Human Resource Management*, 22(17), 3565–3581.

Ashton, C. and Morton, L. (2005). Managing talent for competitive advantage: taking a system approach to talent management. *Strategic HR Review*, 4(5), 28–31.

Bangura, A. K. (2005). Ubuntugogy: an African educational paradigm. *Journal of Third World Studies*, 22(2), 13–53.

Blodgett, J. G., Bakir, A. and Rose, G. M. (2008). A test of the validity of Hofstede's cultural framework. *Advances in Consumer Research*, 35, 762–763.

Buhler, P. M. (2008). Managing in the new millennium: are you prepared for the talent shortage? *Supervision*, 69(7), 19–21.

Busine, M. and Watt, B. (2005). Succession management: trends and current picture. *Asia Pacific Journal of Human Resources*, 43(2), 225–237.

Cappelli, P. (2008). Talent management for the twenty-first century. *Harvard Business Review*, 86(3), 76–81.

Chapman, M. (1997). Preface: social anthropology, business studies, and cultural issues. *International Studies in Management and Organization*, 26(4), 3–29.

Charan, R. (2010) Banking on talent. *People Management*, October 24–25.

Choudhury, A. M. (1986). The community concept of business: a critique. *International Studies of Management and Organization*, 16(2), 79–95.

Cullum, J. and Turnbull, S. (2005). A meta-review of the management development literature. *Human Resource Development Review*, 4(1), 335–355.

Dalton, K. (2010). *Leadership and Management Development: Developing Tomorrow's Managers*. Harlow: Pearson Education Limited.

Debrah, Y. A. and Ofori, G. (2006). Human resource development of professionals: the case of Tanzanian construction industry. *International Journal of Human Resource Management*, 17(3), 440–463.

Duit, R. (1991). On the role of analogies and metaphors in learning science. *Science Education*, 75(6), 649–673.

Eshun, P. A. and Jellicoe, S. A. (2011). The impact of foreign direct investment on the development of the Ghanaian mineral industry. *Asian Journal of Business and Management Sciences*, 1(1), 148–167.

Fasokun, T. O. (2005). Characteristics of adult learning in Africa. In Fasokun, T. O., Katahoire, A. and Oduaran, A. (eds.), *The Psychology of Adult Learning in Africa* (pp. 14–30). Cape Town: Pearson Education.

Grzeda, M. M. and Assogbavi, T. (1999). Management development programs in Francophone sub Saharan Africa. *Management Learning*, 30(4), 413–429.

Gyekye, K. (1994). Talking development seriously. *Journal of Applied Philosophy*, 11(1), 45–56.

The Hofstede Centre (n.d.). Hofstede dimensions. Available at www.geert-hofstede.com/hofstede_dimensions.php. Accessed 22 March 2014.

Hofstede, G. (1980). *Culture's Consequences*. Thousand Oaks, CA: Sage.

Hofstede, G. (2002). Dimensions do not exist: a reply to Brendan McSweeney. *Human Relations*, 55(11), 1355–1361.

Hofstede, G. and Peterson, M. F. (2000). Culture: national values and organizational practices. In Ashmanasy, N. N., Wilderon, C. and Peterson, M. F. (eds.), *The Handbook of Organizational Culture and Climate* (pp. 401–416). Newbury Park, CA: Sage.

Israel, A. (1989). *Institutional Development: Incentives to Performance*. Washington, DC: The World Bank.

Kiggundu, M. N. (1991). The challenges of management development in Sub-Saharan Africa. *Journal of Management Development*, 10(6), 32–46.

Lassiter, J. E. (2000). African culture and personality: bad social science, effective social activism, or a call to reinvent ethnology? *African Studies Quarterly*, 3(1), 1–21.

Lwoga, E. T., Ngulube, P. and Stilwell, C. (2010). Managing indigenous knowledge for sustainable agricultural development in developing countries: knowledge management approaches in the social context. *International Information and Library Review*, 42, 174–185.

McSweeney, B. (2002). Hofstede's model of national cultural differences and their consequences: a triumph of faith – a failure of analysis. *Human Relations*, 55(1), 89–118.

Michaels, E., Handfield-Jones, H. and Axelrod, B. (2001). *The War for Talent*. Boston: Harvard Business School Press.

Minerals and Mining Law 2006 (Act 703) (s. 50). Accra: Ghana Publishing Corporation.

Minkov, M. and Hofstede, G. (2011). The evolution of Hofstede's doctrine. *International Journal of Cross Cultural Management*, 18(1), 10–20.

Mthembu, D. (1996). Discovering the indigenous roots of management. In Lessem, R. and Nussbaum, B. (eds.), *Sawubona Africa: Embracing Four Worlds in South African Management*. Johannesburg: Struik Publishers.

Mumford, A. (1998). Managing learning and developing management. *Human Resource Development International*, 1(1), 113–118.

Myloni, B., Harzing, A. K. and Mirza, H. (2004). Host country specific factors and the transfer of human resource management practices in MNCs. *International Journal of Human Resource Management*, 25(6), 518–534.

Nafukho, F. M. (2006). Ubuntu worldview: a traditional African view of adult learning in the workplace. *Advances in Developing Human Resources*, 8(3), 408–415.

Nyambegera, S. M. (2002). Ethnicity and human resource management practice in sub-Saharan Africa: the relevance of the managing diversity discourse. *International Journal of Human Resource Management*, 13(7), 1077–1090.

Nzelibe, C. O. (1986). The evolution of African management thought. *International Studies of Management and Organization*, 16(2), 6–16.

Ocholla, D. N. and Onyancha, O. B. (2005). The marginalized knowledge: an informatics analysis of indigenous knowledge publication (1990–2004). *South African Journal of Libraries and Information Science*, 71(3), 247–258.

Omolewa, M. (2007). Traditional African modes of education: their relevance in the modern world. *International Review of Education*, 53, 593–612.

Oppong, N. Y. (2013). Towards African work orientations: guide from Hofstede's cultural dimensions. *European Journal of Business and Management*, 5(20), 203–212.

Oppong, N. Y. (2015). Localization of management in multinational enterprises in developing countries: a case study of policy and practice. *International Journal of Training and Development*, 19(3), 223–231.

Oppong, N. Y. and Gold, J. (2013). Talent management in the Ghanaian gold mining industry: a critical exploration. *Universal Journal of Management and Social Sciences*, 3(10), 1–19.

Owoyemi, O. A., Oyelere, M., Elegbede, T. and Gbajumo-Sheriff, M. (2011). Enhancing employees' commitment to organisation through training. *International Journal of Business and Management*, 6(7), 280–286.

Premoli, C. (1998). African gold: potential, problems and opportunities. Special Publication, Sydney, Australia, 14 pp.

Rohan, M. (2000). A rose by any names? The value construct. *Personality and Social Psychology Review*, 4(3), 255–277.

Sagiv, L. and Schwartz, S. H. (2007). Cultural values in organisations: insights for Europe. *European Journal of International Management*, 1(3), 176–190.

Schellekens, L. (2007). Management training and its contribution to economic recovery in Africa. *Journal of Management Development*, 8(5), 40–50.

Taras, V., Kirkman, B. L. and Steel, P. (2010). Examining the impact of cultural consequences: a three decade, multilevel meta-analytic review of Hofstede's cultural values dimensions. *Journal of Applied Psychology*, 95(3), 405–439.

Trompenaars, F. (1993). *Riding the Waves of Culture*. London: Economist Books.

Walumbwa, F. O., Avolio, B. J. and Aryee, S. (2011). Leadership and management research in Africa: a synthesis and suggestions for future research. *Journal of Occupational and Organizational Psychology*, 84(3), 425–439.

Williamson, J. G. (2002). Winners and losers over two centuries of globalization. Paper delivered at the 2002 WIDER Annual Lecture, 5 September 2002, Copenhagen.

6 Building effective provincial administration in Thailand

The role of performance management

Nicha Sathornkich, Piyawadee Rohitarachoon,
Derek Eldridge and Farhad Hossain

Introduction

One major feature of development administration is the quest for devolution of authority from central government to lower tiers of administration. This is a challenging task in respect of maintaining strategic control, establishing account-ability for resources and ensuring compatibility between these two aspects in the devolution process. Decentralization in Thailand from the central government to provincial administrations demonstrates the classic feature of this component of development management which in this case has been enacted through the implementation of a revitalized performance management system.

Since 2002 the Government of Thailand has promoted decentralization of administration and mandated the role of the head of each government agency as a chief executive officer (CEO) with responsibility for implementing a performance management system (PMS) which incorporates a performance agreement (PA) with key performance indicators (KPIs) driving the annual fiscal cycle. All seventy-five provincial managements, excluding Bangkok, are involved (OPDC, 2004a) with their performance being judged under four perspectives, namely effectiveness in meeting citizen needs, quality of services, efficiency of administration and progress on organization development. While the new paradigm for provincial administra-tion aims to effectively utilize personnel, budgets and other resources through a performance management system to improve the living conditions of the people (OPDC, 2004b; Ministry of Interior, 2009), it has not been exempt from contro-versy, both at inception and implementation. Criticisms arise from the questionable application of PMS for decentralization in a public sector which is traditionally centralized, particularly in a time of diametrically opposed political views in the country on what constitutes effective governance (Jatusripitak, 2003; Shinawatra, 2003; Sirisumphand, 2004; Chulalongkorn University, 2005; Bowornwathana, 2010).

The chapter firstly reviews fundamental issues in the application of performance management to decentralization and then refers to the experience of its enactment at provincial level in Thailand. Respondents for the study at both provincial and central levels are identified. The analysis and discussion of findings cover five major development management themes, namely the extent that decentralization has resulted in a self-sustaining provincial administration, how far provincial governors have emerged as CEOs, the degree of impact on capacity building, the effect on service delivery and the value of incentives as related to performance assessment.

Theoretical foundations of the research

The fundamental principles of performance management

Performance management (PM) involves setting strategic goals and performance targets, allocating and prioritizing resources, developing measurements, monitoring and evaluating progress towards those targets and giving feedback to managers (Busi and Bititci, 2006; Hume, 1995). In addition, associated human resource policies and practices assist PM implementation by the identification of core competency requirements and the development of team and individual capabilities (Marchington and Wilkinson, 1997). Such an approach encourages organizations to establish a culture in which individuals and teams take increased responsibility for developing their own skills, improving processes and contributing to the achievement of organizational goals (Talbot, 2010; Philpott and Sheppard, 1992).

Bryson (1995: 7) contended that making effective decisions on strategic priorities depends on analysing both the internal and external environments and understanding the interests of the different groups who are affected. However, because varied stakeholder expectations can constrain clarity on needed actions, a process of bargaining and negotiation is required to avoid conflict (Collier et al., 2001) and to ensure that statements made on the necessary actions do embody real commitment (Mintzberg et al., 1998: 158). To achieve such commitment Bryson (1995: 224–226) suggested that when making decisions leaders should be concerned with five significant factors. First, they should be capable of designing and using both formal and informal communication networks within and with other interested organizations in order to understand how to balance competing demands from stakeholders. Second, leaders must be skilled in dealing with all parties involved in the strategy implementation through negotiation and bargaining as events unfold. Third, leaders need to know who to influence to obtain resources for strategy implementation. Fourth, leaders are required to build winning, sustainable coalitions and alliances so that they can support and defend the required strategy in implementation. Finally, leaders should avoid bureaucratic confinement and encourage challenge to existing restrictions which impede progress.

Fundamental in PMS is the use of a range of feedback indicators meaningful to service delivery and standards which give a holistic picture of an organization's performance, balanced between results and process, financial and non-financial data and the short term and long term. Such comprehensive feedback can potentially satisfy the perspectives of different stakeholders as well as providing vital information for performance improvement (Jackson, 1995a, Kaplan and Norton, 1992). Needless to say, PMS does not always live up to its expectations when introduced into an organization and some potential weaknesses are referred to in the experience revealed below.

Performance management in the public sector

Historically, employment in the public service has demonstrated two unique characteristics. Firstly, it usually has a 'welfare' component which offers a degree of staff security unmatched in other sectors including buffering against unemployment (Commonwealth Secretariat, 1996: 5). Secondly, traditional public management demonstrates large, centralized bureaucracies and the prevalence of 'command and control' systems driven by rules and budgets (Ellingson and Wambsganss, 2001). As reported in many studies, these two aspects can contribute to overstaffing, workplace inertia, inefficient service delivery, a poor management planning cycle, de-motivation of staff and even more seriously corruption (Commonwealth Secretariat, 1998). In response to this potential scenario, performance management has been adopted from the private sector with the aim of improving public service efficiency, effectiveness and responsiveness in order to satisfy the needs of customers and citizens, as well as giving an improved public perception of government (OECD, 1995). Drucker (1989: 89) emphasized that 'nonprofits need management even more than business does, precisely because they lack the discipline of the bottom line' and in line with this idea Radnor and McGuire (2004) suggested that because public services are operated without market competition, performance measurement is implemented as a substitute for market pressures.

In setting the public sector context for building effective performance management, Jackson (1995b: 19–20) recognized the complexity that organizations face: they serve multiple objectives; have a diversity of clients; deliver a wide range of policies and services; and exist within uncertain socio-political environments. Additionally, the public sector is charged with producing 'public values' (Alford, 2001: 5), the legal framework, responses to market failure and interventions to promote equity. Also, outcomes of PMS will undoubtedly include such factors as economy (Jackson, 1995a), effectiveness (Holloway, 1999), efficiency (Lawton and Rose, 1994) and quality of service (Rouse, 1999; Talbot, 2000).

In the development of PMS in the public sector Kerr (2009) referred to the value of mission statements which inevitably express socially desirable outcomes, but cautions that buried within them are goals, which to be purposefully enacted require adequate attention to multiple stakeholder interests. These interests can be complex, unclearly defined and often conflicting (Farnham and Horton, 1999; Rouse, 1997). Consequently, public sector organizations find it a real challenge to identify clear strategic objectives in a changing environment (De Waal, 2001; Heinrich and Marschke, 2010).

Also, a clear focus on public sector goals becomes difficult when cascading down an organization's objectives to subsidiary bodies when 'parenting styles' of central ministries have a strong influence on strategic control and financial control in PMS (De Waal, 2001: 21–24). Strategic control usually implies a situation in which corporate headquarters issues guidelines and the lower levels independently develop their own strategic plans which are then evaluated and perhaps prioritized by headquarters. Financial control necessarily runs in parallel with strategic control with emphasis placed on defining both short- and long-term financial objectives within the overall budget set by headquarters, which then regularly checks on the accomplishment of those objectives. If there is not a clear alignment and linkage between higher-level decision making and operational performance, identified organizational priorities may not be fulfilled, a situation which may be further exaggerated when powerful elected officials and interest groups unduly influence budget funding and thereby potentially ignore the needs of the officially targeted beneficiaries (Osborne and Gaebler, 1992).

At the heart of performance management is the Performance Agreement (PA) governing the goals to be accomplished within a specific time period. An agreement is used as a cascading tool within an organization to hold managers to account by identifying desired results, establishing guidelines on how to achieve those results, formulating frameworks for budgeting and resource allocation and defining account-abilities (GAO, 2000). A PA can potentially enhance teamwork across organizational boundaries, build employee commitment and result in 'synergy in partnership' (Covey, 1995). Further, such an agreement can help maintain the consistency of programme priorities and the continuity of those programmes during leadership transition periods.

Performance management and capacity building

The learning and growth perspective of PM emphasizes the long-term investment in employees, information systems and organizational capabilities (Ellingson and Wambsganss, 2001: 117) which include employee satisfaction, retention and productivity (Kaplan and Norton, 1996). Associated with these outcomes are employee learning (Ellingson and Wambsganss, 2001) and employee participation in decision making (Osborne and Gaebler, 1992), with many studies confirming that goal-setting processes have a positive effect on learning how to perform better in the workplace (Buchner, 2007). In this respect, difficult and specific goals are said to lead to higher performance compared to vague do-your-best goals (Buchner, 2007: 63). However, Mintzberg (1998) claimed that if targets are too precisely defined, it may direct efforts to the disregard of significant areas of activity later discovered to be important.

When looking at the potential for performance to be improved Buchner (2007) suggested that there are five moderators influencing the perception of goal-driven performance: goal importance, goal commitment, self-efficacy on the part of individuals, the value placed on feedback and the degree of task complexity. Perceptions may not be congruent with needs when for instance 'goal displacement' occurs in which individuals substitute means for ends (Wheelen and Hunger, 2000), or when individuals focus on easily measurable activities that attract reward at the expense of real priorities. This can result in sub-optimization in an organization's overall accomplishment and its ability to enhance capacity as the scope for learning is curtailed.

Visible, tangible and comparable measures are fundamental in designing and implementing actions to improve results (Parsons, 2007; Meekings, 1995) but are subject to complex and empirical challenges in their definition (Talbot, 2010: 1).

Successfully designed measures not only enable the management of performance to be steered in a more accurate and effective way but most importantly are 'a means of organizational learning' (Jackson, 1995b: 20). Such learning based on feedback is essential in dealing with unexpected changes, coping with uncertainty and complexity in the environment and creating opportunities for sustainability advantage (Gold, 2007: 339). Also, to maintain their effectiveness, performance indicators need to be continuously reviewed and linked with the organization's strategy, achieving this connectivity being perceived as a learning process (Dixon et al., 1990). In support of this view Jackson (1995b: 25) maintains that some government agencies have demonstrated 'the capacity to learn from information signals that indicators provide, as well as the organizational capabilities to act upon that learning'.

Incentive schemes in performance management

To improve the effectiveness of public services and to reinforce accountability, reform agendas have increasingly advocated the use of incentive schemes based on approaches derived from the private sector (Radnor and McGuire, 2004). Behaviorally based theories suggest that an incentive pay scheme has the potential to create a clear motivational linkage between an individual's performance and rewards derived from the effort extended (Lawler, 1990). However, implementing such a scheme in the public sector may be difficult in many aspects. First, the public sector typically serves many principals who usually pay attention to different dimensions of output and their interests may not align. Burgess and Ratto (2003: 288) stated that in the multi-principals' setting, 'each principal will offer a positive coefficient on the element(s) she is interested in and negative coefficient on the other dimensions. This creates a negative externality on the other principals who have to face lower efforts in those dimensions'.

Second, in the context of multiple outputs not only is it difficult to measure and monitor performance but also to distinguish good performers from the poor ones. Additionally, perverse incentive effects can occur when a job requires individuals to perform several tasks but only some are measured and rewarded (Burgess and Ratto, 2003: 292). As a consequence, individuals are likely to increase effort only on the rewarded tasks.

Third, in many cases in the public sector individuals achieve results as team members contributing to the same output requirements and in these circumstances Burgess and Ratto (2003: 289) suggested that the greater the uncertainty in output measurement and the greater the size of the team, the more complex is the design of an optimal incentive scheme. Also, the free-ride problem is likely to exist when all team members share the same output and are subject to team-based rewards.

Fourth, when introducing financial rewards it sends a message that the relationship between individuals and the organization is a pure market one which may undermine intrinsic motivation (Burgess and Ratto, 2003: 290). Further, Khojasteh (1993) developed a survey based on Herzberg's motivation theory to record perceived dissatisfaction with categorized intrinsic and extrinsic rewards from both public and private sectors' points of view. He found that employees in the public sector placed higher value on achievement and advancement and significantly less value on pay and job security than those in the private sector.

Kohn (1997) further built on these arguments by suggesting that performance-based incentive rewards are only effective for temporary compliance and have little connection with sustaining changes in attitudes and behaviour. Once there is no longer an extra reward available, individuals tend to slip back to their old behaviours. He maintained that such rewards fail for various reasons. First, as discussed above, pay can have limited motivational impacts in the public sector. Second, 'reward punishes' when a received reward is not equal to an expected reward. Third, rewards disrupt relationships and destroy cooperation when individuals compete for them. Fourth, if an assumption that incentives can solve organizational problems is dominant then underlying issues affecting performance are less likely to be discussed. Fifth, rewards discourage risk-taking when individuals avoid risk which may jeopardize their chances of rewards. Finally, rewards undermine intrinsic value, stated as 'The more a manager stresses what an employee can earn for good work, the less interested that employee will be in the work itself' (Kohn, 1997: 22).

Data collection

Fifty-five senior officials were interviewed in five provincial governments in Thailand: Lumphun, Phayao, Phetchaburi, Prachuap Khiri Khan and Samut Songkhram. The inclusion of a province related to the need to achieve a representative sample chosen to reflect varying endowments in local culture and resources. Provinces were also selected on the basis of a demonstrated impact of PM being apparent and that governors were present in the selected provinces for enough time to be familiar with local conditions having personally negotiated the previous PA and seen it through to evaluation.

Key informants in each province included the Provincial Governor, Vice Provincial Governor, Deputy Governor, Chief of Provincial Governor's Office, Chief of Provincial Strategy Group, Policy and Planning Officer and Heads of Provincial Departments. Each interview took approximately 60–90 minutes and visits also offered the chance to observe the work environment in the Provincial Governors' Offices. In addition to public officials, interviewees in each province included private sector representatives with key roles in development such as the Chairman and Vice Chairman of Provincial Chambers of Commerce, Chairman of the Federation of Thai Industries, members of Provincial Tourism Societies, farmers and members of communities as recipients as well as contributors to public services. Staff of central ministries which have functional responsibilities for service provision in the provinces were included as respondents, as well as senior officials in the Ministry of the Interior, which appoints provincial governors and overviews provincial administration and local government.

Findings

The creation of self-sustaining provincial administration

The research reveals that PMS has enabled the four-year State Administration Plan, as agreed by Parliament, to be cascaded to ministries, and provinces which have then agreed their own aligned strategies as embodied in PAs. A Deputy Prime Minister, appointed by the Prime Minister, oversees a group of provinces in the implementation of this process and supports Governors in the quest to deliver the agreed development targets. As a result each province has a well-defined PA stating its service and development intentions, performance targets and associated measures. Furthermore, the research confirms that activities related to each provincial PA receive a significant degree of priority in ministries' budgets. Importantly key Government priorities are being enacted at provincial level, such as those on natural and environmental conservation, drug eradication and energy efficiency.

However, the findings identify that a lack of capacity to fully prepare and manage provincial budgets has a significant impact on management capability to deliver the required results. This is because each province still relies on budget components emanating from several ministries which are a challenge to integrate and manage in a unified manner. Additionally it was reported that sector budget allocations may not be fully sufficient to support PA targeted service provision. While this situation has eased somewhat since 2009 with a province now having the legal authority to prepare its own budget, the supporting processes linked with several ministries involve diversified and sometimes conflicting terminologies and guidelines which provincial staff find difficult to comprehend. As a result, deadlines for procedure completion might not be met, although developments are underway for a revised database with agreed terminologies for mutual utilization and assigned responsibilities for data recording and maintenance.

It is clear from the findings that the involvement of provincial staff in PMS and the production of PAs have contributed significantly to the development of provincial vision and the ability to draw in local resources for development while at the same time taking account of national priorities and functional strategies derived from ministries. However, respondents reported that PA centrally derived targets considered too ambitious can provide a de-motivating effect and can lead to some associated KPIs being set at a sub-optimum level. This is particularly the case when provincial staff believe that expected outcomes in these same areas will be subject to substantial increase in future years. Also, detected was a lack of ability to take goals in some areas forward operationally in line with Bourgeois's (1980: 227) claim that 'agreement on goals without agreement on means correlates with poor performance'. This reflects in some cases a lack of internal provincial process for identifying and choosing means to attain targets. In this respect, Lumphun and Phayao Provinces provide a unique example where there was a goal to increase longan exports but how this was to be done eluded provincial staff. This was eventually resolved by the Deputy Prime Minister overseeing these provinces actively playing a crucial role in leading the public and the private sectors in detailed trade negotiations with Chinese trade representatives.

While evidence has been generated that strategic capability at provincial level has a degree of sustainability as a result of PMS, concerns were raised that PAs are unduly drawn towards the execution of central ministries' requirements at the expense of the development of strategies at provincial level based on the concerns of local communities. As a consequence the provincial PA can focus too heavily on economic aspects and pay limited attention to social issues. The consequence is that provincial managers can neglect responsibilities to fully involve local stakeholders in a dialogue to understand and promote development opportunities at provincial level. Such imbalance has serious implications for leadership roles, motivation and administrative flexibility (Moynihan and Pandey, 2010) with the potential in the long term to be self-defeating in respect of the Government's aim to create self-sustaining provincial administrations.

Additionally, while the provincial vision and strategy are linked with those at the national and ministerial levels, the coordination with local administrations has largely been ignored. Although representatives from local administrations are appointed to provincial management committees, it does not guarantee that local development strategies are aligned and linked to those at the higher level, which may result in government policy not being fully effective at grassroots level.

The emergence of provincial governors as CEOs

PMS introduced new roles and responsibilities for provincial governors and the findings suggest that this has created a shift in the working culture from an administrative approach towards a more managerial one. In all of the provinces investigated, the Governors have become to varying degrees strategic leaders managing provincial development plans and monitoring and evaluating performance of PAs. Senior staff reported that teamwork and participative administration have been stimulated to some extent in all of the provinces to the benefit of citizens and that provincial governors have led this change process. A clear impression is given that old style political control has given way to a significant degree to the idea that a prime responsibility lies with provincial governors as CEOs to utilize personnel and local resources for development. Additionally, both executives and subordinates value the advantages that PMS has brought to their work by an increased ability to identify roles, to formulate necessary actions and to monitor results.

However, the findings indicate that while PMS aims to gather central agencies together in support of the emergent CEO roles of provincial governors, there is limited coordination and cooperation to do this. Each ministry to a significant extent pays attention only to its functional responsibilities with a limited view of holistic provincial development and the challenge of providing multi-dimensional services in support of the well-being of the citizens. The evidence can be seen in the deviation in terminology used for the same service items and the multiple report production for different agencies utilizing the same base information, a common finding concerning inadequate attention to the design of change processes in the public sector (Fryer et al., 2009). These findings are not surprising with central administration reflecting the common public agencies' characteristics of hierarchy, bureaucracy, red tape and rigidity (Ellingson and Wambsganss, 2001) with the working culture of government departments not having shifted to the degree necessary to incorporate procedures to fully promote the interests of provincial administration. Thus while the experience of learning how to build more responsive governance at provincial level may be proceeding under the tutelage of governors, the future potential of devolved functions may be in jeopardy unless further reform at the centre can proceed.

Evidence gathered suggests that all of the provincial governors included in the research have to a significant extent become role models in stimulating continuous learning and improvement amongst staff. They provide encouragement to challenge existing practices, to make changes as necessary and to seek collaboration from various local resources in achieving outcomes. As such the PA has provided a baseline for the creation of a provincial vision which staff and the public have bought into. Also new administrative processes have been created as a result of the identification of KPIs, the negotiation of performance targets, the coordination of inter-sector activities, and the evaluation of performance. One example of how citizens have benefited from new thinking is the creation of 'one stop' points of contact for members of the public with several key service staff being present to deal with local issues at specified times, sometimes on a mobile basis.

However, PMS implementation in provinces is heavily influenced by legislative requirements related to the emergent role of the Provincial Governor as CEO in respect of budget preparation. The demands on management decision making inspired by PA implementation have to some extent outpaced the available legal rights, which crucially puts provincial governors in jeopardy, being unaware of potential misconduct under current legislation. Additionally, with emergent changes provincial governors report the need for legal personnel to advise in the provinces as legislation is often difficult to comprehend and incorporate, which potentially constrains leadership in service improvement and innovation.

Capacity building

Staff development to handle PMS is a critical factor in its potential success. Central agencies have provided development support on PMS implementation and on defining roles and responsibilities in provincial administration through seminars, workshops, road shows, manuals, teleconferences, online training and e-programmes designed for reporting. Additionally, academic institutes have provided research outputs that not only build understanding of the philosophy, concepts and procedures of PMS, but also inform graduates who plan to enter the public service. Apart from formal training provincial governors actively organize events that promote the sharing of knowledge and experience, such as 'Coffee Forums'.

An important benefit from PMS reported by many respondents was the ability to sustain administration and outputs when a provincial governor is transferred elsewhere. In addition, ongoing PMS activity substantially reduces interference from any self-motivated agenda that a new provincial governor may bring which could result in interruption or discontinuation of existing agreed programmes.

An 'operating administration' based on a PA also assists during a new provincial governor's transition period. However, the research reveals crucially that provincial team members' lengths of service in a province are important for the continuation of an effective PMS. Staff believe that success depends on the presence of a critical mass of experienced persons who through mutual understanding can design and deliver agreed PA components, organize relevant stakeholder meetings through their networks, monitor performance and seek collaboration from the wider community as necessary.

It was found that there are several personnel-related issues which inhibit PMS implementation. First, while the emergent learning culture has stimulated the development of new capabilities there is still a deficit in required knowledge and skills if PM is to be fully effective, particularly those related to analysis and planning. Second, frequent relocation of senior staff causes a degree of work system disruption and possible discontinuation of some important activities, because ministry-driven relocation usually happens quickly and a province has little chance in controlling or preparing for this. Third, a significant number of staff in key areas at provincial level suffer work overload, in spite of some efforts to alleviate this. Finally, limited opportunities to participate in training and workshops organized by central agencies result in staff not being prepared appropriately to cope with changes. This is very much in line with findings from the study of two UK public sector organizations which stress the absolute need to train all affected staff on the purposes and potential impacts of PMS (Radnor and McGuire, 2004).

Service delivery

The impact of PMS implementation on service provision has been significant in many ways. First, service improvement is demonstrated because of cycle time reduction and simpler work processes as a result of a special KPI designed for this aspect. Second, more coordination of activities has resulted through the alignment of the work schedules of provincial departments, particularly in the provision of a mobile service to remote villages and communities. Third, the emergence of strengthened teamwork, coordination, and collaboration has resulted in a more harmonious, friendly, and sharing work atmosphere that is apparent to citizens in all the provinces studied.

The increasing involvement of the private sector, academic institutes and citizens in provincial management and development plans, together with the public sector support on community projects, creates a sense of provincial ownership. It results in improved understanding and relationships between the public sector and other sectors within the province and empowers many bodies to work towards provincial development goals. A common feature of this was that respondents from the private sector reported that they felt honoured to be appointed as provincial management committee members in support of policy implementation and service delivery.

Very importantly on the negative side the research reveals that the PA can result in a neglect of services not formally included in it but thought by many provincial stakeholders to be important. The possibility here is that while centrally defined functions and goals may be well served through PMS, local service needs may go unrecognized or be poorly supported because of lack of resource allocation. Locally induced service provision is an important consideration as each province is different in terms of citizens' needs, economic resource potential and cultural endowments. However, the very nature of the PMS experience may over time induce the inclusion of local needs through increased managerial awareness of how resources can be brought together to achieve development targets in a self-sustaining manner.

The value of incentives

The arrangement for incentive payments as reported is one of the most contentious issues facing provincial administrations. When the incentives for top executives are compared with those for other senior staff members it is seen that the amounts allocated are markedly different even though they rely on the same provincial performance score. The incentive schemes for different groups act in an uneven manner with some negative consequences in the quest for improved performance. First, the incentives for different groups can be based on different philosophies and purposes which potentially undermine the equitable and fair intentions implied in PMS implementation. Second, the incentive scheme for local administration is perceived as relatively easy to access on favourable terms when compared to the ones available for the province. Third, monetary incentive results in system distortion because more attention is paid to activities that potentially lead to a high performance score in order to secure a monetary allocation. Fourth, the provincial incentive distribution criteria are tightly linked with the PA, meaning that eligible provincial departments and individuals are limited to those playing a significant part in the PA, which does not cover all required provincial roles and responsibilities. Overall, misunderstanding of the incentive scheme is apparent due to it being perceived as a 'bonus' in the same way as an enterprise distributes an element of profit for distribution when in fact sums for the scheme are limited and involve the use of taxpayers' money. Moreover, there is a possibility that the incentive scheme in its current form can destroy the traditional civil servants' pride in serving the King as it can create greediness, undue competition and selfishness. The key question is how far should monetary incentives be balanced against the intrinsic rewards of public service contribution? It may possibly not be worth distorting important PM benefits by continuing with incentive schemes in their current form.

Concluding remarks

This study offers empirical evidence of the effect of PMS implementation at the provincial level in Thailand, a topic that is essentially part of development management but has been previously under-researched in the Asian context. An important finding is that while much progress has been made towards a self-sustaining process of provincial administration in Thailand, more time is necessary for PMS to fully embed itself given that some key staff still have a limited understanding of its concepts and philosophy, practices and associated learning needs. Additional support is therefore necessary to promote PMS values, methods and behaviours, otherwise decentralization through this approach may only occur in a limited way with the potential for the system to be distorted from its due intentions and possibly misused. Furthermore, the findings suggest that linking and cascading the PA from the provincial level down to the responsibilities of departments and individual posts requires more attention in terms of coordination with budgets. Finally, urgent consideration needs to be given to structural alignment of the incentive scheme so that it is based in the view of Heinrich and Marschke (2010) on measures that actually and realistically represent performance. Otherwise its total withdrawal should be considered.

Finally, while strong initial support from government has enabled PMS to drive decentralization, changes at the political level can, on the other hand, jeopardize the system and disrupt continuous improvement in provincial administration. Unfortunately, the study reveals a recent dilution of government support in terms of PMS implementation that has resulted in uncertainties on the future of strategically driven provincial development plans, putting in doubt what Goodsell (2006: 623) refers to as 'a vision that captures its interpretation of public administration's fulfilled contribution to a democratic polity'.

References

Alford, J. (2001). The implication of 'publicness' for strategic management theory. In G. Johnson and K. Scholes (eds.), *Exploring Public Sector Strategy* (pp. 1–16). Harlow, Essex: Pearson Education Ltd.

Bourgeois, L. J. (1980). Performance and consensus. *Strategic Management Journal*, 1(3), 227–248.

Bowornwathana, B. (2010). Bureaucratic politics and administrative reform: why politics matter. *Public Organisation Review*, 10(4), 303–321.

Bryson, J. M. (1995). *Strategic Planning for Public and Nonprofit Organizations: A Guide to Strengthening and Sustaining Organizational Achievement*. San Francisco: Jossey-Bass.

Buchner, T. W. (2007). Performance management theory: a look from the performer's perspective with implication for HRD. *Human Resource Development International*, 10(1), 59–73.

Burgess, S. and Ratto, M. (2003). The role of incentives in the public sector: issues and evidence. *Oxford Review of Economic Policy*, 19(2), 285–300.

Busi, M. and Bititci, U. S. (2006). Collaborative performance management: present gaps and future research. *International Journal of Productivity and Performance Management*, 55(1), 7–25.

Chulalongkorn University (2005). *Full Report on the Evaluation of Efficiency and Results of Integrated Provincial Strategic Plan Project*. Bangkok: Ministry of Interior.

Collier, N., Fishwick, F. and Johnson, G. (2001). The processes of strategy development in the public sector. In G. Johnson and K. Scholes (eds.), *Exploring Public Sector Strategy* (pp. 17–37). Harlow, Essex: Pearson Education.

Commonwealth Secretariat (1996). *Working Towards Results: Managing Individual Performance in the Public Service*. London: Commonwealth Secretariat.

Commonwealth Secretariat (1998). *Introducing New Approaches: Improved Public Service Delivery*. London: Commonwealth Secretariat.

Covey, S. R. (1995). Performance agreement. *Executive Excellence*, 12(5), 3–4.

De Waal, A. A. (2001). *Power of Performance Management: How Leading Companies Create Sustained Value*. New York: John Wiley.

Dixon, J. R., Nani, A. J. J. and Vollmann, T. E. (1990). *The New Performance Challenge: Measuring Operations for World-Class Competition*. New York: Business One Irwin.

Drucker, P. F. (1989). What business can learn from nonprofits. *Harvard Business Review*, 89(4), 88–93.

Ellingson, D. A. and Wambsganss, J.R. (2001). Modifying the approach to planning and evaluation in governmental entities: a 'balanced scorecard' approach. *Journal of Public Budgeting, Accounting & Financial Management*, 13(1), 103–120.

Farnham, D. and Horton S. (1999). Managing public and private organizations. In S. Horton and D. Farnham (eds.), *Public Management in Britain* (pp. 26–45). Hampshire: Palgrave.

Fryer, K., Antony, J. and Ogden, S. (2009). Performance management in the public sector. *International Journal of Public Sector Management*, 22(6), 478–498.

GAO (2000). *Managing for Results: Emerging Benefits from Selected Agencies' Use of Performance Agreements*. Washington, DC: US General Accounting Office.

Gold, J. (2007). Human resource development. In J. Bratton and J. Gold (eds.), *Human Resource Management: Theory and Practice* (pp. 306–357). Hampshire: Palgrave Macmillan.

Goodsell, C. T. (2006). A new vision for public administration. *Public Administration Review*, 66(4), 623–635.

Heinrich J. and Marschke G. (2010). Incentives and their dynamics in public sector performance management systems. *Journal of Policy Analysis and Management*, 29(1), 83–208.

Holloway, J. (1999). Managing performance. In A. Rose and A. Lawton (eds.), *Public Services Management* (pp. 238–259). Essex: Pearson Education.

Hume, D. A. (1995). *Reward Management: Employee Performance, Motivation and Pay*. Oxford: Blackwell.

Jackson, P. M. (1995a). Introduction: reflections on performance management in public service organizations. In P. M. Jackson (ed.), *Measures for Success in the Public Sector: A Public Finance Foundation Reader* (pp. 1–18). London: The Chartered Institute of Public Finance and Accountancy.

Jackson, P. M. (1995b). Public service performance evaluation: a strategic perspective. In P. M. Jackson (ed.), *Measures for Success in the Public Sector: A Public Finance Foundation Reader* (pp. 9–26). London: Chartered Institute of Public Finance and Accountancy.

Jatusripitak, S. (2003). *World Competitiveness: Integrated Management at the Provincial Level under the National Strategic Plan: Workshop on Leadership Development for Change Management*. Bangkok: Office of the Public Sector Development Commission.

Kaplan, R. S. and Norton, D. P. (1992). Balanced scorecard: measures that drive performance. *Harvard Business Review*, 70(1), 71–79.

Kaplan, R. S. and Norton, D. P. (1996). *The Balanced Scorecard: Translating Strategy into Action*. Boston: Harvard Business Press.

Kerr, S. (2009). *Reward Systems: Does Yours Measure Up?* Boston: Harvard Business Press.

Khojasteh, M. (1993). Motivating the private vs. public sector managers. *Public Personnel Management*, 22(3), 391.

Kohn, A. (1997). Why incentive plans cannot work. In S. Kerr (ed.), *Ultimate Rewards: What Really Motivates People to Achieve* (pp. 15–24). Boston: Harvard Business Review Book.

Lawler, E. E. I. (1990). *Strategic Pay: Aligning Organizational Strategies and Pay Systems*. San Francisco: Jossey-Bass.

Lawton, A. and Rose, A. G. (1994). *Organisation and Management in the Public Sector*. London: Pitman.

Marchington, M. and Wilkinson, A. (1997). *Core Personnel and Development*. London: Cromwell Press.

Meekings, A. (1995). Unlocking the potential of performance measurement: a practice implementation guide. *Public Money and Management*, 15(4), 5–12.

Ministry of Interior (2009). *Plan and Development in Provinces and the Region*. Bangkok: Bureau of Provincial Administration Development and Promotion, Ministry of Interior.

Mintzberg, H. (1998). Five Ps for strategy. In H. Mintzberg, J. B. Quinn and S. Ghoshal (eds.), *The Strategy Process: Revised European Edition* (pp. 13–21). London: Prentice Hall.

Mintzberg, H., Ahlstrand, B. and Lampel, J. (1998), *Strategy Safari: The Complete Guide through the Wilds of Strategic Management*. London: Prentice Hall.

Moynihan, D. P. and Pandey, S. (2010), The big question for performance management: why do managers use performance information? *Journal of Public Administration Research and Theory*, 20(4), 849–866.

OECD (1995). *Governance in Transition: Public Management Reforms in OECD Countries*. Paris: Organisation for Economic Co-operation and Development.

OPDC (2004a). *Public Sector Development for the Benefit of the Thai Citizens*. Bangkok: Public Sector Development Commission.

OPDC (2004b). *Report on 2-Years Performance of the Public Sector Development Commission and the Office of the Public Sector Development Commission (January 2003–September 2004)*. Bangkok, Public Sector Development Commission.

Osborne, D. and Gaebler T. (1992). *Reinventing Government*. Reading, MA: Addison-Wesley.

Parsons, J. (2007). Measuring to learn whilst learning to measure. *Measuring Business Excellence*, 11(1), 12–19.

Philpott, L. and. Sheppard, L. (1992). Managing for improved performance in strategies for human resource management. In L. Philpott and L. Sheppard (eds.), *Strategies for Human Resource Management: A Total_Business Approach*. London: Kogan Page.

Radnor, Z. and McGuire M. (2004). Performance management in the public sector: fact or fiction? *International Journal of Productivity and Performance Management*, 53(3), 245–260.

Rouse, J. (1997). Resources and performance management in public service organizations. In K. Issac-Henry, C. Painter and C. Barnes (eds.), *Management in the Public Sector: Challenge and Change* (pp. 73–104). London: International Thomson Business Press.

Rouse, J. (1999). Performance management, quality management and contracts. In S. Horton and D. Farnham (eds.), *Public Management in Britain* (pp. 76–93). Hampshire: Palgrave.

Shinawatra, T. (2003). *Thailand: The New Context in the World Competitiveness: Workshop on Change Management Development*. Bangkok: Public Sector Development Commission.

Sirisumphand, T. (2004). *Provincial CEOs: Innovation and Challenge in Thai Public Development*. Bangkok: Public Sector Development Commission.

Talbot, C. (2000). Performing 'performance' – A comedy in five acts. *Public Money and Management*, 20(4), 63–68.

Talbot, C. (2010). *Theories of Performance: Organisational and Service Improvement in the Public Domain*. Oxford: University Press.

Wheelen, T. L. and Hunger, J. D. (2000). *Strategic management business policy*. Upper Saddle River, NJ: Prentice Hall.

7 Capacity development for civil service reform in Croatia

Bejan David Analoui and Farhad Analoui

Introduction

When it comes to reform to New Public Management (NPM), Croatia's need to deal with inherent challenges (Antwi and Analoui, 2010) is not unique. The major challenge for public administration has been to create the supporting mechanisms to cope with cultural and economic changes, and to implement public policies (Wilson, 1887; Taylor, 1911; Stoker, 2006). Prior to ascension to the European Union, Croatia's need to strengthen the capacity of its civil service in order to support the creation of a politically neutral, professional and honest civil service to ensure the premises for real transformation in the public sector has been on the table (Analoui, 2009). Public sector reform is invariably related to the establishment of human resource departments and the capacity building (CB) of staff and management through human resource development programmes (Antwi and Analoui, 2010; O'Flynn, 2007; Analoui, 2007).

The undertaking of such reform is an exercise in development management. Development management is a subfield of public administration, and the trends in development management emerge from the particulars of this subfield, as well as broader trends influencing perspectives on public administration globally and historically (Brinkerhoff, 2008). A well-recognized lesson from the implementation of development management initiatives is that the manner in which development management tasks are undertaken influences both effectiveness and results (Brinkerhoff and Crosby, 2002). Thus, attention to process is an integral element of development management. As Thomas (1999) notes, among the distinctive features of managing development is that it involves more than simply achieving tasks to meet immediate goals most efficiently; it also addresses how the processes of task accomplishment can contribute to influencing social dynamics and outcomes, such as empowerment and building capacity.

The primary aim of this chapter is to provide an insight into the development needs of managers, in particular middle managers in charge of the teams and/or operations in the 'Tax Administration' and Ministry of Finance (MoF) in particular, whilst maintaining the integrity of the organization's own processes. In order to achieve this, the chapter was guided by two questions: What category of skills and competencies do managers require in order to remain effective as leaders of their establishment/operations? What are the core competencies required by the managers to achieve increased effectiveness and improved leadership at work?

Based on our findings we argue that a context-sensitive and more holistic focus on human resource development is required for effective CB within the public sector. To that end we provide insights into middle managers' perceptions of undertaking training and development to enhance their competency, and consider the associated challenges and implications for human resource development practice.

The chapter was written with primary data collected using questionnaires, translated to the Croation language and distributed to 213 public sector middle managers in the regional and Zagreb offices and departments. A total of 112 completed questionnaires were received (52.6 per cent response rate) and were analysed descriptively using statistical tools. The questionnaire consisted of 35 items, with the exception of the demographic questions and two open questions, the remaining questions each contain five alternative scores on a Likert scale. These ranged from *Not all all* (1.0), to *Once in a while* (2.0), *Sometimes* (3.0), *Fairly often* (4.0), and *Frequently if not always* (5.0). In addition, 13 semi-structured interviews were conducted purposively amongst the participants.

The rest of the chapter is organized as follows: the next section briefly reviews the literature on the interrelationship between public sector reform and CB, followed by a discussion of the required competencies for capacity building. Finally, relevant conclusions will be outlined.

Public sector reform and capacity building: a brief overview

Pollitt and Bouckaert (2004: 8) define reform in the public sector as 'deliberate changes to the structures and processes of public service or organization with the purpose of getting them to run better'. Kiggundu (2000) emphasizes that in industrialized northern countries, public sector reform was driven by ideology in response to citizen and taxpayer demands for improved public services, a smaller role for governments at all levels, private sector participation, and reduced tax burdens. For transition economies, the goal has been to break down authoritarian institutional structures and expedite democratic development and economic market reforms. Developing countries undertook reform as a direct consequence of the early experiences of structural adjustment programmes (Antwi and Analoui, 2013).

However, this has been a phenomenon which has spread globally, and trends have taken shape by using developed countries with a long history in public administration as a benchmark (Bekke and Meer, 2000). Thus, the 2005 World Public Sector Report distinguishes among three broad models of public administration and management: traditional public administration (the bureaucratic model, characterized by rigid rules, formal procedures and uniform, closed systems), public management, including New Public Management (essentially characterized by its hostility to the one-size-fits-all approach of the traditional public administration and its admiration for business-like efficiency, with emphasis on goals and achievement of objectives), and responsive governance (characterized by accountability, participation, transparency, equalities agenda and sustainability) (see also United Nations, 2005).

In order to reflect the lessons learned from previous experiences, it is argued that public sector reform should be 'strategic, integrative, experimental, knowledge-based, transformational, service- and results-oriented, and participatory citizen-driven. Reform initiatives must also be locally grounded and contextualized, emphasizing the development of broad-based politically, technically and managerially sustainable core competencies and capacities supported by democratic institutional arrangements' (Kiggundu, 2000: 156). It is now proven that public sector reform is invariably related to the CB of staff and management (Antwi and Analoui, 2010). CB/development is a multi-dimensional phenomenon and is defined as:

- 'Capacity building is the ability of individuals, groups, institutions and organizations to identify and solve development problems over time' (Morgan, 1996: 7).
- '... capacity is the combination of people, institutions and practices that permits countries to reach their development goals. ... Capacity building is ... investment in human capital, institutions and practices' (World Bank, 1998: 8).
- Capacity development is 'the process through which individuals, organizations and societies obtain, strengthen and maintain the capabilities to set and achieve their own development objectives over times' (United Nations, 2008: 4).

CB includes and supports strategies for long-term investment in education and learning, and strengthened state and institutional reforms that respond to citizen needs (United Nations, 2008). As described in Alley and Negretto (1999), there is the need for programmes that can be integrated into a country's own systems that enhance the capacity of local people to better serve their own community in a sustainable manner. 'In practice, CB takes a variety of forms, but has been summarised as being the development of *skills*, the development of *structures*, and the provision of *support*' (O'Hare, 2010: 35). Research on CB has revealed organizational CB to be a multi-dimensional concept putting together capabilities, knowledge, resources and human capital to achieve objectives (Sobeck and Agius 2007: 238). The blending of capabilities may involve improving management competencies and/or improving sustainability.

Capability is defined 'as the collective skill or aptitude of an organisation or system to carry out a particular function or process either inside or outside the system' (Baser and Morgan, 2008: 25). The coming together of different capabilities in an effectiveness interrelationship is crucial to the capacity of a system. The five core capabilities that can be found in all organizations and systems (Baser and Morgan, 2008: 26–33) include:

- Capability to act and self-organize.
- Capability to generate development results.

- Capability to relate and survive within the environment and in connection with other actors.
- Capability to adopt and self-renew.
- Capability to achieve coherence.

The capacity of an organization or system is the ability to create public value with competent people committed to generating results, collective capabilities to support and manage the structure for sustainability, and the ability to attract these things together with some sort of integration, synthesis and coherence. O'Hare (2010), summing up the work of Southern (2002), identifies organizational and financial planning; HRM; risk management; performance management; marketing management; strategic management; relationship management and technology management as parts of CB which add to 'change management'.

Capacity development and civil service reform in Croatia

The main characteristics of the respondents discussed here include their age, gender and work experience. The results of the analysis also provide the profile of the organization and its management. It must be noted that the question requesting respondents' date of birth which was used to gather data on the age of the respondents was answered in a number of forms by respondents. These have been interpreted as follows:

a) Where a two-digit number such as '58' or '45' has been entered, this has been interpreted as the age of the respondent.
b) Where a year such as '1952' has been entered this has been interpreted as the respondent's year of birth; the respondent's age has then been calculated by subtracting the year the questionnaire was completed from respondent's year of birth (i.e. 2010 – 1952).

As shown in Figure 7.1, respondents' gender was distributed as follows: the minority of the respondents (n = 36) were male while the remaining respondents (n = 76) were female. The majority of managers are therefore female, with a female-to-male ratio of 2.1:1. This is not surprising since in Eastern European countries including Croatia, women have always been encouraged to work alongside their male counterparts.

The age of respondents ranged from a minimum of 29 to a maximum of 63 years of age; given that the mean age of respondents is 50 years of age, it is reasonable to characterize the middle and senior managers as being 'relatively mature'. This is also partly due to the fact that those who are enjoying the middle and senior management positions have had to accumulate adequate years of service in order to gain the recognition to be selected for and/or appointed to a middle management position (Analoui, 1995). This finding is in line with the view that finds older managers may be relatively more valuable because they have developed important skills and general experience (Wei et al., 2005).

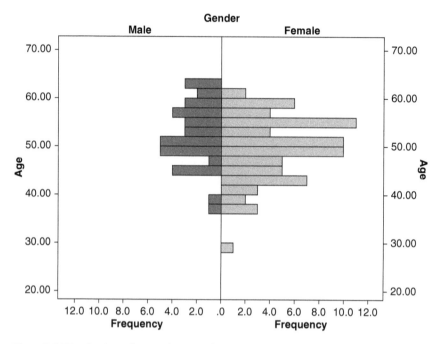

Figure 7.1 Distribution of respondents' age by gender
Source: Field data

This picture has been gradually changing lately especially in the MoF where the HR policies have become more in line with EU countries and attempts have been made to base the promotion on 'performance' rather than age and years of service. However, this in many cases proved rather challenging.

When distributed on the basis of standard age groups (see Figure 7.2) it is clear that the majority of the managers (75 per cent, n = 81) are aged between 46 and 65. This is perhaps to be expected given the seniority of their positions; however, the number of respondents aged between 56 and 65 (22 per cent, n = 24) highlights the necessity for succession planning in the mid to long term. However, the high rate of staff turnover in public sector establishments as a whole, including the MoF, does not allow for accurate succession planning. Further, the data generated through annual performance appraisal is not, as yet, neither accurate nor adequately incorporated into the reward system and/or HR planning policies.

The distribution of respondents' 'Age by Gender' shows that the female members of the workforce are characterized by a wider distribution of age than their male counterparts (see Figure 7.1).

The data shows that respondents have a relatively high degree of work experience in the public sector (see Table 7.1); the minimum and maximum years of work experience range from 10 to 39 years with a mean of 19.5 years of experience.

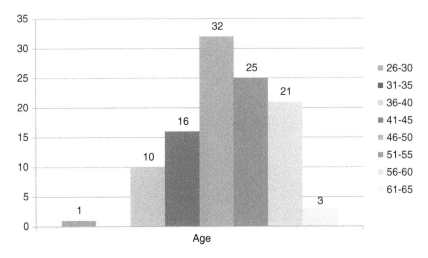

Figure 7.2 Distribution of respondents' age
Source: Field data

Table 7.1 Respondents' work experience

	N	Min	Max	Mean	Std. Deviation
Leadership Experience (Years)	112	10	39	19.5	6.67

Source: Field data

Grouping respondents' work experience by five-year intervals (see Table 7.2) reveals that the majority (60.7 per cent, n = 68) have 19 years of work experience or less. However, it must be noted that some middle and senior managers have worked in other public sector establishments before joining the MoF. This internal move between the ministries and public sector establishments is not frowned up and implicitly condoned throughout the sector. This is largely due to the inability to secure promotions and career advancement in one organization, which forces the individuals to make a horizontal move to benefit from better work-related conditions (Guthrie, 2001; Analoui, 1997).

Cross-tabulating work experience and gender (see Table 7.3) reveals that female respondents have considerably more work experience than their male counterparts. This perhaps suggests that female managers within the organization may be more suitable for future promotion.

Thus, the profile of the respondents can be summarized as being senior and mid-level public sector managers, who are relatively mature, with considerable years of work experience. The majority of the respondents are female, and female managers tend to be the most experienced.

Table 7.2 Respondents' work experience (five-year intervals)

	Frequency	Per cent
10–14	22	19.6
15–19	46	41.1
20–24	19	17.0
25–29	14	12.5
30–34	6	5.4
35–39	5	4.5
Total (n, %)	112	100

Source: Field data

Table 7.3 Work experience and gender cross-tabulation

Work Experience (Years)	Gender		Total
	Male	Female	
10–14	5	17	22
15–19	12	34	46
20–24	7	12	19
25–29	5	8	13
30–34	4	2	6
35–39	2	3	5
Incomplete section			−1
Total	35	76	112

Source: Field data

This profile of respondents, combined with the issues of poor staff retention and a lack of succession planning, provides support for our contention that a greater focus on holistic human resource development practices are necessary for capacity building. Although it is desirable to enhance individuals' competencies through training (Ndou and Sebola, 2015) the long-term effectiveness of development activity will evidently be limited where individuals do not stay within a post or within the organization. Thus, to ensure the long-term effectiveness of capacity building through training it is imperative that both retention and succession planning also be addressed by HR professionals (Analoui, 2007).

Profile of formal management training in Croatia civil service

Training and development is undoubtedly the most relevant strategy by which HR can develop their senior management resources (Winterton and Winterton, 1997; Wang, Hutchins and Garavan, 2009). The results of the survey indicate that the number of respondents who have received formal management training is 29.46 per cent (see Table 7.4). This is clearly limited as 70.54 per cent have not received formal management training. Indeed, up to three years ago, very few managers received formal training simply because the only training available was from the Office of the Civil Service. As one participant asserted, 'the materials are old, the trainers are not familiar with modern training methods and everything takes the form of traditional class room seminars ... very boring'. Recently, due to senior management initiatives, regional grants and loans have been secured, and as a result management training, especially in the areas of HR and its functions, leadership, communication and team development, and management, have been provided to nearly all senior and middle managers in the MoF and Tax Administration throughout the regions.

Cross-tabulating respondents' work experience and management training (see Table 7.5) reveals no apparent relationship between the two. This indicates that the lack of formal management training amongst respondents may be symptomatic of a lack of human resource development activity in the Croatian public sector. This is not surprising. As one participant noted most attention has been paid to 'technical training as opposed to soft skills management training ... besides it is only recently that some organisations have become aware of the importance of HRM and the need for human resource development'. As another manager commented, 'Only recently we have started to enjoy management training. Traditionally, people related training was not available let alone being offered to all middle and senior managers'. Further, little has been done to initiate HRD programmes in the regional offices. 'This is the first time we are provided with management training of this sort ... we should have more of it and on a regular basis', as one of the regional managers commented.

These findings are consistent with those in other settings that have found that training aimed at public sector reform is often inadequate. For example, Pallangyo and Rees (2010) described training received within Tanzanian local government agencies as being poorly coordinated, and not relevant for meeting the needs of employees.

Table 7.4 Respondents who have received formal training

	Frequency (n)	Per cent (%)
No	79	70.54
Yes	33	29.46
Total	112	100

Source: Field data

Table 7.5 Cross-tabulation of respondents' work experience and receipt of formal training

Work Experience	Received Formal Management Training		Total
	No	Yes	
10–14	18	4	22
15–19	32	14	46
20–24	13	6	19
25–29	8	5	13
30–34	4	2	6
35–39	3	2	5
Total	78	33	111

Source: Field data

As shown (see Table 7.5), there seems to be a tendency amongst older participants to receive less formal training than those participants with fewer years of experience. This is largely due to the prevailing perceptions amongst the middle and senior managers with more years of experience that 'they don't need it', and that 'training should be given to the younger ones'. It was observed that there seems to be a belief amongst the more experienced participants that needing training is an admittance of questionable performance. Clearly, the HR department has to continue with its recent efforts to change the managers' perception, especially those with more years of experience, of the value of development activity.

The data analysis reveals four main findings with important implications for HR policy in the organization:

- Female respondents have considerably more experience than their male counterparts. This indicates that the HR policy for promotion within the organization should place equal emphasis on the promotion and enhancement of male and female staff.
- A relatively large portion of respondents (22 per cent, n = 24) are aged between 56 and 65. This indicates that the organization should pay attention to succession planning as 22 per cent of senior managers are likely to retire in the mid to long term.
- This also indicates that the organization may benefit from a tailored training and development programme that will allow them to pass on the knowledge and experience gained throughout the present initiative to future senior managers.
- There is a need to raise awareness amongst the managers, especially those of greater years, and those with more than 20 years of experience about the importance of training throughout one's career.

Required competences for capacity building: a discussion

The purpose of this section is to identify the categories of competencies required for capacity building as perceived by middle and senior managers. Data was collected from 112 respondents who were asked to respond to open-ended questions. The questions required them to detail the skills they perceived as being most important for CB. Participants in the survey responded in their native language (Croatian) which was translated, accurately, by a senior in-house translator in the department of Human Resource Management, which was further cross-checked by an independent translator to ensure accuracy; the rate of accuracy was determined as 99 per cent.

The survey used four categories of classification originally proposed by Analoui (2002): These are:

a) *People Related* – skills and competencies concerned with the management of people and relationships, for example communication and negotiation;
b) *Task Related* – skills and competencies related to carrying out day-to-day tasks;
c) *People and Task Related* – skills and competencies relating to the interrelationship between the previous two categories, which are difficult to separate, such as the management of the tax core group, which requires the use of both people and task skills for effective completion of work activities; and
d) *Self and Career Development* – competencies required to develop oneself in relation to career advancement.

A thematic analysis of the data was carried out, using three individuals to code and cross-check data to ensure validity and reliability of the data. The scores have been coded as follows: 3 most important, 2 important, 1 least important (see Table 7.6).

The overall ranking of the data indicates that managers perceived 'people related' (34.6 per cent) and 'self and career development' (29.8 per cent) as the most important categories of competencies for CB rather than 'task related' (26.8 per cent).

Table 7.6 Ranking of competencies required for capacity building

	Most Important		Important		Least Important	
	F	%	F	%	F	%
People Related	32	28.1	46	40.4	49	43.4
Task Related	43	37.7	21	18.4	12	10.6
People and Task Related	16	14.0	3	2.6	5	4.4
Self and Career Development	23	20.2	44	38.6	47	41.6

Source: Field data

This is not unusual simply because most managers have already acquired a good understanding of the task and the job in hand by the time they reach middle and senior positions. It is at this time that they become aware of the importance of their own career development and the need to acquire people related skills and competencies (Analoui, 1995; Cappelli and Crocker-Hefter, 1996; Harrison, 2009).

The public sector in Croatia, like other newly formed EU states, has previously focused on the task-related rather than people-related aspects of the job. This is mainly due to the preference shown by the 'traditional' style of management used to manage the task and people in these establishments. With modernization of the public sector and globalization, senior management of many public sector organizations have recognized the importance of managing people in order to achieve a higher degree of performance at work (Cascio, 2014).

Unlike others, the MoF senior management realized the importance of acquiring relevant and specific competencies for achieving improved performance and began a systematic training of both middle and senior managers, in the area of people-related skills and competencies. This, however, does not mean that task-related aspects of the position are less important. Managers expressed the view that they also felt that those with more 'soft' managerial skills and competencies seem to be more successful in their work. As one asserted, 'It boils down to working with people. They are the ones who get the job done. We [managers] need to get them on board so that they do the job willingly … the old days of *do as I tell you* are gone, today it is about the policies and the ability to handle the people that matters most'.

This view is also in line with findings in the extant literature which suggests that middle and senior managers tend to be concerned with acquisition of people, and self and career development knowledge, skills and competencies as they move on to a more senior position (Al-Madhoun and Analoui, 2003).

Interestingly, the design of the management courses and seminars offered to middle and senior managers reflects this concern. It was probably the first time (2010–11) that managers of a public sector organization within Croatia had been exposed to people- and self-related issues and topics such as communication, team building and management, leadership and motivation, and more importantly the self-related aspects such as self-perception, identification of one's preferences and career development. As one manager mentioned, 'it is the first time ever we have had access to this kind of management training … it is a shame but true that most courses and training [in management] in Croatia are ineffective. The design is traditional, class room based and not good'. Another regional manager said, 'It is not a secret. This is the first time we are experiencing these topics. We realised that we need these skills but couldn't have access to them'.

As shown (see Table 7.7) three categories of skills and competencies are reported to be important. As mentioned earlier this is due to the lack of access to appropriate management training on the part of the managers. However, they are aware that people-related skills and competencies alone 'will not do' and that they should have a combination of all four categories (see Figure 7.3). However, as one summarized, 'The higher up you go the more of your time is spent on dealing with people issues.

Table 7.7 Overall ranking of competencies required for capacity building

Ranking	Category	Cumulative Score	%
1	People Related	237	34.6
2	Self and Career Development	204	29.8
3	Task Related	183	26.8
4	People and Task Related	59	8.6

Source: Field data

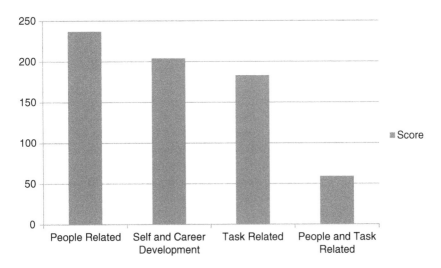

Figure 7.3 Overall ranking of competencies required for capacity building
Source: Field data

This is unavoidable and calls for more training in this area'. As a female manager expressed, 'Men should learn how to deal with employees ... the macho style of management nowadays is resented by the employees. ... After all you can't get the job done without others ... it is impossible'. The literature in the area of CB also confirms the importance of the training and for improving management capacity amongst the middle and senior public sector managers.

It is also observed that most managers were becoming aware that Croatia was going to join the EU soon and that they may find themselves competing with other managers across Europe. As one summarized, 'Soon we will be expected to deliver and that needs more and more of these kinds of training'. However, the general observation made confirms the view that the MoF and one or two other ministries and public sector organizations are in the minority in terms of adopting a planned and systematic training for their employees. The civil service as a whole requires more attention to become ready for accession.

On the whole, the managers showed that they:

a)   are aware of their need to acquire new managerial knowledge, skills and competencies to increase their effectiveness;

b)   had a greater need for the development of people- and task-related skills and competencies rather than those that are purely task related;

c)   appreciated the modern type of management training they had recently received;

d)   are conscious of the fact that joining the EU requires them to learn and know more to be on par with their counterparts in Europe; and

e)   are aware that the public sector as the whole needs to do more to meet its capacity target to join the EU in 2013.

Commentary on the Croatian experience of capacity building within the MoF

In the recent past, due to low salaries, unclear recruitment, and scarce tools required to perform one's task, especially at the local level, there has been capacity erosion at the individual level in public organizations (OECD, 2009). Similar experiences were reported in the MoF in which was found that provision of learning and development opportunities for middle and senior management had been neglected. As with other public sector training programmes (see for example, Pallangyo and Rees, 2010) it was reported that the training provided prior to the 2008–2011 period did not meet the needs of employees.

Mengesha and Common (2007) aptly argue that the civil service can only achieve CB when human resources management practices are efficient and can accommodate the necessary reforms. In initiating and implementing CB processes, it is imperative to allow organizations to operate and deliver their own directives by having internal policies, procedures and frameworks that enable actors to achieve the organization's goals (United Nations, 2008).

In line with this view, the MoF invested in human resource CB. In the undertaking of this initiative the MoF did not act alone. The MoF developed a virtuous relationship (OECD, 2009) with external organizations. It was the renewed participation and interest from donors including the World Bank and Central Funds in the Netherlands that allowed for the CB building programme to be undertaken.

It was apparent from undertaking the programme that the needs of managers were focused mainly on three areas of skills and competencies: *people related, self and career development*, and *task related*. In addition to a prior lack of adequate training and development, it was revealed that employee retention was problematic, and that there was a lack of adequate succession planning.

In light of this, the researchers believe that a context sensitive and holistic focus on human resource development is requisite for effective human capacity building within the public sector. To that end, an understanding of capacity building ought to include and emphasize strategic and sustainable aspects. Thus, capacity building is defined here as 'a strategic and informed process of strengthening and developing the competences and capabilities by which individuals, organisations, and societies make effective use of resources (human and otherwise), and adopt and adapt to the environment, in order to achieve their own goals on a sustainable basis'.

Concluding remarks

The discussion of the Croatian public sector and MoF in particular demonstrated that public sector reform has gone through a number of conceptual changes from traditional to modern approaches, which relies heavily on the effective operation of human resources. Unfortunately, the development of HRM in newly established states such as Croatia in Europe has been slow and in many cases has amounted to merely relabeling personnel management to HRM. In Croatia, the public sector is characterized by a typical unreformed civil service. However, the observations made revealed that the MoF has made deliberate and decisive steps towards establishing and operationalizing a modern HRM department to achieve its strategic objectives.

The MoF has been involved in the programme of CB with the intent to strengthen individuals' competencies, and to enable related departments and agencies to perform functions, solve problems, and set and achieve objectives in a sustainable manner. Since capacity involves capability to act and self-organize, generate development results, relate, adopt and self-renew, and achieve coherence, the strategy to achieve these includes education, learning, training and development. It is therefore not surprising to see that MoF uses CB as a vehicle for achieving its objectives. However, such programmes require continuity and sustainability to ensure that progress continues and individual capabilities increase to meet new challenges.

Development management is a complex process, and may be influenced by a range of intra- and extra-organizational factors. It is a process that the MoF has engaged with whole-heartedly, and with an awareness and cognizance of its importance. Undoubtedly, it can be concluded that these attempts by the HRM department to modernize the MoF have been by and large successful. The provision of the modern management development programmes to middle managers has, to a large degree, increased the awareness of the respondents of the importance of learning and personal growth, and the necessity to view the MOF as a service organization which is accountable to clients and has to constantly improve its internal processes to increase the quality of the services and products expected from it.

References

Alley, K. and Negretto, G. (1999). *Literature Review: Definition of Capacity Building and Implications for Monitoring and Evaluation*. New York: UNICEF, Division of Evaluation, Policy and Planning.

Al-Madhoun, M. and Analoui, F. (2003). Management and development: the training programs for small and Micro Enterprises in Palestinian Territories. *Management Research News*, 26(6), 39–67.

Analoui, F. (1995). Management skills and senior management effectiveness. *International Journal of Public Sector Management*, 8(3), 52–68.

Analoui, F. (1997). How effective are senior managers in the Romanian public sector? *Journal of Management Development*, 16(7), 502–516.

Analoui, F. (ed.) (2002). *The Changing Patterns of Human Resource Development*. Aldershot: Gower.

Analoui, F. (2007). *Strategic Human Resource Management*. London: International Thomson Business Press.

Analoui, F. (2009). Challenges for successful reform: an international perspective. *Journal of Management Development*, 28(6), 489–494.

Antwi, K. B. and Analoui, F. (2010). Challenges of making donor-driven public sector reform in sub-Saharan Africa sustainable: some experiences from Ghana. *International Journal of Public Administration*, 33(12–13), 635–647.

Antwi, K. B. and Analoui, F. (2013). Challenges of making donor driven public sector reform in Africa sustainable: some experiences from Ghana. In Rees, C. J. and Hossain, F. (eds.), *Public Sector Reform and Transitional Countries: Decentralisation and Public Sector Reform* (pp. 55–68). Abingdon: Routledge.

Baser, H. and Morgan, P. (2008). Capacity, change and performance. *European Centre for Development Policy Management*. Study Report (ECDPM Discussion Paper 59B). Maastricht: ECDPM.

Bekke, A. J. G. M. and Meer, F. M. (eds.) (2000). *Civil Service Systems in Western Europe*. Cheltenham: Edward Elgar Publishing.

Brinkerhoff, D. (2008). The state and international development management: shifting tides, changing boundaries and future directions. *Public Administration Review*, 68(6), 985–1001.

Brinkerhoff, D. and Crosby, B. (2002). *Managing Policy Reform: Concept and Tools for Decision-Makers in Developing and Transitioning Countries*. Bloomfield, CT: Kumarian Press.

Cappelli, P. and Crocker-Hefter, A. (1997). Distinctive human resources are firms' core competencies. *Organizational Dynamics*, 24(3), 7–22.

Cascio, W. F. (2014). Investing in HRD in uncertain times now and in the future. *Advances in Developing Human Resources*, 16(1), 108–122.

Guthrie, J. P. (2001). High-involvement work practices, turnover, and productivity: evidence from New Zealand. *Academy of Management Journal*, 44(1), 180–190.

Harrison, R. (2009). *Learning and Development* (5th ed.). London: Chartered Institute of Personnel and Development.

Kiggundu, M. N. (2000). Civil service reforms: limping into the twenty-first century. In Minogue, M., Polidano, C. and Hulme, D. (eds.), *Beyond the New Public Management: Changing Ideas and Practices in Governance* (pp. 155–171). Cheltenham: Edward Elgar.

Mengesha, G. H. and Common, R. (2007). Public sector capacity reform in Ethiopia: a tale of success in two ministries. *Public Administration and Development*, 27(5), 367–380.

Morgan, G. (1996). *Creative Organisation Theory*. Newbury Park: SAGE Publication.

Ndou, S. D. and Sebola, M. P. (2015). Capacity building in local government: an analysis for application of competency-based training in South Africa. *The Business & Management Review*, 6(5), 90–100.

OECD (2009). From good principles to a better practice: an OECD-DAC perspective on capacity development. Issues brief 3. Available at www.oecd.org/dac/governance-peace/governance/docs/43868693.pdf. Accessed 28 June 2016.

O'Flynn, J. (2007). From new public management to public value: paradigmatic change and managerial implications. *Australian Journal of Public Administration*, 66(3), 353–366.

O'Hare, P. (2010). Capacity building for community-led regeneration: facilitating or frustrating public engagement? *International Journal of Sociology and Social Policy*, 30(1/2), 32–47.

Pallangyo, W. and Rees, C. J. (2010). Local government reform programs and human resource capacity building in Africa: evidence from local government authorities (LGAs) in Tanzania. *International Journal of Public Administration*, 33(12–13), 728–739.

Pollitt, C., and Bouckaert, G. (2004). *Public Administration Reform: A Comparative Analysis.* Oxford: Oxford University Press.

Sobeck, J. and Agius, E. (2007). Organizational capacity building: addressing a research and practice gap. *Evaluation and Program Planning*, 30(3), 237–246.

Southern, R. (2002). Understanding multi–sectoral regeneration partnerships as a form of local governance. *Local Government Studies*, 28(2), 16–32.

Stoker, G. (2006). Public value management a new narrative for networked governance? *The American Review of Public Administration*, 36(1), 41–57.

Taylor, F. W. (1911). *The Principles of Scientific Management.* New York: Harper and Row.

Thomas, A. (1999). What makes good development management? *Development in Practice*, 9(1–2), 9–17.

United Nations Department of Economic and Social Affairs (2005). *Unlocking the Human Potential for Public Sector Performance: World Public Sector Report 2005* (Vol. 3). United Nations Publications.

United Nations (2008). *Capacity Development Practice Note.* New York: UNDP.

Wang, J., Hutchins, M. and Garavan, T. N. (2009). Exploring the strategic role of human resource development in organizational crisis management. *Human Resource Development Review*, 8(1), 22–53.

Wei, L.Q., Lau, C.M., Young, M.N. and Wang, Z. (2005). The impact of top management team demography on firm performance in China. *Asian Business & Management*, 4(3), 227–250.

Wilson, W. (1887). The study of administration. *Political Science Quarterly*, 2(2), 197–222.

Winterton, J. and Winterton, R. (1997). Does management development add value? *British Journal of Management*, 8(1), 65–76.

World Bank (1998). *Assessing Aid: What Works, What Doesn't, and Why.* Oxford: Oxford University Press.

8 Training entrepreneurs and policy makers for poverty reduction in Africa

Spirituality in business perspective

Aminu Mamman, Hamza B. Zakaria and Motolani A. Agbebi

Introduction

Material and non-material poverty is one of the main challenges facing Africa today (World Bank, 2009, 2013). In fact, it can be argued that all other challenges and problems confronting Africa today stem from poverty. Corruption and poor governance on the continent are directly associated with poverty. Several approaches have been used to address poverty in Africa. These approaches started with structural adjustment policies in the 1980s. This was followed by the Economic Growth approach in the 1990s. Also, the perennial Foreign Aid approach is still pursued, although to a limited extent. Following the Global Poverty Report in 2000, International Trade has been advocated as a potential solution to solving Africa's economic challenges, which are fuelling poverty. After the questionable outcomes of poverty reduction papers of the mid-1990s, the Poverty Reduction Strategy and Millennium Development Goals (MDGs) have been another initiative advocated and pursued to address poverty. This approach has been successful to a limited extent. Sustainable Development Goals (SDGs) is the latest initiative post the expiration of the MDGs in 2015. The common thread that runs through all the initiatives is the acknowledgment of the role of the private sector in development and poverty reduction. However, the limitation of this approach is the inadequate attention paid to the SME sector, especially the informal sector. This is in spite of the fact that about 90 per cent of the working population in most African counties are employed in the small and medium-sized enterprise (SME) formal and informal sector of the economy (Mamman et al., 2015).

It is also important to note that increasingly most Africans meet their daily needs for food, water, housing, education and health through the private sector (Business Action for Africa, 2010). Most of the providers of such needs are in the SME sector. Therefore, the potential of the SME sector in eradicating poverty in Africa is huge. This chapter discusses the role of SMEs in poverty reduction through economic growth and employment. It highlights the roles of national governments and international institutions in supporting the SME sector in order to play its role in poverty reduction. The chapter advances a novel approach for developing the SME sector through training entrepreneurs and policy makers using the concept of spirituality to ensure a collaborative approach instead of an individualistic competitive western approach.

Arguments for and against SMEs in economic growth and poverty reduction

There are arguments for and against state support for SMEs. Those in favour of support argue that through their business activities SMEs provide efficiency, innovation and productivity to the wider economy. Therefore, support to the sector will lead to social benefits, especially in the area of poverty reduction given the dominance of the sector in the economy (Beck and Demirgüç-Kunt, 2004; Beck, Demirgüç-Kunt and Levine, 2005). This argument is also buttressed by the belief that institutions and financial market failure impede SME progress and therefore they need state support. The second argument for state support of the SME sector relates to the point we made earlier. Proponents of the SME sector argue that SME growth boosts employment; therefore state subsidies targeted at the sector will help reduce poverty (Beck and Demirgüç-Kunt, 2004). In spite of the potential benefits of the sector and the arguments by its proponents, critics argue that large firms are better at providing sustainable employment and boosting the natural productivity through efficiencies derived from economies of scale. Proponents of large firms also argue that large firms provide higher wages and non-wage benefits than SMEs. This means the former are more likely to reduce poverty than the latter. What this argument fails to acknowledge is the absence of adequate large firms in Africa to provide those advantages that will lead to poverty reduction. In fact, even in developed countries, the majority of people are employed in the SME sector, not in large-scale organizations. One of the arguments in favour of SMEs that proponents of large firms challenge is the labour-intensive nature of SMEs. Proponents of large firms argue that SMEs are no more labour intensive or better at creating jobs than large firms. In fact, the proponents of large firms argue that economic growth is the result of natural endowment, policy and institutions, rather than the prevalence of SMEs (Beck and Demirgüç-Kunt, 2004). Therefore, state support for SMEs without natural endowment, policy and institutions will not lead to economic growth, employment and poverty reduction.

The argument that a poor business environment affects all firms, large and small, should not deter states from supporting SMEs for at least two reasons. First, large firms are more able to deal with some of the challenges of a poor business environment. For example, they have more resources to address poor infrastructure and bureaucratic bottlenecks affecting their business. The shorter life span of SMEs compared to larger firms in Africa is partly attributable to the latter's ability to deal with challenges of the business environment. Despite the arguments against SME support, it is widely agreed that the private sector, where SMEs are the dominant players in Africa, provides the main avenue for pro-poor growth and eradicating poverty on the continent. Hence, experts and international development practitioners and institutions have argued for carving a role for the private sector in development. For example, the OECD (2006) has published detailed guidelines and arguments for private sector development, which will address the challenges of poverty. Similarly, Business Action for Africa (2010) has provided a detailed account and cases of how multi-national companies in developing countries are developing partnerships with the local business and communities in Africa to address unemployment and poverty. How can the SME sector be developed to support poverty eradication? This is the question that preoccupied the attention of policy makers and experts on the subject of poverty and the role of SMEs in development.

Developing the SME sector for poverty eradication

In the last few decades, there have been attempts to understand the role of SMEs in development and how to enact policies to enable the sector to deliver on its potential. What is glaringly obvious from the studies undertaken in the sector is that there are clear requirements of the sector if it is to achieve the potential observed and demonstrated around the globe (OECD, 2004). Research evidence suggests that in order to develop the sector and to achieve the objectives of growth, employment and poverty reduction, the following issues have to be addressed. First, there have to be cross-cutting policies and strategies that affect many areas of the economy and thus will stimulate and support SME growth through entrepreneurial pursuit (OECD, 2004). Prominent areas that are considered relevant to SME development include sound and appropriate economic policies, conducive business environments for SMEs to operate in, and the integration of a national development strategy with an SME development strategy.

The second requirement for successful SME development that will foster poverty reduction is the inclusion of all stakeholders in the formulation and implementation of strategies for SME development. This is because interchange and corporation across the stakeholders will foster ownership of the strategies and engender the implementation of them, and that will make the strategies politically credible and sustainable (OECD, 2004: 16). The third condition for SME development is the integration of SMEs into the local, regional and international/global markets. This condition requires significant infrastructural and institutional development, which will enable service delivery for SMEs. OECD (2004) argue that capacity building of institutions charged with the responsibility of executing SME development strategies is essential and critical. Finally, within the African context at least, women account for a significant proportion of SME operators, especially in the informal sector. Therefore, any initiative that is aimed at developing the sector must include a specific strategy for women in the sector. In fact, OECD (2004: 6) points out that 'Enhancing women's ability to participate in SME development should be taken into account at every level, as women account for an important share of private sector activity and contribute most to poverty reduction. Gender dimensions need to be mainstreamed throughout SME development strategies and programs'.

The conception and implementation of SME development in Africa

African governments have embarked on developing the SME sector as means of economic growth and poverty reduction in the last two decades (Beck et al., 2005; Fjose, Grunfeld and Green, 2010; Klapper, 2002; Olawale and Garwe, 2010; World Bank, 2013). The conception and sometimes the implementation of the

SME development agenda have been aided by international institutions and donor agencies such as the UNIDO, ILO, DFID, SIDA, USAID, etc. The institution that has a long, coherent and sustained track record of SME development in Africa is the International Labour Organization (ILO). The institution has used its flagship employment programme called SEED (Sustainable Employment and Economic Development) to champion small enterprise development in Africa and developing countries in general (Vandenberg, 2006). SEED's approach to SME development focuses on developing business environments for SMEs through sound policies, laws and business regulations that will generate conducive environments for the establishment, and sustainable operation of SMEs. The ILO's approach to SME development also sees the role of business associations as critical to the development of appropriate policies and their implementation. Hence, the initiatives encourage SME operators to form business associations to enable them to have representation in policy formulation (Vandenberg, 2006). Another element of the approach is the encouragement of public–private partnerships between the state and the SME sector, especially in the area of infrastructure development where the poor and the unemployed will directly benefit. Apart from infrastructure development, public–private partnerships in service delivery (e.g. in health and education) are also encouraged because these services are predominantly provided by the private sector, especially in the urban slums and rural areas.

The ILO and other international development institutions have recognized that market access for SMEs is a major challenge for their development. Therefore, the SEED program has initiated measures to improve market access to micro- and small-scale entrepreneurs in Africa and developing countries (Vandenberg, 2006). One of the essential ingredients for developing a business is the service that will help the business enhance its capacity to operate effectively and sustainably. SMEs rely on other businesses or public organizations for such services. However, relying on donors or the state for business services such as market information or information regarding the changes in the business environment is becoming increasingly unsustainable economically. Therefore, as part of the SEED initiative, the ILO has focused on helping to find a sustainable approach to self-funding of business development services, such as capacity building training and user-pay access to market information (Vandenberg, 2006).

Another feature of the ILO's approach to SME development that will contribute to poverty reduction is the mainstreaming of gender equality and youth entrepreneurship. As pointed out by Vandenberg (2006: 33), 'Women face particular barriers in their struggle against poverty and often require targeted support in starting and expanding enterprises'. The young and the unemployed members of African societies form a significant proportion of the population. They are untapped resources for the development of the SME sector that will contribute to poverty reduction and enhance economic growth in ways that will benefit all. It has been noted that 'To focus attention and action, the UN Secretary General initiated the Youth Employment Network (YEN), which is a partnership between the United Nations, The World Bank, and the ILO. The latter is the lead agency. SEED has been contributing to YEN, notably in entrepreneurship working group' (Vandenberg, 2006: 34).

There are other specific support initiatives provided by states and international development agencies geared towards the development of the SME sector in Africa (Commission for Africa, 2005; Business Action for Africa, 2010). These include micro-finance and vocational training support to start and improve small business enterprises. Small businesses all over the world are notorious for their limited shelf lives. This issue is even more critical in Africa where the business environment is much harsher than most parts of the world. This calls for a different approach to supporting the sector in Africa. This is where this chapter departs slightly from the existing capacity building approach adopted by many institutions and governments around the world. We will elaborate on this in the following sections.

Building capacity of SMEs in Africa

We argue in this chapter that the starting point for building the capacity of SMEs and the development of the sector as a whole should be from the training of policy makers and SME operators, as well as those wishing to join the sector. The strategies for developing the sector discussed above will not be realized if those charged with the responsibility for implementing them have serious 'moral' deficiencies. The curriculum for such training should therefore be based on the concept of spirituality and system thinking, where policy makers and SME operators will be immersed in the principles and behavioural outcomes of spirituality. We provide the following arguments for the use of spirituality as the foundation of training and developing policy makers for effective and sustainable development of the SME sector. The first argument is that systems, structures and policies by themselves do not deliver desirable outcomes if the operators within the systems, structures and policies are not in tune with the foundation on which the systems, structures, and policies are built. We argue that spirituality will bring operators of SMEs and policy makers in tune with the concept of collaboration rather than competition. This is essential for implementable SME policies and sustainable business for poverty reduction.

Secondly, the failure of SME policies is largely due to the lack of implementation or inadequate implementation by people who are devoid of spiritual intelligence, rather than a lack of professional or technical skills. The idea of having representatives of SMEs in a policy-making body assumes that the agent (SME representative) will represent the interest of the principal (i.e. SME sector). However, evidence consistently demonstrates that agents in Africa abdicate their responsibilities and engage in individualistic rent-seeking behaviour (Buchanan, 1980; United Nations, 2009) due to lack of spiritual intelligence. Therefore, professional skills that are devoid of spiritual intelligence have proved to be inadequate in guaranteeing proper behaviour. Thirdly, some policies are deliberately enacted with a rent-seeking agenda or sectional agenda due to lack of spiritual intelligence. Thus, no amount of professional and technical training will compensate for the absence of spiritual intelligence. This is why, in spite of the highly educated and professional people making policies and running businesses, SMEs and the sector continue to be saddled with self-inflicted problems that are avoidable if only Africa will develop a critical mass of spiritually intelligent people to enact appropriate policies and implement them. Finally, we argue that the limited shelf-life of SMEs in Africa and the challenges they face is a function of the business environment and the low level of spiritual intelligence of the SME operators as a collective entity, not at an individual level. If the SME sector can develop a critical mass of spiritually intelligent operators, the operators will be able to mitigate some inherent challenges of the business environment. The following sections discuss how traditional entrepreneurial training has been conceived and delivered. The sections will then discuss how spiritually intelligent policy makers and SME operators can be developed in Africa.

Current approach to training SME operators for development

It is widely acknowledged that the business environment is not the only challenge to SME development in Africa. Lacking the necessary skills required to run a successful SME is one of the most significant weaknesses of SME operators in Africa (OECD, 2004; Cheloti, 2005). For example, a study funded by the German Technical Cooperation Agency (GTZ) reported that Kenyan entrepreneurial training is handicapped by the lack of adequate training providers and the limited scope of training (Cheloti, 2005). Similarly, an OECD (2004) study also indicates that there is a high need for entrepreneurial and vocational skills in developing countries to ensure economic growth and poverty reduction. The OECD (2004: 32) also pointed out that:

> the linkages between education and training strategies are still weak, resulting in weak market signals for policy makers and administrators. Although entrepreneurs may not be citing quality of education and training as a major obstacle to their business in large surveys, this may be due more to the survey designs.

It is in recognition of this need for business skills in the SME sector that governments, donors and international institutions such as UNIDO, World Bank and ILO have invested a lot of moral and financial support in the development of business skills in the SME sector of developing countries, especially in Africa. The most prominent institution engaged in developing business skills in developing countries is the ILO. Using two key training programs, namely 'Start Your Own Business' (SYB) and 'Start and Improve your Business' (SIYB), the ILO has trained thousands of entrepreneurs and small business operators in Africa (Trulsson, 2002). By most measures the ILO program has been very successful. According to the ILO (2012):

> SIYB is a management-training programme with a focus on starting and improving small businesses as a strategy for creating more and better employment, particularly in emerging economies. The overall objective is to contribute to economic development and to the creation of new and better jobs.

The ILO does not directly provide the training itself, but rather operates like a franchise system of service delivery under its technical cooperation intervention model. It enters into agreement with training providers in the public and private sector to provide the training using its methodology and tools. Specifically, the ILO supports business development service (BDS) providers to improve the skills required to implement, monitor, manage and finance training programmes. It also helps BDS providers to set up a sustainable training system at the national level in developing countries. The aim is to support and contribute to sustainable economic growth and employment generation (Trulsson, 2002).

The ILO training program uses four toolkits to deliver the main objective of the program. The first component focuses on potential entrepreneurs that do not have any business ideas, but do have the ambition of starting their own business. This component is aptly called Generate Your Business Idea (GYB). After going through GYB, the trainee is supposed to generate a concrete idea that is implementable. The second component of SIYB is called Start Your Business (SYB). This training program focuses on those people who have a clear business idea that is implementable, but do not know how to implement it. The ILO (2014: 3) indicates that 'The programme is a combination of training, field work, and after training support activities and consists of two sub-programmes'. These two sub-programmes are 'the SYB Business Awareness, where participants assess readiness to start a business both in conceptual and financial terms; and the SYB Business planning that teaches them how to prepare a business plan and asses its viability' (ILO, 2014: 3).

The third component of the programme focuses on people who are already in business and need to improve on business productivity and problem-solving skills. Trainees are exposed to good management principles and practice in the areas of marketing, human resource management, operational management, financial management and overall strategic management. The fourth and final component of the SIYB program is called Expand Your Business (EYB). This component is for existing entrepreneurs with growth orientation, that is, entrepreneurs who want to expand their existing business irrespective of whether the business is a micro enterprise or a medium-sized enterprise (Trulsson, 2002). EYB provides trainees with practical tools to implement and realize fast business growth and profits (ILO, 2014). This program includes both training and non-training elements.

Another institution that provides training and non-training support to SMEs is the International Finance Corporation (IFC). This is part of the World Bank Group. IFC collaborates with many institutions, foundations and programmes to support SMEs in Africa and developing countries (IFC, 2011). For example, as part of its Business Edge program of Intervention, IFC uses farmer and SME training products to offer entrepreneurs the training they need to expand their businesses. Using farmer and SME training products, IFC offers free online toolkits for entrepreneurs to learn how to access finance, product and market information to enable them run a successful business. The training offered by institutions and local organizations have been making an impact on the perception of the need to develop business skills in Africa. However, we argue that within the context of poverty reduction, there is more room for improvement in the approach to SME training. A new approach is needed for the following reasons.

First, in spite of the acknowledgement of the role of policy makers and implementers in supporting skills development in the SME sectors, the existing training approach does not fully integrate them in the methodology. It is necessary for policy makers and implementers to appreciate not only the importance of the sector, but the challenges they face and the solution needed in the operation of successful business enterprises. Second, a new approach is required regarding the philosophy and rationale for training SME operators. The current approach is based on a Western individualistic competitive 'winner takes all' mentality. In a poverty-ridden African context, this approach is not sustainable, as demonstrated by the shorter life span of SMEs. A more Afrocentric collaborative approach is required. This is why there is need to integrate policy makers and implementers in the training system. Third, it is important to appreciate that there is a lot of poverty amongst self-employed SME operators. Setting up and running a business might not be the road out of poverty (Lambrech and Beens, 2005). Therefore, the new approach should not only focus on technical and professional skills required for running a successful business, but also explore whether working for the entrepreneur would be a better way out of poverty. This point has policy implications for resource allocation and support. A training approach that will integrate policy makers in the system will provide the opportunity to access the best way to allocate scarce resources more efficiently rather than assuming that whoever volunteers to join the entrepreneurial route will necessarily get out of poverty.

Integrating spirituality in policy formulation and SME development

We argued earlier that there is need for an Afrocentric approach to SME development in Africa. This is because professional and technical skills are inadequate to deliver the desired outcomes in terms of sustainability and poverty reduction. Hence we advocate the use of spirituality as the foundation for SME development in Africa. Spirituality has been described by Roehlkepartain et al. (2006: 139) as 'the essential potentiality for addressing the ultimate questions that are intrinsic to the experience of being human'. Experts on spirituality argue that people who are spiritual demonstrate ultimate concern through personal goal strivings (Apter, 1985; Emmons, 1999; Jaworski, 1996; Pargament and Park, 1995). These concerns in a nutshell refer to the meaning of life, what one finds meaningful as well as the search for what is meaningful in whatever what one does. It should be noted that most experts distinguish religion from spirituality. While the former is concerned largely about the sacred/divine and organized practices, the latter focuses on the individualistic 'secular' search for meaning and purpose (Bigger, 2008; Mamman and Zakaria, 2016; Zinnabauer et al., 1997). For the purpose of this chapter and indeed for the practical nature of the paper, we adopt the secular perspective of spirituality. We therefore adopt the following explanation of spirituality:

> We need to regard spirituality as a quest for personal meaning-making at the highest level, which includes intellectual, ethical, social, political, aesthetic and other such dimensions. It makes a quality of reflection which is holistic in

scope, transcends material needs and ambitions, and transforms the personality in positive ways. (Bigger, 2000:3)

People who are *spiritual* demonstrate ultimate concerns through their pursuit of personal goals (Apter, 1985; Emmons, 1999; Jaworski, 1996; Pargament and Park, 1995; Mamman and Zakaria, 2016). Therefore, spirituality is personal but at the same time experiential and integrative – where transcendence, morality, belonging, connectedness, meaning and purpose are all included in conception (Bigger, 2008: 62). Bigger's explanation with emphasis on belonging, connectedness, and meaning further highlights the relevance of integrating spirituality in training policy makers and SME operators. From a training perspective, when meaning is embedded in entrepreneurial training and development of policy makers, it will enable trainees to appreciate the connection between their behaviour and long-term implications of their actions that will affect them and their community at large. The current individualistic winner takes all approach which focuses on competition is devoid of appreciating the long-term implications of one's action on the business environment and the sustainability of the business. The principles of spirituality, if properly applied, will ensure policy implementation and engendering of appropriate behaviours on the part of the SME operators.

Developing spirituality and spiritual intelligence amongst policy makers and SME operators

According to Bigger (2008), spirituality is an experiential exercise. In other words, a person's vocation provides an opportunity for experimentation and reflection on the meaning of one's purpose and how it is achieved through the vocation one chooses to pursue. According to Chaudhary and Aswal (2013: 1510), 'to be spiritual is to think, act and interact from an awareness of self as spirit not form'. To be spiritual is to be spiritually intelligent (Chaudhary and Aswal, 2013; Mamman and Zakaria, 2016). Thus, policy makers and SME operators can only demonstrate spiritual behaviour if they are able to develop spiritual intelligence. They must acquire the characteristics of spiritually intelligent people (Mamman and Zakaria, 2016). Zohar (2005) described a spiritually intelligent person as someone who has the following characteristics: self-awareness; spontaneity; being vision and value led; compassion; holism; celebration of diversity; field independence; humility; urge to ask the why question; ability to reframe; positive use of adversity; and sense of vocation. This means that these characteristics can be the foundation for developing a training and development curriculum for policy makers and SME operators in Africa. This should enable them to acquire the relevant skills to behave in a collaborative way rather than individualistic competitive way.

Zohar and Marshall (2004: 26) in a later publication described spiritual intelligence as how 'we address and solve problems of meaning and value, the intelligence with which we can place our actions and our lives in a wider, richer, meaning-giving context, the intelligence with which we can assess that one course of action or one life path is more meaningful than another'. This latter definition fits perfectly with the issues and challenges facing Africa today. We argue that African policy makers and public servants are facing critical issues surrounding meaning and values associated with the choices they make as custodians of public property. Therefore, the development of spiritual intelligence should help them improve on the decisions and choices they make for the betterment of their 'humanness'. In fact, Chaudhary and Aswal (2013: 1510) argued that, to be spiritually intelligent is to use what one knows in the right way, at the right time, in the right place, with the right intention. Chaudhary and Aswal's explanation further buttresses our argument that developing spiritual intelligence rather than developing more *professional* and *technical skills* should be the focus of a new approach to developing SMEs and policy makers and implementers in Africa (Mamman and Zakaria, 2016). If African policy makers and SME operators can use their knowledge and skills in line with Chaudhary and Aswal's (2013: 1510) definition of spiritual intelligence, the strategies for developing the sector are more likely to deliver desirable outcomes.

Using spirituality to train policy makers and SME operators

There are certain traits that will engender appropriate behaviour in every endeavour. If such traits can be developed amongst policy makers and SME operators it will be possible to ensure SME development and poverty reduction in Africa. Experts have argued that some people have certain spiritual behavioural traits that enable them to find overall satisfaction in life and influence others significantly through their behaviours (Emmons et al., 1998; Emmons, 1999, 2000). Therefore, identifying such people or developing them should make a significant contribution to the development of the SME sector in Africa. Arguably, if a critical mass of policy makers and SME operators can be developed in key sectors of the economy and the governance system, appropriate policies can be enacted and implemented effectively given that such people would be deriving personal satisfaction from the effective implementation of such a policy rather than engaging in rent-seeking behaviour, which has been the major cause of policy failures in Africa (Mamman et al., 2015). The following sections demonstrate how three of the spiritual behavioural traits can impact on policy making and the management of SMEs. We demonstrate how policy makers and SME operators can benefit from being sensitized regarding the positive impact such traits on policy formulation and implementation as well as running a successful business.

TRANSCENDING THE MATERIAL IN PUBLIC OFFICE AND IN RUNNING A BUSINESS

For many, if not most Africans, starting a business or pursuing a career in the public sector is solely for material gains. This attitude is undoubtedly one of the main causes of rent-seeking behaviour by public servants and the winner-takes-all mentality of SME operators. Unfortunately, this approach ultimately leads to material impoverishment in the long run. It has been argued that one of the important components of spiritual traits is the ability to transcend the physical and the material (Emmons, 2000; Slife, Hope and Nebeker, 1999). This trait enables a person to sense a synchronicity to life and to develop a bond with humanity (Emmons, 2000; Piedmont, 1999). Developing such a bond will ensure the development of a conducive environment for the business to thrive since the business is an extension of the community of human beings. Referring to several authors such as Piedmont (1999), Emmons (2000: 10) points out that transcendence is regarded as a form of art 'capable of developing capacities of the mind such as attentional training and refining awareness'. From the practical point of view, transcendence should enable people to develop a strong bond with humanity rather than own tribe, religion, race or nationality. *Transcendent* people derive pleasure and satisfaction not from material acquisition or achievements but from the sense of rising above such acquisition and achievements (Dyer, 2007; Mamman et al., 2015). The strong bond with humanity enables people with such traits to have wider perspective to the purpose of the economic activity, which leads to inclusive behaviours (Feinstein and Krippner, 1988; Fowler, 1981; Seaward, 1995). Within the context of poverty reduction in Africa, developing and using people with spiritual traits in the public and the private sectors should make a significant difference in the fight against poverty and underdevelopment through the SME sector.

This spiritual trait (i.e. transcendence) should be used in all poverty reduction interventions targeting SMEs and policy making. For example, training and development programs on entrepreneurship as well as public policy making should have a specific section that advocates the virtues of greater purpose (non-material) for businesses (i.e. SME). Similarly poverty-reduction policy formulation should not focus on material poverty only given that spiritual poverty can be the main cause of material poverty. Technical skills related to policy making or running a business should be anchored to the greater purpose (e.g. societal development). People should know why the skills are important to them and the wider society and, most importantly perhaps, how the skills can contribute to the eradication of poverty (Mamman et al., 2015: 76).

SANCTIFYING DAILY ACTIVITIES IN PUBLIC OFFICE AND IN BUSINESS

In line with the doctrine of spirituality, there should be a greater meaning in what one does regardless of how minor the task. Most importantly, there should be a connection between what one does with the greater purpose which is beyond the material. This is the only way to determine if what one does is worthwhile, which leads to happiness. To achieve this state requires *sanctification of daily activities*. Therefore, this is one of the important spiritual traits that should make a significant impact on the behaviour of policy makers and business operators. This trait provides another opportunity to put into practice the concept of transcendence by policy makers, public office holders and SME operators (Mamman et al., 2015). According to Emmons (2000: 11), 'To *sanctify* means to set apart for a special purpose'. Therefore, there should be a superior and bigger purpose even in the mundane minute activity. This concept should appeal to Christians and Muslims. For example, in Islam, worship (*Ibadah*) is not only rituals such as praying and fasting, but whatever a *Muslim* does 'appropriately' is also worship (Mamman et al., 2015). This means that sanctification of policy-making activities or conducting daily business activities should take a different dimension in the minds of policy makers and SME operators (Mamman et al., 2015). *Sanctification* should enable them to be fully conscious of the wider implications of their daily activities on the society since spiritually endowed people bond with humanity at large rather than sectional interest. In fact, Monk et al. (1998) argued that through sanctification people see the divine even in ordinary activities. According to Emmons, Cheung and Tehrani (1998), when work is spiritualized through sanctification, people become 'imbued with a sense of the sacred, [and] these goals take on a significance and power not found in secular strivings' (Emmons, 2000: 12). Undoubtedly, within the African context where religion is revered, leveraging the notion of sanctification to change the attitudes and behaviour of policy makers and business operators should appeal to all concerned.

Spiritualization of daily activities through sanctification can be achieved through training given that the dominant religions on the continent (Christianity and Islam) advocate the use of daily endeavours to achieve greater good and salvation (Mamman et al., 2015). However, the challenge in achieving this is that in the African context religious teachings are applied exclusively rather than inclusively. For many Africans, religion is practiced in the churches and mosques, not necessarily in daily interaction with fellow humans, which spirituality preaches. This is the main reason we advocate the use of spirituality as a foundation for training and developing policy makers and SME operators in Africa. However, in a training setting, public office holders/policy makers and SME operators should be provided with clear evidence of the material and non-material benefits of sanctifying their daily activities. There are several practical personal development materials, books and case studies that can help achieve this objective (Mamman et al., 2015: 77).

BEHAVING VIRTUOUSLY IN POLICY MAKING, IMPLEMENTATION AND BUSINESS OPERATION

We argued earlier that the traditional training approach which focuses on professional and technical skills does not elicit the required cooperative behaviour that is needed for the Afrocentric business environment context and policy implementation of SME development strategies. This because the training methodology does not inculcate the idea of behaving in the interest of the community but rather in the interest of the business and the career of the trainee. Virtuous behaviour is one of the key traits that will ensure that trainees behave in a way that benefits the self and others (Emmons, 2000). We argue that the new approach to training policy makers and SME operators should include a provision that instils virtuous behaviour. Spiritually endowed people demonstrate virtuous behaviour consistently (Mamman et al., 2015: 78). Such people show forgiveness, express gratitude, exhibit humility and compassion and display sacrificial love (Emmons, 2000). Self-control is another important element of virtuous behaviour which we believe is critical to policy formulation, implementation and running a sustainable SME. According to Baumeister and Exline (1999) self-control is at the heart of success in every human endeavour. Self-control or lack of it is a significant determinant of other human limitations such as anger, pride, greed, lust and envy. *Control these and you are on your way to success*, the perennial philosophy suggests (Mamman et al., 2015: 78). Emmons (2000: 13) also pointed out that 'Virtues connect to both motivation, representing ultimate concerns, and to effective action. Conceiving of these inner qualities as virtues, implies that these are sources of human strength that enable people to function effectively in the world'. Virtue is so important to the point that some writers argue that it is the closest characteristic of a person that defines who (s)he is (Zagzebski, 1996). Good virtues have universal application. No culture or religion or race has a monopoly of good virtues (Mamman et al., 2015: 78). This makes it easier to advocate the inculcation of good virtues amongst public servants and SME operators. It is a challenge, however, to preach it to those who are spiritually impoverished. Such people would appreciate the benefits and application of good virtues but only to their inner circle, such as those with whom they share religious affiliation, social class affiliation, or racial or tribal affiliation (Mamman et al., 2015: 78). Virtuous behaviour is the manifestation of the first two spiritual traits. Both policy makers and SME operators can make a significant contribution to poverty reduction if they behave in a virtuous manner. Indeed, most successful business people demonstrate such traits because to do so makes business sense (Mamman et al., 2015: 78).

Conclusion

This chapter acknowledged the role of the private sector and SMEs in the fight against poverty in Africa. It highlights the challenges and arguments for and against the use of the SME sector as an avenue for job creation, economic growth and poverty reduction. The chapter sets out to provide another perspective to dealing with poverty in Africa using training SMEs and policy makers as the foundation. We argue that the focus on technical and professional training in policy making or provision of courses on how to set up and run a business with some financial support is not enough to enable the private sector to address the challenges of poverty on the continent. Therefore, we advocate the integration of spirituality in the training of policy makers and SME operators in Africa.

References

Apter, M. J. (1985). Religious states of mind: a reversal theory interpretation. In Brown, L. B. (ed.), *Advances in the Psychology of Religion* (pp. 62–75). Oxford: Pergamon.
Baumeister, R. F. and Exline, J. (1999). Virtue, personality, and social relations: self-control as the moral muscle. *Journal of Personality*, 67(6), 1165–1194.
Beck, T. and Demirgüç-Kunt, A. (2004). SMEs, growth, and poverty. *Public Policy for the Private Sector Note 268*. Washington, DC: World Bank.
Beck, T., Demirgüç-Kunt, A. and Levine, R. (2005). SMEs, growth, and poverty: cross-country evidence. Available at http://siteresources.worldbank.org/DEC/Resources/84797-1114437274304/SME_Beck_Demirguc-Kunt_Levine_revised_032005.pdf. Accessed 20 September 2015.

Bigger, S. (2000). Spiritual and religious education and antiracism. In Leicester, M., Mogadil, S. and Mogadil, C. (eds.), *Values in Education and Cultural Diversity* (pp. 15–24). London: RoutledgeFalmer.

Bigger, S. (2008). Secular spiritual education? *Education Futures*, 1(1), 60–70.

Buchanan, J. (1980). Rent-seeking and profit seeking. In Buchanan, J., Tullock, G. and Tollison, R. D. (eds.), *Towards a Theory of Rent-Seeking Society*. College Station: Texas A&M Press.

Business Action for Africa Report (2010). Business Partnership for Development in Africa. Available at www.acadfacility.org/downloads/news/2010/2010_article_businesspartnerships.pdf. Accessed 12 August 2015.

Chaudhary, B. and Aswal, M. (2013). Imparting spiritual intelligence curriculum in our classrooms. *European Academic Research*, 1(7), 1508–1515.

Cheloti, D. (2005). The fight against poverty and unemployment in Kenya. In Dornberger, U. and Fromm, I. (eds.), *Private Sector Development and Poverty Reduction: Experience from Developing Countries*. GTZ. Available at www.uni-leipzig.de/sept/workshop/haikou/downloads/Proceedings_PrivateSectorDevelopmentAndPovertyReduction.pdf. Accessed 7 June 2015.

Commission for Africa (2005). *Our Common Interest*. London: Office of the Prime Minister.

Dyer, W. (2007). Change *Your Thoughts, Change Your Life*. New York: Hay House.

Emmons, R. A. (1999). *The Psychology of Ultimate Concerns: Motivation and Spirituality in Personality*. New York: Guilford Press.

Emmons, R. A. (2000). Is spirituality an intelligence? Motivation, cognition, and the psychology of ultimate concern. *The International Journal for the Psychology of Religion*, 10(1), 3–26.

Emmons, R. A., Cheung, C. and Tehrani, K. (1998). Assessing spirituality through personal goals: implications for research on religion and subjective well-being. *Social Indicators Research*, 45(1–3), 391–422.

Feinstein, D. and Krippner, S. (1988). *Personal Mythology: The Psychology of Your Evolving Self*. Los Angeles: Jeremy P. Tarcher.

Fjose, S., Grunfeld, L. A. and Green, C. (2010). SMEs and growth in sub-Saharan Africa: identifying SMEs roles and obstacles to growth. MENON-publication no. 14/2010.

Fowler, J. (1981). *Stages of Faith: The Psychology of Human Development and Search for Meaning*. New York: Harper Collins.

IFC (2011). Small and medium enterprises. *Telling Our Story*, 5(1), 8.

ILO (2012). *Start and Improve Your Business – Global Tracer Study 2011*. Geneva.

ILO (2014). *Start and Improve Your Business: Implementation Guide*. Available at www.ilo.org/wcmsp5/groups/public/---ed_emp/---emp_ent/---ifp_seed/documents/publication/wcms_315262.pdf. Accessed 11 November 2015.

Jaworski, J. (1996). *Synchronicity: The Inner Path of Leadership*. San Francisco: Berrett Koehler.

Klapper, F. D. (2002). *Small and Medium-Sized Enterprises Financing in Eastern Europe*. World Bank Policy Research Working Paper 2933.

Lambrecht, J. and Beens, E. (2005). Poverty among self-employed business people in a rich country: a misunderstood and distinct reality. *Journal of Developmental Entrepreneurship*, 10(3), 205–222.

Mamman, A., Kanu, M. A., Alharbi, A. and Baydoun, N. (2015). *Small and Medium-Sized Enterprises (SMEs) and Poverty Reduction in Africa*. Newcastle: Cambridge Scholar Publishing.

Mamman, A. and Zakaria, H. (2016, in press). Spirituality and Ubuntu as the foundation for building African institutions, organizations and leaders. *Journal of Management, Spirituality and Religion*, 2016. Available at http://dx.doi.org/10.1080/14766086.2016.1159976.

Monk, R. C., Hofheinz, W. C., Lawrence, K. T., Stamey, J. D., Affleck, B. and Yamamori, T. (1998). *Exploring Religious Meaning* (5th ed.). Upper Saddle River, NJ: Prentice Hall.

OECD (2004). Promoting SMEs for development. Second OECD Conference of Ministers Responsible for SMEs. Istanbul, Turkey. Available at www.oecd.org/cfe/smes/31919278.pdf. Accessed 18 September 2015.

OECD (2006). Promoting pro-poor growth: Private sector development. Available at www.oecd.org/dac/povertyreduction/36427804.pdf. Accessed 20 September 2015.

Olawale, F. and Garwe, D. (2010). Obstacles to the growth of new SMEs in South Africa: a principal component analysis approach. *African Journal of Business Management*, 4(5), 729–738.

Pargament, K. I. and Park, C. L. (1995). Merely a defense? The variety of religious means and ends. *Journal of Social Issues*, 51(2), 13–32.

Piedmont, R. L. (1999). Does spirituality represent the sixth factor of personality? Spiritual transcendence and the five-factor model. *Journal of Personality*, 67(6), 985–1013.

Roehlkepartain, E. C., King, P. E., Wagener, L. and Benson, P. L. (2006). *The Handbook of Spiritual Development in Childhood and Adolescence*. London: Sage Publications.

Seaward, B. L. (1995). Reflections on human spirituality for the worksite. *American Journal of Health Promotion*, 9(3), 165–168.

Slife, B. D., Hope, C. and Nebeker, R. S. (1999). Examining the relationship between religious spirituality and psychological science. *Journal of Humanistic Psychology*, 39(2), 51–85

Trulsson, P. (2002). Constraints of growth-oriented enterprises in the Southern and Eastern African Region. *Journal of Developmental Entrepreneurship*, 7(3), 331–339.

United Nations (2009). *Rethinking Poverty: Report on the World Social Situation*. New York. Available at www.un.org/esa/socdev/rwss/docs/2010/fullreport.pdf. Accessed 30 July 2015.

Vandenberg, P. (2006). *Poverty Reduction Through Small Enterprises: Emerging Consensus, Unresolved Issues and ILO Activities*. Geneva: ILO.

World Bank (2009). *Global Monitoring Report: A Development Emergency*. Washington, DC.

World Bank (2013). *World Development Report: Jobs*. Washington, DC.

Zagzebski, L. T. (1996). *Virtues of the Mind: An Inquiry into the Nature of Virtue and the Ethical Foundations of Knowledge*. Cambridge: Cambridge University Press.

Zinnabauer, B. J., Pargament, K. I., Cowell, B. J., Rye, M. and Scott, A. B. (1997). Religion and spirituality: unfuzzing the fuzzy. *Journal for the Scientific Study of Religion*, 38, 412–425.

Zohar, D. (2005). Spiritually intelligent leadership. *Leader to Leader*, 38(Fall): 45–51.

Zohar, D. and Marshall, I. (2004). *Spiritual Capital: Wealth We Can Live By*. San Francisco: Berrett Koehler Publishers, Inc.

Part III

Development management

Actors, practices and lessons

9 Navigating through the maze of development actor pluralism

Actor interfaces and development management in Africa

Justice Nyigmah Bawole and Farhad Hossain

Introduction

Development as a concept has several dimensions. These include economic, social, political, legal, institutional, technological, environmental, religious and cultural (Corbridge, 1995). Similarly, development issues have become more complex over the years necessitating the enhancement of the creative capacities of several actors looking for innovative solutions to problems with which they are confronted (Le Bellu and Le Blanc, 2010). Even more importantly, it is generally acknowledged that development occurs due to some deliberate actions carried out by particular agents or by an authority ordered to achieve improvement in existing conditions (Ranis, 2004). Put differently, development does not happen per chance but it is carefully planned and orchestrated by a number of actors and institutions working in concert.

In an endless changing context, where emerging issues raise questions for the development community, particularly on how development processes have been and are being designed, supported and managed, it becomes imperative to critically review the various roles of development actors and to find out how they interrelate with each other. This is extremely important in the context of development actor pluralism in the developing world, especially in Africa.

This chapter seeks to identify the main development actors in Africa and to understand the various ways in which these actors interrelate with each other towards development management in the region. The major development actors in Africa are explored with emphasis on their interrelationships and interfaces as they work towards development on the continent. The chapter ends with a summary and some conclusions.

The concept of development

Development is inevitably an emergent and contested concept – different meanings have arisen through continuing critical debates. As a core concept in the social sciences since the enlightenment era, it has been tagged 'the central organizing concept of our time' (Cowen and Shenton, 1995). Thus, because of its centrality, there is considerable divergence over its conceptualization. For instance, whereas some economists are quick to equate development to economic growth, others have quite broader definitions thereby making it complex, ambiguous and amorphous (Thomas, 2004).

It must also be quickly pointed out that development occurs in different parts or ways, at different speeds and driven by different forces (Bellù, 2011). Seers (1969) contends that a country could only be said to have developed if its answers to all three key questions indicate visible decline in the identified variables. These questions are: What has been happening to poverty? What has been happening to unemployment? And what has been happening to inequality? She adds that it will be strange to call the result 'development' if one or two of these central problems have been growing worse, even if per capita income doubled. Such a position highlights the view of development as a process that goes beyond mere economic growth as economists argue.

In spite of the contestation of viewpoints in the literature, the notion of development encompassing 'change' in a variety of aspects of the human condition seems to be a common theme. Dokurugu (2011) contends that development should place emphasis on the human beings who are the ultimate beneficiaries and not on institutions and physical development. This human-centred development approach also necessitates that development policies and their implementation be evolved locally by the people. This is based on the recognition that actors and beneficiaries are more likely to feel involved in a specific issue which has an impact on them, rather than by more general aspects of participatory development.

Multiple actors and development management

Development management seeks to achieve a greater focus on sustainable and higher quality development and greater community benefit than under previous planning legislations (Davids, 2012). It includes a wide number of planning activities such as designing, analysing, influencing, promoting, engaging, negotiating, decision making, co-ordinating, implementation, compliance and enforcement. At their regional seminars on development management in November and December 2007, the Department for Communities & Local Government (DCLG) defined development management in the context of its role in delivering sustainable development as an 'end-to-end management of the delivery chain for sustainable development' (Planning Officers Society Enterprises, 2007). Although, this definition largely relates to spatial planning, the term is also about actively stimulating institutional and organizational changes that increase human freedom and wealth, and consequently the level of development. It represents a deliberate, conscious and informed attempt to move institutions and organizations towards higher levels of efficiency and effectiveness in a way which is faster than their autonomous rate of progressive change and in a more co-ordinated manner.

There is some consensus around the management of the development process, which draws on a range of theories and approaches. Development management is largely built around a theory-led approach to the role of institutions and organizations in development (Hydén, 1983; Preston, 1996). This chapter is however aligned to its alternative, the actor-oriented approach pioneered by Norman Long (2001). As opposed to the structural, institutional and political economy analysis,

Long argued that one way out of the bottlenecks of development research will be 'to adopt an actor-oriented perspective that explores how social actors (both local and external to particular arenas) are locked in a series of intertwined battles over resources, meanings and institutional legitimacy and control' (Long, 2001: 3). Therefore, this perspective focuses on how development agencies, governments and local leaders come together towards a common purpose and pool their resources to implement a good change (Chambers, 2004) in society (Schuurman, 1993).

The utility of the actor interface perspective in understanding social change and development is its recognition of the central significance of 'human agency', self-organizing processes and the mutual determination of the 'internal' and 'external' factors and relationships (Schuurman, 1993, Long and Long, 1992; Long, 2001).

This approach focuses on the life worlds and interlocking projects of various actors, and requires delving more deeply into the social and cultural discontinuities and ambiguities inherent in 'battlefields of knowledge' (Long and Long, 1992). According to Long and Jinlong (2009), the social and cultural discontinuities and ambiguities involved shape the relations between local actors, development practitioners, other interested parties and even researchers.

Long (2001) further observes that in introducing a development project or program to any society, it is important that emphasis is put on creating the most efficient social interface (Bossman, 2004) possible in order to avoid encountering social discontinuities and other possible obstacles. This is because discontinuity of a development project gives the indication that actors are in a process of 'devising ways of bridging, accommodating, or struggling against each other's different social and cognitive worlds' (Long, 2001). Interface analysis therefore helps in dealing with the social discontinuities and works at characterizing the different organizational and cultural forms that may have an influence on the reproduction or transformation of social discontinuities (Kontinen, 2004; Booth, 1994). To ensure a certain level of continuity in social interface, relationships must be analysed as an integral part of the processes of negotiation, adaptation and transformation of meaning. Thus, as noted by Kontinen (2004), it should cover the whole span of an intervention.

In this chapter, the actor-oriented approach is operationalized as any approach in which the actors in development are given definite roles, some as givers and others as receivers and some even as administrators on the sideline, but always in such a way that there is no sign of a top-down approach and that the whole process becomes actor-driven (Schuurman, 1993; Long, 2001 cited in Bossman, 2004). Based on this, there seem to be several fronts of relationship between these actors thereby implying an interface and a form of agency. These actors work on behalf of each other for their own direct or indirect benefit(s) (Long, 2001).

Development actors in Africa

Over the past decades, national, regional and local governments across the globe have infused innovation into their organizational approaches to create new development agencies and tools as well as other entities that have specific tasks in pursing their development agendas (Haque, 2004).

This has brought into the picture several actors, institutions and agencies who are engaged in everyday struggles and negotiation over livelihoods and resources in managing development projects and programs in Africa. Ohno and Shimamura (2007) argue that ideally, top leadership such as the central government would provide a long-term development vision backed with a strong political will to realize that vision. This is then followed 'by mobilizing and utilizing both domestic and external resources, [as] the technocrats of central economic agencies are crucial as they have the responsibility of translating the vision into concrete action plans' (Ohno and Shimamura, 2007).

This responsibility includes formulating development plans and strategies, articulating priority policies, programming public investment and managing resources within hard-budget constraints. Technocrats are responsible for the coordination of various development stakeholders, such as line ministries, other central governmental agencies, local governments, traditional institutions, multinational donors, non-governmental organizations and private/corporate organizations (through their corporate social responsibility initiatives), all in the bid to facilitate the implementation of projects and the delivery of essential public service. The various actors involved in this complex web of development are discussed below.

Multinational donors

Notions of state, development and governance have changed in contemporary times. A central concept of governance and development today is one of networks, with the state moving from a 'provider state' to a 'facilitator state' (Stoker, 1998). The state is expected to secure development through networks with multinational donors along with various donor organizations. It is in this regard that international donors such as the World Bank, the United Nation Development Program (UNDP), the United Nations Educational, Scientific and Cultural Organization (UNESCO), Deutche Gesellschaft fur Technische Zusammenarbeit (GTZ), UK's Department for International Development (DFID), the Danish Development Agency (DANIDA) and the U.S. Agency for International Development (USAID) have taken centre stage and contributed enormously particularly to development in Africa and other third-world nations.

It is pertinent to note that these donor agencies, largely Western, tend to be propositivist oriented and formulate purely rational solutions and processes to tackle the development challenges of countries across the globe. These agencies often lack appropriate perspectives on the unique social, cultural and ecological conditions affecting development in developing countries particularly in Africa. Their prescriptions tend to work in highly formalized western societies but often fail in Africa with large informal associations and networks. Riggs and MacKean (1964) argue that development and change must be made relevant to the context. If there is any consensus today in the development world, it is that the point of departure for any policy or project should be a sound understanding of the context and its challenges. If local actors are to take effective ownership of a project, then the project must be responding to their needs. Yet in reality, the process of identifying these needs is all too often disconnected from the actual expectations of the inhabitants and institutions involved. These donors are often driven by constraints on their side, in particular the need to disburse funding, which wins out over adapting to the context.

Be this as it may, these donor agencies over time have adopted collaborative mechanisms to partner and network with local agencies such as NGOs, and national as well as local government institutions with a better understanding of development challenges of the continent (Haque, 2004). This enhances successful implementation of their development agendas and as observed by Stoker (1998), these actors are able to enforce accountability, transparency, responsiveness, procedural simplicity and moral governance because they fund national governments' development projects and NGO activities in several sectors of Africa.

It is reported for instance that, in Malawi, because of the relatively low capacity at the district level, donor agencies consider NGOs to be better advocates for community needs and key actors in the policy formulation process. This accounts for increased donor support, increased space and of course expanded role of NGOs within the decentralization process and in development management. Decentralization therefore opens up avenues for more engaging relations between local government actors and civil society within the decentralized space. This underscores the link between decentralization and increased NGO influence across the continent (Kadzamira and Kunje, 2002; Ulleberg, 2009).

Central government

Traditionally, development is considered as being in the domain of the central government. Theories of the emergence of socialist, welfare and even capitalist states emphasize the primary role of central government in bolstering development (Aidukaite, 2004; Hicks, 1999). Central governments are expected to provide a national strategic framework, define policies and initiate various efforts towards national development (Ohno and Shimamura, 2007). In Africa and other developing countries, governments have rolled out elaborate plans, along which they were to pursue development. Unfortunately most of these development plans have not yielded the desired results (Ake, 2001).

At the turn of the twenty-first century, the United Nations Millennium Development Goals (MDGs) were adopted as a blueprint for development by all countries in the world and leading development institutions. Efforts by central governments coupled with international aid notwithstanding, most African countries failed to meet most of the targets of the eight MDGs (Maathai, 2011). Whereas some countries in the region recorded improvements in their national indicators, wide disparities among provinces/districts were also recorded. Africa currently seems to be a fragmented continent, economically and socially, and the continent's challenges particularly on the human and social fronts are becoming increasingly alarming. Consequently, several calls are being made for African governments to take up their traditional responsibility of providing their citizens with public services such as security, education and health care.

In Ghana for example, the 1992 Constitution mandates the National Development Planning Commission (NDPC) to make proposals for the development of the country (Ghana, 1992). It further enjoins the state in article 36(1) to take all necessary action to ensure that the national economy is managed in such a manner that it will maximize the rate of economic development and to secure the welfare, freedom and happiness of every person in Ghana. The Government is further mandated to provide adequate means of livelihood and suitable employment and public assistance to the needy. Development of the country is to be even and balanced in all regions and every part of each region of Ghana. This is to improve the conditions of life in the rural areas, and generally, redress any imbalance in development between the rural and the urban areas of Ghana by the effective utilization of available resources.

In carrying out all these developmental functions, the central government through its technocrats formulates national development plans and collaborates with respective agencies and organizations such as donors for financial assistance, district assemblies and NGOs towards effective implementation of these plans on behalf of the State.

Metropolitan/municipal district assemblies (MMDAs)

Development has a significant local dimension and many researchers believe that localities are better positioned to stimulate development as they directly interface with the local people (Ayee, 2000b; Adamelekun, 1988; Asante, 2003). Local jurisdictions have been identified as an appropriate scale to address developmental challenges and MMDAs have a critical role to play in promoting economic development at the local level. Through the decentralization process, local jurisdictions serve as channels for central governments' policies and programs to trickle down to the most remote areas and hinterlands of Africa (Adamelekun, 1988; Asante, 2003).

Local governments have considerable authority over local land use, markets, housing and plans to address growth-related problems that are considered as important aspects of development (Ayee, 2000b). In Ghana, for example, a whole ministry exists for the coordination of development in local and rural areas. Local government as a form of decentralization provides services including basic health care and education, social welfare, internal transport, maintaining law and order, local works and housing, firefighting and other emergency services, traffic regulation, streetlight maintenance, water supply, environmental services, garbage collection/ waste management, etc. (Ayee, 2000b; Adamelekun, 1988). In delivering these services MMDAs are guided by the core responsibility of being the principal agent for advancing the cause of equal opportunity, redistribution of wealth and poverty reduction. Local governments are therefore the vehicle for development (Ayee, 2000b; Adamelekun, 1988).

Despite their control by the central government, Sakyi (2008) notes that local governments collaborate with central governments and other local actors such as local producers and their associations, community-based organizations, as well as NGOs (for capacity initiatives) and donors (for development funds) to contribute and manage development actions of their communities. However, Bawole and Hossain (2014) note that such collaborations have been largely tokenistic and cosmetic. As argued by Helmsing (2003), local governments have an important facilitating role in creating a favourable business environment and infrastructural conditions towards local economic development (LED).

Non-governmental organizations (NGOs) and civil society organizations (CSOs)

In the international development discourse, the complementary role of NGOs, civil society and the state is universally acknowledged and unequivocal (Tvedt, 1998; Mercer, 2002). Osborne and Gaebler (1992) note that cooperation between civil society and political society and between the state and citizens facilitate governance and ultimately development. Therefore, underpinned by democratic assumptions of engagement, participation, wider debates and the politics of development, NGOs and CSOs have become key development actors in modern times. Michael Bratton (1989) highlights the contribution of NGOs to development and argues that they are significant bolsterers of development by virtue of their participatory and democratic approach.

Accordingly, NGOs and other CSOs are key agents in donor-, government- and World Bank–funded development projects and programmes across the globe (O'Dwyer and Unerman, 2007; Mercer, 2002). They have become the main service providers in Africa and other developing countries where state capacity is deemed weak and in sectors where the government is unable to fulfil its traditional role of providing basic public services such as education, environmental sanitation and health care (Bratton, 1989; Kaldor et al., 2003; Bendell, 2000; Mercer, 2002). As affirmed by Mayhew (2005), international support for NGOs has been fuelled, at least in part, simply by disillusionment at governments' failure to meet donor objectives especially in Africa.

Ulleberg (2009) indicates that most NGOs have now moved beyond filling government developmental gaps to capacity building activities. NGOs also interface with local communities and collaborate with district assemblies on areas which require expertise such as climate change and complex sanitation challenges. They also assist in developing the capacity of local government (Kadzamira and Kunje, 2002) to ensure that the local assemblies are efficient in policy formulation and implementation and are able to sustain development actions within their jurisdictional areas (Ulleberg, 2009).

Funding and patronage of NGO activities by international donors have contributed to the proliferation of NGOs and other civil society organizations across Africa (Davids, 2012). In Ethiopia, for instance, USAID conditions development assistance by giving part of the aid directly to NGOs (Mayhew, 2005). This has led critics to accuse NGOs that accept this type of funding of compromising their autonomy (Degnbol-Martinussen and Engberg-Pedersen, 1999). Sen (2006) argues that few of the major policy initiatives of recent times have allowed any sort of autonomy while still giving the impression of doing so. Nelson (2006: 709) equally observes that 'states and donors exert considerable influence on the strategic choices, programmatic practices and political orientation of NGOs'. But confidence in NGOs has lately waned in Africa. Notwithstanding, their status and utility as small scale, flexible, dynamic, adaptive, local, efficient and innovative makes them crucial and complementary to state action. They remain a preferred option by donor organizations and institutions, governments as well as civil society as far as development on the continent is concerned (Bratton, 1989; Davids, 2012).

Traditional authorities

There is no disagreement over the role of traditional authorities in governance and consequently development management (Ayee, 2000a; Boafo-Arthur, 2006). In Africa, traditional rulers are regarded as the legitimate leaders of their people and despite recent debates about the relevance of the institution, chiefs still command great influence in their areas of jurisdiction. Amenta and Ramsey (2010) argue that this is because the institution is deeply ingrained in formal and informal procedures, norms, routines and conventions put into place as a structure above the individual level and constraining or constituting the interests and political participation of actors.

A unique character of traditional institutions is that they share common histories, interests and aspirations with their people. Chiefs are in touch with the developmental needs and interests of their people and are better equipped to articulate them than are government-appointed administrators, who are mostly accountable only to the political élite (Dokurugu, 2011).

In Ghana for example, traditional authorities, despite their chequered colonial history (Ayee, 2000a), are still at the centre of governance and development particularly at the grassroots. This is aptly captured by Aidoo (1978: 48) who notes that 'You cannot go to any village and … start propagating an ideology or political programme or anything in the air … the chiefs are very important if we are going to think about participation of all the people in government'.

In contemporary times, most traditional rulers in Africa have demonstrated the knack to promote development even beyond their areas of jurisdiction. The developmental role of the modern day chief is forcefully brought home by the Asantehene, Otumfuo Osei Tutu II who admonishes his colleagues:

> Our predecessors engaged in inter-tribal wars, fighting for conquest over territories and people. Today, the war should be vigorous and intensive against dehumanization, poverty, marginalization, ignorance and disease.… Chieftaincy must be used to propel economic development through proper lands administration, through facilitating investments in our communities, and through codification and customs and traditions making it impossible for imposters to get enstooled and creating unnecessary situations for litigation. (Cited in Ayee, 2007)

The Otumfuo Education Fund initiated by the Asantehene is a major undertaking in this regard and does not only benefit his subjects but also Ghanaians of other ethnic extraction. Kleist (2011) notes how other chiefs interviewed in his study were engaged in a range of activities to attract or collaborate with NGOs or other donors to further the cause of development in their traditional areas.

The prominence and importance of chiefs is strengthened with the guarantee of chieftaincy in Ghana's constitution. In Ghana, the 1992 Constitution further recognizes the role of chieftaincy in several key national institutions such as the Council of State. Among other duties, chiefs provide advice to the central government and help in the administration of the districts, regions and the nation as a whole. In pursuit of their traditional functions, these chiefs are guided by strong goals of sustained human and economic development and modernization (Ayee, 2000a).

A major source of financing for development by chiefs in Africa is royalties from minerals, timber and other natural resources that are extracted in their jurisdictional areas. Awuah-Nyamekye (2014) however highlights how governments in Ghana for example are reluctant to pay these royalties. He argues that traditional councils and owners of stool lands like the municipal and district assemblies depend on these royalties to provide social developments like awarding bursaries to deserving students and teachers and also run the secretariats of traditional and divisional councils inter alia. Therefore, delays in payment of these royalties undermine the ability of traditional institutions to deliver the much-needed development in their areas.

Related to this, the clan system, a network of kinship and families that transcends community boundaries and is found in almost all African countries, also plays a developmental role (Mohan and Zack-Williams, 2002). Membership of these clans and kinship groups is exclusively by birth. One born into a particular family/clan automatically belongs to it. These groups serve as platforms for nurturing values like service, communal feeling, solidarity and cohesion. Families and clans are basic units of organization and focal institutions for uniting their members and promoting a sense of belonging among people in rural communities (Lentz, 1995). They create in individuals a sense of citizenship and civic responsibility; essential ingredients for mobilization and development.

Corporate organizations (through CSR)

Corporate social responsibility (CSR) as a concept entails the practice whereby corporate entities voluntarily integrate both social and environmental responsibilities in their business philosophy and operations (Zain, 2008). This practice stems from the notion that business is part of society, and therefore has community and national obligations, a philosophy rooted in the cultural and economic history of many African countries. In modern times therefore managers of multinational companies (MNCs) have found the need to give back to the societies in which they operate mainly because of the realization that their immediate and macro environments have a direct impact on the attainment of the corporate goals, objectives and mission statements.

In Africa, corporate organizations contribute to development by giving donations and gifts as well as offering social services related to safety, health and environment, education schemes, medical benefits, fundraising and others like regeneration of deprived communities, reclamation of derelict land and creation of new regeneration jobs (Siwar and Noramelia, 2004). Visser (2006) notes that they also help to improve the governance, ethical, social, labour and environmental conditions of societies and developing countries in which they operate, while remaining sensitive to prevailing religious, historical and cultural contexts.

Both international and local corporate organizations in Africa utilize CSR as a formal and informal way of expressing their gratitude for sustained business operations. The various development strategies and programmes position firms to have close relationships with their host communities. Carroll (1991, 1998) presents a four-part pyramid that sheds light on how CSRs play out in a developing country context (see Figure 9.1). The model is considered as an indicator of the relative emphasis to be placed on various responsibilities and aspects of development in Africa. From Carroll's pyramid, economic responsibilities get the most emphasis in developing countries followed by philanthropy and then legal issues. Receiving less attention is ethical responsibilities.

In executing their CSR initiatives, businesses evaluate their available resources and engage stakeholders to identify what their developmental needs are. This ensures that the projects offered are tailored to the needs of communities so they fully benefit from them. During such interactions, corporate businesses interface with the local assembly, traditional authorities and opinion leaders within the respective communities.

Thus, from the local authority, they require information to determine who, where and what meets their criteria for intended projects. From traditional authorities, clan and opinion leaders, businesses require information regarding the unique social, cultural, religious and ecological conditions affecting the development projects they wish to implement in the communities. National and local governments also give approval for such projects to commence. Such collaborative mechanisms with local institutions help foster grassroots development, ownership, accountability and sustainability of development projects.

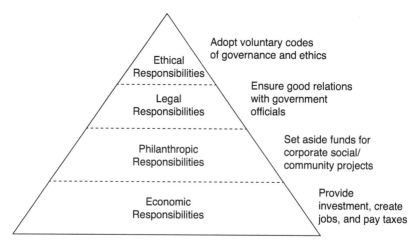

Figure 9.1 CSR pyramid for developing countries
Source: Carroll (1991)

Individual citizens, opinion leaders and youth associations

Within the democratic space, a lot of emphasis is placed on the involvement of citizens in governance and development (Svara and Denhardt, 2010; Lentz, 1995). Thus, citizens are not left out when it comes to development of their local areas. In African communities there exist several primary forms of social organizations and associations which serve as rallying points for individuals in the community to be engaged in development. These groups usually pursue social development objectives although it must be noted that some also have economic objectives (Lund, 2006). The associations are mostly made up of the youth but there are also those formed along gender lines. In Ghana, for example, there are women groups engaged in self-help projects (known as 'nnoboa' in Akan) in the communities which support group members through granting of soft loans from group resources or acting as mediums for the disbursement of credit from external agencies (which could be from CSR of corporate financial institutions operating locally) in support of individual members' varied economic activities. These economic activities, which include shea butter processing, pito (traditional drink) brewing, dawadawa spice processing, petty trading, weaving of mats and baskets, livestock and poultry, crop farming and collection of fire wood as kitchen fuel, are often resourced by the local assemblies and locally based NGOs.

From such groups, influential opinion leaders emerge and they lead the charge for development in their areas. The formation of the youth associations in particular often emanate from the recognition among the youth that they will take over from their leaders and that the future of their communities is in their hands. They therefore take up challenges that will bring about development of the entire community. These associations generally meet on scheduled times but also on festive occasions such as Christmas, New Year and festivals to discuss and plan development for their areas.

As far as development is concerned, such groups form the critical mass to offer self-help assistance in the form of manual labour for development projects in the communities. They sometimes engage in the construction of social infrastructure (schools, health facilities and social centres) and feeder roads (Lentz, 1995). They support their traditional authorities in various developmental activities in the community such as the protection of natural resources in the community – water bodies, anti-bushfire watchdogs, economic trees against bushfires and the protection of crops by ensuring that all animals are quarantined during the rainy season.

In addition, they organize themselves to provide communal or group labour in farming-related activities – sowing and harvesting on their husbands' farms, construction, rehabilitation and plastering of houses in the off-season. 'Kotaa' groups for instance assist individual members by pooling labour to assist each other to carry out farm work and construction-related works. These groups seek to benefit from the principle of synergy by pooling labour for economic production and social development in Ghana (Lentz, 1995).

The utility of such groups and leaders is that they serve as the base of development ensuring participation of citizens in the development of their regions. When participation is secured, development projects are owned and shared by all citizens leading to greater sustainability (Lentz 1995; Lund, 2006).

Actor networks and development management

The discussions above give an indication of how development assumes a multi-stakeholder dimension involving networks of increasing complexity. Involvement of multiple actors does away with the relatively simple, top-down development management structures of the past centring only on governments and donors, replacing them with more complex patterns.

On the African continent, the new horizontal forms that draw together approximately-peer organizations such as public–private partnerships and/or vertical forms that cut across levels from the addition of community participation to insertion into the global value chains result in networks that define development management. These networks are also characterized by the proliferation particularly of information and communication technologies which have become ever-more deeply woven into development management, just as they are into the fabric of society (Hanseth et al., 2004).

Actor pluralism and networks promote partnerships and complementary interactions characterized by collective knowledge and co-production and co-monitoring of development programs. Donors for instance become catalysts and the facilitator of dialogue and agenda set by various central governments. Various coalitions of actors from civil society and the private sector ensure that in their implementation various national and local governments comply with set standards with traditional authorities, individual citizens, opinion leaders and youth associations serving as a critical support base of development ensuring participation and ownership of projects. And of course in Africa, this dynamic relationship cannot happen outside the traditional and religious regulations in the various communities, with most traditional authorities providing the land for development projects.

Overall the reflexes thus established contribute to more effective and transparent development action because the various actors are able to position themselves as the driving force behind proposals and programs over which citizens have an effective means of control.

Conclusion

This chapter has attempted to identify and characterize differing actor practices, strategies and rationales, the conditions under which they arise, how they interlock, their viability or effectiveness for solving specific problems, and their wider social ramifications on the development process in Africa. Hinging on the actor-centred approach, it highlighted the need to see development as a complex process with many different agents, and which takes place in a rapidly changing world.

As desirable as development is, this chapter highlights the fact it does not occur per chance but rather due to some deliberate action carried out by particular agents or by an authority. This is consistent with the notion of networking, a central concept of governance and development in an endless changing contemporary context.

In Africa, it is this realization that has brought into the picture several actors, institutions and agencies who are engaged in everyday struggles and negotiation over resources in managing development projects and programs. Therefore although central governments have been expected to deliver development, they do so with a number of actors and these include various international donors, district assemblies, non-governmental organizations (NGOs) and civil society organizations (CSOs), traditional authorities, corporate organizations (through CSR), individual citizens, opinion leaders and youth associations.

These actors interrelate with each other as they play their different and unique developmental roles. Therefore, a well-organized collaborative framework within which these actors and agencies work is required to bring about the much-desired development on the African continent.

References

Adamelekun, D. O. M. L. (1988). *Local Government in West Africa since Independence*. Lagos: University of Lagos Press.

Aidoo, A. K. (1978) 'Chieftaincy', in Republic of Ghana, *Proceedings of the Constitutional Drafting Commission held at the Kwame Nkrumah Conference Centre*.

Aidukaite, J. (2004). The emergence of the post-socialist welfare state – the case of the Baltic States: Estonia, Latvia and Lithuania. Doctoral Dissertation. Södertörn University College.

Ake, C. (2001). *Democracy and Development in Africa*. Washington, DC: Brookings Institution Press.

Amenta, E. and Ramsey, K. M. (2010). Institutional theory. In Leicht, K. T. and Jenkins, J. C. (eds.), *Handbook of Politics: State and Society in Global Perspective*. New York: Springer.

Asante, F. A. (2003). *Economic Analysis of Decentralisation in Rural Ghana*. Germany: Peter Lang.

Awuah-Nyamekye, S. (2014). *Managing the Environmental Crisis in Ghana: The Role of African Traditional Religion and Culture with Special Reference to the Berekum Traditional Area*. Newcastle upon Tyne: Cambridge Scholars Publishing.

Ayee, J. R. A. (2000a). Chieftaincy and the new local government system, paper presented at a symposium on the theme 'Chieftaincy and Modern Politics', as part of a series of symposia on Chieftaincy in connection with its Photo Exhibition on Asante Kings of the Twentieth Century, organized by the Institute of African Studies, University of Ghana, Legon on 7 June 2000.

Ayee, J. R. A. (2000b). Decentralization and good governance in Ghana, unpublished paper of May 2000 prepared for the Canadian High Commission, Accra, Ghana.

Ayee, J. R. (2007). Traditional leadership and local governance in Africa: the Ghanaian experience. Paper presented as the Fourth National Annual Local Government Conference on the theme 'Traditional Leadership and Local Governance in a Democratic South Africa: Quo Vadis', held from 30–31 July 2007 at the Southern Sun–Elangeni, Durban.

Bawole, J. N. and Hossain, F. (2014). Marriage of the unwilling? The paradox of local government and NGO relations in Ghana. *Voluntas: International Journal of Voluntary and Nonprofit Organizations*, 26(5), 2061–2083.

Bellù, L. G. (2011). Development and development paradigms: a (reasoned) review of prevailing visions. Food and Agriculture Organization of the United Nations. Available at www.fao.org/docs/up/easypol/882/defining_development_paradigms_102en.pdf. Accessed 22 July 2015.

Bendell, J. (2000). Introduction: working with stakeholder pressure for sustainable development. In Bendell, J. (ed.), *Terms for Endearment: Business* (pp. 14–30). Sheffield: Greenleaf Publishing/New Academy of Business.

Boafo-Arthur, K. (2006). Chieftaincy in Ghana: challenges and prospects in the 21st century. In Odotei, I. and Awedoba, A. (eds.), *Chieftaincy in Ghana: Culture, Governance and Development* (pp. 145–168). Accra: Sub-Saharan Publishers.

Booth, D. (ed.) (1994). *Rethinking Social Development: Theory, Research and Practice*. Burnt Hill and Harlow: Longman Scientific and Technical.

Bossman, W. (2004). An analysis of the actor-oriented approach as tool in international development cooperation. Doctoral Thesis. University of South Africa.

Bratton, M. (1989). The politics of government-NGO relations in Africa. *World Development*, 17(4), 569–587.

Carroll, A. B. (1991). The pyramid of corporate social responsibility: toward the moral management of organizational stakeholders. *Business Horizons*, 34(4), 39–48.

Carroll, A. B. (1998). The four faces of corporate citizenship. *Business and Society Review*, 100(1), 1–7.

Chambers, R. (2004). *Ideas for Development*. IDS Working Paper 238. Sussex: IDS.

Corbridge, S. (ed.) (1995). *Development Studies: A Reader*. London: Edward Arnold.

Cowen, M. P. and Shenton, R. W. (1995). The invention of development. In Corbridge, S. (ed.), *Development: Critical Concepts in the Social Sciences* (Volume 1, pp. 27–45). London: Routledge.

Davids, I. (2012). *Participatory Development in South Africa: A Development Management Perspective*. Pretoria: Van Schaik.

Degnbol-Martinussen, J. and Engberg-Pedersen, P. (1999). *Aid-Understanding International Development Cooperation*. London: Zed Books.

Dokurugu, A. Y. (2011). Traditional authority, peace and socio-economic development in the Dagbon Kingdom of Ghana. Thesis. Kwame Nkrumah University of Science and Technology.

Ghana, Republic of (1992). *Constitution of the Republic of Ghana, 1992*. Tema: Ghana Publishing Corporation.

Hanseth, O., Aanestad, M. and Berg, M. (2004). Introduction: Actor-network theory and information systems. What's so special? *Information Technology & People*, 17(2), 116–123.

Haque, M. S. (2004). Governance based on partnership with NGOs: implications for development and empowerment in rural Bangladesh. *International Review of Administrative Sciences*, 70(2), 271–290.

Helmsing, A. H. J. (2003). Local development: new generations of actors, policies and instruments for Africa. *Public Administration and Development*, 23(1), 67–76.

Hicks, A. M. (1999). *Social Democracy & Welfare Capitalism: A Century of Income Security Politics*. Ithaca: Cornell University Press.

Hydén, G. (1983). *No Shortcuts To Progress: African Development Management in Perspective*. London, Heinemann: University of California Press.

Kadzamira, E. C. and Kunje, D. (2002). *Changing Roles Of Non-Governmental Organisations in Education in Malawi*. Washington DC: USAID.

Kaldor, M., Anheier, H. and Glasius, M. (eds.) (2003). *Global Civil Society 2003*. Oxford: Oxford University Press.

Kleist, N. (2011). Modern chiefs: tradition, development and return among traditional authorities in Ghana. *African Affairs*, 110(441): 629–648.

Kontinen, T. (ed.) (2004). *Development Intervention: Actor and Activity Perspectives*. Helsinki, Finland: Center for Activity Theory and Developmental Work Research and Institute for Development Studies, University of Helsinki.

Le Bellu, S. and Le Blanc, B. (2010). How to characterize professional gestures to operate tacit know-how transfer. *The Electronic Journal of Knowledge Management*, 10(2), 142–153.

Lentz, C. (1995). 'Unity for Development' youth associations in north-western Ghana. *Africa*, 65(3), 395–429.

Long, N. (2001). *Development Sociology: Actor Perspectives*. London and New York: Routledge.

Long, N. and Jinlong, L (2009). The centrality of actors and interfaces in the understanding of new ruralities: a Chinese case study. *Journal of Current Chinese Affairs*, 38(4), 63–84.

Long, N. and Long, A. (eds.) (1992). *Battlefields of Knowledge: The Interlocking of Theory and Practice in Social Research and Development*. London and New York: Routledge.

Lund, C. (2006). Twilight institutions: public authority and local politics in Africa. *Development and Change*, 37(4), 685–705.

Maathai, W. (2011). Challenge for Africa. *Sustainability Science*, 6(1), 1–2.

Mayhew, S. H. (2005). Hegemony, politics and ideology: the role of legislation in NGO-government relations in Asia. *Journal of Development Studies*, 41(5), 727–758.

Mercer, C. (2002). NGOs, civil society and democratization: a critical review of the literature. *Progress in Development Studies*, 2(1), 5–22.

Mohan, G. and Zack-Williams, A. B. (2002). Globalisation from below: conceptualising the role of the African diasporas in Africa's development. *Review of African Political Economy*, 29(92), 211–236.

Nelson, P. (2006). The varied and conditional integration of NGOs in the aid system: NGOs and the World Bank. *Journal of International Development*, 18(5), 701–713.

O'Dwyer, B. and Unerman, J. (2007). From functional to social accountability: transforming the accountability relationship between funders and non-governmental development organisations. *Accounting, Auditing & Accountability Journal*, 20(3), 446–471.

Ohno, I. and Shimamura, M. (2007). *Managing the Development Process and Aid: East Asian Experiences in Building Central Economic Agencies*. GRIPS Development Forum.

Osborne, D. and Gaebler, T. (1992). *Reinventing Government*. Boston: Addison-Wesley Publishing Co.

Planning Officers Society Enterprises (2007). *Development Management: Initial Guidance*. Available at www.planningofficers.org.uk/downloads/pdf/DMSP_Initial_Guidance_18_12_07.pdf. Accessed 21 October 2015.

Preston, P. (1996). *Development Theory. An Introduction*. Oxford: Blackwell.

Ranis, G. (2004). Human development and economic growth. *Yale University Economic Growth Center Discussion Paper* (887).

Riggs, F. W. and MacKean, D. D. (1964). *Administration in Developing Countries: The Theory of Prismatic Society* (p. 227). Boston: Houghton Mifflin.

Sakyi, E. K. (2008). Implementing decentralized management in Ghana: the experience of the Sekyere West District Health Administration. *Leadership in Health Services*, 21(4), 307–319.

Schuurman, F. J. (1993). Development theory in the 1990s. In Schuurman, F. J. (ed.), *Beyond the Impasse: New Directions in Development Theory*. London: ZED Books Ltd.

Seers, D. (1969). The meaning of development. *International Development Review*, 11(4), 2–6.

Sen, K. (2006). Viewpoint: capacity building and the state. Ontrac 34, 1–3. Oxford: INTRAC. Available at www.intrac.org/resources_database.php?id=287. Accessed 27 July 2015.

Siwar, C. and Noramelia, M. W. (2004). Corporate social responsibility (CSR), costs for R&D and financial performance in developing countries: a case study in Malaysia. In *The 2004 Corporate Social Responsibility and Environmental Management Conference Proceedings, Nottingham* (pp. 285–294).

Stoker, G. (1998). Governance as theory: five propositions. *International Social Science Journal*, 50(155), 17–28.

Svara, J. H. and Denhardt, J. (2010). The connected community: local governments as partners in citizen engagement and community building. *Promoting Citizen Engagement and Community Building*, 4–51.

Thomas, A. (2004). *The Study of Development*. Paper prepared for DSA Annual Conference, 6 November, Church House, London.

Tvedt, T. (1998). *Angels of Mercy or Development Diplomats? NGOs and Foreign Aid*. Oxford: James Currey.

Ulleberg, I. (2009). The role and impact of NGOs in capacity development from replacing the state to reinvigorating education. Paris: International Institute for Educational Planning, UNESCO. Available at http://unesdoc.unesco.org/images/0018/001869/186980e.pdf. Accessed 20 October 2015.

Visser, W.,(2006). Revisiting Carroll's CSR pyramid: an African perspective. In Pedersen, E. R. and Hunicke, M. (eds.), *Corporate Citizenship in Developing Countries* (pp. 29–56). Copenhagen: Copenhagen Business School Press.

Zain, M. (2008). Social responsibility in business: Friedman & Carroll's differing views on business responsibilities. Available at maria-zain.suite101.com › Business & Finance › Business Management. Accessed on 29 October 2015.

10 Managing local development in Africa

Empirical evidence from Northern Ghana

Francis Nangbeviel Sanyare, Farhad Hossain and Christopher J. Rees

Introduction

During the last few decades, the public sector in developing countries has been viewed as a key player to achieving poverty reduction and sustainable development (Crawford and Hartman, 2008; Dijk, 2008; Steiner, 2008). To secure this, governments have focused efforts on ensuring an effective and efficient public sector. It is no longer doubtful that the development performance of countries is intricately pivoted on the quality of their public institutions (Tillema, Mimba and van Helden, 2010: 204). As the world brings an epoch of implementing the Millennium Development Goals (MDGs) to a close, and while many anxiously anticipate a post-2015 development agenda, the anticipated gains of programs implemented to achieve the MDGs in transitional countries remain elusive. At the heart of this failure is the lack of 'the things that give life to democracy', such as 'Capable, reliable, and transparent [public] institutions […] and a vibrant private sector and civil society […]' (Obama, 2009).

In theory, this emphasis on an effective and efficient public sector is attributable to the rise in prominence of New Public Management (NPM), as well as reinventing trends of governments (see Jan van Helden, Johnsen and Vakkuri, 2008; Tillema et al., 2010). A central objective of these initiatives was to streamline governance and administrative systems to meet the current world order and to enable countries to deal with the emergent challenges of the twenty-first century (Ohemeng, 2009). Often, such reforms aim to reduce the size of government and to increase efficiency and effectiveness of core public sector processes (Liou, 2007). The pace of implementing such programs is, however, known to leave increasingly complex gaps with which public administration institutions have to grapple. One implication is that managers of local administrations face an enormous challenge to be efficient and effective in the midst of dwindling resources – financial, human, technical – and institutional capacities. Thus there is the need to be innovative and to improve systems and strategies for delivering services (Andersen, 2010; Berry, 2007). However, to achieve this would require the right balance of enhanced local capacities. This enhanced capacity is envisaged to guarantee that societal challenges are effectively addressed by achieving the desired ends for citizens in service delivery and to ensure that they (public organizations) always achieve a high premium for their constituents, without compromising efficiency (Ohemeng, 2009). However research suggests that in spite of decades of reformation, the quality of public service delivery has remained abysmally low (Tillema et al., 2010: 204).

One way to achieve the benefits of efficiency and effectiveness in public organizations is through decentralized local administrative reform. Researchers suggest that decentralization involves important aspects of the political governance structure such as degree of responsiveness, a participatory structure and political conformance (Tillema et al., 2010: 207). This notwithstanding, recent research into the decentralized local administration in Ghana has often focused on how it engenders local development (Crawford, 2004a, 2004b) and leads to poverty reduction (Crawford, 2008a; Steiner, 2008); the constraints to implementation (Antwi, Analoui and Cusworth, 2007; Barima and Analoui, 2010; Sakyi, 2008a); and management of decentralized departments (Sakyi, 2008b). The administrative challenges which these institutions face are rarely discussed within the context of Africa and Ghana. This chapter therefore seeks to discuss these contextual challenges to local administrations in the developing country context.

Both primary and secondary data were collected for this study. A qualitative case study approach involving 45 purposely selected key informants was used. The choice of this approach enabled a contextually intensive exploration into decentralized local administration so as to gain insights typically not achievable through other approaches (Yin, 1994). A thematic qualitative data analysis technique was used. This allowed us to identify, analyse and report patterns (themes) within the data.

Theoretical perspectives

Decentralized public administration

Decentralization is highlighted as an epitome of public sector reform (Rees and Hossain, 2010), with a proven ability to improve effectiveness and efficiency in developing countries (Pallangyo and Rees, 2010). There is agreement among some researchers that a drive towards decentralized management is a direct consequence of an apparent unresponsiveness, wastefulness and overcentralization of national bureaucracies (Ahwoi, 2010; Awortwi, 2011). As Feldheim (2007: 253) concludes, the goal of administrative decentralization was to achieve improvement in organizational performance as well as to meet increasingly complex customer expectations through continual analysis and improvement of the process of providing such services, which are not inert in nature. Others maintain that the gravitation towards this kind of reform was born out of the American concept of 'quality initiative', through which continual employee empowerment is emphasized (Feldheim, 2007; Hays and Whitney, 1997).

There is no wonder that almost all developing countries have come to accept administrative decentralization as a core process to acquire better services for their local populations (Haque, 2010). Through decentralized public administration, relevant needs-based provision of services would accrue due to increased participation and greater public oversight (Haque, 2010; World Bank, 1998). Contrary to centralized administration, decentralized organizations are said to be flatter, and more innovative in their approach (Crawford, 2009). Decentralized administration empowers and engages employees in the decision-making processes, allowing for timely and personalized responses to clients or citizen needs (Berman, 1995; Feldheim, 2007). This brings internal and external customer satisfaction, and is premised on an organizational commitment to quality, the use of continual data analysis and a shared commitment to the process of empowered employees and enlightened management (Feldheim, 2007). Experiences however, indicate that decentralized administration is neither necessarily effective nor responsive and there is no guarantee that the needs of local people would always be addressed (McCarney, 1996). The argument that the assumptions underlying the efficacy of local pubic administrations are universally applicable has thus been questioned in the extant literature. For the concept of employee empowerment to become accepted and entrenched, organizational leaders need a shared vision for greater achievement, and higher levels of productivity. This requires a shift in culture, in ways that allow power sharing and collective responsibilities, which will then lead to a collective sense of ownership of decisions and implementation processes. However, as Feldheim suggests, such a culture is premised on the assumption that organizational players are intrinsically motivated to succeed, and in addition, that the organization must value and empower the individuals who work there (Feldheim, 2007: 253). This appears to be a compromised case among decentralized local administrations of developing countries. Unlike the case of so-called egalitarian societies, local public administration in developing economies is mostly laid-back (Ellison, 2006), and bear a charge of being corrupt and non-transparent, thus making achievements of employee empowerment for effective and efficient delivery of public goods and services in real terms a far cry. These issues further muddy the chances of ensuring genuine accountability to local people.

Efficiency and effectiveness in decentralized public administration?

The literature suggests that the inability of some public bureaucracies in transitional countries to perform is mostly based on overall systemic poor performance and institutional weaknesses (Antwi et al., 2007). The new public management (NPM) type of decentralized administration is praised as a strategic means for local administrations to reach autonomy, and to measure and reward organizational and individual performance (Antwi et al., 2007: 3) necessary to facilitate the delivery of high-quality citizen-valued services (Sakyi, 2008b).

In theory, NPM-decentralized local administration would be based on the market ideology of capitalism (Feldheim, 2007), and hence when applied at the level of decentralized local administration, would profoundly change the nature of public service where the emphasis moves away from traditional administration's hierarchy and job roles to performance and individual accountability. By default, perceived inefficiencies of the centralized bureaucracies are minimized through empowerment of local administrative employees. It also has the ability to introduce, within the public sector, the performance incentive and the discipline that exist in a market environment; therefore, NPM is said to bring the benefits of efficiency and effectiveness to public sector activities and to serve public purposes by allowing governments to learn from the private sector despite contextual differences. It is not by accident that many transitional country governments have embraced NPM as the framework to modernize governments and re-engineer the public sector (Ayeni, 2002; Hope, 2001). In managerial parlance, such an arrangement would promote a culture of performance orientation where highly centralized, hierarchical structures give way to a more localized, decentralized management atmosphere in which decisions on resource allocation and services delivery are made closer to the point of delivery. This provides the scope for feedback from clients and other interest groups (Hope, 2001), while supporting capacities at the centre for policy guidance as well as allowing the state to respond to the myriad of interests in flexible, cost-effective ways. Given that public bureaucracy has underperformed in the past, applying NPM principles therefore means an emphasis on problem solving and good governance.

However, the achievement of NPM-influenced reforms is only manifest when capacity and openness to change takes centre stage in public administration. Regrettably, however, there often exists a set of complex institutional mechanisms that constrain the implementation of various policies in a timely and effective manner (Hope, 2001). This makes it interesting to examine the nature of these constraints.

Perspectives on capacity for effective performance

The literature on local governance establishes a strong relationship between capacity and performance (Bergh, 2010). Antwi et al. (2007) highlight the fact that building (local) capacities is essential for Africa's strategic development agenda. This is in recognition that the contrary, that is, inadequacy of local capacity, is often cited as a significant contributor leading to the (re)centralization of public services (see Antwi et al., 2007: 5). For instance, the literature on decentralized public administration in developing countries is replete with highlights of apparent capacity gaps which affect the resolve to realize the goals of carrying forward the decentralization process. This inadequate capacity has implications for sustained, long-term development. This appears contrary to the wide implementation of NPM-driven public sector reforms which emphasize a performance culture in public organizations. One basic understanding of such a demand on public organizations is the need for a calibre of highly capable, skilled and motivated public sector workers. Therefore, the goal of delivering citizen–desired services at the local level calls for enhancing both 'human and institutional capacity' (Barima and Analoui, 2010).

Conceptually, capacity could mean different things to different people. Bergh (2010), following Morgan (2006), describes capacity as an embryonic state. In that perspective, capacity is said to proceed from an intricate mix of attitudes, resources, strategies and skills, both tangible and intangible. Others perceive capacity as a multi-dimensional and complex set of attributes, which include the state of awareness, knowledge, skills, self-confidence and actions (Tandon, 2001). From a systems perspective, Tandon (2001: 13) adds that (institutional) capacity 'can be defined as the totality of inputs needed by an actor to realise its purpose'. At the local level, this would ensure that such institutions are able to function effectively as 'institutions of local self-governance'. For Barima and Analoui (2010: 637), capacity includes the power or ability of something – a system, an organization, a person – to independently perform and produce or deliver an activity properly and efficiently.

Broadly speaking, from the view of government, capacity generally would involve the government's ability to effectively coordinate all sectors of its economy in ways that respond to pressures from both within and outside the boarders of the nation. Internally, it speaks to the government's ability to plan, manage and sustain development processes of their economies and societies (Larbi, 1999; Barima and Analoui, 2010). The UNDP (as cited by Barima and Analoui, 2010), sees capacity as the ability of individuals and organizations or organizational units to perform functions effectively, efficiently and sustainably. In addition to the above, and thinking organizationally, capacity would reflect in part what has become the organizational memory, and the commitment, as well as the technical know-how and proficiency of the people engaged in delivering the needed services. Tandon (2001) divides the potential capacity within any given organization into three types: intellectual capacity, institutional capacity and material capacity. Decentralized administrative capacity is manifested in two ways: (1) policy capacity, which would include institutional capacity, is reflected in procedures, systems, structures, decision making, competence, accountability, and networking abilities; and (2) material capacity, which could include resources, physical assets, funds, and infrastructure. We focus on a decentralized local administration's capacity because, as Asante and Ayee (2004:1) suggest, 'it is one of the most important reasons for implementation of decentralized programs in sub-Saharan Africa'.

Empirical observations on the capacities of local administration for effective performance

Availability of strong policies, systems and regulation

Effective performance of local administrations largely hinges on the availability of clear policies, structures and frameworks that everybody understands. Essentially, these serve as guides to the functioning of public officials and the entirety of organizational arrangements within which they work. The 1992 Constitution of Ghana and the Local Government Act of Ghana (Act 462) amply spell out broad national policies and frameworks within which the decentralized public administration is carried out. On this basis, the overall policy framework for local government operations appears to be directly derived from prevailing national development policies.

The legal regime confers on the local agencies considerable freedom to act within their jurisdictions. Even though local government authorities are theoretically free to carry out their business in accordance to the local needs and in the best interest of the people, the data indicate the contrary. This freedom is effectively curtailed by so-called 'requirements' on local administrations to tailor activities and performance strictly to prevailing national development policies. Further, the local administrations' constitutional mandate to act as independent planning and implementation agents within their jurisdictions is subsumed by central government sector ministries who have extended their monitoring and oversight responsibilities to act as agents that provide specific directives and guidelines within which decentralized departments in every local government authority is supposed to function. The data further reveal that the local administration's policies and procedures are not different from those which pertain at the national level. This is because government and sector ministries supplant the otherwise participatory bottom-up planning approach, and insist, contrary to constitutional provisions, that local level plans must be strictly tailored to fit broad national development plan guidelines. While this may respond to the central government's desire to ensure a balance in national development and consistent application of administrative process to reflect the national development priorities, a recent report found the contrary. It found that national development policies drastically change with changing political orientations in the country (see Daily Graphic, 2011). This changing nature of central government administrative and development polices imposes impediments on local governments' ability to strategically adopt local development plans, administrative structures, procedures and process over time. This would not be the case if local administrators' actions were truly locally driven. The study further reveals that local administrators face enormous daily dilemmas in pursuance of their duties. For instance, respondents echoed that over a period of ten years (that is, between January 2000 and January 2010), guidelines for local development planning changed from the Ghana Vision 2020 document to the Ghana Poverty Reduction Strategy (GPRS I), Growth and Poverty Reduction Strategy (GPRS II), and the Ghana Shared Growth and Development Agenda. Thus, by implication, within a ten-year period, the country has experienced two democratic governments, each changing its policy focus in short intervals with telling consequences for local level administrations which then struggle to design systematic programmes that respond to the needs of their populations. Often times, this situation forces a local administration to adopt a reactionary or knee-jerk strategy to deal with emerging issues. It further impacts on a local administration's capacities for fixity of purpose. That is, their abilities to strategically ground local development and administrative policies lie constantly in flux.

In most transitional countries, the social structure of local communities is based on mutual trust and reliability; such an elusive and constantly changing policy environment causes local administrators to 'lose face' with local communities. This is often compounded by their inability to implement previous plans prepared with the participation of such communities. The adoptive skills of local administrations are overstretched because, in such a continually changing environment and with limited control over policies, to be responsive to community needs and yet remain innovative becomes a perilous business.

Financial and budget planning

Financial discretion, coupled with the capacity to plan and implement locally devised policies, is essential for the proper functioning of local government organizations. Decentralized local governments in developing countries are variously challenged by the lack of fiscal decentralization in real terms (Crawford, 2008a; Jütting et al., 2005). This remains a norm in Ghana as decentralized local governments are systematically denied self-determination in the use of allocated resources in accordance with local realities.

Often lacking in viable taxable and other internally generated income sources, local administrations rely mainly on the District Assemblies Common Fund (DACF), a central government financial transfer, which constitutes over 80 per cent of most district assemblies' yearly expenditure (Banful, 2009); thus, the DACF remains a vital source of income for all local governments. In theory, local administrations are free to utilize this and other funds in accordance with their own budgets developed through a participatory process. However, the data from this study suggest that local autonomy in allocation or utilization is mere rhetoric. As Banful (2009) contends, this is because of occasional political manipulation of the formula for sharing the common fund, and of tinkering with funds for purposes other than those originally intended in ways that effectively defeat the true meaning of decentralized local administration. The interference in the management of this fund reduces the role of the district assemblies to sheer receptors or implementers of central government directives. This is aptly captured by Domfeh and Bawole's (2009) assertion that local government agencies have become merely administrative hubs for central government. For example, as regards the preparation and execution of financial budgets, local administrators are rendered ineffective and incapable of effectively bringing on board the local realities of communities they serve. The views of senior district administrators interviewed are summed up by the comments of one senior district administrator presented below:

> We are not allowed to prepare the budgets here […] but you know that a budget is well executed when the one executing it took part in preparing it […] they (central government) sit down in Accra and direct us to use matrixes (which is developed at the central government level). Every matrix is a set of activities both service and investment and when we get down there [Accra] we must allocate the money to those activities in the matrix […] sometimes we may have a local problem with say the district education service but we are not allowed to go beyond what is in the given matrix. Because of this we go and come and they have given us the activities short of what is on the ground here […] and when we give them the budget estimates they further cut it making it difficult for us to function.

This lack of freedom and discretion effectively renders the constitutional responsibility of local administrations to plan, harmonize and coordinate the implementation of all local integrated development moribund. Although local administrations can often anticipate the arrival of the DACF, they do not have any capacities to predict how much they are likely to receive. As Banful (2009) suggests, this is because no district assembly can adequately predict the variables that affect the allocation they get. These variables are changed yearly. In effect, this renders financial planning capacity ineffective.

Further, it is commonplace to find instances where the central government directs local administrations to spend a given percentage of their share of the District Assemblies Common Fund (DACF) on government-identified priorities. For instance, respondents point out that the government has often directed that 1 per cent of DACF be given to the district directorate of health to carry out malaria prevention programs. The central government points an accusing finger at a perceived 'acute shortage' of skilled personnel at the local level as justification for its reluctance to allow local administration a free hand to operate. As claimed by one district administrator, there is this 'funny feeling at the national level that there is inadequate managerial capacity at the district level', for which reason the central government does not want to let go. Sakyi (2008b) found the same phenomenon when he studied decentralized health administration in the Sekyere West district of Ghana.[1] In theory, decentralized administrations have control over financial budget and expenditure decisions but in practice, these decisions are subject to directives from the central government or its relevant ministry to which local administrators must comply without questioning. This, in our view, incapacitates local administrators' ability to operate in a decentralized manner.

Adequacy and reliability of funds

The above issues translate directly to financial inadequacies at the local level. The data overwhelmingly suggest funding as the main capacity challenge to proper functioning of the local administrations. As mentioned earlier, local administrations depend heavily on the District Assemblies Common Fund (DACF) to run their major projects and programs. Two other sources were highlighted by the interviewees, that is, internally generated and donor funds. All three sources, the data reveal, are challenge-infected and hence cannot be relied upon. Accordingly:

> We don't have adequate resources to implement our activities. You see, the inadequate resources stem from the fact that before we do our [local] planning we always look at the District Assemblies Common Fund, which is a major source [sic] of funding ... then we also make projections of the donor funding we are going to get [...] In most cases donor funding tends not to come in or they come not in accordance to the quantities that we are expecting. As for the internally generated funds, they always go into fuel and other running cost, hardly do we execute any physical projects with our internally generated funds. (Senior local administrator)

In addition to the restrictive and inadequate nature of the common fund, there are also practical issues not far removed from the policy challenges. Not only is the common fund insufficient, it is also distributed in an untimely way. For example, in one of the local government administrations surveyed, it was revealed that they received the second quarter transfers of their share of the Common Fund for 2010 in the first quarter of 2011. District assemblies invariably face catastrophic income shortages on one hand and enormous performance expectations from local communities on the other. This limits their capacities to be fluid in delivering locally relevant services. In effect, the realities surrounding the flow of funds bear little resemblance to the attractively presented plans that are drawn up and lodged at the assembly. In the words of a respondent (community development officer), 'without money you cannot carry out any project and if you even start and along the line there is no money to complete, it would be standing there […]'.

Two factors account for this income incapacity. First, local administrations do not have a viable tax collection base as central government is said to hold on to all 'lucrative tax centres, while local government has access to only low yielding taxes such as basic rates and market tolls' (Crawford, 2008b; Nkrumah, 2000). However, the literature suggests that tax raising abilities of local administrations are critical ingredients to the capacities of such administrations to function properly (Jütting et al., 2005). Incidentally, because local administrations are left with uneconomic tax bases, interviewees pointed out that it was not economically wise to invest the rather meagre funds available to collect low yielding taxes because these districts are largely scattered and sparsely populated with very little or no taxable local economic activities. For this reason, some assemblies generate as little as 5 per cent of their income internally. It is estimated that up to 97 per cent of the population in some local administration jurisdictions are peasant farmers; they fall within the poorest occupational group in rural Ghana, and therefore tax revenues are very insignificant.

Secondly, the DACF, the main source of income for local administration, is often subject to heavy 'deductions at source'. Upon conducting a recent due diligence audit, one of the districts interviewed realized that almost 47 per cent of their share of the Common Fund had been deducted by the central government for other purposes for which they had no hand in determining. Another district pointed out that during the last quarter of 2010, for instance, after the government deductions, they were in a deficit. The districts point out that the central government makes such deductions to fund certain 'national policies' which were introduced without the budgetary allocations that were needed. This is probably why Crawford (2008b: 253) opined that local administration revenues in Ghana remain limited and 'subject to central government "earmarks" over its expenditure'.

Entity autonomy and freedom to function

As already observed, there is very little leverage for local government authorities to function effectively and efficiently. The literature on decentralization in Ghana has highlighted the need for an unambiguous delineation of functions between the local and central government as a sure condition for success (Crawford, 2008a: 252;

Jütting et al., 2005). Our findings coincide with Crawford's (2008a: 252) that contrary to provisions of District Assemblies Act 462, 1993, the abilities of district assemblies to implement their functions as per Act 462 is limited. In a situation where there is limited fiscal decentralization, local administrations are bound to be perpetually dependent on the whims and caprices of the central government which effectively curtails their function as independent units. This finding confirms a recent report of the Institute of Economic Affairs that 'although the 1992 Constitution places emphasis on the importance of decentralization, the reality on the ground is different and that real power resides in the central government, not the local government' (see Daily Graphic, 2011).

Strikingly, we find that the rarity of capacity in quality and quantity as identified by Sakyi (2008b: 315) is very much part of the larger organizational deficiency of local administrations in Ghana. It may well have accounted for the inability of a large proportion of local administrators to recognize that the full autonomy of their administration is necessary to ensure proper functioning as truly responsive to the interest of local communities. We note that long-standing attachment to central government has probably led local administrations to accept such dependency as the norm. Some local administrators opined that they are not mature enough to be autonomous. It appears such fears are fuelled more by an incomplete understanding of the decentralized administrative system in itself than anything else. For instance, some interviewees in this study seem to misconstrue the insufficiency of local funds enough to suggest that local administrations should not be fully autonomous. This appears contrary to recognizing that the half-hearted attitude by the central government to fully implementing decentralization is to blame for the financial incapacities at the local level. For example, one of those in favour of local–central dependence at the local level argued that

> this is because, they have not been able to get enough funds […] in order to meet all our needs […] assuming they decentralised us and they ask us to pay ourselves, how can we pay ourselves? The internally generated funds in this district are so small and the data we have [for tax purposes] are not also reliable, so if they decentralise us we would run into financial crisis. (Senior officer in charge of Finance)

It would appear this consideration may be blamed for a lacklustre attitude of some local government administrators to be innovative and seek out alternative sources of funding for local activities. In addition, the data show that the various decentralized departments which are under the district assembly are resource starved. They lack the budget and logistics needed to carry out daily duties resulting in the underperformance of the local administration. This situation leaves departments powerless to deliver their annual action plans and to act promptly to deal with emergent situations. In the words of one interviewee:

> We have no budget at all to run our services so we depend on other organisations (NGOs) and the district assembly, […] so when I am in the field and I see

issues that are directly related to my department, I feel shy [and incapable] to reveal my mother department to the people [...] all because I don't have my own. (Head of a decentralized department)

This finding in itself suggests an uneasy relationship between the decentralized departments and the local administration in terms of control and utilization of district-wide budgets. The decentralized departments, according to the findings of this study, receive budgets directly from their mother ministries in Accra; they implement their own programs and in most cases view the local administration as an external entity when it comes to dealing with budgets. Research shows that an 'estimated 85% of government funds at the district level are not controlled by the district assembly' (Crawford, 2008a: 250). On the whole this mistrust in itself is a constraint to the proper functioning of the entire local administration. When asked if their local administration has the autonomy and freedom to function as an entity one respondent clearly identified the lack of empowerment felt at the local level:

it depends, for instance, there are certain projects that are awarded by the central government, as we are sitting now [...] when an issue related to this department is reported [...] we should act immediately, [but] the assembly would have to call Accra to come and sort it out for them [...] so certain things are done at the national level and others are done at the local level [...] I would say that we do not have the freedom and ability to do everything.

Indeed, this feeling of powerlessness is likely, in the long run, to quell any desire among public officials based at the local level to act in the interest of local people. It further dampens the passion to deliver public services in an effective and efficient manner, leading logically to underperformance. Another peculiar hindrance in the ability to deliver effective and efficient services to local people observed from this study is the lack of incentive to motivate actors within laid down structures at the local level. This has implications for local administrations' capacities to 'plan, initiate, co-ordinate, manage and execute policies in respect to matters affecting local people' as contained in Article 240[2][b] of the 1992 Constitution of Ghana. For instance, members of the district assembly, area councils and unit committees work on a voluntary basis. They point out that, at times, they have to use their personal resources to carry out activities of the district assembly and this serves as a disincentive to perform effectively. The local administrators opined that the local administration does not have a budget to support the activities of these units; while they could reasonably expect some extra provision from central government, this is not forthcoming.

Local institutional, personnel capacities and competencies

Perceptions of the availability of local capacities to effectively plan implement and generally deliver effective and efficient services at the local level appeared mixed. Interestingly, some interviewees interpreted questions about personnel capacities to mean their own abilities and hence were quick to defend that there is adequate and capable personnel at the district level, citing their own levels of education and qualifications as evidence of this competence. It is important to note, however, that personnel capacities go beyond the mere schooling of administrators. It involves other competencies such as innovation, leadership skills, institutional memories and indeed astute social and emotional abilities to function within the chaotic nature of local government, as summarized by one interviewee:

> I would say there is the human capacity … but the issue of competencies is still a problem, not all of them have the capacities to function as is required … material capacity and technical know-how is not sufficient, we need more training … we need more in all aspects, but in terms of human resources we need more particularly in the quality.

Even though some respondents stated the view that appropriate human resources are available, we found that, in terms the adequacy of personnel capacity, there is a great deal of insufficiency. In fact, some local administrators agreed that there are issues of inadequacy of personnel capacities. For example, one interviewee stated: 'in most cases at the assembly level only two or three people have a semblance of the capacity we need to function … when those people are not there then there are problems … so there is an issue of capacity'.

The dearth of capacities within various decentralized departments becomes even more prominent when viewed in terms of personnel's abilities to realistically develop workable plans and co-ordinate related activities. We observe that this is an area where acute capacity challenges are apparent in many decentralized local administrations. In addition to non-availability of personnel to carry out evidence-based planning, decentralized departments themselves do not fully appreciate the need for planning. Further, those who do plan, plan directly with their mother ministries. This approach, in effect, circumvents and then isolates the local government. In addition, even though the district coordinating unit together with stakeholders from decentralized departments can discipline non-performing or offending staff, the highest form or action they can take against such staff is to suspend them; dismissal, or even transfer, is not an option. Indeed, our findings coincide with Sakyi's (2008a: 314) finding that 'the degree of transfer of authority in respect to human resource matters' remains a 'taboo' area in which district administrators can only meddle at their own peril.

Again, it is observed that due to interferences from above, there is a scarcity of staff commitment to follow due process. For instance, when it comes to the award of local contracts, a majority of those who win contracts are not qualified to execute them; yet, due to their political patronage, such contracts are awarded to them. Local administrators with a responsibility to monitor the delivery of services are powerless and unable to follow due process in carrying out their duties. The result is the delivery of sub-standard jobs at best. Further, perceptions of other institutional capacities are not altogether very different. The study found that, even when there is a modicum of personnel capacity and competence coupled with a willingness to deliver high-quality services, material and logistical insufficiencies effectively block this enthusiasm. Local administrations are without the very basic tools to enhance their performance. Decentralized departments go without adequate arrangements for transport and logistical needs that would enable them to perform. In the words of one interviewee:

> we have two offices, at least you would have expected that when you come you would see computers, but look at it … not even curtains!!, so generally, the constraint facing the assembly in its development drive is logistics.

Conclusions

The chapter has addressed the question of capacity constraint of local public administrations to effective and efficient performance. We note that governments have variously justified many actions on the basis of the promise of NPM reforms and that Ghana's decentralized local administration is no exception. So much has been promised under the umbrella of NPM-type local administration: empowerment, downward accountability, and efficiency and effectiveness to say the least. It is indicative from our findings that, due to contextual and cultural differences between institutions implementing NPM reforms, the outcomes vary greatly; this is explained by the apparent 'ambiguous nature of the NPM and the strength of national cultures and institutional patterns' (Pollitt, Thiel and Homburg, 2007: 2). Thus, we conclude that, in Ghana, it is difficult to say that NPM-type decentralization has led to efficiency and effectiveness in decentralized local administration.

Some of the major preconditions for realizing efficiency and effectiveness in decentralized local administration include the existence of strong local capacity, vibrant and properly functioning local institutions and a strong local political capacity (Smoke, 2003, 2006). We have found, contrary to the above, that there is a paucity of local capacity in terms of quality and quantity for organizational effectiveness in the quest to address local development needs. This incapacity tends to become more prominent as one moves laterally along the decentralized departments within the local administration. In particular, it would appear that without these local capacities, decentralization could be said to have occurred in a vacuum.

There is no doubt that decentralized local administration holds promise in the provision of services that are locally relevant and acceptable to all stakeholders. However, this appears a far cry from the experiences within local administrations where financial and managerial incapacity are more of a daily reality. Our findings echo the fact that, in Ghana, decentralization, in functional terms, is yet to arrive at the local level. We conclude that, on the whole, the inability of local administrations to perform as expected can be attributed to a variety of deficiencies coupled, importantly, with central government's lacklustre attitude towards real decentralization. Decentralization, as outlined in LGA 1993, Act 462, is found to be severely compromised by central government's reluctance to fully decentralize (Crawford, 2008b) in ways that would ensure that such local administrations are able to function effectively as institutions of local self-governance. In addition to larger organizational deficiency of local administrations, a significant proportion of local administrators themselves fail to recognize that the full autonomy of their administration is necessary to ensure proper functioning in a manner that is truly responsive to the interest of local communities.

When operating effectively, decentralized local administrations become relevant to the lives of the people that they serve (Grindle, 2007). In recognition of this perspective, enormous expectations are placed upon local administrations in Northern Ghana from citizens who are seeking better health and education services, economic opportunities, and security. There is therefore pressure on local administrations to create public value in services delivery in ways that contribute to a meaningful public life. It would appear from the evidence adduced in this study that local administrations, confronted by various capacity challenges, are struggling with how best to carry citizen expectations and statutory responsibilities for the provision of public services including socio-economic development at the local level.

New public management–type decentralization which, some claim, has been applied at the local level in Ghana, appears to have failed to cast off the centralizing powers of central government in order to operate in a decentralized manner in accordance with the dictates of Local Government Act 462 and the provisions contained in the 1992 Republican Constitution. As the literature suggests, for the benefits of NPM-type decentralized local administration to accrue at any point in the public service, fundamental changes to the basic administrative culture, management systems and central government support is a necessity (Asante and Ayee, 2004). Further, reliance on hierarchical structures should be curtailed while the operational autonomy of line managers and agencies at the local level should be facilitated. It is important that increased local capacity and openness to change takes centre stage in local public administration where important decisions on planning services delivery and resource allocation are made close to the point of delivery.

Note

1   This is in the southern sector of the country while our study focused on the northern sector.

References

Ahwoi, K. (2010). *Local Government and Decentralisation in Ghana.* Accra: Unimax Macmilan.

Andersen, J. A. (2010). Assessing public managers' change-oriented behavior: are private managers caught in the doldrums? *International Journal of Public Administration*, 33(6), 335–345.

Antwi, K. B., Analoui, F. and Cusworth, J. W. (2007). *Human Resource Development Challenges Facing Decentralized Local Governments in Africa: Empirical Evidence from Ghana.* Paper presented at Leadership, Learning, Institutes and Public Service: A conference for leaders who shape and deliever leaning and development. Accra, Ghana.

Asante, F. A. and Ayee, R. A. (2004). Decentralization and poverty reduction. University of Ghana. Available at www.isser.org/Decentralization_Asante_Ayee.pdf. Accessed 3 August 2011.

Awortwi, N. (2011). An unbreakable path? A comparative study of decentralization and local government development trajectories in Ghana and Uganda. *International Review of Administrative Sciences*, 77(2), 347–377.

Ayeni, V. (2002). *Public Sector Reform in Developing Countries: a Handbook of Commonwealth Experiences*. London Publication Unit, Commonwealth Secretariat.

Banful, A. B. (2009). Do institutions limit clientelism? A study of the District Assemblies Common Fund in Ghana (D. S. a. G. Division, Trans.). *IFPRI Discussion Paper 00855*. Washington: International Food Policy Research Institute.

Barima, A. K. and Analoui, F. (2010). Challenges of making donor-driven public sector reform in sub-Saharan Africa sustainable: some experiences from Ghana. *International Journal of Public Administration*, 33(12), 635–647.

Bergh, S. I. (2010). Assessing the scope for partnerships between local governments and community-based organizations: findings from rural Morocco. *International Journal of Public Administration*, 33(12), 740–751.

Berman, E. (1995). Employee empowerment in state agencies: a survey of progress. *International Journal of Public Administration*, 18(5), 833–850.

Berry, F. S. (2007). Strategic planning as a tool for managing organizational change. *International Journal of Public Administration*, 30(3), 331–346.

Crawford, G. (2004a). Democratic decentralisation in Ghana: issues and prospects. *POLIS Working Paper No. 9*. Leeds: School of Politics and International Studies, University of Leeds.

Crawford, G. (2004b). The European Union and democracy promotion in Africa: the case of Ghana. *POLIS Working Paper No. 10*. Leeds: School of Politics and International Studies, University of Leeds.

Crawford, G. (2008a). Decentralization and the limits to poverty reduction: findings from Ghana. *Oxford Development Studies*, 36(2), 235–258.

Crawford, G. (2008b). Poverty and the politics of (de)centralisation. In Crawford, G. and Hartman, C. (eds.), *Decentralisation in Africa: A Pathway Out of Poverty and Conflict?* Amsterdam: Amsterdam University Press.

Crawford, G. (2009). 'Making democracy a reality'? The politics of decentralisation and the limits to local democracy in Ghana. *Journal of Contemporary African Studies*, 27(1), 57–83.

Crawford, G. and Hartman, C. (2008). Introduction: decentralisation as a pathway out of poverty and conflict? In Crawford, G. and Hartman, C. (eds.), *Decentralisation in Africa: A Pathway out of Poverty and Conflict?* Amsterdam: Amsterdam University Press.

Daily Graphic. (2011). Ghana needs national development policy – IEA Survey. Available at http://news.myjoyonline.com/news/201103/62111.asp. Accessed 12 August 2011.

Dijk, M. P. v. (2008). The impact of decentralisation on poverty in Tanzania. In Crawford, G. and Hartman, C. (eds.), *Decentralisation in Africa: A Pathway out of Poverty and Conflict?* Amsterdam: Amsterdam University Press.

Domfeh, K. A. and Bawole, J. N. (2009). Localising and sustaining poverty reduction: experiences from Ghana. *Management of Environmental Quality: An International Journal*, 20(5), 490–505.

Ellison, B. A. (2006). Bureaucratic politics as agency competition: a comparative perspective. *International Journal of Public Administration*, 29(13), 1259–1283.

Feldheim, M. A. (2007). Public sector downsizing and employee trust. *International Journal of Public Administration*, 30(3), 249–270.

Grindle, M. S. (2007). *Going Local: Decentralisation, Democratization and the Promise of Good Governance*. Princeton and Oxford: Princeton University Press.

Haque, M. S. (2010). Decentralizing local governance in Thailand: contemporary trends and challenges. *International Journal of Public Administration*, 33(12), 673–688.

Hays, S. W. and Whitney, S. B. (1997). Reinventing the personnel function: lessons learned from hope-filled beginning in one state. *American Review of Public Administration*, 27(4), 324–342.

Hope, K. R., Sr. (2001). The New Public Management: context and practice in Africa. *International Public Management Journal*, 4, 119–134.

Jan van Helden, G., Johnsen, Å. and Vakkuri, J. (2008). Distinctive research patterns on public sector performance measurement of public administration and accounting disciplines. *Public Management Review*, 10(5), 641–651.

Jütting, J., Corsi, E., Kauffmann, C., McDonnell, I., Osterrieder, H., Pinaud, N. and Wegner, L. (2005). What makes decentralisation in developing countries pro-poor? *The European Journal of Development Research*, 17(4), 626–648.

Larbi, G. A. (1999). *The New Public Management Approach and Crisis States*. Geneva: UNRISD.

Liou, K. T. (2007). Introduction. *International Journal of Public Administration*, 30(3), 227–229.

McCarney, P. L. (ed.). (1996). *The Changing Nature of Local Government in Developing Countries*. Toronto: University of Toronto Press Incorporated.

Morgan, P. (2006). *Case Study on Capacity, Change and Performance: The Concept of Capacity*. Maastricht: European Centre for Development Policy Management.

Nkrumah, S. A. (2000). Decentralisation for good governance and development: the Ghanaian experience. *Regional Development Dialogue*, 21(1), 53–67.

Obama, B. (2009). Obama Ghana Speech. Full text available at www.huffingtonpost.com/2009/07/11/obama-ghana-speech-full-t_n_230009.html. Accessed 28 January 2011.

Ohemeng, F. L. K. (2009). Constraints in the implementation of performance management systems in developing countries. *International Journal of Cross Cultural Management*, 9(1), 109–132. doi: 10.1177/1470595808101158.

Pallangyo, W. and Rees, C. J. (2010). Local government reform programs and human resource capacity building in Africa: evidence from local government authorities (LGAs) in Tanzania. *International Journal of Public Administration*, 33(12), 728–739.

Pollitt, C., Thiel, S. v. and Homburg, V. (2007). New Public Management in Europe. Available from ESCP-EAP European School of Management, http://publishing.eur.nl/ir/darenet/asset/11553/BSK-2007-004.pdf. Accessed 20 March 2011.

Rees, C. J. and Hossain, F. (2010). Perspectives on decentralization and local governance in developing and transitional countries. *International Journal of Public Administration*, 33(12), 581–587.

Sakyi, K. E. (2008a). Factors constraining public sector reform implementation in Africa: a Ghanaian case study. *African Administrative Studies*, 70, 1–24.

Sakyi, K. E. (2008b). Implementing decentralised management in Ghana: the experience of the Sekyere West District Health Administration. *Leadership in Health Services*, 21(4), 307–319.

Smoke, P. (2003). Decentralisation in Africa: goals, dimensions, myths and challenges. *Public Administration and Development*, 23(1), 7–16.

Smoke, P. (2006). Fiscal decentralisation policy in developing countries: bridging theory and reality. In Bangura, Y. and Larbi, G. (eds.), *Public Setor Reform in Developing Countries: Capacity Challenges to improve Services*. London: Palgrave Macmillan.

Steiner, S. (2008). Constraints on the implementation of decentralisation and implementation for poverty reduction – the case Of Uganda. In Crawford, G. and Hartman, C. (eds.), *Decentralisation in Africa: A Pathway out of Poverty and Conflict?* Amsterdam: Amsterdam University Press.

Tandon, R. (2001). Capacity building for effective local self-governance. *Participation & Governance*, 7(20), 13–17.

Tillema, S., Mimba, N. P. S. H. and van Helden, G. J. (2010). Understanding the changing role of public sector performance measurement in less developed countries. *Public Administration and Development*, 30(3), 203–214. doi: 10.1002/pad.561.

World Bank. (1998). *Rethinking Decentralisation in Developing Countries*. Washington, DC: World Bank.

Yin, R. (1994). *Case Study Research: Design and Methods* (2nd ed.). Thousand Oaks, CA: Sage Publications.

11 HRM in small and medium-sized enterprises in China

Towards a theoretical framework of determinants and HRM practices

Shaoheng Li and Christopher J. Rees

Introduction

Small and medium-sized enterprises (SMEs) across the world play an increasingly important role in stimulating national and global economies, promoting technology and innovation, and enhancing social stability by reducing poverty and creating employment opportunities (Atherton and Fairbanks, 2006; Ayyagari et al., 2011; Cunningham, 2011). Given that China is in a transitional economy, SMEs considerably impact on the development of the whole nation. For example, it has been reported that, in China, SMEs make up 99 per cent of registered firms and account for 80 per cent of job creation, 60 per cent of GDP, 50 per cent of tax revenue and 66 per cent of patent inventions (Cunningham, 2010, 2011; Xinhua Net, 2011).

SMEs in China face great challenges and difficulties. It is noted that managerial problems are one of the key issues that constrain SME growth, for example, shortage of skilled workers and managerial talents, deficiency of incentive mechanisms, insufficient training and an unstructured compensation system (Cooke, 2012; Cunningham and Rowley, 2008; Rutherford et al., 2003). It is necessary to address HRM issues to facilitate the sustainable development of SMEs. As suggested by Cunningham and Rowley (2008: 361), 'HRM may provide a vehicle for SMEs to reduce the problems they face'.

However, SMEs are largely under-researched in existing HRM literature, especially in China. One review of 265 articles relating to HRM in China published in 34 leading journals from 1998 to 2007 showed that SMEs are absent from ten major researched topics (Cooke, 2009a). Multinational corporations, joint ventures and large state-owned enterprises tend to be favoured as studying targets (Li and Sheldon, 2010). Although some contributions have been made, the number, the scope and the depth of research publications on the subject remains sparse and limited (Warner and Rowley, 2010). Given the significant role of SMEs and the dearth of research in that area, the main objective of this chapter is to develop and present a framework to study the determinants and HRM practices in SMEs in the mainland of China.

The chapter commences by addressing the complex interpretation of the term 'SME' with reference to the context of China. Then it presents a comprehensive picture of diverse HRM practices by functions in SMEs. Based on previous theoretical work, including concepts drawn from the Harvard framework, institutional theory and the framework of HRM in developing countries, it further identifies three broad types of factors that shape HRM practices in Chinese SMEs, namely organizational, institutional and cultural factors. A conceptual framework is then proposed in the final sections of the chapter. The contributions and limitations are discussed in the conclusion.

The term 'SME'

There is no universal definition of SME due to its dynamic nature and regional and sector differences. Various parameters are employed to define it, such as the number of employees, annual revenue, the amount of invested capital, value of fixed assets and production capability (De Kok et al., 2013; Harvie and Lee, 2002). It is noted that the number of employees tends to be the most widely used criterion (De Kok et al., 2013). In addition, an SME may be interpreted by multiple indicators or a mono standard; these multiple perspectives exacerbate the debatable classification of the term.

China has upgraded SME classifications four times since the People's Republic of China (PRC) was founded (Cunningham, 2011) yet the issue remains complex as SMEs are not only defined by quantitative measures but also interpreted by qualitative means. The latest quantitative criteria, 'Provisions on the Standards for SMEs', were released in 2011, according to which SMEs are made up of micro, small and medium enterprises (PRC, 2011). The criteria highlight the great variance in lower and upper limits of the definition across sectors. For instance, in wholesale and warehousing industries, an enterprise with fewer than 200 people falls into the category of SMEs whereas in the information transmission sector, the cut-off point increases ten times to 2,000 people.

Apart from quantitative definitions, SMEs in China can be qualitatively categorized by geographic location of registration and ownership structure. Cunningham (2011) presented an illustration where SMEs are categorized as rural and urban SMEs. Rural SMEs consist of town and village enterprises (TVEs), private enterprises (PEs) and self-employed individuals (SEIs) while urban SMEs are made up of state-owned enterprises (SOEs), collective-owned enterprises (COEs), PEs, SEIs and other ownership forms (mainly joint ventures). It needs to be emphasized that privately owned SMEs account for the majority of SMEs while SOEs are typically large-sized (ibid.).

It can be seen that the classification of SMEs in China is multi-dimensional and is evolving along with their development in a dynamic environment. Thus, it is necessary to revisit the definition when examining SME issues.

Current situation of HRM practices in SMEs

The nature of HRM in SMEs is typically viewed as personalized, informal, flexible, ad hoc, complex, short-term and even contradictory (Harney and Dundon, 2006; Richbell et al., 2010; Singh and Vohra, 2009). Given the broad range of HRM practices, this chapter focuses on those under five generic HR functions, namely planning, recruitment and selection, training and development, performance management and reward management.

HR planning practices appear to be largely absent and ignored in comparison with others in SMEs. It is also an extremely under-researched area except in a few cases. A survey of 89 SMEs in Vietnam reveals that only 16 per cent of them have written HRM plans (Nguyen and Bryant, 2004). In a similar vein, Singh and Vohra (2009) found that a quarter of the participant Indian SMEs (N = 143) conduct formal HR planning on a regular basis. With respect to Chinese SMEs, little attention has been paid to planning practices in literature (see Cunningham, 2010).

Practices under the **recruitment and selection (R&S)** domain are widely adopted in SMEs as those cannot be avoided as long as an organization operates. However, it is claimed that the practices are typically informal and low cost as SMEs are generally constrained by insufficient financial budget, inaccessibility to resources and lack of professionals with HRM expertise (Barrett and Mayson, 2007; Cunningham, 2010; Young-Thelin and Boluk, 2012). A number of researchers suggest that SMEs predominately adopt walk-in, employee referral, government agencies and newspapers as recruitment sources and select candidates by reference checks, resume review and interviews (Kotey and Slade, 2005; Singh and Vohra, 2009; Wiesner and McDonald, 2001; Young-Thelin and Boluk, 2012).

Cunningham's (2010) research consisting of 114 SMEs in China indicates that four-fifths of firms are engaged in R&S practices and further concludes recruitment is the most frequently involved HR function. It is observed that SMEs are able to source talents from a broader labour market but the methods and techniques remain informal such as prevalent internal and interpersonal network-based recruitment (ibid.).

Training and development (T&D) practices seem to be eschewed by the vast majority of SMEs (Nguyen and Bryant, 2004; Richbell et al., 2010). Arguably, this neglect of a cornerstone of HRM may be attributable to five factors associated with the very nature of SMEs:

1 *Cost*: The cost of investments in people appears to be in conflict with limited financial budget (Storey, 2004).
2 *Long-term orientation*: Long-term orientation of development programs seems to be incompatible with the short-term outlook and shorter lifespan of SMEs (Cunningham, 2010). As noted by Nguyen and Bryant (2004: 607), 'practices that have longer term implications are … least likely to be adopted (in SMEs)'.
3 *Employers' perceptions*: They believe employees are competent and do not perceive skill shortage as a problem (Richbell et al., 2010).
4 *Job hopping*: Owners/managers are concerned about possible job hopping if their employees' capabilities are enhanced by training (Cassell et al., 2002).
5 *Lack of HRM professionals*: Even if owners/managers are willing to engage in T&D, the lack of HRM professionals would lead to practical problems in formulating policies and implementing activities.

Some contributions have been made in different contexts where two main points can be elicited from existing studies. First, on-the-job, in-house training is the most widely used method in SMEs (Kotey and Slade, 2005; Richbell et al., 2010; Wiesner and McDonald, 2001), though, notably, managerial employees are more likely to receive formal, external T&D opportunities in comparison with non-managerial employees (Kotey and Slade, 2005). Second, in relation to China, Cunningham's (2010) study suggests that although many SMEs engage in T&D, the contents are mainly task-orientated in which little emphasis is placed on long-term employee development.

Performance management (PM) plays a vital role in HRM system as it aligns different HR functions to take effect together (Boxall and Purcell, 2003). Nevertheless, the practices in SMEs tend to be informal and ad hoc, as reflected by the absence of measurable criteria and rating scales, irregular implementation of appraisals, failures to provide feedback and limited use of appraisal results (Barrett and Mayson, 2007; Cassell et al., 2002; Kim and Gao, 2010; Nguyen and Bryant, 2004). Singh and Vohra's (2009) survey in India shows appraisal criteria are, in the main, based on supervisors' personal observations. On the other hand, an optimistic picture is presented by Kotey and Slade's (2005) investigation in Australia in which performance appraisals are adopted by 80 per cent of SMEs with clear rating scales and the results are linked to training for poor performers.

In China, Western PM has been viewed to be in contradiction with traditional Chinese culture (Cooke, 2012). Limited focus has been placed on the SME sector with the exception of two studies. The findings of Cooke's (2009b) research indicate that only one third of private firms (N = 65) have formal appraisals relating to rewards. Further, Kim and Gao (2010) found that smaller family firms rarely implement formal appraisal and provide feedback.

Reward management (RM) is crucial for SMEs as remuneration is weighted more heavily on attracting and retaining talents compared with larger corporations where other highly valued items might be offered such as sufficient T&D opportunities (Cardon and Stevens, 2004). Inconsistent findings have been suggested in previous literature. In the UK, Bacon and Hoque (2005) found that only 16 per cent of private SMEs (N = 388) employ performance-related pay. By contrast, Singh and Vohra (2009) revealed that 70 per cent of the surveyed Indian SMEs state the basis for reward is working performance and over 50 per cent of them adopt annual increments and bonus. Similarly, Wiesner and McDonald (2001) reported that performance-based pay is present in over 90 per cent of the sampled Australian SMEs.

In respect of China, RM practices have been evolving since the 'iron rice bowl' era. The principle of pay is shifting from systems promoting egalitarianism and respect for age/seniority to systems emphasizing performance and responsibility, especially in the private sector (Cooke, 2012; Kim and Gao, 2010). It is noted that RM is an under-researched topic (Cooke, 2012). Although Kim and Gao's (2010) research investigated small family firms, the specific compensation practices were not mentioned as the objective of the study was to examine the size effect. Given that the vast majority of SMEs are in the private sector, three main characteristics of firms in the private sector, as summarized by Cooke (2012), should provide some clues. These characteristics are (1) compositions of compensation package remain simple; (2) performance-related pay is adopted by increasing employers; and (3) pay levels are predominately determined by employers where there is little space for employees to negotiate (ibid.).

Based on the review above, some key points can be summarized as follows. Planning practices tend to be the least underexplored area. Informal and low-cost methods and techniques remain prevalent in R&S. T&D opportunities are limited, especially for grassroots employees. PM is generally characterized by subjective criteria, irregular implementation and poor use of appraisal results. The means of rewards in SMEs are simple but performance is usually taken into account. Some inconsistent findings imply the diversity of HRM practices in the SME sector due to numerous influential factors. On the one hand, evidence suggests that HRM practices in Chinese SMEs share some features in common. On the other hand, they have unique characteristics attributed to the ideology and culture. Thus, it is necessary to look at the factors that shape HRM practices in Chinese SMEs.

Factors influencing HRM practices in SMEs

It is well documented that a wide range of factors may influence the adoption of HRM practices in SMEs. The link has been theoretically underpinned by several established HRM frameworks and theories.

The Harvard framework illustrates the connection between HRM choices and two broad factors, namely stakeholder interest and situational factors (Beer et al., 1984). Institutional theory, particularly new institutionalism, is also helpful in understanding determinants of HRM practices (Tsai, 2010). It is argued that in order to obtain legitimacy and survive, organizations need to comply with institutional expectations, which would generate homogeneity over time (Paauwe and Boselie, 2003). Focusing on the HRM field, Paauwe and Boselie (2003: 61) interpret three mechanisms of forming isomorphism as (1) 'coercive: implementation as a result of regulatory pressures', i.e. laws, regulations, conventions and labour union requirements; (2) 'mimetic: imitation as a result of uncertainty and trends/fads', which suggests organizations could imitate competitors' policies/practices to avoid uncertainty or implement certain fashionable practices; and (3) 'normative: management control system, depending on the professionalization of an employee group', which indicates that the workforce's professional level is influential to practices.

It is apparent that those theories are rooted in Western societies which inherently reflect Western features. Whether they could be applied to other contexts such as China remains debatable despite the contributions made by various scholars (Cooke, 2009b, 2012; Cunningham, 2011; Cunningham and Rowley, 2008; Warner, 2010, 2011). Given that China is a developing country vis-à-vis the criteria of the World Bank (2012), a HRM framework proposed by Budhwar and Debrah (2001) focusing on the developing world is found to be relevant at this juncture.

Budhwar and Debrah's framework illustrates that there are three levels of factors shaping national patterns of HRM, namely 'national factors' consisting of culture, institutions, business environment and sector, 'contingent variables' such as firm size, age, ownership, current life-cycle stage, various stakeholders' interests, trade unions and HR strategies, and 'organisational strategies and policies' (Budhwar and Debrah, 2001: 6). The framework has some strengths and weaknesses which need to be addressed. Unlike Western-focused models, it places a particular emphasis on developing countries, which paves the way of theoretical understanding of HRM in a different context. In addition, it highlights a finite set of national factors that have greater impacts rather than encompassing all elements (Taylor et al., 1996). Thus, those key factors could be adopted and examined with priorities by researchers (Budhwar and Debrah, 2001). But the framework separates HR strategies and organizational strategies at two different levels. Though the proactive role of HR strategies is stressed, the matching and integration between them is relatively important (Holbeche, 2009).

By drawing on some concepts from the theories and frameworks discussed above, this chapter, with a particular focus on SMEs in China, proposes a framework outline in Figure 11.1. The framework highlights three broad types of factors shaping HRM practices in SMEs in China, namely organizational, institutional and cultural factors. They are elaborated in the following sections.

Organizational Factors

Organizational factors relate to firms' attributes and features, such as size, age, sector, ownership, geographical location, presence of HRM professionals/department, managerial style and current employees.

There is substantial evidence that firm size is a key predictor in explaining variation of HRM practices in SMEs. In other words, the bigger firms are, the more likely they are to adopt formal HRM practices (Bacon and Hoque, 2005; Richbell et al., 2010; Singh and Vohra, 2009). Though the effect is well documented, it should not be considered in isolation as certain patterns of HRM practices tend to be shaped by

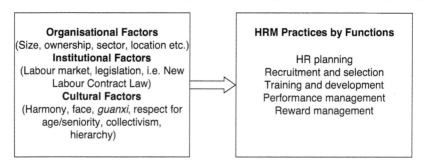

Figure 11.1 A framework of determinants and HRM practices in SMEs in China
Source: Compiled by the authors

the interplay of diverse parameters rather than a sole factor (Harney and Dundon, 2007; Tsai, 2010). For instance, size is directly associated with resource availability (Kim and Gao, 2010). Sector is another parameter that contributes to homogeneity and heterogeneity within and across industries (Urbano and Yordanova, 2008). According to Tsai's (2010) investigation, the adoption of HRM practices is homogenous within the high-tech industry in Taiwan. Urbano and Yordanova's (2008) empirical research suggests differences exist in subsectors of tourism. Ownership has been found influential as well. As noted by Kotey and Folker (2007), family firms are less likely to adopt professional training programs than non-family firms.

The effect of geographic location remains ambiguous, especially in China. Kim and Gao (2010) compare family firms located in eastern-coastal and inland areas and argue that location exerts little effect on variations in HRM practices. However, some researchers demonstrate it has significant influence on HRM choices (Ding et al., 2000). By analysing 62 JVs and SOEs in China, Ding et al. (2000) claim that the more southern and coastal the locations of firms, the more likely these firms are to employ sophisticated HRM practices, especially in relation to labour contract systems. Different regions in China vary tremendously in the conditions of economic environment. A more developed region tends to be beneficial to businesses because of its attractiveness for investment and the existence of richer pools of talent and markets (Warner et al., 2002). Thus, given the great gap in different areas of China, location needs to be considered as an influence on HRM practices in SMEs. There are additional organizational factors that could be influential, for example, the presence of HR personnel/department (Urbano and Yordanova, 2008), owners/managers' discretion/involvement (Singh and Vohra, 2009; Tsai, 2010), managerial style and current employees (Harney and Dundon, 2007).

It is noted that most organizational factors are globally generic in SMEs while institutional and cultural factors relating to Chinese characteristics tend to be exclusive to SMEs in China.

Institutional factors

Institutional factors are mainly concerned with political, legal, social, historical and economic dimensions. Given its broad coverage, this chapter mainly focuses on two aspects, legislation and the labour market, as they are sensitive to employment issues.

As discussed previously, the effect of legislation in shaping HRM practices has been theoretically underpinned by the coercive mechanism of institutional theory and the Harvard framework. Given various legislations that may impact on SMEs, the present discussion mainly considers the new Labour Contract Law of PRC (referred to as LCL hereafter). The rationale of the focus lies in three aspects. First, LCL is one of the most recently promulgated laws in China as it was enacted in 2008 (MHRSS, 2016). Second, the priority of LCL is concerned with employment relations in corporations, especially in relation to the regulation of informal employment activities in the private sector (Cooke, 2012). Third, the LCL has been the subject of heated debates but lacks exploration.

The LCL is widely regarded as a remarkable improvement upon the earlier Labour Law which failed to address increasing tensions in the private sector and rising labour disputes (Cooke, 2012; Wang et al., 2009). Employers tend to avoid establishing formal employment relations with employees in order to escape legal monitoring (Cooke, 2012). It was reported by a nationwide survey in 2005 that the labour contract signing rate was less than 20 per cent in the private sector (Xinhua Net, 2007). The LCL aims to create a stable and long-term employment relation by enhancing the labour contract system which particularly reinforces the legal protection of employees who are under informal employment, such as temporary employees and agency workers (Cooke, 2012). From firms' perspectives, it is viewed as a heavy burden due to increased labour cost mainly linked to social insurance premiums and redundancy pay: as noted by Chan (2012: 24), 'labour costs did increase for small and medium-size labour intensive businesses in low-end enterprises'.

The introduction of the non-fixed-term labour contract in the LCL (article 14) seems to be a particularly controversial issue (Cheng, 2009). The article stipulates that when the employee has been working ten years or more consecutively for the employer, and/or a fixed term contract was concluded twice prior to the renewal, a non-fixed-term labour contract shall be concluded unless the employee requests otherwise (MHRSS, 2016). It is questioned whether the introduction is reminiscent of the 'iron rice bowl' and 'job for life' era as it appears to set restrictions on terminating the employment contract (Cooke, 2012: 168). Overall, the LCL has a profound influence on regulating HRM policies and practices, especially for SMEs in the private sector.

The condition of the labour market significantly impacts on HRM practices in SMEs as it is directly associated with workforce supply. Evidence elicited from Harney and Dundon's (2006) study of six SMEs in Ireland shows that staffing practices are particularly affected. It is found that a small pool of qualified candidates in the labour market leads to more investment in recruitment practices, such as increased use of external agencies (ibid.). Investment in training practices may also be required if new recruits are not adequately skilled.

It is argued that the Chinese labour market is now more market-oriented than it used to be (Warner, 2011). During its development, there are three conflicts and problems embedded in the Chinese labour market. First of all, it remains at the 'nascent stage' (Zhu and Warner, 2005: 360), which is attributed to its late emergence in the 1980s after the introduction of economic reforms (Warner, 2011). These immaturities are reflected in the absence of sufficient regulations, effective monitoring mechanisms and transparent information systems (Zhu and Warner, 2005). As mentioned earlier, in order to avoid legal penalties, employers tend to be resistant in building formal relationships and regularizing employment practices, which conflicts with employees' growing self-awareness of protecting their own rights and interests in security, social insurance premiums, working hours and conditions (Cooke, 2012).

In addition, the situation of the Chinese labour market is complicated by the coexistence of two distinct employment styles. Along with the developing openness of the Chinese market, the western employment system introduced by MNCs has been challenging traditional Chinese employment styles characterized by 'master-servant employment relations', which is prevalent in small private firms (Zhu and Warner, 2005: 360). The situation becomes more complex when these two styles are mixed in varying degrees. This duality of influences compounds the generally accepted difficulty of designing effective employment systems.

Finally, the skilled labour shortage versus surplus unskilled workforce forms another conflict in the Chinese labour market (Cooke, 2012; Cunningham and Rowley, 2008). This structural imbalance is disadvantageous to both parties. A tremendous amount of unskilled labour is unemployed or trapped in low-wage jobs whereas numerous employers, especially SME owners, experience talent shortages due to their inability to attract and retain talent in the face of fierce competition from larger firms operating in the jobs market (Cooke, 2012; Cunningham and Rowley, 2008). Under such tough circumstances, SMEs are forced to enhance their HRM practices in staffing, T&D and compensation to better cope with the problems.

Cultural factors

National culture plays a vital role in affecting take-up and outcomes of HRM practices (Warner, 2010). Despite its gradually fading impact, especially on younger generations, Confucian ideology undoubtedly remains deep-rooted in social norms and values in the Chinese society (ibid.). Confucianism emphasizes harmony, *guanxi* (that is, relationship), preservation of face, respect for age/seniority, collectivism and hierarchy (Cooke, 2009a; Cunningham and Rowley, 2007; Wang et al., 2005).

Harmony, *guanxi* and preservation of face interact with one another and form complex interpersonal dynamics (Wong et al., 2010). Preservation of face tends to maintain harmony and build friendly relationships; harmony is created by maintaining good relationships and face (Cunningham and Rowley, 2007; Wong et al., 2010). *Guanxi* can be interpreted as interpersonal relationships, which are crucial in Chinese society (Chen and Tjosvold, 2007). It is claimed that *guanxi* could offer significant advantages in business and careers, such as assistance in gaining access, obtaining information/resources and being accepted as an insider in a relatively short period of time (Cunningham and Rowley, 2007). It is suggested that collectivism-orientated HRM practices are prevalent in some East Asian countries (Zhu et al., 2007). Those practices put a great emphasis on a team rather than an individual, for instance, selection with a preference of people who possess teamwork spirit, and training with a focus on enhancing team cooperation and the distribution of incentives based on team performance (ibid.).

These relationship-focused cultural facets constrain the formalization of HRM practices on the one hand and yet facilitate positive HRM-related outcomes on the other hand. For example, it is argued that performance appraisal seems to be contradictory with keeping face and harmony as a notable distinction between excellent and poor performers would result in an undesirable atmosphere (Chow, 2004). Appraisals could impair employees' face and break established relationships, especially when negative feedback is provided, which may set obstacles in other aspects of management. In addition, selection, promotion and career development opportunities may be biased by *guanxi* as acquaintances in the network tend to be considered with high priorities (Chen and Tjosvold, 2007; Zhu et al., 2013). A survey indicates that employees widely believe *guanxi* outweighs abilities and performance in finding a job and getting promotion (Zhu et al., 2013). Nevertheless, there are some benefits that could be brought by *guanxi*. Evidence suggests loyalty, organizational commitment and intention to stay can be strengthened by *guanxi-based* network (Hom and Xiao, 2011). Also, the cost of recruitment can be largely reduced by using established *guanxi* (Cunningham, 2010).

Respect for age/seniority and stress on hierarchy is derived from Confucian rules that define social orders and culturally acceptable behaviour. Ensuing relationships within the home and wider social settings are 'dominant-subservient' in nature (Wang et al., 2005: 314), for example, requiring that the younger should obey the older brother. The rules attempt to maintain harmonious relationships and enhance individuals' conformity with the permanently hierarchical social order (Cunningham and Rowley, 2007). Those ethical values are mirrored in some HRM practices, such as seniority-based pay, seniority allowance, high priorities of seniors in promotion and less involvement of employees in decision making (Zhu et al., 2012). Based on a sample of 2852 questionnaires regarding preferred HRM practices by employees, Cai et al.'s (2011) analysis suggests a great emphasis on seniority, loyalty and group orientation.

Overall, in China, traditional culture influences HRM practices in many ways. The impacts are, however, complicated as both benefits and constraints can be produced. Schlevogt (2001) suggests the cultural influences on management practices are greater in the private sector than in the public sector. Thus, it is rational to consider cultural factors when examining HRM practices in SMEs.

Conclusion

The sustainable development of SMEs exerts a profound impact on economic growth and poverty reduction, especially in developing countries. In order to shed light on people management in SMEs in China, this chapter has explored management practices from a human resource perspective. For example, it has examined the dual classification system of SMEs in China. Large variances in quantitative criteria have been noted across various sectors. The use of a qualitative classification system for SMEs in China adds more complexity to definitional issues. Given the evolving nature of the classification of SMEs, it will undoubtedly be necessary to revisit this subject over time. The chapter has also reviewed the current situation of HRM practices in Chinese SMEs; this remains an under-researched area despite the existence of some prominent contributions.

The chapter expands the knowledge on SME HRM practices in China. A theoretical framework with a particular focus on Chinese SMEs is proposed to address the role of organizational, institutional and Chinese cultural factors in shaping HRM practices. The framework provides a theoretical underpinning that is designed to assist examinations of underlying relationships between determinants and HRM practices in future empirical research. With respect to practical implications, this work helps SME owners and HR practitioners to isolate and understand the impact of, and interrelationships between, these factors on effective HRM practices. Moreover, it has the potential to contribute to national policy development in relation to SMEs in China, particularly by understanding how the labour market and the new Labour Contract Law impact on management practices in the SME sector. Hopefully, the framework will prove beneficial to policy makers when formulating and refining development polices.

However, it is acknowledged that there are many possible determinants (for example, global institutions) and HRM practices in other functions (for example, employee relations, health, safety and well-being) beyond the framework. This research calls for more attention, exploration and practical action from academics, practitioners and policy makers to assist SME development in China.

References

Atherton, A. and Fairbanks A. (2006). Stimulating private sector development in China: the emergence of enterprise development centres in Liaoning and Sichuan provinces. *Asia Pacific Business Review*, 12(3), 333–354.

Ayyagari, M., Demirguc-Kunt, A. and Maksimovic, V. (2011). Small vs. young firms across the world: contribution to employment, job creation, and growth. *Policy Research Working Paper Series 5631*, The World Bank.

Bacon, N. and Hoque, K. (2005). HRM in the SME sector: valuable employees and coercive networks. *The International Journal of Human Resource Management*, 16(11), 1976–1999.

Barrett, R. and Mayson, S. (2007). Human resource management in growing small firms. *Journal of Small Business and Enterprise Development*, 14(2), 307–320.

Beer, M., Spector, B., Lawrence, P. R., Mills, D. O. and Walton, R. E. (1984). *Managing Human Assets*. New York: Free Press.

Boxall, P. and Purcell, J. (2003). *Strategy and Human Resource Management*. Basingstoke: Palgrave Macmillan.

Budhwar, P. S. and Debrah, Y. (2001). Introduction. In Budhwar, P. S. and Debrah, Y. (eds.), *Human Resource Management in Developing Countries* (pp. 1–15). London: Routledge.

Cai, Z., Morris, J. L. and Chen, J. (2011). Explaining the human resource management preferences of employees: a study of Chinese workers, *The International Journal of Human Resource Management*, 22(16), 3245–3269.

Cardon, M. S. and Stevens, C. E. (2004). Managing human resources in small organizations: what do we know? *Human Resource Management Review*, 14(3), 295–323.

Cassell, C., Nadin, S., Gray, M. and Clegg, C. (2002). Exploring human resource management practices in small and medium sized enterprises. *Personnel Review*, 31(6), 671–692.

Chan, K. (2012). The global financial crisis and labor law in China. *Chinese Economy*, 45(3), 24–41.

Chen, N. Y. F. and Tjosvold, D. (2007). Guanxi and leader member relationships between American managers and Chinese employees: open-minded dialogue as mediator. *Asia Pacific Journal of Management*, 24(2), 171–189.

Cheng, Y.Y. (2009). New changes in regulation on the implementation of the Employment Contract Law of the People's Republic of China as well as its influence on enterprises. *Journal of Beijing Vocational College of Labour and Social Security*, 3(1), 9–13.

Chow, I. H. (2004). The impact of institutional context on human resource management in three Chinese societies. *Employee Relations*, 26(6), 626–642.

Cooke, F. L. (2009a). A decade of transformation of HRM in China: a review of literature and suggestions for future studies. *Asia Pacific Journal of Human Resources*, 47(1), 6–40.

Cooke, F. L. (2009b). Performance and retention management in Chinese private firms: key challenges and emerging HR practices, AIRAANZ Annual Conference, Newcastle, Australia.

Cooke, F. L. (2012). *Human Resource Management in China: New Trends and Practices*. Abingdon: Routledge.

Cunningham, L. X. (2010). Managing human resources in SMEs in a transition economy: evidence from China. *The International Journal of Human Resource Management*, 21(12), 2120–2141.

Cunningham, L. X. (2011). SMEs as motor of growth: a review of China's SMEs development in thirty years (1978–2008). *Human Systems Management*, 30(1), 39–54.

Cunningham, L. X. and Rowley, C. (2007). Human resource management in Chinese small and medium enterprises: a review and research agenda. *Personnel Review*, 36(3), 415–439.

Cunningham, L. X. and Rowley, C. (2008). The development of Chinese small and medium enterprises and human resource management: a review. *Asia Pacific Journal of Human Resource*, 46(3), 353–379.

De Kok, J., Deijl, C. and Essen, C.V. (2013). Is small still beautiful? Literature review of recent empirical evidence on the contribution of SMEs to employment creation. ILO Report, Eschborn: GIZ.

Ding, D. Z., Goodall, K. and Warner, M. (2000). The end of the 'iron rice-bowl': whither Chinese human resource management? *International Journal of Human Resource Management*, 11(2), 217–236.

Harney, B. and Dundon, T. (2006). Capturing complexity: developing an integrated approach to analysing HRM in SMEs. *Human Resource Management Journal*, 16(1), 48–73.

Harney, B. and Dundon, T. (2007). An emergent theory of HRM: a theoretical and empirical exploration of determinants of HRM among Irish small- to medium-sized enterprises (SMEs). *Advances in Industrial and Labor Relations*, 15, 103–153.

Harvie, C. and Lee, B. (2002). East Asian SMEs: contemporary issues and developments – an overview. In Harvie, C. and Lee, B. (eds.), *The Role of SMEs in National Economies in East Asia* (pp. 1–20). Cheltenham: Edward Elgar Publishing.

Holbeche, L. (2009). *Aligning Human Resources and Business Strategy (2nd Edition)*. Oxford: Elsevier.

Hom, P. W. and Xiao, Z. (2011). Embedding social networks: how *guanxi* ties reinforce Chinese employees' retention. *Organizational Behavior and Human Decision Processes*, 116(2), 188–202.

Kim, Y. and Gao, F.Y. (2010). An empirical study of human resource management practices in family firms in China. *The International Journal of Human Resource Management*, 21(12), 2095–2119.

Kotey, B. and Folker, C. (2007). Employee training in SMEs: effect of size and firm type – family and nonfamily. *Journal of Small Business Management*, 45(2), 214–238.

Kotey, B. and Slade, P. (2005). Formal human resource management practices in small growing firms. *Journal of Small Business Management*, 43(1), 16–40.

Li, Y. and Sheldon, P. (2010). HRM lives inside and outside the firm: employers, skill shortages and the local labour market in China. *The International Journal of Human Resource Management*, 21(12), 2173–2193.

Ministry of Human Resources and Social Security (MHRSS) of PRC (2016). The Law of the People's Republic of China on Labour Contract. Available at www.mohrss.gov.cn/SYrlzyhshbzb/zcfg/flfg/fl/201605/t20160509_239643.html. Accessed 28 June 2016.

Nguyen, T. V. and Bryant, S. E. (2004). A study of the formality of human resource management practices in small and medium-size enterprises in Vietnam. *International Small Business Journal*, 22(6), 595–618.

Paauwe, J. and Boselie, P. (2003). Challenging 'strategic HRM' and the relevance of the institutional setting. *Human Resource Management Journal*, 13(3), 56–70.

People's Republic of China (PRC) (2011). Provisions on the standards for SMEs. Available at www.gov.cn/zwgk/2011-07/04/content_1898747.htm. Accessed 20 April 2014.

Richbell, S., Szerb, L. and Vitai, Z. (2010). HRM in the Hungarian SME sector. *Employee Relations*, 32(3), 262–280.

Rutherford, M. W., Buller, P. F. and McMullen, P. R. (2003). Human resource management problems over the life cycle of small to medium-sized firms. *Human Resource Management*, 42(4), 321–335.

Schlevogt, K. A. (2001). The distinctive structure of Chinese private enterprises: state versus private sector. *Asia Pacific Business Review*, 7(3), 1–33.

Singh, M. and Vohra, N. (2009). Level of formalisation of human resource management in small and medium enterprises in India. *The Journal of Entrepreneurship*, 18(1), 95–116.

Storey, D. J. (2004). Exploring the link, among small firms, between management training and firm performance: a comparison between the UK and other OECD countries. *The International Journal of Human Resource Management*, 15(1), 112–130.

Taylor, S., Beechler, S. and Napier, N. (1996). Toward an integrative model of strategic international human resource management. *Academy of Management Review*, 21(4), 959–985.

Tsai, C. (2010). HRM in SMEs: homogeneity or heterogeneity? A study of Taiwanese high-tech firms. *The International Journal of Human Resource Management*, 21(10), 1689–1711.

Urbano, D. and Yordanova, D. (2008). Determinants of the adoption of HRM practices in tourism SMEs in Spain: an exploratory study. *Service Business*, 2(3), 167–185.

Wang, H., Appelbaum, R. P., Degiuli, F. and Lichtenstein, N. (2009). China's new Labour Contract Law: is China moving towards increased power for workers? *Third World Quarterly*, 30(3), 485–501.

Wang, J., Wang, G. G., Ruona, W. E. A. and Rojewski, J. W. (2005). Confucian values and the implications for international HRD. *Human Resource Development International*, 8(3), 311–326.

Warner, M. (2010). In search of Confucian HRM: theory and practice in Greater China and beyond. *The International Journal of Human Resource Management*, 21(12), 2053–2078.

Warner, M. (2011). Labour markets in China: coming to terms with globalization. In Benson, J. and Zhu, Y. (eds.), *The Dynamics of Asian Labour Markets: Balancing Control and Flexibility* (pp. 134–147). Abingdon: Routledge.

Warner, M., Goodall, K. and Ding, D. Z. (2002). Implementing China's people-management reforms. In Warner, M. and Joynt, P. (eds.), *Managing across Cultures: Issues and Perspectives (2nd Edition)* (pp. 168–177). London: Thomson Learnin.

Warner, M. and Rowley, C. (2010). Chinese management at the crossroads: setting the scene. *Asia Pacific Business Review*, 16(3), 273–284.

Wiesner, R. and McDonald, J. (2001). Bleak house or bright prospect? Human resource management in Australian SMEs. *Asia Pacific Journal of Human Resources*, 39(2), 31–53.

Wong, A. L. Y., Shaw, G. H. and Ng, D. K. C. (2010). Taiwan Chinese managers' personality: is Confucian influence on the wane? *The International Journal of Human Resource Management*, 21(7), 1108–1123.

World Bank (2012). How we classify countries. Available at http://data.worldbank.org/about/country-classifications. Accessed 28 February 2014.

Xinhua Net (2007). Understanding labour contract law: misunderstanding of non-fixed term labour contract. Available at http://news.xinhuanet.com/politics/2007-11/19/content_7101995.htm. Accessed 25 April 2014.

Xinhua Net (2011). Survival crisis hits China's small businesses. Available at http://news.xinhuanet.com/english2010/indepth/2011-07/31/c_131021370.htm. Accessed 10 April 2014.

Young-Thelin, L. and Boluk, K. (2012). A case study of human resource practices in small hotels in Sweden. *Journal of Human Resources in Hospitality & Tourism*, 11(4), 327–353.

Zhu, C. J., Cooper, B. K., Fan, D. and De Cieri, H. (2013). HR practices from the perspective of managers and employees in multinational enterprises in China: alignment issues and implications. *Journal of World Business*, 48(2), 241–250.

Zhu, Y. and Warner, M. (2005). Changing Chinese employment relations since WTO accession. *Personnel Review*, 34(3), 354–369.

Zhu, Y., Warner, M. and Rowley, C. (2007). Human resource management with 'Asian' characteristics: a hybrid people-management system in East Asia. *The International Journal of Human Resource Management*, 18(5), 745–768.

Zhu, C. J., Zhang, M. and Shen, J. (2012). Paternalistic and transactional HRM: the nature and transformation of HRM in contemporary China. *The International Journal of Human Resource Management*, 23(19), 3964–3982.

12 Empowerment through small business development in Alexandra, South Africa

Patricia Agupusi

Introduction

The development of small, medium- and micro-sized enterprises (SMMEs) is seen globally, and especially in developing countries, as a key strategy for economic growth, job generation and invariably poverty reduction. Since 1994 South Africa has been promoting small businesses as an engine for economic growth and socio-economic integration. More recently, due to the continued rise in unemployment in South Africa, there has been a renewed focus in the sector not simply as a catalyst for growth but more importantly as the key to job generation and poverty reduction, especially among historically disadvantaged groups.

Poverty reduction is a major challenge facing South Africa since the end of apartheid. Data from the poverty and inequality research undertaken by the Human Sciences Research Council (HSRC) in 2005 indicates that 57 per cent of South Africans, of which over 95 per cent are black, are living below the poverty line (Leibbrandt et al., 2010; Bhorat and Kanbur, 2006).[1] The persistently high level of poverty in South Africa is attributed partly to the jobless growth of the economy, and has led to an emphasis on small business development as a catalyst for job creation and poverty alleviation. In 1996 the White Paper for Small Business Development Act was introduced to redefine the role of small businesses in the new South Africa. This chapter aims at adding to current knowledge by looking at the synergies between SMME development and poverty alleviation and their potential contribution to Alexandra's transformation programme.

The choice of Alexandra for the study was based on its history of neglect during the apartheid era which has made it one of the most impoverished towns in South Africa, notwithstanding that it borders the most affluent part of Johannesburg. The core objective of the chapter is to investigate the relationship between small business development and poverty alleviation in Alexandra. This is done through a critical examination of the development and impact of government programmes, and private sector initiatives on poverty alleviation through SMMEs in Alexandra.

Providing the poor with access to productive income and opportunities is critical to poverty reduction in Alexandra. There are several South African poverty alleviation programmes such as welfare provision through social security and pensions. However, the country cannot afford to support more than 50 per cent of the population living below the poverty level with welfare payments. Hence there has been an increase in the promotion of wealth creation rather than unsustainable wealth redistribution. One key strategy is an emphasis on wealth creation, especially among the black population, through entrepreneurship development with the popular slogan 'Entrepreneurship, the life-blood of the nation'. In addition, the non-sustainability of equity transfer and several loopholes in the Black Economic Empowerment Programme have pushed the need for multidimensional strategies for poverty reduction. This is what has led to the renewed commitment by the government and the private sector to small business development as a pivotal tool for poverty alleviation through skills training and job creation.

The key question is whether poverty can be reduced through SMME development, particularly in the context of Alexandra, South Africa. To address this question, the paper examines the SMME framework as it relates to poverty alleviation. It provides the socio-economic background of Alexandra and the challenges of SMME development in poverty alleviation. It identifies the roles of the private sector and the government and the challenges faced by entrepreneurs. Finally, the paper examines how the different initiatives created by the government and the private sector to provide financial support, training and mentoring will translate into more sustainable businesses that create jobs and skills transfers which will contribute to poverty reduction in Alexandra.

The central argument is that SMME promotion has the potential to contribute to poverty alleviation and the transformation process in Alexandra. The recent Strategy Paper on Small Business Development[2] also recognizes micro enterprises and survivalists as the key to poverty alleviation through income generation, particularly in rural and impoverished towns such as Alexandra.

The research applies critical content analysis of secondary material complemented with primary data obtained through semi-structured interviews with key informants including local development agencies, entrepreneurs and potential entrepreneurs. Lack of comprehensive data on SMMEs is one of the major challenges of studying small businesses in South Africa. However, in the last few years data collection in the formal sector has improved, although not in the informal sector, which is significant in poverty alleviation. The dearth of empirical information is highest in the informal sector and is partly attributed to inadequate research and the difficulty of recording the frequent entries into and exits from the sector.

To obtain the maximum amount of information, I intend to triangulate multiple data sources to describe the different SMME sectors and how they contribute to poverty alleviation in Alexandra. Most information on SMMEs in this chapter is drawn from the Global Enterprises Monitor (GEM) on South Africa, the DTI Annual Review of Small Business and the Alexandra Development Forum. Primary data from semi-structured interviews with key informants complement these sources.

Overview of small business in South Africa

Globally, the concept of small business is diverse and depends on the level of each country's economic development. The lack of a clear and homogeneous definition of small businesses can affect research findings and the understanding of its contribution to socio-economic development. There are different characteristics of small business such as entrepreneurship, ownership and management, labour status, the formal and informal economy and the size of the entity (Annual Review of Small Business in South Africa, 2004). Meanwhile, what constitutes the size of a small business varies from one economy to another. In developed countries such as the US, businesses with fewer than 500 employees are considered small, while in developing countries such as South Africa the number employed may be considerably smaller.

According to South Africa's 1996 National Small Business Act, an SMME is seen as 'a separate and distinct business entity, including co-operative enterprises and non-governmental organisations, managed by one owner or more persons which, including its branches or subsidiaries, if any, is predominantly carried on in any sector or sub-sector of the economy' (National Small Business Act, 1996: 2). SMMEs in the South African context are classified into five categories (see Table 12.1).

Micro enterprises are considered as businesses with a turnover below the VAT registration limit of R300,000. Many informal and micro enterprises provide the livelihoods of millions of people in South Africa (Annual Review of Small Business in South Africa, 2004). Table 12.1 sets out the definition of small business in South Africa.

According to the most recent Small Business Annual Review, small businesses make up about 95 per cent of all enterprises in South Africa (Annual Review of Small Business in South Africa, 2004: 50). Non-VAT-registered businesses operating in the informal sector number between 1.8 and 2.5m. Small businesses contribute 45 to 50 per cent of GDP. The remaining percentage is contributed by big businesses and the public sector. Formal small businesses employ 50 to 60 per cent of the labour force, increasing to 75 per cent when the informal sector is included (ibid.: 63).

With the understanding that there are fundamental differences in aspects such as the policies and structure of small, medium, micro and survivalist enterprises, this chapter uses the term small business to encompass these categories.

Table 12.1 National Small Business Act 1996: definition of SMEs

Size of enterprise	Number of employees	Annual turnover	Gross assets
Medium	Fewer than 100–200, depending on industry	Under R4m to R50m, depending on industry	Under R2m to R18m, depending on industry
Small	Fewer than 50	Less than R2m to R25m, depending on industry	Less than R2m to R4.5m, depending on industry
Very Small	Fewer than 10 to 20, depending on industry	Less than R200.000 to R500,000, depending on industry	Less than R150,000 to R500,000, depending on industry
Micro	Fewer than 5	Less than R150,000	Less than R150,00

Since the late 1980s, the employment share of big businesses has been in decline, while that of small business has increased. The increase in small businesses' job absorption within the jobless growth economy has led to increased support for small business in South Africa. The 1996 White Paper for Small Business Development was a hallmark in small business development. Since then the White Paper has been reviewed and amended to accommodate some institutional changes that offer differential support programmes for formal and informal SMMEs.

Institutional framework for small business development in South Africa

Several institutions and mechanisms have been introduced by the South African government through its Department of Trade and Industry (DTI). The two key government agencies established for small business development are the *Small Enterprises and Development Agency (SEDA)* and *Khula Enterprises Limited*. These institutions have initiated a range of programmes aimed at fostering new business start-ups and capacity building. For a long time the government did not have a support agency for micro and survivalist businesses. Although a few NGOs and CBOs were involved in this sector, the lack of government support left a big gap in the development of the survivalist and micro enterprises sector. In 2004, the *South Africa Micro-credit Apex Fund* (SAMAF) was created within Khula to provide them with financial support. SAMAF operates mainly with cooperatives and community development agencies, which work directly with small business owners in rural areas and townships. Table 12.2 explains some of these institutions.

Table 12.2 Government development institutions for small business

Institutions	Activities
SEDA	SEDA offers a range of business development services. It provides non-financial services through integrated support agencies across the nation with more than 284 Enterprise Information Centres in the municipalities across the nation.
Khula Enterprises	Khula facilitates access to finance for small businesses. It has various financing products and works with major commercial banks and private organizations such as Business Partners. Khula's operations involve loans and credit guarantees through commercial banks. It also offers a mentorship programme.
National Empowerment Fund (NEF)	NEF provides various start-ups for small businesses and rural and community transformation. Its financing capacity ranges from R250,000 to R10m. NEF focuses specifically on disadvantaged individuals.
Industrial Development Corporation (IDC)	IDC generates its funds independently of the government. It provides various sector-focused financing products ranging from R1m, with specific focus on SMEs and empowerment.

Institutions	Activities
South Africa Micro Finance Apex Fund	SAMAF is modeled on the Grameen Bank in Bangladesh. It provides loans of up to R10,000 to micro and survivalist enterprises in poor areas. Its main focus is poverty alleviation.
Gauteng Enterprise Propeller (GEP)	The GEP is a Gauteng Provincial Government (GPG) agency established under the auspices of the Department for Economic Development to provide non-financial and financial support and to co-ordinate stakeholders for the benefit of SMMEs in Gauteng.

Within Khula there are other products, such as the Umsobomvu Youth Fund (UYF), which provide support for young people. In addition to the government institutions listed in Table 12.2, private organizations provide financial and non-financial support to potential entrepreneurs with a special focus on previously disadvantaged individuals (PDI). The Business Partners collaborate with Khula to provide funds for business start-ups and existing businesses. Anglo Zimele, a subsidiary of Anglo American, promotes enterprises with a special emphasis on PDI. The Business Place provides non-financial support to entrepreneurs and is one of the few business support centres based in Alexandra. Commercial banks are also involved in small business development through community banking.

Small business and poverty alleviation

Promotion of small business for poverty reduction in developing countries has been gathering momentum among governments and international development agencies. For example, the UNDP has been developing 'Growing Sustainable Business (GSB)' initiatives for poverty reduction in other developing countries such as Tanzania, Zambia, Ethiopia, El Salvador and Serbia and Montenegro. The initiatives focus on a cutting edge business model that engages a range of local partners.[3] In South Africa, the importance of the promotion of SMMEs as a tool for poverty reduction is noted in the Strategic Framework for Small Business.[4] A critical aspect of this framework is the broad scope of participants it will encompass, especially in the informal sector, which comprises very small, micro and survivalist enterprises. Survivalist businesses mainly represent a set of activities by people unable to secure regular formal employment or access to the formal economic sector, while micro enterprises often involve the owner, family members and at most four paid employees. Very small enterprises usually apply better business skills and are more organized, with greater potential for growth into the formal economy. These sectors predominantly comprise Alexandra's small business activities. They may act as a stepping stone into the formal sector and subsequently bridge the gap between the first and second economies typified by Alexandra and its affluent neighbours. Figure 12.1 illustrates the relationship between poverty alleviation and small business development.

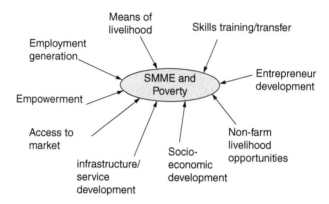

Figure 12.1 Small business development and poverty alleviation
Source: Modified from Rogerson (2006)

Sectors of SMMEs with an advantage in Alexandra, such as transport, construction and tourism, have the potential for providing the linkages needed to attract economic development in the community. There are some inherent advantages in promoting SMMEs for poverty reduction, such as through skills learning and transfer, especially in areas where there is an acute shortage of skills. One key benefit is job creation through the employment of others or self-employment, thereby creating livelihoods for many people. SMMEs can also provide access to markets for the poor, much-needed infrastructure improvements and service in the community. SMME activities are expected to contribute to the transformation process.

Poverty and small business development in Alexandra

In 1912 Alexandra was made a Native Township wherein blacks were allowed to rent and own property. The town falls within Region 7 of the Municipality of Johannesburg. It is located 3 km from Sandton, the financial heart of Johannesburg. Alexandra borders the industrial areas of Wynberg, Limbro Business Park and Bruma Commercial Park. Smith (2002) describes the distance as just a few steps: 'It amazes me the short quick steps – two to be exact – between Sandton and Alexandra. You get Sandton, Wynberg Industrial area, Alexandra. Is it really possible to make these steps even shorter? Although it is located next to the most affluent business district and one of South Africa's highest income residents, the life and living conditions of Alexandrians are the exact opposite of their affluent neighbours'. As a result of a long history of neglect during the apartheid era, Alexandra remains one of the most impoverished and densely populated townships with 60 per cent of its population unemployed compared to 22 per cent in Gauteng (Bozzoli, 2004; Rogerson, 2006; Kirsten and Rogerson, 2002).

There is a long-term problem of structurally unemployed individuals in Alexandra who have never had a job or who have been laid off from mines or factories due to the transition to the high-tech economy. It is increasingly difficult for them to find a job in the present-day labour market, which requires highly skilled labour (Bhorat, 2001; Chandra and Nganou, 2001). As a result, many individuals are left to employ themselves as their only possible means of livelihood.

Since 1994 there has been series of programmes to transform Alexandra. These include the Presidential Renewal Project (PRP), involving all stakeholders. There is also small business development and local economic development. The lives of many Alexandrians have improved since 1994, but a huge proportion of the population is still impoverished.

The town is characterized by poor infrastructure, inadequate services, high crime and a severe environment that earns it the title of 'Dark City' (Mgquba and Vogel, 2004; Rogerson, 2006). According to the 2001 census, 50 per cent of people over 20 years of age are without schooling and about 50 per cent of people aged 2–24 are currently not receiving education, the highest incidences in Gauteng. As a result of previous apartheid laws that discouraged black entrepreneurship, small business development is in its early stages and lacks adequate infrastructure and an enabling business environment. There are also limited business service providers in Alexandra. In addition most business activities operate at an informal, survivalist level.

According to the Alexandra Chamber of Commerce there are approximately 4000 small businesses, with survivalist-level enterprises dominating this number. This is in line with the recently-published FinMark survey of 6,000 households, which found that typical township businesses are in the retail (65 per cent) and services (24 per cent) sectors. Most of the existing micro businesses employ fewer than nine people, and are mainly kept in the family. The lack of alternative livelihoods is frequently cited as the primary motivation for starting up new businesses. Some of the retailers interviewed showed high entrepreneurial drive but lacked the necessary skills and knowledge to grow their businesses beyond the survivalist level. This explains the high number of survivalist enterprises and the stagnation of small business in Alexandra. This trend is not peculiar to Alexandra, as it is a common pattern in other parts of South Africa.

This chapter concurs with Horn's (1995) argument that it is misleading to conceive of all participants in small businesses as entrepreneurs. The GEM analysis distinguishes between necessity and opportunity entrepreneurial motivation. Opportunity entrepreneurs are those who take advantage of a business opportunity, while necessity entrepreneurs are those who venture into business because there is no better livelihood option (GEM, 2008). Perhaps, the majority of business owners in Alexandra are within the necessity level, but it does not follow that these levels are irrelevant in small business development, especially considering the subsector's contribution to the provision of means of livelihoods to owners and their employees. The role of necessity entrepreneurs in poverty alleviation through job creation, including in the informal sector, cannot be denied. It is likely that some will progress from survivalist to micro and formal businesses. Meanwhile, in an environment where most of the population is neither educated nor has formal employment skills, the tendency to enter into informal (necessity) business is high as an alternative livelihood strategy. In addition, recession conditions in the formal sector are the core explanation for the surge in survivalist enterprises in often already-overtraded income niches such as tuck shops, spazas[5] and hawking operations (Rogerson, 1996).

There has been a continuous decline in jobs in the traditional sector (manufacturing, mining and agriculture), which absorbs unskilled labour. The growing service sectors are intrinsically skilled-labour intensive and thus have no demand for unskilled labour. With the majority of the unemployed in Alexandra unskilled, the chances of getting work in this sector or in the commercial and industrial hub remain very low, at least in the short and medium term. This increases the poverty levels of Alexandra's residents. In order to tackle the poverty rate a multifaceted approach must include enterprise development. Small business in itself is insufficient as a poverty alleviation strategy, even though the sector could contribute significantly to poverty alleviation.

Key features of small business in Alexandra

According to the local chamber of commerce, transport and tourism are the dominant SMME sectors; trading additionally takes a major share of the number of small businesses. Small businesses in Alexandra are still in their early stages, at an average age of five years old. The tourism sector has been attracting the attention of the public and private sectors and researchers. For the most part this is due to Alexandra's strategic place in the history of South Africa, especially during the apartheid era.

As a result of the rejuvenation of the tourism sector and its contribution to employment generation there has been an initiative by the government towards making Alexandra a tourist destination (Rogerson, 2006: 51). The tourism sector is seen as a lever for promoting small businesses through local entrepreneurs providing such services as tour guiding and handicrafts (Rogerson, 2006). The sector has also attracted linkages with key players in tourism from Sandton, such as the Southern Sun Group, and local stakeholders in the Alexandra (Pro-Poor Tourism in Practice, 2004)[6].

Development business support agencies in Alexandra

There are very few development support agencies in Alexandra. Notwithstanding the government's claimed commitment to small business development for poverty reduction in rural areas and impoverished townships, there is no government business support agency in Alexandra. SAMAF, a government agency whose primary goal is poverty alleviation through provision of financial support to informal and micro-enterprises in rural areas and impoverished towns, has no outlet in Alexandra. When I spoke with officials of SAMAF in Johannesburg, I was told that they had organized a couple of workshops in Alexandra, but the response had been poor.

One of the two private business support agencies in Alexander observes the situation differently. During an interview it was explained that most agencies avoid

Alexandra because of preconceived ideas which can be traced to impressions of high violence and crime in Alexandra. The problem is also related to these agencies' lack of knowledge and understanding of the Alexandrian environment. These drive up the cost of doing business in the area considerably. This is also the key reason for low private sector investment in the area, despite the town's tourism potential.

Private sector initiative for SMME development in Alexandra

Alexandra is strategically placed due to its proximity to Sandton and other key commercial areas. The private sector's initiative to support SMMEs in Alexandra includes skills training, outsourcing and information dissemination. There are high expectations that big companies will partner with small businesses in Alexandra through supply chain linkages. For example, the tourism sector in Alexandra is targeted to develop strong linkages between Alexandra and Sandton through Southern Sun Hotels (Pro-Poor Tourism in Practice, 2004; Rogerson, 2006). Southern Sun operates six five-star hotels and is expected to contribute to enterprise development in the area. The partnership is in line with the South African Black Economic Empowerment transformation initiatives and provides mutual benefits for both Southern Sun and Alexandra (Rogerson, 2006: 51). It is also a means of promoting a link with the neighbouring commercial community of Alexandra through enterprise development, skills and job creation (Kaplan, 2004). Southern Sun outsources some of its services such as cleaning and housekeeping operations to Alexandra-based enterprises and supports local restaurants in terms of training. There is also an initiative to market township tours using residents as tour guides. These initiatives have contributed to the thriving of the service sector in the area.

Other private sectors are also involved in enterprise development in the town. An entrepreneur involved in skills training explained that she is in partnership with a private training agency in the city which usually recruits most of her training clients: 'At least people are getting a paid job which provides them with a good income. A little improvement in skills adds value to one's income; it makes a lot of difference to the life of young people in the community'.

An entrepreneur with an advertising agency commented that although he is based in Alexandra and about 70 per cent of his clients are from the city he has no links with private or public organizations. He explained that it can be very difficult securing clients as he is competing with big, well-established names with plentiful resources. He argued that stepping out is most important for a businessman: 'Having my own business has given me more confidence financially, and I employ people from the community in addition to offering other community services'.

Key constraints to SMME development in Alexandra

Interaction with entrepreneurs in Alexandra revealed that the major constraints to doing business there are similar to those faced by their counterparts in other townships and rural areas of South Africa. These constraints limit the contribution

SMMEs could make to poverty reduction. One issue is lack of business management skills and skilled labour: although some local business centres provide training for entrepreneurs, they still have very low business acumen. Interaction with business owners and service providers indicated that this lack of basic business management skills is affecting business growth. A private service provider commented that entrepreneurs in the community still have a long way to go. Some do not keep accounts, nor do they have a bank account. Some spend their capital because they cannot distinguish between business capital and profit. This leads to business stagnation and collapse.

There is an extreme shortage of skilled labour in Alexandra. Business owners disclosed that it is very difficult to find an employee with enough training in Alexandra. The cost of employing people from outside is rather high, and those with skills prefer to work in Johannesburg rather than Alexandra. An advertising agency owner explained that although he has trained his five permanent employees he still has to do some of the key work himself in order to produce acceptable quality of work. The local chamber of commerce agrees that outsourcing to local entrepreneurs is discouraging because of their poor service. Business owners tend to look outside Alexandra for skilled employees, thereby denying the contribution that small businesses could make to poverty alleviation within the community.

Another concern is poor infrastructure: lack of essential infrastructure is another obstacle to business development. Although there is some development going on in Alexandra due to the transformation programme, key infrastructure and services such as water, a reliable telephone system and ADSL that could facilitate business are not adequately available. The local chamber of commerce is planning a strategy to attract businesses and service providers to Alexandra so that residents will benefit through skills transfer and job creation, but poor infrastructure has hindered this move. Entrepreneurs are also affected by poor infrastructure. One such entrepreneur commented that his desire is to open an Internet café, but due to poor Internet access and the cost of operation, he cannot. A graphic designer has to rely on the Internet in the office of a local business service provider, and a spaza shop owner commented that as there is no major outlet for goods in bulk she has to travel out of Alexandra: 'It costs a lot to travel outside Alexandra for bulk purchases. In the end there is little or no profit out of the business, because no one will buy if prices are too high'.

Crime and negative public perception is also an issue: Alexandra is known for its politically intense and violent environment, but it is crime that has given it its bad image. Crime and violence are seen by the residents as issues of the past that have been exaggerated. On the other hand, most business service providers outside Alexandra avoid it because of the high crime rate, which makes the cost of doing business very high. Alexandrian entrepreneurs interviewed did not see crime as their primary problem; rather, the lack of capital and access to markets was cited as the key constraint to small business development.

As just noted, access to capital and bureaucracy is a key constraint. Lack of capital and the complexities of obtaining loans from financial institutions and government development agencies were cited as major hindrances to small business development.

The inhibitive policy framework discourages entrepreneurs from seeking funds to start up new or expand existing business. In terms of support intervention, a huge information gap has been identified between local business service providers and entrepreneurs. There is a lack of government support agencies which could fill the gap left by the small number of private business service providers. Indeed, while there are businesses support agencies in nearby Johannesburg, most entrepreneurs are ignorant of their availability and how they might access them.

The few that have knowledge of some of the services and incentives available for them are discouraged due to the complexity and bureaucracy involved in obtaining any kind of support. The Strategy Business Partnerships Report shows that red tape costs businesses R79bn annually in South Africa (SBP, 2006). Entrepreneurs in Alexandra argued that the process of obtaining support from the government is not only difficult and discouraging but it is also based on 'who you know' and political connections. A number of key players within the sector confirm this, but also argue that most of these entrepreneurs are not coming forward, and that those that come do not present viable business ideas. The question is how can this gap be bridged?

Summary

This chapter has sought to critically analyse the activities of small businesses and their contribution to poverty alleviation and transformation in Alexandra. It is observed that small businesses form a very significant part of Alexandra's economic activity and are pivotal to its transformation process.

Considering the socio-economic make-up of the community, small businesses can contribute greatly to poverty alleviation. Due to the history of discouragement of entrepreneurship and the culture of working for 'the boss' there is still an absence of entrepreneurial culture, and education for young people in a way that could encourage them to enter business. Small businesses are faced with a series of constraints which impede their development and consequently poverty alleviation.

Although the government accepts responsibility for ensuring that there is adequate support for SMMEs in all communities and addressing the needs of disadvantaged and marginalized black entrepreneurs, its presence is still to be felt in Alexandra. There is a claim that the government does not consult with organizations that represent businesses, despite its goal of promoting the sector for transformation and poverty alleviation.

It has also been identified that the elaborate government policies and established support institutions for small business development focus mostly on the formal sector and neglect the informal sector, where the majority of the poor are to be found. A few incentives, such as SAMAF and the Mafisa micro loan for the informal and semi-formal sectors, lack the capacity and drive for implementation.

Small businesses in Alexandra are predominantly semi-formal to informal, but current policy on small business development neglects this sector. The micro and survivalist sectors which are dominant in the town are clearly contributing to the basic needs and greater well-being of their participants. Nevertheless, this sector could raise living standards and provide employment for residents if there were a coherent and constructive policy to enhance its dynamism. The chosen policy must understand the constraints on this sector.

Concluding remarks

The government is yet to identify potential sectors, disaggregate various sets of problems according to each sector (such as the service, retail and construction sectors) and address them specifically. Maximizing growth and a pro-poor policy for small businesses will contribute further to poverty alleviation and general transformation in Alexandra. Using SMMEs to target poverty alleviation therefore requires a diverse strategy that accommodates and involves the very poor, who lack skills and formal education for business management. Approaches such as microfinance, skills and business management training are therefore paramount in ensuring SMME strategy implementation for poverty reduction.

Notes

1   The poverty income line in South Africa is R1,290 per month. Recent data (2015) from StataSA shows only a slight decline in poverty at 53.8 per cent.
2   Unlocking the Potential for South Africa Entrepreneurs (DTI, 2006).
3   Growing Sustainable Business for Poverty Reduction: www.undp.org/business/gsb.
4   Unlocking the Potential for South Africa Entrepreneurs (DTI, 2006).
5   Small shops and kiosks.
6   For further study on tourism and poverty alleviation, see Rogerson (2006).

References

Annual Review of Small Business in South Africa (2004). Department of Trade and Industry (DTI).
Bhorat, H. (2001). *Fighting Poverty: Labour Markets and Inequality in South Africa*. Juta and Company Ltd.
Bhorat, H. and Kanbur, S. R. (2006). *Poverty and Policy in Post-Apartheid South Africa*. Cape Town: HSRC Press.
Bhorat, H., Lundall, P. and Rospabe, S. (2002). *The South African Labour Market in a Globalizing World: Economic and Legislative Considerations*. Geneva: International Labour Organisation.
Bozzoli, B. (2004). *Theatres of Struggle: Popular Rebellion and the Death of Apartheid*. Edinburgh: Edinburgh University Press.
Chandra, V. and Nganou, J. (2001, November). Obstacles to formal employment creation in South Africa: evidence from recent firm surveys. In *DPRU Conference, Johannesburg, November.*
Department of Trade and Industry (DTI) (2006). Unlocking the Potential for South Africa Entrepreneurs. Available at www.dedea.gov.za/Economic%20Development%20 Legislation/Integrated%20SME%20Strategy%20-%20Summary%202005.pdf. Accessed 28 July 2016.
Global Entrepreneurship Monitor (GEM) (2008). Global Entrepreneurship Monitor, 2008 Executive Report (online). Available at http://entreprenorskapsforum.se/wp-content/ uploads/2010/02/GEMGlobal-Report_2008.pdf. Aaccessed 8 July 2013.
Horn, P. (1995). Self-employed Women's Union. *South African Labour Bulletin*, 19, 34–38.

Kaplan, L. (2004). Skills development in tourism: South Africa's tourism-led development strategy. *GeoJournal*, 60(3), 217–227.

Kirsten, M., and Rogerson, C. M. (2002). Tourism, business linkages and small enterprise development in South Africa. *Development Southern Africa*, 19(1), 29–59.

Leibbrandt, M., Woolard, I., Finn, A. and Argent, J. (2010). Trends in South African income distribution and poverty since the fall of apartheid. OECD Social, Employment and Migration Working Papers.

Mgquba, S. K. and Vogel, C. (2004). Living with environmental risks and change in Alexandra Township. *South African Geographical Journal*, 86(1), 30–38.

National Small Business Act, No. 102 (1996). Republic of South Africa. Available at www.thedti.gov.za/sme_development/docs/act.pdf. Accessed 4 July 2016.

Pro-Poor Tourism in Practice (2004). Pro-Poor Tourism Pilots in Southern Africa. Available at www.pptpilot.org.za. Accessed 28 July 2016.

Rogerson, C. M. (1996). Urban poverty and the informal economy in South Africa's economic heartland. *Environment and Urbanization*, 8(1), 167–179.

Rogerson, C. M. (2006). Pro-poor local economic development in South Africa: the role of pro-poor tourism. *Local Environment*, 11(1), 37–60.

Smith, S. (2002). Tripping through Alexandra. *The Johannesburg Africa News*. Accessed from http://iafrica.com/news/specialreport/wssd_focus/features/154147.htm (no longer available online).

Strategy Business Partnerships (SBP) (2006). *Business Bridge for Business Growth and Business Partners 2006*. Available at www.sbp.org.za. Accessed 28 July 2016.

13 Existing governance structure in international NGOs

A constraint to organizational decision-making

Carol Brunt

Introduction

Governance structure shapes not only an organization's decision-making procedures but defines stakeholder relationships and the process of employee participation. The direct approach to employee participation, either consultative or delegative, is management driven (Wilkinson et al., 2010). It is an approach that is widely held by human resource (HR) professionals in the UK in the belief that the application of HRM policies and practices can resolve any intrinsic conflict between employees and employers (Coats, 2004; Bacon and Storey, 2000). Greater participation of employees in decision-making often results in enhanced employee commitment and contribution, lower levels of absence and reduced turnover, and improved performance (Guest and Peccei, 2001).

While stakeholder theory shapes our understanding of salience and employee participation in organizational decision-making (Mitchell et al., 1997), middle management assumes an important stakeholder role in the organizational hierarchy, particularly for multinational corporations (MNCs). Given the centralized determination of HR policies in MNCs (Mamman et al., 2009; Ferner et al., 2011) middle management can play a pivotal role in policy implementation and employee participation, particularly in subsidiary offices where their presence on the ground provides the international face of the organization and an important link to head office. However, in the non-profit sector, we know little of management processes among international non-governmental organizations (NGOs) (Lewis, 2007). Based on stakeholder theory and the experience of stakeholder relations in the for-profit sector, I would expect that in the non-profit sector, middle management would also play a pivotal role in policy implementation and employee participation.

The findings presented in this chapter draw on data from a larger, qualitative multiple case study of HR management processes in six INGOs, representative of the most common types of large INGOs operational in the development aid sector in East Africa. Senior management teams at field level are comprised of Country/Executive Directors and Heads of Departments. Programme Managers responsible for implementation have closer relations to staff and comprise the majority of middle management. Among senior management, the ratio of expatriates to Kenyans is 3:2, whereas for middle management positions including programme managers, the rate is 1:4 expatriates to nationals. There is no definitive correlation between the level of management and nationality as many organizations have positioned national staff within the senior management ranks. The figures provide some detail of management composition. In addition, expatriates do not necessarily refer only to Western-based staff but include international hires from around the world.

Field research was undertaken between January and June 2011. Selected agency documents were reviewed for evidence of decision-making at management meetings and on important management issues, as well as INGOs' espoused values. A total of 36 semi-structured interviews were conducted. A cross-section of management from each of the agencies were interviewed to decrease the likelihood of research subjectivity that would have occurred if speaking only to senior management. In employing a qualitative approach, the study was dependent on the veracity of the input (Tomlinson, 2005) gathered from management representatives of the respective participant agencies. The application of content analysis to coded transcripts was helpful in identifying management attributions (D'Aveni and MacMillan, 1990) and patterns of decision-making within existing governance structures.

This chapter presents details of an exploration of the impact of governance structure on middle management's contribution to organizational decision-making in the non-profit sector, contributing to our understanding of 'conventional management theory in the development context' (Thomas, 1996: 9). The findings in this study reveal the influence of governance structure on opportunities for middle management to participate in organizational decision-making. Senior management resident at international headquarters influence local management participation in organizational decision-making at field level. This research facilitates a critical reflection on INGO management and the contribution of middle management to organizational decision-making. It is a structural approach for its ability to highlight organizational hierarchy as a governance mode (Puranam and Vanneste, 2009: 13). Governance structure is emphasized for its authoritative control in shaping stakeholder relations between senior management (both at headquarters and in the field), middle management and staff in the country offices as they participate in organizational decision-making.

Stakeholder theory as a vehicle for exploring governance structure

The study of corporate governance includes those relationships between stakeholders that shape the process of organizational decision-making and who retain control over organizational resources (Aguilera and Jackson, 2003). Dominating the study of corporate governance, agency theory (Golden-Biddle and Rao, 1997) reflects top management control over the decision-making process, and positions middle management in a representational rather than an empowering role (Sundaramurthy and Lewis, 2003). In contrast to agency theory, stakeholder theory presents an inclusive framework to an examination of corporate governance that acknowledges the interests of all parties in relation to the firm, and, in doing so, provides a stakeholder driven model for the organization (Freeman, 1984; Donaldson and Preston, 1995).

The importance of stakeholder theory is found in its multiplicity as a descriptive method to understand an organization's internal and external environments, a predictive role that links strategic management to organizational objectives, and a normative aspect that prioritizes the value of stakeholder interests (Donaldson and Preston, 1995: 70–71). As Donaldson and Preston (1995: 74) state, 'recognition of these ultimate moral values and obligations gives stakeholder management its fundamental normative base'. Given the adoption by INGO management of a stakeholder approach in their own project development processes, the use of stakeholder theory in this analysis is salient, particularly for its recognition of shared organizational values and beliefs that form the backbone of INGO principles.

Corporate governance structures reflect an organizational hierarchy whose centre of decision-making, retention of power and authority, and control of information flow (Kerr, 2004) rests at the pinnacle of the organization at its headquarters, with senior management and the Board of Directors. As a stakeholder group, senior management's decision-making process and outcomes are shaped by management cognition of their inter-organizational domain as they seek to define organizational reality in their own terms. For their part, middle management assume a facilitative role responsible for programme implementation and leadership of organizational change.

Middle management as important stakeholders

Employees are readily identified stakeholder groups. Scholars also recognize management as important stakeholders (Kotter, 1978; Freeman, 1984). Organizational decisions are shaped firstly by stakeholder (management) cognition (Adher and Helfat, 2003; Golden-Biddle and Rao, 1997), and then further influenced by inter-organizational domain (Aguilera and Jackson, 2003), management experience and demographic background (Knight et al., 1999). Our recognition of management as stakeholders encourages reflection of management roles and role differentiation within the management hierarchy.

On the one hand, senior management's interpretation of organizational reality demonstrates trade-offs within their inter-organizational domain, evident in their resultant choices and actions (Barton, 1966; Clegg et al., 2011) such as that of discord management. While corporate governance structures amalgamate multiple stakeholders with differing interpretations of organizational reality under one umbrella, the amalgamation creates an arena for possible discord. A lack of agreement among senior management stakeholders can undermine strategic direction (Knight et al., 1999) and organizational performance (Voss et al., 2006). Alternatively, the ability of senior decision-makers to voice dissent has been shown to improve the quality of decision-making and team commitment (Dooley and Fryxell, 1999) among senior management.

For their part, middle management have a key role as facilitators (Miles and Snow, 2008) and change agents in the introduction of new policies and procedures (Huy, 2002; Luscher and Lewis, 2008). For middle management, communication and experience sharing assist in their facilitative role in maintaining organizational stability while fostering organizational continuity (Huy, 2002; Balogun and Johnson, 2004). Group process shapes management's 'mental models' (Knight et al., 1999: 459) of organizational strategy. As a process of sense making, middle management participates in a 'conversational and narrative process' in order to 'create and maintain an inter-subjective world' (Balogun and Johnson, 2004: 524).

However, despite their facilitative role (Huy, 2002) as champions of organizational change, middle managers have been referred to as 'change recipients' (Balogun and Johnson, 2004: 543) for the challenges they face from hierarchical barriers and senior management control as they balance conflicting organizational demands for stability and continuity.

In MNCs, standardization of management practices, governance structures and systems, as well as placing headquarters staff in key management positions often characterizes the structures of field offices. The standardization of management practice or convergence of practice includes HRM policies developed at headquarters and transferred to subsidiary offices (Mamman et al., 2009). The practice creates, in effect, mirror images of the organization worldwide with country offices operating in a different cultural context than that of the home office.

Middle management's role in-country positions them as intermediaries between senior and lower levels of the organization. It is a role that is compromized by centralized decision-making at organizational headquarters as illustrated in the following example. In an examination of management decision-making and governance structure among MNCs, research suggests decision-making at more senior levels constrains local innovation and input that would be under the purview of middle management.

Using a large-scale survey of MNCs in host countries, Ferner et al. (2011) query the extent to which central decision-making in these firms dominates subsidiary autonomy over human resource policy. In doing so, their analysis broadens the discussion of management decision-making and governance structure to include organizations operating across geographic borders and cultures to encompass multinational companies where the locus of organizational decision-making remains at the firm's headquarters.

> To the degree that organisational governance rules and practices are determined by actors beyond the jurisdiction of the host business system, the scope for institutional self-determination and for indigenous experimentation and innovation is likely to be constrained. (Ferner et al., 2011: 484)

In the non-profit sector, governance principles and management roles demonstrate a unique intersection in a sector where managers gravitate to employment for greater job satisfaction derived from intrinsic rewards, scheduling freedoms, and greater discretion in how they perform their work (LeRoux and Feeney, 2013).

Management in the non-profit sector can play a transformational role in leading change within an organizational culture shaped by shared values and beliefs (Jaskyte, 2004) that encourage participation as an organizational principle. Should organizational change challenge the shared values and beliefs at the heart of NGOs, middle management could find itself caught in a conundrum between a role as change agent and commitment to the set of shared values and beliefs that drew them to the organization. The introduction of more commercial, business-oriented procedures in the UK charity retail sector demonstrates the collective challenges faced by middle managers in their ability to champion organizational change and implement organizational directives.

In a survey of shop managers, 64 per cent of respondents agreed/strongly agreed that 'too many decisions are made by head office' without consultation of branch managers, and 51 per cent of shop managers agreed/strongly agreed with the statement that 'I would like more opportunity to influence decisions made by the charity' (Parsons and Broadbridge, 2004: 238). The new procedures introduced by senior management at the charity shops created pushback from local shop managers as the shift to results/profit generation clashed with the branch managers' identification with underlying volunteering principles (Parsons and Broadbridge, 2004).

Non-governmental organizations (NGOs) operating in the international arena or INGOs are viewed as alternative providers in the provision of basic services (Chambers, 1986; Hyden, 1983; Suleiman, 2013; World Bank, 1991) to local communities in the developing world. Funders who rely on INGOs for delivery of basic services do not query organizational governance principles. As some scholars contend, the principles of good governance reflect an ideological approach rather than an empirical reality (Edwards and Hulme, 1996; Suleiman, 2013). Examined more closely, the outward face of the NGO demonstrates a unified organizational identity when threatened (Golden-Biddle and Rao, 1997). This unified organizational identity belies the top-down decision-making that isolates local managers and provides token rewards to staff (Parsons and Broadbridge, 2004).

Corporate governance is responsible for shaping stakeholder relations in the for-profit and non-profit sectors. Characterized by control between management stakeholders, corporate governance positions middle managers in representational rather than empowering roles (Sundaramurthy and Lewis, 2003). Recognizably, management are an important stakeholder group (Kotter, 1978; Freeman, 1984) whose interpretation of organizational reality impacts organizational decision-making process and outcomes. At senior levels, strategic direction and organizational performance are vulnerable to missteps (Knight et al., 1999; Voss et al., 2006). Among middle management, shared experience among peers contributes to sense making of organizational reality and supports their facilitation role in maintaining organizational stability while fostering organizational continuity (Huy, 2002; Balogun and Johnson, 2004) in the face of organizational change.

Middle management in INGOs in Kenya

Stakeholder theory (Freeman, 1984; Mitchell et al., 1997; Donaldson and Preston, 1995) has been identified as useful both in conceptualizing stakeholder relationships and in the identification of those persons who can provide insights into the INGO management process through their discourse. As noted earlier, management is an important stakeholder group (Kotter, 1978; Freeman, 1984), and I identify management sub-groups comprised of senior management at headquarters, and senior and line management in the field as important stakeholders for INGOs. It is the line management in the field, those Programme Managers that comprise middle management within each INGO and tasked with the responsibility of implementation of organizational policies and procedures, that are the focus of analysis.

What makes middle management as stakeholders of particular interest is their key role in facilitating organizational change. Drawing on the anthropological writings of van Ufford (1993), I envisage INGO governance structure as a ladder with INGO headquarters at the top and staff in the country offices at the bottom. Based on his own NGO experience, van Ufford characterized stakeholder relations among different stakeholder groups by what he perceives as their ignorance of, and lack of familiarity with, the actions of other stakeholders within the NGO's operating environment. I adopt his characterization to conceptualize the relationships between stakeholder groups within the INGO as institution.

The following definitions describe each of the stakeholder groups:

INGO headquarters: refers to the centre of operations of the INGOs and includes the Board of Directors. They are collectively considered responsible for much of the policy and programmatic decision-making in the organization. For the participant agencies in the study, headquarters are located in North America or Europe.

Senior management: refers to those managers in the organization who hold decision-making power in-country including Country Directors, Assistant Country Directors, and Heads of Departments such as Finance. Some of those holding senior positions may be expatriates while others may be national staff from the country of operation.

Line management: refers to managers who are directly accountable to senior management as described above and responsible for implementing organizational policies as well as programmes and projects in the field. With multiple staff below them, these managers are positioned in the middle of the hierarchy, as intermediaries between senior management and front-line staff. Middle management positions are primarily held by national staff from the country of operation.

Staff: refers generally to all employees who do not hold management positions within INGOs. These positions are operational in nature with direct report to line management. They also act as a key interface between the INGO itself and its external environment including local communities as stakeholders.

The INGO as institution refers collectively to the headquarters located primarily in the North, to senior and line management as well as staff operating in the field or country office of the respective INGO. It is a formal governance structure that shapes organizational decision-making and relationships between stakeholders. There is a differential in the institution between the global level of operations situated at its northern-based headquarters, where organizational strategy, human resource policies and practices are drafted, and the country level of the institution that is responsible for implementation, albeit with some amendments to reflect national labour legislation in host countries.

There is a unidirectional information flow between stakeholder groups as those located at headquarters retain ultimate control over the outcomes of decision-making processes. Their decisions flow downwards from headquarters to senior management to line management as well as to staff. Moreover, the governance structure perpetuates potential tensions and mutual dependencies between each stakeholder group, as each group seeks to retain its power and control over the stakeholder group below them.

INGO governance structures reflect hierarchical organizations that reinforce power differentials among stakeholder groups. The impact of these INGO governance structures and the accompanying unidirectional information flow undermines the pivotal facilitation role of line managers in their role as middle management, minimizing opportunities to participate in decision-making that might have been available in flatter governance structures. The hierarchical structures themselves reinforce stakeholder relations in a configuration that challenges middle management's responsibilities for ensuring organizational stability and continuity in the face of organizational change. This finding is not surprising. A study of ten UK-based NGOs found that most agencies had a formal structure with clearly defined hierarchies at headquarters level that was replicated at the country level (Billis and MacKeith, 1993: 13–14).

The home-country effect (Muller-Camen et al., 2001), a process whereby organizational policies from headquarters are imposed on field offices located in host countries, is very much in evidence among NGOs creating a mirror image of the organization worldwide irrespective of country of operation.

Organizations in this study have a variety of mechanisms to facilitate the participation of staff in organizational decision-making. These mechanisms range from those that are management-led such as staff meetings and strategic planning sessions to those led by the staff themselves such as staff councils. An examination of interviewee discourse confirms that all agencies encourage staff participation. The HR Manager is acknowledged as the link between staff and management in all agencies with one exception.

INGO documentation confirms a hierarchical management structure that is responsible for shaping management stakeholder relations and ensuring the unidirectional information flow downwards from INGO headquarters to the field offices. Hierarchical governance structures shape the process of organizational decision-making on major management issues within participant INGOs. Interviewees identify institutional growth, reductions in program budgets, and staffing and compensation as issues that are significant to the organization. Despite the presence of participatory mechanisms for staff, and purported encouragement of staff participation, there is no evidence of an upward information flow from staff to middle management to senior management.

While organizational hierarchy is acknowledged as a constraining factor on organizational decision-making (McCourt and Brunt, 2013), INGO governance structure and organizational hierarchy are examined in detail in order to identify impacts on middle management's role and contribution to organizational decision-making. Table 13.1 outlines staff participation in organizational decision-making at each participant agency, and provides details of staff input as well as management response to staff input on major management issues. As a presentation of overall research findings, it surfaces the controlling role of senior management both at headquarters and in the field in the decision-making process.

The details contained in Table 13.1 highlight the hierarchy of internal decision-making that exists in each of the participant agencies as headquarters and

Table 13.1 Staff participation in organizational decision-making

Agency	Issues		Staff Input		Management Response	
B	1	Reduction in program budgets	1	Limited consultation	1	Decisions by HQ, regional team
	2	Increase partner-led programmes	2	Resource mobilization, seek employer action on recruitment, retention and compensation issues	2	Favourable response
C	1	Strategic direction	1	Limited consultation	1	Senior management level decision-making
	2	Staffing and compensation	2	Limited consultation	2	HQ and Country Director make decisions
D	1	Reduction in program budgets	1	None	1	HQ and senior management level decision-making
	2	Staffing and compensation	2	None	2	Country Directors make decisions
E	1	Programme growth	1	Limited consultation	1	Senior management and HQ level decision-making
	2	Staffing and compensation	2	Requested reclassification	2	Country Director supported introduction of new salary band from HQ
F	1	Programme growth	1	Limited consultation	1	Country Director makes unilateral decisions on management restructuring
	2	Staffing and compensation	2	Detailed input on policy changes concerning R&R, accommodation, leave	2	Under consideration by management
G	1	Programme growth	1	None	1	Country Director unilaterally decides to expand geographic scope
	2	Staffing and compensation	2	Contributions to HR review conflict with management; day to day issues regarding allowances and leave	2	Programme Director and Country Director made final decisions; management approval

senior management retain control of decisions on major management issues. Not all agencies identify with all three of these major management issues. Staff input on major management issues such as institutional growth, reductions in program budgets, and staffing and compensation is minimal as final decisions remain with senior management at headquarters (Brunt and McCourt, 2012). Noticeably, the analysis finds a lack of contribution by middle management in management discourse on all issues of organizational decision-making.

In three agencies (Agencies E, F and G), senior management in the field contributed to decisions by headquarters on institutional growth. Senior management at Agency E worked in tandem, both in the field and at headquarters, to direct institutional growth. At Agencies F and G, Country Directors took decisions on program growth unilaterally within the overall framework established by headquarters for institutional growth. Faced with reductions in program budgets, headquarters at Agencies B and D led decision-making on the reductions with assistance from senior management in the field offices.

At Agencies C, D, E and G, Country Directors were identified as responsible for decisions on staffing and compensation. However, headquarters at Agencies C and E assumed the lead for decisions on staffing and compensation. At Agency D, decision-making on staffing and compensation issues were taken unilaterally by the Country Director. Agency G is an anomaly and stands apart as the only agency to include Program Directors as middle management in the decision-making process.

Analysis of decision-making patterns

Organizational decision-making among the stakeholder groups identified earlier can be grouped into five broad patterns: INGO headquarters takes unilateral decisions, INGO headquarters assumes a lead role with some input from senior management in the country of operation, senior management in-country assumes a lead role with some input from INGO headquarters, unilateral decision-making by senior management in-country or senior management collaboration with line/middle management in-country.

An examination of management decision-making processes in INGOs in Kenya finds clustering around headquarters/senior management and senior management/headquarters combinations with a notable absence of middle management participation. All of the identified major management issues are financially driven, and as such, decisions on these issues hold great importance for senior management both at headquarters and in the field in terms of accountability and retention of control of essential resources. Senior management decision-making leaves little room for participation in organizational decision-making by line management at field level, suggesting that meaningful engagement by middle managers is compromised by immoveable governance structures.

Examined in more detail, governance structures of the participant INGOs are strict hierarchies with headquarters at the pinnacle of the organization. Each country office constitutes its own mini-hierarchy comprised of senior and line management as well as agency staff. The governance structure marginalizes the voice of line managers who as middle management are key drivers of organizational change with responsibility for balancing organizational stability and continuity (Huy, 2002).

INGO headquarters serves as the control centre for decision-making on major management issues such as institutional growth, reductions in program budgets, and staffing and compensation by either leading decision-making or establishing decision-making frameworks. Driven from the top, decision-making follows strict hierarchical lines. This seemingly top-down control contrasts with espoused collaborative participation principles that purportedly guide INGO actions. We know that the flip side of control is collaboration that occurs among stakeholders in the development of a trust-seeking relationship. The presence of both control and collaboration within an organization can create a reinforcing governance paradox (Sundaramurthy and Lewis, 2003) that underlies organizational decision-making. Hence, consideration of both control and collaboration can turn a negative influence into a positive force for organizational behaviour (Smith and Berg, 1987). This suggests that:

Proposition #1: An organization can embrace the paradoxical existence of collaboration and control present in INGOs.

In other words, INGOs can respond to the paradox and encourage middle management participation in organizational decision-making. By doing so, INGOs signal an organizational inclusiveness that addresses the existing duality between organizational principles and practices of participation, and provides real opportunities for collaboration among all stakeholders across the organization. From an organizational behaviour perspective, embracing organizational paradox would resolve underlying tensions in these organizations created by existing duality and incongruence between theory and practice. The current exclusion of middle management from organizational decision-making reinforces rather than resolves duality with respect to participation.

Management cognition and interpretation of organizational reality play an important role in organizational decision-making. At senior management level, reality is shaped by trade-offs between individual choices and actions (Clegg et al., 2011) to forge a singular, unified organizational identity. The formation of organizational identity could include input from middle management provided that there are no reprisals for opposing interpretations. However, middle management may fear backlash from senior management for appearing to undermine senior management's drive for unanimity. In which case, should the risk be perceived as significant or too great to bear, they may refrain from providing senior management with discretionary information (Detert and Burris, 2007). There are benefits to acknowledging dissenting voices at the senior level. Acknowledgement of dissent can improve the quality of decision-making (Dooley and Fryxell, 1999). Senior management could recognize the salience of middle management input to the benefit of INGO performance. This suggests that:

Proposition #2: In developing its stakeholder approach, organizations that recognize the salience of middle manager input can strengthen the productive role of middle managers as change agents.

There are limitations to this analysis. The larger research study on which this chapter is based is constrained in its examination of INGO decision-making processes. The questions posed to interviewees focused on the two-year period immediately preceding the actual interviews in 2011, thereby restricting the review period to 2009–2011. The choice to bound the period under review reflects my attempt to ensure comparability of responses both within and across agencies. A more longitudinal approach to the study of INGO management process could uncover greater detail of governance structures and their potential impact.

Further research could examine how internal and external stakeholders to the organization interpret the absence of middle management participation in organizational decision-making. As mutual exchange occurs among and between organizations in the process of forming and reforming coalitions and cooperative relations in development projects, stakeholder feedback could provide useful input. The contribution of this research lies in its detail of the INGO management process. The propositions present an opportunity to balance stakeholder control and collaboration, thereby signalling inclusivity as a means to overcome the constraints posed by existing governance structures.

Concluding thoughts

Stakeholder theory and analysis provides an inclusive framework to examine governance structures of INGOs operating in Kenya. It serves to uncover a multiplicity of stakeholder relationships that might otherwise have gone unnoticed and hidden from view. The pivotal role of middle management as facilitators and change agents in maintaining stability and fostering continuity highlights a somewhat forgotten stakeholder group in the organizational decision-making process and exposes a lack of inclusivity.

Management decision-making faces new challenges across geographic borders and cultures as governance structures are imported from northern-based headquarters locations. NGOs operating internationally experience similar challenges as firms in the for-profit sector through imported governance structures that leave little room for indigenous contribution from middle management.

The findings in this study provide new insights into the INGO management process. For organizations whose shared values and beliefs suggest inclusive and participatory principles of participation, management implementation is often constrained by the organization's own institutional governance structures.

References

Adher, R. and Helfat, C. E. (2003). Corporate effects and dynamic managerial capabilities. *Strategic Management Journal*, 24(10), 1011–1025.

Aguilera, R. and Jackson, G. (2003). The cross-national diversity of corporate governance: dimensions and determinants. *Academy of Management Review*, 28(3), 447–465.

Bacon, N. and Storey, J. (2000). New employee relations strategies in Britain: towards individualism or partnership. *British Journal of Industrial Relations*, 38(3), 407–427.

Balogun, J. and Johnson, G. (2004). Organisational restructuring and middle manager sensemaking. *Academy of Management Journal*, 47(4), 523–549.

Barton, R. (1966). Reality and business policy decisions, *Academy of Management Journal*, 9(2), 117–122.

Billis, D. and Mackeith, J. (1993). *Organising NGOs: Challenges and Trends in the Management of Overseas Aid*. London: Centre for Voluntary Organisations.

Brunt, C. and McCourt, W. (2012). Do INGOs walk the talk? Reconciling the 'two participations' in international development. *Journal of International Development*, 24(5), 585–601.

Chambers, R. (1986). Normal professionalism, new paradigms and development. *IDS Discussion Paper* 227. Brighton: IDS.

Clegg, S., Kornberger, M. and Pitsis, T. (2011). *Managing and Organisations – An Introduction to Theory and Practice*. 3rd Edition. London: Sage Publications.

Coats, D. (2004). Speaking up! Voice, industrial democracy and organisational performance (online). Available at www.theworkfoundation.com/assets/docs/publications/142_Speaking_Up.pdf. Accessed 11 June 2010.

D'Aveni, R. and MacMillan, I. (1990). Crisis and the content of managerial communications: a study of the focus of attention of top managers in surviving and failing firms. *Administrative Science Quarterly*, 35(4), 634–657.

Detert, J. R. and Burris, E. R. (2007). Leadership behaviour and employee voice: is the door really open? *Academy of Management Journal*, 50(4), 869–884.

Donaldson, T. S. and Preston L. E. (1995). The stakeholder theory of the corporation: concepts, evidence, and implications. *Academy of Management Review*, 20(1), 65–91.

Dooley, R. and Fryxell, G. (1999). Attaining decision quality and commitment from dissent: the moderating effects of loyalty and competence in strategic decision-making teams. *Academy of Management Journal*, 42(4), 389–402.

Edwards, M. and Hulme, D. (1996). Too close for comfort? The impact of official aid on nongovernmental organisations. *World Development*, 24(6), 961–973.

Ferner, A., Regaskis, O., Edwards, P. K., Edwards, T., Marginson, P., Adam, D. and Meyer, M. (2011). HRM structures and subsidiary discretion in foreign multinationals in the UK. *The International Journal of Human Resource Management*, 22(3), 483–509.

Freeman, R. E. (1984). *Strategic Management: A Stakeholder Approach*. London: Pitman Publishing.

Golden-Biddle, K. and Rao, H. (1997). Breaches in the boardroom: organisational identity and conflicts of commitment in a nonprofit organisation. *Organisation Science*, 8(6), 593–611.

Guest, D. E. and Peccei, R. (2001). Partnership at work: mutuality and the balance of advantage. *British Journal of Industrial Relations*, 39(2), 207–236.

Huy, Q. N. (2002). Emotional balancing of organisational continuity and radical change: the contribution of middle managers. *Administrative Science Quarterly*, 47(1), 31–69.

Hyden, G. (1983). *No Short Cuts to Progress: African Development Management in Perspective*. London: Heinemann Educational Books.

Jaskyte, K. (2004). Transformational leadership, organisational culture, and innovativeness in nonprofit organisations. *Nonprofit Management and Leadership*, 15(2), 153–168.

Kerr, J. (2004). The limits of organisational democracy. *Academy of Management Executive*, 18(3), 81–95.

Knight, D., Pearce, C. L., Smith, K. G., Olian, J. D., Sims, H. P., Smith, K. A. and Flood, P. (1999). Top management team diversity, group process and strategic consensus. *Strategic Management Journal*, 20(5), 445–465.

Kotter, J. P. (1978). *Organisational Dynamics: Diagnosis and Intervention*. London: Addison Wesley.

Leroux, K. and Feeney, M. (2013). Factors attracting individuals to nonprofit management over public and private sector management. *Nonprofit Management and Leadership*, 24(1), 43–62.

Lewis, D. (2007). *The Management of Non-Governmental Development Organisations*. London: Routledge.

Luscher, L. S. and Lewis, M. (2008). Organisational change and managerial sensemaking: working through paradox. *Academy of Management Journal*, 51(2), 221–240.

Mamman, A. Nabil, B. and Adeoye, A. (2009). Transferability of management innovation to Africa: a study of two multinational companies' performance management system in Nigeria. *Global Business Review*, 10(1), 1–31.

McCourt, W. and Brunt, C. (2013). Inherent constraints and creative possibilities: employee participation in Kenya. *International Journal for Human Resource Management*, 24(10), 1997–2018.

Miles, R. E. and Snow, C. C. (2008). *Organisational Strategy, Structure and Process*. Stanford: Stanford University Press.

Mitchell, R. K., Bradley R. A. and Donna J. W. (1997). Toward a theory of stakeholder identification and salience: defining the principle of who and what really counts. *Academy of Management Review*, 22(4), 853–886

Muller-Camen, M., Almond, P., Gunnigle, P., Quintanilla, J. and Tempel, A. (2001). Between home and host country: multinationals and employment relations in Europe. *International Relations Journal*, 32(5), 435–448.

Parsons, E. and Broadbridge, A. (2004). Managing change in nonprofit organisations: insights from the UK charity retail sector. *Voluntas*, 15(3), 227–242.

Puranam, P. H. and Vanneste, B. S. (2009). Trust and governance: untangling a tangled web. *Academy of Management Review*, 34(1), 11–31.

Smith, K. K. and Berg, D. N. (1987). *Paradoxes of Group Life*. San Francisco: Jossey-Bass.

Suleiman, L. (2013). The NGOs and the grand illusions of development and democracy. *Voluntas*, 24(1), 241–261.

Sundaramurthy, C. and Lewis M. (2003). Control and collaboration: paradoxes of governance. *Academy of Management Review*, 28(3), 397–415.

Thomas, A. (1996). What is development management? *Journal of International Development*, 8(1), 95–110.

Tomlinson, F. (2005). Idealistic and pragmatic versions of the discourse of partnership. *Organisation Studies*, 26(8), 1169–1188.

van Ufford, P. Q. (1993). Knowledge and ignorance in the practices of development policy. In Hobart, M. (ed.), *An Anthropological Critique of Development* (pp. 135–160). London: Routledge.

Voss, Z., Cable, D. M. and Voss G. B. (2006). Organisational identity and firm performance: what happens when leaders disagree about 'who we are?' *Organisation Science*, 17(6), 741–755.

Wilkinson, A., Gollan, P. J., Marchington, M. and Lewin, D. (2010). Conceptualizing employee participation in organisations. In Gollan, P. J., Lewin, D., Marchington, M. and Wilkinson, A. (eds.), *The Oxford Handbook of Participation* (pp. 3–25). Oxford: Oxford University Press.

World Bank (1991). *The World Development Report 1991 – The Challenge of Development* (online). Available at www.worldbank.org. Aaccessed 4 May 2011.

14 Managing the Millennium Development Goals (MDGs) in developing countries

Lessons from a local district in Ghana

Albert Ahenkan

Introduction

The issues of the Millennium Development Goals (MDGs) have moved to the core of the international development agenda since the adoption of the Millennium Declaration in 2000 by world leaders, committing the world to a new global partnership to reduce extreme hunger, poverty and poor health and expand the choices of the poor. They are probably the most discussed global development goals in recent years. The MDGs are particularly interlinked in developing countries and Ghana in particular, with each contributing to the occurrence of the other and hence the need for an integrated approach to accelerate their achievement. The world, united by common values and striving with renewed determination to improve human development, set eight time-bound measurable goals and targets that aim to eradicate extreme poverty and hunger, achieve universal primary education, promote gender equality and empower women, reduce child mortality and improve maternal health, combat HIV/AIDS, malaria and other diseases, ensure environmental sustainability, and develop global partnerships for development (World Bank, 2012; UNDP, 2011; UNICEF, 2010).

Even though the MDGs are global, they can most effectively be achieved through action at the local level. The MDGs therefore provided a development framework as a blueprint for local authorities to direct and consolidate their development efforts toward the achievement of the MDGs. Progress on the attainment of the MDGs is often measured and reported at the national, regional and international levels through global, regional and national MDG Reports. Nevertheless, while MDGs have become the common development framework at the global level, they are in themselves the subject of debate when it comes to their implementation at both national and district levels.

In September 2000, Ghana committed to tracking these eight time-bound MDGs and associated indicators. MDGs have since been mainstreamed into the country's successive medium-term national development policy framework, the Ghana Poverty Reduction Strategy (GPRS I), 2003–2005, and the Growth and Poverty Reduction Strategy (GPRS II), 2006–2009. With many countries trying to decentralize development process, it is important that the global targets be set in local contexts, reflecting local reality, aspirations and priorities. In Ghana, development action takes place at the local level and it is equally at the local level that real action on the MDGs will be achieved. Local authorities were mandated to essentially create their own, unique poverty reduction, health and environment policies and strategies, in consultation with all the stakeholders, especially the poor and vulnerable, to achieve the MDGs (GPRSP, 2006). Local development programmes and actions are therefore very crucial drivers in achieving these global targets.

Unfortunately, while progress towards the MDGs is monitored, evaluated and analysed using national aggregated figures, very little or no effort has been made to assess the local performance of the MDGs and targets at the district and local level. The overall assessment of Ghana's progress toward the MDGs in 2010 reveals that, while progress has generally been positive, tangible results have been mixed across indicators (NDPC, 2010). The achievements related to the MDGs have been largely centred on the national aggregate figures with no concrete empirical data on the achievements at the district and local levels. The achievements reported at the country level are aggregate figures that may not reflect the actual situation on the ground. In other words, the reported aggregated data on achievements may vary widely across various districts and localities in Ghana. For instance, the national report on MDG monitoring and evaluation fails to differentiate between national and district level achievements. However, conditions at the district and local levels are likely to be different or worse than the averages for the nation, especially in the low income and vulnerable communities in Ghana.

It is therefore difficult to provide a true assessment of development realities and progress of MDGs in Ghana without contextualizing the actual progress of the MDGs. Localization and mainstreaming of the MDGs will help to highlight the local dimensions in development efforts of the country. Localizing MDGs in Ghana is an important way to align the global MDGs with national long-term planning and PRSP processes. The main objective of this study is to assess the progress of MDGs beyond the national level using the Tain District in Ghana as a case study. This study focuses on MDGs 1, 2, 5 and 7c (i.e. poverty, education, health and water and sanitation). These four MDGs are selected because they are also interlinked with Goals 3, 4, 6 and 8.

The study was conducted in the Tain District in 2015. The Tain District was one of districts created in June 2004, in the Brong Ahafo Region. It is situated at the northwest of Sunyani (Regional Capital). It lies within latitudes 7½ and 8o 45` North and longitudes 2o 52` West and 0o 28` East. In terms of land area, the Tain District covers 4,125 square kilometers. The district shares common boundaries with Wenchi District to the east, Jaman North to the west, Sunyani West to the south and Berekum District to the southwest. It is also bounded by the Bole District of the Northern Region to the northeast, Kintampo South to the southeast and La Cote d'Ivoire to the northwest. Nsawkaw, the district capital, is 18 miles from Wenchi, the capital of the Wenchi District Assembly, from which Tain was carved out.

In order to achieve the objectives of the study, the case study design within the qualitative paradigm was used. This method was deemed appropriate because the researcher examines in detail many features of a few cases at a point in time often in a qualitative form (Neuman, 2007). The literature review also generated essential information that informed the design of research instruments to guide the collection of primary data and information in the field. The qualitative data collection instruments used for this study were the in-depth interview (IDI) and focus group discussion (FGD). The data for the study was collected in four months (December 2012–March 2013). The data collection method was deemed appropriate because the research is a case study and therefore required an instrument that affords the respondent the opportunity to provide in depth and unrestricted information about the subject. For the IDIs, a total of 15 respondents were selected through purposive sampling because of their personal experiences in the local actions and MDGs programmes in the district. The respondents were key actors in the district including the District Planning Officer, District Health Director, Health and Sanitation Committee Chairman, District Agriculture Extension Officers, Nurses, Midwives, Community Health Nurses and Assemblymen. These categories of people were selected because of their role in the implementation of various initiatives towards the achievement of the MDGs. A total of two FGDs were conducted each consisting of nine (9) members which lasted for sixty minutes. An FGD has advantages when gathering information or exploring opinions, norms, values, experiences and practices, wishes and concerns. In addition, the study also critically reviewed secondary data from the annual reports of the Tain District Assembly, the Medium Term Development Plan, annual report of the Tain District Education Service, as well as the annual report of the Tain District Health Administration.

The chapter is divided into five sections. The first section is the introductory section and covers the background, objective and the methodology of the study. The second section presents an overview of the MDGs and some of the indicators. The third section presents a brief report of the progress of the MDGs in Ghana. The fourth section analyses progress and challenges in the implementation of the SD Agenda at the local level. The conclusion and the way forward moving into the new sustainable development goals form the last section.

Overview of the Millennium Development Goals

The Millennium Development Goals (MDGs) were identified as the roadmap for meeting the commitments of the Millennium Declaration and have been internationally accepted as a common global development framework. The eight MDGs have development targets and indicators to guide the realization of these goals. The MDGs provide a clear and precise, jointly agreed-upon framework that is applicable in all countries toward poverty reduction and human development. The eight goals are a call to action, to mobilize development efforts involving national governments, local governments and development partners to direct their activities toward achieving the MDGs by the year 2015. Each country has committed to setting such targets and to publishing annual reports assessing progress in relation to each goal. The goals are interlinked and provide a platform for joining together and following up on all the commitments made at the various UN global summits held in the 1990s (UN, 2006). Table 14.1 shows the eight MDGs and some core indicators for monitoring progress.

Table 14.1 MDGs and some indicators

MDGs	*Core indicators*
Goal 1: Eradicate extreme hunger and poverty. Target: Halve, between 1990 and 2015, the proportion of people whose income is less than one dollar a day.	• Average household income • Proportion of households with income less than the poverty threshold
Goal 2: Achieve universal primary education. Target: Ensure that, by 2015, children everywhere, boys and girls alike, will be able to complete a full course of primary schooling.	• Gross Primary Enrolment ratio • Net Primary Enrolment ratio • Proportion of 6–12-year-old children who are not in school
Goal 3: Promote gender equality and empower women. Target: Eliminate gender disparity in primary and secondary education, preferably by 2005 and to all levels of education not later than 2015.	• Ratio of females to males in basic schools • Number of women in District Assembly governance
Goal 4: Reduce child mortality. Target: Reduce by two-thirds, between 1990 and 2015, the under-five mortality rate.	• Under-five mortality per 1,000 in the districts • Trend of child mortality in the districts
Goal 5: Improve maternal health. Target: Reduce by three-quarters, between 1990 and 2015, the maternal mortality ratio.	• Proportion of women who died due to pregnancy-related causes • Trend of maternal deaths in the districts • Proportion of births attended by skilled health personnel
Goal 6: Combat HIV/AIDS, malaria and other diseases. Target: Have halted by 2015, and begun to reverse, the spread of HIV/AIDS.	• HIV prevalence rate in the district • Reported cases of Malaria
Goal 7: Ensure environmental sustainability. Target: Integrate the principles of sustainable development into country policies and programmes and reverse the loss of environmental resources. Target: Halve, by 2015, the proportion of people without sustainable access to safe drinking water and sanitation facilities.	• Proportion of land area covered by forest in the district • Proportion of households without access to safe water in the district • Proportion of households without access to sanitary toilet facilities in the district • Quality of water bodies and their management
Goal 8: Develop a global partnership for development. Target: Develop and implement strategies for decent and productive work for youth.	• Unemployment rate of 15–24 year olds • Population with access to affordable essential drugs on a sustainable basis • Development focus of private organizations working in the district

Source: Fielmua and Bandie (2011); UNDP (2010)

Ghana's MDG Progress

Ghana's progress has been mixed. Targets such as halving extreme poverty (MDG 1a), halving the proportion of people without access to safe drinking water (MDG 7b), universal primary education (MDG 2a) and gender parity in primary school (MDG 3) have been attained. Substantial progress has been made in reducing HIV prevalence (MDG 6c), access to ICT (MDG 8f) and reducing the proportion of people suffering from hunger. However, only slow progress has been made on full and productive employment (MDG 1b), equal share of women in non-agriculture wage employment and women's involvement in governance (MDG 3), reducing under-5 and child mortality (MDG 4), reducing maternal mortality (MDG 5), and reversing environmental resource loss and improving sanitation (MDG 7) (UNDP, 2015).

Ghana met the target of halving extreme poverty in 2006 ahead of the 2015 deadline. The population living below the national lower poverty line (i.e. extreme poverty) dropped from 36.5 per cent in 1991 to 18.2 per cent in 2006. This trend is consistent with the new measures of poverty used in the 2012/13 Ghana Living Standards Survey (GSS, 2014). Using the new lower poverty line of GH¢792.05, extreme poverty declined further from 17 per cent to 8 per cent between 2006 and 2013. The proportion of the population living below the national upper poverty line declined from 51.7 per cent in 1991 to 28.5 per cent in 2006, just 2.6 percentage points away from the MDG target. In spite of the improvement in the poverty situation at the national level, high incidence and depth of poverty remains a challenge in the three northern regions. The growth performance of Ghana over the years, the growing role of social sector programmes including national health insurance, as well as critical investments in physical and social infrastructure, have played a considerable role in ensuring advances in reducing poverty and achieving better human development outcomes (World Bank, 2012; UNDP, 2015).

Progress towards the achievement of the MDGs in the Tain District

A number of initiatives are being pursued by the local authorities towards the achievement of the MDGs in the Tain District. The key action towards the achievement of the MDGs is the implementation of the District Medium Term Development Plans (DMTDP). MDGs have since being mainstreamed into the country's successive medium term national development policy framework, the Ghana Poverty Reduction Strategy (GPRS I), 2003–2005, and the Growth and Poverty Reduction Strategy (GPRS II), 2006–2009. The DMTDP is the overarching development policy document of the district, which aims to sustain development, eliminate poverty and hunger, and improve health of the population of the district. The DMTDP covers all key sectors of the district's economy, thus incorporating a number of activities to address the MDGs. The IDIs with the District Planning officer and the review of the DMTDP reveal that the assembly is actively pursuing a number of programmes including free maternal healthcare, capitation grant and a school feeding programme, among others. This section discusses the progress made towards the achievement of the Millennium Development Goals in the district. It examines the progress made and challenges of the selected goals.

Goal 1: hunger and poverty

Hunger

Food security is an important issue in the achievement of the MDGs. The MDG target for food security seeks to halve between 1990 and 2015 the proportion of people who suffer from hunger. The study reveals that the Tain District is on track of achieving Goal 1 on hunger. The district is food secured and the incident of mal-nourished children is minimal. The district has made good progress in term of food security. It is able to produce enough for the inhabitants within to the extent of being able to export some of the food products outside the district. This is how the agriculture extensions officers and some community members put it during the FGDs:

> We are able to produce enough for the inhabitants within and to the extent of exporting some of the food products to other neighboring district ... apart from food crops, the district is also a major producer of cashew for export.
>
> The issue of food insecurity is not a problem in the district. About 80% are food crop farmers, food is not a problem ... the problem is that we produce to feed ourselves with very little to sell to generate income.
>
> In terms of availability, accessibility and affordability we do not have any major problem. The only problem is that during bumper seasons we cannot store and most produce go waste which is bad for us. But food is not really a problem here. (Ayamga, 2014)
>
> Our agriculture is rain-fed in this district. In most cases, we do farming during two seasons: March–July and August–November. We cannot predict the rains, we use past experience and in some years it fails us. At times you plant your seeds but the rains will not come at the right time or even when the rains come at wrong time.

Poverty

The Tain District's performance in eradicating poverty has not been quite as remarkable. The incidence of poverty represents the number of persons whose incomes or consumption levels fall below the poverty line and can be classified as poor in the district. Though poverty incidence has declined marginally at the district level, there are worrying trends in terms of disparities across the communities in the district. The incidence of poverty remains very high using the consumption and income data of the district. Over 40 per cent of the district population were found to be below the upper poverty line (TDA, 2012). The poverty level in the district also manifests itself in terms of low incomes due to small farm sizes, poor road network, poor housing conditions, high level of child labour and high illiteracy. Using the Tain District poverty profile, it was also evident that poverty in the district is varied with some communities being poorer than others. It ranges from severe poverty areas to less poor areas. The high poverty incidence also reflects in the distribution of poverty in the district. The data reveals that the Sabiye Area Council is the most poverty stricken, followed by the Banda Ahenkro and Kyekyewere Area Councils. The zones with the least poverty are the Badu Town and Seikwa Area Councils. The poverty incidence in the district could largely be explained by varied economic activities of the communities, individuals and households. Poverty is highly endemic among food crop farmers. This is how the District Planning Officer (DPO) put it:

> Poverty is one of the factors dragging down the progress of this district; it is a stumbling block towards our effort to achieving a good standard of living for the people. This is because over 80% of the people are peasant farmers engaged in the production of maize, yam, groundnuts and other cereals ... but I can say that poverty is more stricken in some part of the district than others.
>
> Agriculture, which is the greatest contributor of the district's revenue, and the main survival of the people in the district has been affected by prolonged drought and erratic rainfall in recent years but as for food is not a problem at all in the district. We are food secure.

One farmer said:

> Many of us are poor in terms of cash not food ... in this community everybody produces some food crops so nobody buys from fellow farmer except people who come from other big cities to buy ... this year for instance a bag of maize sells at only GHC50.00 ... master what can this money do.

The high incidence of poverty in the district and among food crop farmers in rural areas should engage the attention of policy makers and relevant stakeholders.

Goal 2: education

Goal 2 of the MDGs seeks to achieve universal primary education with a target of ensuring that children everywhere, boys and girls alike, will be able to complete a full course of primary schooling. Two indicators under consideration in this chapter in assessing the district's education performance in the MDGs are the Gross Enrolment Ratio (GER) and Net Enrolment Ratio (NER) in primary education and the basic education completion rates. The Tain District has made some improvements particularly in the areas of preprimary enrolment. At the kindergarten (KG) level, the NER has increased from 75.0 per cent in 2006 to 95.0 per cent in 2012, which is higher than the national average (GES-Tain, 2012). The 2012 district education report also indicates that 79 per cent of children of primary school-going age in the district are actually in school though this is lower than the national figure of 83.9 per cent. Available data and trend analysis on MDG 2 of achieving universal primary education show that the district is not on track to achieving the gross enrolment target for primary school by 2015 as the NER is decreasing. At the primary level, the NER has rather reduced from 79.0 per cent in 2006 to 72.0 per cent in 2012. However, the completion rate for the primary level has increased from 88.2 per cent in 2006 to 90.4 per cent in 2012.

Education beyond primary school though is also critical to ensure sustained progress toward other goals such as employment, poverty reduction, and health-related MDGs. Although the performance of the district toward universal primary school enrolment is very good, this progress is yet to translate into commensurate primary completion rates. The study reveals that the completion rate at basic level (junior high school) increased marginally from 54.8 per cent in 2006 to 57.7 per cent in 2012, which is not encouraging to achieve this goal and other goals by 2015. An interview with the District Director of Education reveals that though some progress has been made in terms of GER at the primary school level, there are a number of challenges facing the district. The progress was driven by specific public interventions underpinned by the government to achieve universal primary education. This is how the District Director of Education (DDE) and some teachers describe the situation.

> Although we have some challenges the district has achieved good progress in terms of primary enrolment in the district. This is due to various reforms and new policy measures instituted by the government such as the school feeding programme, capitation grant and free school uniforms. (DDE)
>
> I'm not surprised at the poor completion rate at the Junior High School level because of the attitude of some parents towards education. Some parents take their wards to farm during class hours especially during planting season. (Basic School Teacher)
>
> The problem is also the distance to school. Some pupils especially in the remotest part of the district do not have access to basic school in their community. The pupils have to walk about 4 kms to the nearest school and therefore when it rains they do not go to school … or where the elderly child that leads them is sick all the pupils stay at home. (Basic School Teacher)
>
> Some of the children start trading activities at a very tender age and therefore find it difficult to attend school. They make money at tender age and therefore see no need for schooling. (Basic School Teacher)
>
> In some communities the parents prefer their girls to marry after the JSS instead of pursuing the SHS. Some of them as earlier as 15 and 16 years. Once the husband is a worthy man that is okay for the family because he can take care of the girl … that is the reason why you see that the NET is a little higher for girls than boys at the primary school but lower at the JHS. (DDE)
>
> Some parents in the district prefer to use children as farm helps instead of school due to poverty and ignorance and illiteracy. (DDE)

The Gender Parity Index, which measures the ratio between boys' and girls' enrolment rates, has a balance parity of 1 which means a balance between the enrolment for girls and boys at the pre-school level. At the primary level it is 0.98 and it is 0.88 at the junior high school level. On the MDG 3 target of ensuring gender parity, especially at the primary and junior high school (JHS) levels, trends show that the district is on track in achieving both targets, although primary level parity has stagnated at 0.98 since 2006. Several policy measures have accounted for the appreciable improvement in the rate of enrolment in basic schools in the district. In 2010, quite a number of policy interventions were carried out to reinforce the attainment of universal primary education. These include the strengthening of the capitation grant initiative and expanding coverage of the school feeding programme in the district. During the FGDs with some assembly members, a number of challenges were identified as to why the district might not achieve most of the MDG 2 targets by 2015:

> Master, not that we don't want to send them to school. When you have no money to give to the child in the morning, the best option is to take him to farm to assist you. In the farm you will cook and all of you will eat.
>
> In my village for instance, there is no school nearby and so my small girl cannot walk alone to school … they promise to build school here but for years now no school and most people only send their children to school when they relocate to Badu town where there are basic schools.
>
> We received a teacher from the GES to teach in our community but he stayed for only 8 days and went to the district office to change the place to another village because he complains we do not have room where he would sleep … imagine this, the government pays you so you should rent a room yourself.
>
> In this community most of the boys when they complete the JSS they do not further their education … they go to learn a vocation such as carpenter, mechanic or tailoring in Sunyani or Kumasi so I think is better for the child to go to learn vocation after primary education instead wasting three years in JHS and then continue to the same vocation … you understand?

Goal 3: promote gender equality and empower women

In terms of women empowerment, women are seriously underrepresented in major political positions in the Tain District. The study tracked the goal of promoting gender equality and empowering women in the district through participation of women in decision making in the district. The proportion of seats held by women in the Tain District Assembly is one of the indicators used. The study reveals that progress towards increasing the number of women in the assembly suffered a setback with the reduction of the number of women elected into the district Assembly during the 2010 elections, declining from 8 in 2006 to 5 out of the 48 assembly members. Out of the five assemblywomen only one was elected while the other four are government appointees. This reduced the proportion to below 10 per cent.

Goal 5: improve maternal death

Goal 5 of the MDG seeks to reduce by three-quarters the maternal mortality between 1990 and 2015. Although there were no records of maternal deaths in the 1990s in the district since the district was created in 2004, available statistics from the annual health report of the district indicates a consistent reduction in institutional maternal mortality rate from 208/100,000 live births in 2008 to 193/100,000 live births in 2011. This figure could be misleading since the study did not track unreported maternal deaths in the communities due to lack of records on such deaths. However, this downward trend is significant in the achievement of MDG 5. If this trend should continue the district is likely to achieve MDG Ghana national target of 185 per 100,000 live births by 2015. There has also been an increase in access to professional assistance at delivery over the past five years, from 52 per cent in 2003 to 67 per cent in 2011.

Though maternal health care has improved over the past 8 years, extra effort is required for the Tain District to achieve the MDG 5 target of reducing maternal mortality rate by three-quarters by 2015. An in-depth interview with the District Director of Health, the midwives and the community nurses identified a number of challenges. Table 14.2 indicates the doctor/patient ratio of the district.

The progress on maternal health could be derailed due to institutional and socio-cultural challenges in the district. IDIs with the health professionals show that human resources is one the greatest challenges facing health-care delivery in the district. The ratios of nurses and doctors to patients is unacceptably high in the district. It is one of the highest in the country. In an interview with the District Director of Health this is how he summed the challenge:

> My brother the doctor patient ratio of this district is me versus the entire population of the district.
>
> Another big challenge is that the district does not have a blood bank and when you refer a pregnant woman to Wenchi where they can get blood some women refuse to go for fear of blood transfusion … they go to their community and then resort to see traditional birth attendant.

A critical element in maternal health is care provided by skilled professionals during pregnancy and childbirth. The study reveals that over 20 per cent of women do not

Table 14.2 Doctor/patient, nurse/patient and paramedic/patient ratios in the district

Indicator	Baseline
Doctor to population ratio	1:51,778
Nurse to population ratio	1:5,778
Paramedics to population ratio	1:3,452

Source: Tain District Health Directorate (2012)

deliver in a health facility because some of them thought it was unnecessary to do so. Others cited lack of money; accessibility problems like distance to a health facility, transportation problems, not knowing where to go and unavailability of someone to accompany them were also stated as reasons. During the IDIs with midwives and FGDs with community health nurses, a number of socio-cultural factors that could hamper the effort achieved on maternal health in the district were identified:

> Poverty is one of the factors that prevent pregnant mothers from coming early to the facility during labour especially those who stay far away due to lack of money for transport … others also give excuse of husbands not around to give them money. (Midwives and CHN Respondents, IDI)
>
> Although the antenatal care services are free most do not come and when ask them they would mention lack of money to travel to come. (CHN Respondents, IDI)
>
> Poor transport network and vehicles to convey the expectant mother from their communities to the health facility force others to attend to the TBAs nearby to deliver them. Some men also refuse to give money to their pregnant wives to attend hospital. This creates problem especially where the woman is not economically empowered. (FDG)

Some pregnant women shared their concerns during the FGD:

> Transportation is a problem. Most of the communities are not accessible especially during rainy seasons and therefore we have no option but to deliver at home. (FDG)
>
> Lack of financial access hinders us in several ways. When you are going for scan, an amount of GHC30.00 will be charged and when you don't have this amount they will not provide the service. This affects us because you would not know the exact condition of your baby which is sometimes worrying. (FDG)
>
> I refuse to go for a scan requested by the doctor because after all that will not change the sex of my baby. Whatever I am carrying in my stomach will not change so why should I travel all the way to Sunyani and pay GHC30.00 for that purpose. (FDG)
>
> I refuse antenatal care because I did not feel ill during the pregnancy period. I always take herbs as advised by my mother. (FDG)

The issue of religion and maternal health also arises in the district. Some women prefer to consult their pastors on delivery options. One respondent during the FGD said:

> My pastor monitored the progress of my baby till delivery and I had no problem. (FDG)

IDIs with the District Director of Health, the midwives, nurses as well as pregnant women involved in the FGD reveal a lot of maternal health challenges in the district that can affect the achievement of MDG 5 by 2015 if not addressed.

Goal 7c: improving access to water and sanitation

The drinking water and sanitation targets within MDG 7 are to halve by 2015 the proportion of people without sustainable access to safe drinking water and improved sanitation. The provision of water and sanitation services in Ghana remains a critical challenge for the realization of the Millennium Development Goals. Improving water services and uses are essential for increasing hygiene and sanitation service levels that affect the productive lives of people, enhancing enrolment and retention of girls in school, enhancing women's dignity and ability to lead, reducing morbidity and mortality, reducing pre- and post-natal risks and preventing vector- and water-borne diseases (Ministry of Water Resources, Works and Housing, 2007). Water and sanitation are cross-cutting elements of the MDGs. Improving access to water is essential for increasing hygiene and sanitation service levels, which improve the lives and productivity of people. On MDG 7c, the Tain District is not on track of achieving the target on halving the proportion the population without access to safe water and improved sanitation by 2015.

The study reveals that the inadequate access to safe water and sanitation is a perennial problem in rural and urban areas of the district. Though the Tain District's medium-term development plan and other related development priorities give focus to improved rural water supply and sanitation, the district will not be able to achieve MDG 7c on access to improved sources of water and sanitation by 2015. Though the district statistics indicate that the proportion of the population that uses improved drinking water has increased during the last five years, less than 50 per cent of the population has access to improved sources of drinking water. In all the communities, boreholes constitute the major improved source, followed by public taps/stand pipes in three communities; only a few households have pipe-borne water in their dwellings. Rivers and streams make up the largest proportion of unimproved sources of drinking water in the district. The IDIs reveal this in the discussion:

> Though significant progress on water has been made many people in the district still lack safe drinking water, majority are relying on boreholes and streams as sources of drinking water. With only three (what?) to go the district is unlikely to meet the MDG water and sanitation target by 2015 … the situation is difficult. We have plans to serve all these communities either boreholes or piped water but our challenge is funding. (DPO)
>
> Most of the boreholes in my electoral area are broken down for five years without repairs. The community has gone back to use the streams and rivers. The streams have also become very erratic in recent year. (Assemblyman)

Some concerns from community members:

> Our challenge in this community is lack of access to good drinking water. Our borehole broke down for two years now and we have reported it to the assemblyman but no action has been taken so we have to go back to the stream.

The cattle are destroying our drinking water. They also drink from it. How can human beings and animals drink from the same source? Walk through it. We are sharing our drinking water with animals. This is bad but we have no option. The government promised us a borehole last year but it didn't come.

On sanitation, the situation is not encouraging. Apart from a few houses in the entire district which have access to a water closet type of toilet, the majority of the population (over 80 per cent) in the district are not using improved sanitation facilities. Though Badu, Nsawkaw and Seikwa have access to water from pipes, the population is not in position to use a water closet in their houses since water has not been extended to most of the houses. According to the district sanitation statistics, 70 per cent of the total population use open dumping as their system of disposing of solid waste in their communities, a situation which serves as a breeding ground for mosquitoes in gutters and stagnant waters. If the current trend continues, these numbers will remain unacceptably high by 2015 and the district would stand the risk of not achieving MDG 7 on access to water and sanitation. The annual health report of the district reveals that over 80 per cent of the top ten diseases in the district are poor environmental health and sanitation related. Malaria alone accounts for 50 per cent of all the top ten diseases in the district. Figure 14.1 depicts the top ten diseases in the district in 2012.

The challenges facing the Tain District's efforts towards meeting the MDG 7 target on water and sanitation are enormous and require an urgent multi-stakeholder action plan to address them. These concerns were raised during the IDIs with key actors:

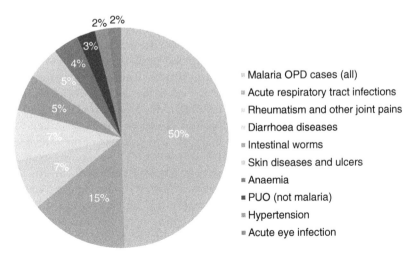

Figure 14.1 Top ten diseases in the Tain District

As stakeholders in local development we believe that improving access to potable water and sanitation is critical to achieving favourable health outcomes, which in turn facilitate economic growth and sustained poverty reduction and the overall achievement of the MDGs but our challenge is inadequate funding and therefore we have to manage with the small resources we have. (DCD)

Imagine women do not have toilet in this community. Ask me where do we go? We use the bushes with the men. We used to have a toilet here until it collapsed last year and the men are not getting one for us. (Assemblywoman)

I have made provision for WC in my house but there is no water so I don't use it ... the situation is bad ... we all use this KVIP but the place is not well kept. The odor is very bad for us so most people refuse to use it. (Opinion Leader).

Conclusion

The overall assessment of the progress toward the achievement of MDGs in the Tain District reveals that, while progress towards the achievement has generally been positive especially with some targets, the performance has been mixed across indicators and based on the current trends, the overall pace of progress was insufficient to achieve all the MDGs by the target date of 2015. Although the Tain District has made significant progress in the area of food security, education and health, the progress towards poverty reduction, maternal health, access to improved water and sanitation is not encouraging. The evidence gathered in the study suggests that scaling up efforts to accelerate progress toward achieving the MDGs in the district is possible if measures are put in place.

Towards new Sustainable Development Goals

The new SDGs form a cohesive and integrated package of global aspirations the world commits to achieving by 2030. Building on the accomplishments of the MDGs, the SDGs address the most pressing global challenges of our time, calling upon collaborative partnerships across and between countries to balance the three dimensions of sustainable development – economic growth, environmental sustainability and social inclusion. Ghana has adopted the Sustainable Development Goals as a new development agenda beyond 2015. To achieve these ambitious goals beyond 2015, Ghana needs to be guided by experiences gathered in the execution of policies and programmes within the MDG framework. The country will need to focus on tackling some of the MDGs that were not attained. Fortunately, the MDGs have dovetailed into the SDGs and any unfinished business can be addressed within the new context. Furthermore, the implementation and monitoring of the SDGs can be localized to address issues of inequality and socio-economic disparities more effectively as well to ensure broader ownership and facilitate the achievement of SDGs in record time.

References

Ayamga, P. (2014, November 12). Personal Interview.

Fielmua, N. and Bandie, R. D. B. (2011). An assessment of MDGs performance at the local level in Ghana: a case study of West Gonja District. *European Journal of Social Sciences*, 23(4), 614–625.

Ghana Education Service (GES)-Tain District (2012). Annual Education Report.

Ghana Poverty Reduction Strategy Paper (GPRSP) (2006). IMF Country Report No. 06/225. Available at www.imf.org/external/pubs/ft/scr/2006/cr06225.pdf. Accessed 17 December 2015.

Ghana Statistical Service (GSS) (2014). Ghana Living Standards Survey (GLSS6): Poverty Profile in Ghana. Accra: Ghana Statistical Service.

Ministry of Water Resources, Works and Housing (2007). Ghana National Water Policy, Accra.

National Development Planning Commission (NDPC) (2010). Ghana Millennium Development Goals Report, UNDP. Accra, Ghana.

Neuman, L. W. (2007). *Basics of Social Research: Qualitative and Quantitative Approaches*. Second edition. Boston: Allyn & Bacon.

Tain District Assembly (TDA) (2012). Tain District Medium-Term Development Plan (TDMDP).

Tain District Health Directorate (2012). Annual District Health Report.

United National Development Programme (UNDP) (2011). Assessing progress in Africa toward the Millennium Development Goals. MDG Report 2011.

United National Development Programme (UNDP) (2015). Ghana Millennium Development Goal Report 2015. Accra: UNDP.

United Nations (UN) (2006). Localizing the Millennium Development Goals: a guide for local authorities and partners. Nairobi, Kenya.

United Nations Children's Fund (UNICEF). (2010). Progress for children: achieving the MDGs with equity. New York: United Nations Children's Fund.

United Nations Development Programme (UNDP) (2010). *Ghana Millennium Development Goals Report*. Accra: UNDP.

World Bank (2012). The Millennium Development Goals, Popular Mobilization, and the Post-2015 Development Framework Policy. Research Working Paper no 6282.

15 Public–private partnerships in highways

The Indian experience

Manisha Verma

Introduction

Development is known to depend on and is determined in significant ways through physical and service infrastructure. The State is charged with the mandate to ensure that policy frameworks are in place to provide an enabling environment for development to take place. In the changing policy environment with multiple non-State actors influencing policy making, different models and approaches to governance have emerged. Partnership with the private sector through a formalized and structured framework is one of these.

Public–private partnerships (PPPs) are being increasingly viewed as an attractive alternative to the traditional modes of delivery of services. A preponderance of PPPs has been observed in highways, expressways, airports, ports, railways, and power production and distribution. Lately some social sector services such as health, education, slum development and urban municipal services have adopted forms where private expertise is utilized in delivery of services. Within PPPs, roles and responsibilities are divided between the two partners. The government can access financial, technical and managerial resources of the private sector in construction and management of public services. It can allocate several substantial risks to the private partners during asset creation and service management. PPPs are claimed to cut down on time and cost overruns. The framework provides a life-cycle approach to asset creation and provisioning of services.

Emerging experience from different countries has revealed serious flaws in the claims of economic superiority, effectiveness and profitability of PPPs. They are being questioned on various accounts of transparency, accountability, equity and excessive profiteering by the private partners, whereas grave concerns have been expressed about elite and agency capture. Critics also suggest a subtle political power shift towards the private sector based on its capital power, through the partnerships. Lately, there has been consensus among scholars on the crucial role that the State partners are required to play within these partnerships to make them more effective. Literature suggests a fundamental rethink on the role of the State agencies within PPPs as there are serious dimensions of public policy and governance which need to be reconsidered from a public interest perspective.

This chapter aims to present learning from the Indian experience of PPPs in highways from a public policy perspective, highlighting the governance issues within the partnerships. A distinctive feature of the Indian experience is that the State partners are found largely responsible for many of the problems that impact the delivery outcomes within these partnerships. This has resulted in lack of interest within the private sector to invest in PPPs. On the other hand, the private partners have also been charged with fairly serious issues such as excessive profiteering through land grabbing and manipulation of the contractual provisions, elite capture, etc. The chapter attempts to critically explore the underlying inter-linked causal factors covering the institutional, financial, politico-bureaucratic and socio-economic structures to understand the reasons causing these issues. PPPs in national and state highways, both operational and under construction, have been studied, thus offering a view of the governance issues of PPPs during both these crucial stages from a national and regional perspective within a federal framework of governance from a developing country, i.e. India. The chapter underscores the crucial role the State agencies need to play in governance of PPPs. While concluding, measures are suggested to strengthen the structures and mechanisms within both the public and private partners to improve service delivery outcomes within the PPP framework.

What made PPPs popular and acceptable

The growth of PPPs is credited to the implicit assumption that the market stands for better efficiencies in production and delivery of services, and partnering with the market is perceived to improve efficiency gains for the government.

PPPs are argued to infuse private capital in public infrastructure projects. Many debt-ridden and cash-strapped governments find this aspect helpful to fill the 'infrastructure deficit'; this also enables releasing the scarce resources for other social objectives. Large infrastructure projects have several substantial financial, commercial, operational, engineering and manpower risks. The government retained many of these in the contractual mode of delivery. It was found ill-equipped to handle them satisfactorily; the contractor did not have sufficient incentive to invest in and manage the different risks of construction and maintenance, and to provide efficiency in cost and quality (Hrab, 2004). Within PPPs the governments can transfer a large number of these to the private partners who are claimed to handle them more efficiently due to their flexible and more agile incentive-based and profit-oriented structures of management. PPPs enable the private partners to bring in their arguably more efficient technological, manpower and managerial capabilities in infrastructure development and management which enhances the quality of services; public sector–provided services have been found to be generally of poor quality with serious issues of sustainability largely due to their weak incentive systems that do not encourage staff performance and rarely promote innovation. Market knowledge and skills in technologically intense fields, discipline and entrepreneurial spirit of the private partner, its project financing and management skills, effective organization and innovation (Field and Peck, 2003) have been cited as reasons for the growing interest in this mode of service delivery.

Within a PPP, services are bundled under one concessionaire or a consortium of developers. According to the transaction cost theory (Williamson, 1998) this leads to reduction in several transaction costs (which are substantial in such multi-actor and multi-agency ventures) thereby resulting in lowered total project cost. This argument is supported by the theory of value-for-money and lifecycle approach to asset development and operation of PPP projects. The contracting mode was criticized for time and cost overruns, the burden of which was borne by the taxpayers by way of an enhanced project cost and delayed services. Because of the involvement of the private sector, it is widely believed that PPP projects do away with the time and cost overruns while providing services of superior quality. Moreover, contracts are known to have limitations when neither specifications of the products nor performance indicators are clearly defined. This is more pronounced in the case of infrastructure projects which are characterized by a high degree of product ambiguity, require specialized knowledge of different organizations, and include investments that have long gestation periods. In such cases, partnerships have been found to mitigate the hazards of uncertainty and ambiguity (Klijn and Teisman, 2000).

Overall, the wide acceptance of PPPs is argued to reflect the transformation of the State–market relationship. PPPs emerged as a form of governance which is argued to be midway between a purely 'State-directed' or 'market-oriented' way for provisioning of public goods (Hodge and Greve, 2009). In addition to providing a mix of resources of the government and the private sectors, PPPs are claimed to be devoid of their dysfunctions (Börzel, 1997).

Worldwide experience of PPPs: brief critical review

Comprehensive review of worldwide experience of PPPs has revealed that there is sufficient and growing evidence to suggest that countries need to deliberate and debate whether PPP is the appropriate mode for delivery of public services. Scholars (Hodge, 2009; Boase, 2000) have advised to be cautious and even sceptical about them.

PPPs have been termed as a Faustian bargain (Flinders, 2005; Peters and Pierre, 2004). There have been serious concerns in respect to their governance aspects including transparency, accountability, equity and efficacy under all conditions, and the risk of being captured by the elite (Rosenau, 1999; Peters and Pierre, 1998). Moreover, doubts have been expressed regarding their 'social desirability' (Vining and Boardman, 2008: 11). Studies of PPPs in the OECD and capitalist countries have found serious flaws with their claims of economic superiority, effectiveness and profitability (Shaoul, 2009; Smith, 2009; Hodge and Greve, 2007; Pollock et al., 2007; Walker and Walker, 2000). Analysts have been wary of the veracity of measures used to determine VfM (value for money) and cost effectiveness of these projects, pointing out that inaccurate discount rates, and flimsy and unprofitable risk analysis based on subjective criteria are often employed for estimation (Ball et al., 2007; Fitzgerald, 2004). Studies (Pollock et al., 2007) have revealed flawed evidence to support claims of improved time and cost overruns. PPPs have been charged with allegations of excessive profiteering (Toms et al., 2009), hidden wealth transfers to the financiers, and deliberate attempts by governments to showcase their perceived efficiency and inflated savings (Shaoul, 2009). Shaoul (2011) suggests a subtle political power shift towards the private sector based on its capital power via PPPs.

Additionally, several issues have been pointed out with the public partners such as lack of clear government objectives and poorly defined sector policies, low credibility of government policies, inadequate legal and weak regulatory and supervisory mechanisms, poor risk management and complex decision-making processes (Kwak et al., 2009; Li et al., 2005; Zhang, 2005). Lack of a competent market to fulfil the presumed arrangements, marked difference between norms and practices of administration, and ascriptive rather than achievements-based criteria for allocation and distribution of recourses are observed to impede success of PPPs in many countries (Peters, 2001). Furthermore, political, social economic and administrative contexts have been found to result in various forms of barriers to their acceptance in some low-income countries (Clarke, 2000; Hentic and Bernier, 1999; Haque, 1996).

Role of the State in governance of PPPs

In view of the increasing concerns about several fundamental issues within these partnerships, there is growing convergence among scholars that the role of the State does not diminish when the private sector gets involved in provisioning of services; it merely changes as the government needs to assume new responsibilities (Allard and Trabant, 2007; Grimsey and Lewis, 2005). Rejecting demands for a 'minimalist State', there appears to be increasing support for an active role of the State within the partnerships (Peters, 1998; Weiss, 1997; Evans, 1995), as the State is acknowledged as the key source of constitutional legitimacy with legal authority and social mandate to seek and protect the public interest, ensure equity, continuity and stability of services, prevent discrimination or exploitation, and ensure social cohesion (Goodsell, 2006; Osborne and Gaebler, 1992; Badie and Birnbaum, 1983). Scholars (Kjaer, 2004; Jessop, 2003) advocate an enlarged role of the State for engaging in a wider process of formulating policies and mechanisms for allocating and coordinating recourses; influencing and structuring the economic and market space; and transit from the role of the financer, controller and commander to a wider one of regulator and facilitator (Goodsell, 2006).

PPPs in highways in India

A distinct and visible policy shift in favour of PPPs in various sectors, predominantly in infrastructure, is evident in India. The central government is increasingly depending on private sector participation to supplement government efforts which will be focused on providing infrastructure to remote areas and rural roads (Planning Commission, 2010). Reliance on the private sector is reflected in the figures of the 12th Five Year Plan (FYP):[1] fifty per cent of the planned investment of about US$1 tn is expected to come from the private sector. Private sector financing was about 30–35 per cent in the 11th FYP (2007–2012), while it was 25 per cent during the 10th Plan. Investments being projected in the road sector over the next decade indicate a 40 per cent rise. Of the total investments, 60 per cent is expected to come from the private sector (Financial Express, 2011a). This is estimated to account for 28 per cent of total investment in infrastructure planned by emerging economies, and is next only to China (PIB, 2010).

According to the World Bank (2010), India is now the largest market for private participation in infrastructure in the developing world. India attracted US$71.9 bn in infrastructure in 2010, which is an 85 per cent increase from 2009. This is the highest investment in any developing country in 2009–2010. A study by Cambridge University and the Royal Bank of Scotland (RBS, 2011) concluded that emerging countries will spend about US$20 tn in the next 20 years on infrastructure, registering a growth of 158 per cent; India is listed as one of the countries that are expected to benefit substantially from this growth. Sector-wise, roads will see the second maximum investment (US$4.2 tn) after power (US$12.7 tn).

The central government created the National Highways Authority of India (NHAI), a statutory autonomous body under the National Highways Authority (NHA) Act, 1988 for enhanced focus on development of highways. It functions under the Ministry of Road Transport and Highways (MoRTH) and is the nodal body for development of national highways, whether under the government-funded or the PPP mode. Within the states, the governments have set up their own bodies to build and maintain state highways. PPP projects are of two kinds in India – BOT (toll) and BOT (annuity). Within the former, the private partners collect tolls from the users to recover their investment; some may be shared with the government if they are in a revenue-sharing agreement. These are built, operated and maintained by the private partner while for the latter the government pays back the entire private investment with interest in installments. The government operates and maintains these projects through private agencies.

Critical analysis of PPPs in highways in India

PPPs were the preferred mode in highways till 2013. Since then, there has been a rethinking regarding their being effective modes of service delivery. The central government has decided to award more than 50 per cent of road projects through the contractual mode in 2013 (PIB, 2013). What significantly differentiates the Indian experience is that the government has been found responsible for many problems affecting highway PPPs. According to recent estimates, infrastructure projects (including highways) worth INR 15 lakh crores are stuck due to various forms of administrative delays and hurdles, and funding problems.

The following sections will deeply analyse the underlying structures and mechanisms causing this.

Delayed environment clearance

The central government has created a structured and legal framework for selection and approval of the concessionaires through model concession agreements, a viability gap funding mechanism, and the formation of high level committees for approval of PPP projects. State governments have their own mechanisms often reflecting the standards protocols created by the central government. Some states provide additional viability gap funding to attract investors. The frameworks clearly define the roles and responsibilities of the two partners, reasons for project termination, change in scope of work, situations for seeking arbitration etc.

Despite this, a large number of PPP projects have languished during the past two to three years by as much as two to five years resulting in escalated project cost, stalled projects, piling cases of arbitration and litigation, and huge inconvenience to the users. The central Ministry of Statistics and Programme Implementation has identified environmental clearance and land acquisition as prime factors causing maximum cost and time overruns in PPP projects. The well-known infrastructure developer GMR pulled out of the much publicized Kishangarh-Udaipur-Ahmedabad highway project due to delayed environmental clearances. The Comptroller and Auditor General of India has pegged the loss caused by this termination at INR 32,500 crore.

As per the division of risks and responsibilities, the central Environment Ministry has to provide environment and forest clearances for projects that pass through forest and non-forest lands; these become more stringent when the route is through protected forests, wildlife and bird sanctuaries. Although the clearances are supposed to be accorded before the construction begins, it seldom happens in practice. Due to financial compulsions, in most cases the developers begin the construction in stretches that do not pass through forests, while the process of seeking clearances continues, although the highway can be made completely operational only when these stretches are connected. So even if patches are completed elsewhere, in absence of environmental clearance the project cannot be completed and made operational.

In addition to the environmental clearance, the state government has to prepare a proposal for seeking central clearance for felling and scientific stacking of trees when the highway passes through a forested area. This is reviewed and approved by the central Forest Ministry. The state is also required to select an agency for undertaking these tasks, which need to be completed before construction can begin. This approval is also delayed by years by the central Ministry in several projects. To cut their losses, some of the bigger developers undertake the activity of felling and stacking the trees themselves; the smaller ones however find it difficult due to their limited resources. According to the concession agreement, the government should reimburse the charges of felling and stacking. In a large number of cases this takes a long time due to slow administrative procedures. What is reimbursed is as per the government-approved rates which are much lower than the market prices at which the concessionaires get the work done. This has led to many developers pulling out of prominent PPP projects.

Evidence reveals that the proposals get stuck in the central Environment Ministry either because they are not thorough in their details (which warrants their reformulation at the state level), or NHAI has not deposited in time or delayed deposition of the Net Present Value (NPV) of the forest resources with the state forest department. A significant reason is centralization of powers to accord clearances in the central ministry thus resulting in the inordinate delay. Earlier regional offices were delegated powers to approve proposals up to a certain financial value. Not only the highways sector, but the infra sector as a whole has been affected by these delays. Recently (January 2014), the Minister for Environment widely perceived to be responsible for the delays was replaced in order to expedite these clearances. Several hundred uncleared files have been recovered from her office. According to reports, the new minister has cleared projects worth INR 1.5 lakh crore in the month since he took charge (Economic Times, 2014).

Problems associated with land acquisition

Land acquisition is identified as one of the most critical elements in timely completion of PPP projects in India. It is found to push back projects by as much as 2 to 4 years, at times. The national Parliamentary Standing Committee on Transport formed to monitor progress in roads projects has found land acquisition to be one of the major causes for delay in projects (Economic Times, 2011).

'Land' is a state subject, which means that the state governments, and not the central government, acquires land for all infrastructure projects including national highways. As per the concession agreement, 80 per cent of the land, free of encumbrances, is to be handed to the concessionaires before construction starts. This is found to almost never happen. In practice the concessionaires begin work as soon as 50 per cent of the land is available so as to meet their project schedules, while acquisition of the remaining land by the government goes on simultaneously. When land is provided in discontinuous patches, which happens often, it is of little use, as although some stretches of the highway can be constructed, the project as a whole cannot be operationalized with broken intermittent links. Over the years the constructed sections also start demanding maintenance even without being used for transport.

One of the major problems with land acquisition in India, till 2013, was caused by the archaic Land Acquisition Act of 1894 which was used to offer compensation packages to the landowners across various parts of the country. The poor rates of compensation, which were not revised for many years, resulted in landowners, mostly poor rural farmers, refusing to part with their land for government projects, choosing to sell to private developers for higher rates. The cause included in the Act that defined reasons for acquisition of land for 'public purpose' was too broad and general. This was misconstrued and misused by the state governments to purchase and divert prime land for purposes which did not serve any public cause. As the need for land for infra projects grew, without commensurate rates for compensation many parts of the country witnessed demonstrations, and sometimes armed rebellions by the agitating landowners as a show of protest. In May to June 2011, the state of Uttar Pradesh saw armed clashes between farmers and the state police force in the 165 km Yamuna-Greater Noida expressway project. The farmers were paid as little as INR 50 per sq. m. in an area while the same land was being sold at INR 1,500 per sq. m. by the private developer with a staggering 3,000 per cent mark-up (The Pioneer, 2011). The agitation assumed a political hue when the opposition parties, at the centre and state, supported the farmers.

To address the cause of these country-wide demonstrations, and to boost infrastructure projects most of which were severely affected by the old Land Act, the national government enacted the Right to Fair Compensation and Transparency in Land Acquisition, Rehabilitation and Resettlement Act, 2013 (also known as the Land Act, 2013). Under the new Land Act, landowners in rural areas will be given four times the prevailing market value as compensation for their land; rates are twice the market value in urban areas. The Act has a sharper definition of 'public purpose' (its loose definition had earlier lent to its wide and rampant misuse). Also, consent of at least 80 per cent of project-affected people is mandatory before acquisition for a PPP project, with a detailed plan for their rehabilitation and resettlement along with livelihood options; evidence from the Yamuna Expressway suggests that many original landowners lost almost their entire livelihood while the compensation was not sufficient for them to generate alternative livelihoods. The new Act have been criticized by private developers. They perceive that the cost of procuring land will increase many-fold, hiking up the project cost. Financing such projects may become very costly for them, they feel. Some states, such as Maharashtra, have raised concerns about the impact this Bill will have on development projects.

Land acquisition is India is worsened by the poor and unsystematic land records in the country coupled with the practice that on record the property is very frequently undervalued compared to its market value to avoid a part of the transaction tax. This makes the compensation, based on the sale deed, substantially lower than the market rates even after escalation is factored in. Due to these issues, some projects often end in litigation and arbitration which delays projects considerably as in the Indian judicial system getting a judgement in land matters is a time-consuming process due to huge pendency of cases[2] (Mendelsohn, 1981). The Dwarka Expressway, even after more than five years, was only 35 per cent complete in 2012 on account of problems with land acquisition and multiple court cases (Times of India, 2012a).

Another aspect of land acquisition that substantially delays infra projects is that it is a lengthy process over many stages from the date of notification for acquisition to its actual possession (during these stages, in some projects sometimes the developer has to compensate the landowners in addition to the government as they may not move out from their land, expecting additional compensation from the private developers). Furthermore, as 'land' is a state subject and highways fall within the administrative jurisdiction of states, for national highways the national agencies have to depend on the state agencies for land acquisition. This requires close coordination between them which may become an issue when in the federal setup the governments at the centre and state do not follow the same political allegiance.

Moreover, government functionaries at the district level are required to closely liaise with the landowners during the many stages. As the district level revenue officers are engaged with various administrative and developmental works of the state government, the task of land acquisition tends to get prolonged. Remarkably such problems have not been noticed in the state highway projects, reflecting problems of ownership of projects at the national and state levels. Developers and NHAI officials are of the view that there is a heightened sense of ownership in state projects among the state functionaries, which is observed to be missing in their involvement in national projects.

Land grabbing by private partners

A significantly distinct feature of PPPs in India (highways, civil aviation and metro rail) is the extent to which they have been used by the private sector to grab prime land. Collusion between the State functionaries and the private developers, rent-seeking behaviour of officers for extending favour, poor accountability structures, archaic land laws which provided for very low compensation, discretionary policymaking favouring a few, crony capitalism, and a booming real estate and land market in the country seem to have contributed to this state of affairs.

In many PPP projects the central or state governments offer land surrounding the project at a substantially low price to the concessionaires as an 'incentive' to invest in the projects, on the alleged pretext that the projects are otherwise unviable (read the case of Odisha at Business Standard, 2011). The government has been charged with misusing the clause of 'public purpose' in the old Land Act to procure land for private developers at cheap prices (Times of India, 2013). The developers have been found to develop this for commercial purposes or sell it to other developers at higher prices, generating huge profits (the Supreme Court has pulled up the Gujarat state government for unlawfully allowing transfer of land from one company to another [Business Standard, 2014]). Critics argue that these gains are not shared with the original landowners nor are ploughed back to the community. Since the Indian economy is primarily agrarian, the original landowners lose out on almost their entire livelihood while the compensation is not sufficient to generate alternative livelihoods. As noted earlier, in the Yamuna-Greater Noida expressway in Uttar Pradesh, the developers reportedly colluded with the state government and amassed prime tracks of land used for commercial development with the landowners getting pittance compensation (The Pioneer, 2011). The role of government functionaries in acquiring land on behalf of the private sector has been so rampant that the State has been called 'the real estate agent' of corporate India (Business Standard, 2010). The Comptroller Auditor General of India has rapped politicians and ministers in Maharashtra for favouring a private land developer, and for framing regulations and amendments propelled by private and public interest (Hindustan Times, 2012). In the scam surrounding the US$620 mn highways projects funded by World Bank, it has been alleged that the concessionaire diverted huge funds to realty development in India and abroad (Times of India, 2012b).

This easy availability of prime land in the name of PPP projects has led many real estate developers and construction companies to transform themselves into infrastructure concessionaires.

While the New Land Act has been formulated to balance the needs of development with fair compensation and equity, it is too early to say to what extent it will be successful in dealing with these deep rooted issues.

Do PPPs always provide better services?

It is claimed that PPPs cut down time and cost overruns, and provide better services. Available data however contradicts this claim.

The Comptroller and Auditor General (CAG) of India carried out a performance audit of eight BOT and annuity projects of the 17 projects taken up for execution under PPP mode between March 1998 and April 2003. Only five were completed in time while there was a delay of as much as 42 months in many (Indian Express, 2008). According to a World Bank report of 2009, as many as 40 per cent of road projects suffer from cost overruns of anything between 25 and 50 per cent (Financial Express, 2011b).

Recent emerging evidence has revealed that many concessionaires have been found to under-report traffic in projects which have a revenue and profit-sharing arrangement with the government. This has strengthened the perception of PPPs leading to loss to public exchequer. For example, in the high-traffic Delhi-Gurgaon expressway, where NHAI gets 50 per cent of toll revenue, under-reporting of traffic has caused huge revenue loss. A Parliamentary Committee have made scathing remarks on the glaring discrepancy between the revenue collected and traffic reported (Times of India, 2011; Lok Sabha Secretariat, 2009). A Public Interest Litigation admitted in the Supreme Court alleges that the concessionaires have recovered their investment of INR 5.50 bn in the three years of operation while its concession period is for more than 20 years. The concessionaire Delhi Gurgaon Super Connectivity Limited (DGSCL) has been removed under charges of gross irregularities, failing to provide services to the tens of thousands of passengers who pass through the 32-lane toll plaza every day, and causing huge traffic pile-ups during peak hours.

Factors shaping PPPs in highways in India

Misalignment of goals of the partners

I argue that a significant reason for delays in administrative approvals which have shaped PPPs in highways in India is that not all government agencies treat the private developers as partners. It is only the executing government agency that considers the concessionaires as partners to some extent. For others they continue to be the 'private sector' and are treated as 'glorified contractors'. I further argue that that the slow-footing of administrative approvals and clearances seems to be motivated by a tacit understanding among some public functionaries that the private partner will 'do anything' to expedite the works. Within the contractual mode the government functionaries followed up on approvals and clearances, as the contractor had no incentive to begin work unless these were provided. In the PPP mode, since revenue generation is dependent on timely completion of the project and revenue, active follow up by the private partners themselves tends to generate opportunities for rent-seeking. This appears to be welcomed by a large part of the bureaucracy as such opportunities did not exist in the contractual mode.

Secondly, there appears to be a general mistrust in the private sector among the public functionaries. The traditional mistrust for private profit within the public sector emanating from its socialistic structure seems to have further accentuated the diffidence among the public functionaries to accord timely clearances. This seems to be strengthened by several highly publicized cases where the private sector has not acted as a responsible partner and indulged in opportunistic behaviour aimed at making illegitimate gains at the cost of the users through acts such as land grabbing, under-reporting of traffic and manipulation of contract obligations. I argue that these are largely responsible for misalignment of goals and priorities between the two sets of partners, causing lack of trust in the private sector and poor support for PPP projects from different government agencies.

Advocacy by policymakers

Despite the almost dismal performance of PPPs in highways in recent times and the weakening interest by the private sector in them, the central Railways and Civil Aviation Ministries continue to announce PPP projects. PPPs also figure prominently in the budget speech of the Finance Minister every year. Some state governments also prefer the PPP mode for delivery of services. I argue that political economy within a region is a potent factor shaping PPPs in India. A section of policymakers, politicians and bureaucrats are observed to project the idea that PPPs are and will be the panacea for all infrastructure ills of the country. There seems to be a concerted effort to inflate the infrastructure deficit within the country, and many times to project an artificial and unrealistic infrastructure scarcity along with the inability of the government to take up the financial burden of the projects. These projections are not based on available evidence from sectors which already have experience with PPPs. Moreover, PPPs in other sectors will also be operating within the same politico-bureaucratic-administrative structures within which PPPs in highways function.

However, some experts have been opposed to the philosophy of adopting PPPs when other frameworks may be better suited for India. The high powered Working Group on Urban Transport of the Planning Commission (Planning Commission, 2012) led by Mr. E. Shreedharan, former head of the much acclaimed government-owned and operated Delhi Metro project and an eminent technocrat, has opined that the PPP mode does not work for urban metro-rail projects in India primarily because the revenue models within the country are not evolved enough to support such partnerships, and the government is better located to undertake these projects. This has been borne out by the pulling out of Reliance Infra from the Delhi Metro Airport link after a protracted legal battle; the government-owned Delhi Metro Rail Corporation (DMRC) has taken over the operations (The Hindu, 2013).

Concluding remarks

The underlying implicit assumption favouring PPPs is that the market stands for better efficiencies in production and delivery of services, and partnering with the market is perceived to improve efficiency gains for the government. Despite the theoretical prescriptions on PPPs claiming their superiority over the services provided by the public sector through the contractual mode, the Indian experience suggests that these contractual collaborations between public and private agencies require deft handling. Manipulation of the contracts by the private sector coupled with poor contractual administrative skills in a large part of the bureaucracy has resulted in PPPs often causing loss to the taxpayer and the exchequer. PPP projects in highways have suffered due to the problems elaborated upon in the chapter. The slow pace of development of the highway network in the country has in turn impacted economic and regional development.

PPPs are typically claimed to coalesce strengths of the private and the public partners, while doing away with the dysfunctionalities of the two sectors. PPPs in the infra sector in India have demonstrated that they are not devoid of these dysfunctionalities of the State and the market, and the projects continue to be affected by inadequacies of present structures of administration and bureaucracy, and market imperfections. Misalignment of goals has resulted in a 'trust' deficit. Aligning these sectors with a common public objective may require understanding of the basic fundamentals that govern the State and the market, while creating governance structures and mechanisms that ensure accountability of both the partners; the capacity of governments to effectively manage these complex new relationships thus assumes critical importance. The State needs to ensure that the PPPs do not result in capitalizing the gains and distributing losses among the taxpayers.

There is consensus among scholars that the focus of discussion and debate on PPPs needs to shift from the first generation technical and managerial matters to larger and more important dimensions of governance and public policy to understand 'who gets what' in the final analysis, as PPPs are likely to constitute a significant component of public policy. Governments need to carefully consider each case and decide whether a PPP is the appropriate mode within the given structural context in which they operate. Many deficiencies in public services can be largely mitigated through reforms of State institutions. Rather than follow stereotypes, governments may explore innovative collaborations with the private sector that would meet different developmental goals of the country and not try to fit one size to all, while still deriving maximum benefit from the usage of private sector resources and expertise. Clarity regarding the choice of a framework for service delivery, not necessarily based on economic and revenue criteria alone, may serve as a valuable instrument to guide policy choices and support their wide acceptance.

Notes

1   Five Year Plans (FYP) are five-year-long plans for various sectors of the economy and social development of the country.
2   According to an estimate there are nearly 30 m cases pending in the various courts of India. Available at www.rtiindia.org/forum/2385-nearly-30-million-cases-pending-courts.html. Accessed 14 August 2011.

References

Allard, G. and Trabant, A. (2007). Public private partnerships in Spain: lessons and opportunities. *IE Business School Working Paper no. EC8-115-1*, 10-7-2007, Madrid.

Badie, B. and Birnbaum, B. (1983). *The Sociology of the State*. Chicago: University of Chicago Press.

Ball, R., Heafey, M. and King, D. (2007). The Private Finance Initiative in the UK. *Public Management Review*, 9(2), 289–310.

Boase, J. P. (2000). Beyond government? The appeal of public private partnerships. *Canadian Public Administration*, 43(1), 73–92.

Börzel, T. A. (1997). What's so special about policy networks? An exploration of the concept and its usefulness in studying European governance. *European Integration online Papers (EIoP)*, 1, 1–28.

Business Standard (2010). The state as real estate agent for corporate India, 7 October 2010. Available at www.business-standard.com/india/news/the-state-as-real-estate-agent-for-corporate-india/410486/. Accessed 12 October 2010.

Business Standard (2011). CAG raps govt for fixing land rate to suit buyers, 24 August 2011. Available at www.business-standard.com/india/news/cag-raps-govt-for-fixing-land-rate-to-suit-buyers/446780/. Accessed 24 August 2011.

Business Standard (2014). SC pulls up Gujarat Minister Anandiben on land deal, 23 January 2014. Available at www.business-standard.com/article/pti-stories/sc-pulls-up-gujarat-minister-anandiben-on-land-deal-114012301168_1.html. Accessed 23 January 2014.

Clarke, G. (2000). The decline of Levathian: state, market and civil society in South-East Asia 1986–1998. In S. P. Osborne (ed.), *Public-Private Partnerships: Theory and Practice in International Perspective* (pp. 149–162). London: Routledge.

Economic Times (2011). Focus on roads rather than filling coffers: par panel to NHAI, 27 March 2011. Available at http://economictimes.indiatimes.com/news/economy/infrastructure/focus-on-roads-rather-than-filling-coffers-par-panel-to-nhai/articleshow/7798187.cms. Accessed 28 March 2011.

Economic Times (2014). Cleared projects worth Rs 1.5 lakh crore: M Veerappa Moily, 12 January 2014. Available at http://articles.economictimes.indiatimes.com/2014-01-12/news/46113053_1_posco-project-steel-plant-forest-advisory-committee. Accessed 12 January 2014.

Evans, P. (1995). *Embedded Autonomy: States and Industrial Transformation*. Princeton, NJ: Princeton University Press.

Field, J. E. and Peck, E. (2003). Public-private partnerships in healthcare: the managers' perspective. *Health and Social Care Community*, 11(6), 494–501.

Financial Express (2011a). India eyes record road expansion, 18 June 2011. Available at http://www.financialexpress.com/news/india-eyes-record-road-expansion/805172/0. Accessed 18 June 2011.

Financial Express (2011b). NHAI selects 101 firms to directly bid for projects, 21 July 2011. Available at http://news.indialocals.com/read/2011/07/05/LJRkMzZmBGx5KmD4ZQtjAj==/full-story-nhai-selects-101-firms-to-directly-bid-for-projects. Accessed 21 July 2011.

Fitzgerald, P. (2004). *Review of Partnerships Victoria Provided Infrastructure*. Melbourne: Growth Solutions Group. Available at www.un.org/esa/coordination/Alliance/PPPInfrastructure .pdf. Accessed 25 December 2010.

Flinders, M. (2005). The politics of public–private partnerships. *The British Journal of Politics and International Research*, 7(2), 215–239.

Goodsell, C. T. (2006). A new vision for public administration. *Public Administration Review*, 66(4), 623–636.

Grimsey, D. and Lewis, M. K. (2005). *The Economics of Public Private Partnerships*. Cheltenham, UK: Edward Elgar.

Haque, M. S. (1996). The contextless nature of public administration in third world countries. *International Review of Administrative Sciences*, 62(2), 315–329.

Hentic, I. and Bernier, G. (1999). Rationalization, decentralization and participation in the public sector management of developing countries. *International Review of Administrative Sciences*, 65(2), 197–209.

The Hindu (2013). Delhi Metro takes over operations of Airport Express Line. Available at www.thehindu.com/news/cities/Delhi/delhi-metro-takes-over-operations-of-airport-express-line/article4869374.ece. Accessed 1 July 2013.

Hindustan Times (2012). CAG indicts ministers for land misuse, 18 April 2012. Available at www.hindustantimes.com/India-news/Mumbai/CAG-indicts-ministers-for-land-misuse/Article1-842218.aspx. Accessed 18 April 2012.

Hodge, G. (2009). Delivering performance improvements through public private partnerships: defining and evaluating a phenomenon. *International Conference on Administrative Development: Towards Excellence in Public Sector Performance*. Riyadh, Saudi Arabia, 1–4 November 2009.

Hodge, G. and Greve, C. (2007). Public–private partnerships: an international performance review. *Public Administration Review*, 67(3), 545–558.

Hodge, G. and Greve, C. (2009). PPPs: the passage of time permits a sober reflection. *Economic Affairs*, 29(1), 33–39.

Hrab, R. (2004). Private delivery of public services: public private partnerships and contracting-out. *Panel on the Role of Government in Ontario Research Paper no. 21*. Available at http://papers.ssrn.com/sol3/papers.cfm?abstract_id=694582. Accessed 21 October 2011.

Indian Express (2008). NHAI invites CAG ire over project delay, 15 December 2008. Available at www.indianexpress.com/news/nhai-invites-cag-ire-over-project-delay/398514/. Accessed 5 April 2011.

Jessop, B. (2003). Governance and meta-governance: on reflexivity, requisite variety and requisite irony. In H. P. Bang (ed.), *Governance as a Social and Political Communication* (pp. 142–172). Manchester: Manchester University Press.

Kjaer, A. M. (2004). *Governance*. Cambridge: Polity Press.

Klijn, E. H. and Teisman, G. R. (2000). Governing public-private partnerships: analysing and managing the processes and institutional characteristics of public-private partnerships. In S. P. Osborne (ed.), *Public-Private Partnerships: Theory and Practice in International Perspective* (ch. 5). London: Routledge.

Kwak, Y. H., Chih, Y. Y. and Ibbs, C. W. (2009). Towards a comprehensive understanding of public private partnerships for infrastructure development. *California Management Review*, 51(2), 51–78.

Li, B., Akintoye, A., Edwards, P. J. and Hardcastle, C. (2005). Critical success factors for PPP/PFI projects in the UK construction industry. *Construction Management and Economics*, 23(5), 459–471.

Lok Sabha Secretariat. (2009). COPU report on public private partnership in implementation of road projects by national highways authority of India in respect of Delhi – Gurgaon project. *C.P.U. NO. 934*. Department of Road Transport, Ministry of Road Transport and Highways, New Delhi: Lok Sabha.

Mendelsohn, O. (1981). The pathology of the Indian legal system. *Modern Asian Studies*, 15(4), 823–863.

Osborne, D. and Gaebler, T. (1992). *Reinventing Government*. Reading, MA: Addison-Wesley.

Peters, B. G. (1998). 'With a little help from our friends': public-private partnerships as institutions and instruments. In J. Pierre (ed.), *Partnerships in Urban Governance: European and American Experiences* (pp. 11–13). New York: Palgrave.

Peters, B. G. (2001). *The Future of Governing*. Lawrence, KS: University of Kansas.

Peters, B. G. and Pierre, J. (1998). Governance without government? Rethinking public administration. *Journal of Public Administration Research and Theory*, 8(2), 223–243.

Peters, B. G. and Pierre, J. (2004). Multi-level governance and democracy: a Faustian bargain? In I. Bache and M. Flinders (eds.), *Multi-Level Governance* (pp. 75–92). Oxford: Oxford University Press.

PIB (Press Information Bureau) (2010). *Speech by the Chairman, NHAI on Investors/Lenders Conference*, 12 May 2010. NHAI, Government of India. Available at http://pibmumbai.gov.in/scripts/detail.asp?releaseId=E2010PR846. Accessed 16 October 2010.

PIB (2011). Highlights of economic survey 2011–12. Available at http://pib.nic.in/archieve/esurvey/esurvey2011/eng2011.pdf. Accessed 16 June 2011.

PIB (2013). 7300 Km of highways to be awarded during 2013–14; more than 50% projects to be taken up on EPC mode. Press Information Bureau, Government of India. Available at http://pib.nic.in/newsite/erelease.aspx. Accessed 16 April 2013.

The Pioneer (2011). Billionaire land-grabbers, 11 March 2011. New Delhi edition, p. 7.

Planning Commission (2012). *Recommendations of Working Group on Urban Transport for 12th Five Year Plan*. Available at planningcommission.nic.in/.../hud/wg_%20urban%20Transport.pdf. Accessed 5 June 2012.

Planning Commission (2010). *Annual Report to the People on Infrastructure 2009–2010*. Planning Commission, Government of India. Available at http://planningcommission.nic.in/reports/genrep/rep_apinfra.pdf. Accessed 10 January 2011.

Pollock, A., Price, D. and Playe, S. (2007). An examination of the UK Treasury's evidence base for cost and time overrun data in UK Value-for-Money policy and appraisal. *Public Money and Management*, 27(2), 127–133.

RBS (Royal Bank of Scotland) (2011). Infrastructure spending in emerging markets to almost triple over the next twenty years, 29 September 2011. Available at www.rbs.com/media/news/press-releases/2011-press-releases/2011-09-30-infrastructure.ashx. Accessed 19 November 2011.

Rosenau, P. V. (1999). The strengths and weaknesses of public-private policy partnerships. *American Behavioral Scientist*, 43(1), 10–34.

Shaoul, J. (2009). Using the private sector to finance capital expenditure: the financial realities. In A. Akintoye and M. Beck (eds.), *Policy, Finance & Management for Public-Private Partnerships* (pp. 27–46). Oxford: Blackwell

Shaoul, J. (2011). 'Sharing' political authority with finance capital: the case of Britain's public private partnerships. *Policy and Society*, 30(3), 209–220.

Smith, A. L. (2009). PPP financing in the USA. In A. Akintoye and M. Beck (eds.), *Policy, Finance & Management for Public-Private Partnerships* (pp. 199–211). Oxford: Blackwell.

Times of India (2011). New counter to check revenue loss on e-way, 23 May 2011. Available at http://articles.timesofindia.indiatimes.com/2011-05-23/delhi/29573727_1_toll-plaza-nhai-official-toll-revenue. Accessed 23 May 2011.

Times of India (2012a). Deadline shifted as Dwarka e-way trips on land hurdles, 4 May 2012. Available at http://timesofindia.indiatimes.com/city/delhi/Deadline-shifted-as-Dwarka-e-way-trips-on-land-hurdles/articleshow/12987437.cms. Accessed 4 May 2012.

Times of India (2012b). World Bank funds for national highway diverted to realty projects? 4 May 2012. Available at http://timesofindia.indiatimes.com/india/World-Bank-funds-for-national-highway-diverted-to-realty-projects/articleshow/12989246.cms. Accessed 4 May 2012.

Times of India (2013). *CAG raps Haryana body for land deal –'Gurgaon land sold at a loss of 439cr'*. Available at http://epaper.timesofindia.com/Default/Client.asp?Daily=CAP&showST=true&login=default&pub=TOI&Enter=true&Skin=TOINEW. Accessed 13 March 2013.

Toms, S., Asenova D. and Beck, C. M. (2009). Refinancing and profitability of UK PFI Projects. In A. Akintoye & M. Beck (eds.), *Policy, Finance and Management for Public-Private Partnerships* (ch. 4). Oxford: Blackwell.

Vining, A. R. and Boardman, A. E. (2008). Public-private partnerships in Canada: theory and evidence. *Canadian Public Administration*, 51(1), 9–44.

Walker, B. and Walker, B. C. (2000). *Privatization: Sell Off or Sell Out? The Australian Experience*. Sydney, Australia: ABC Books.

Weiss, L. (1997). Globalization and the myth of the powerless State. *New Left Review*, 225(225), 3–27.

Williamson, O. E. (1998). Transaction cost economics: how it works; where it is headed. *De Economist*, 146(1), 23–58.

World Bank (2010). *Private Participation in Infrastructure Database*. PPI data update note 58, August 2011. Available at http://ppi.worldbank.org/features/September-2011/2011-South-Asia-PPI-infrastructure-note.pdf. Accessed 5 September 2011.

Zhang, X. (2005). Critical success factors for public–private partnerships in infrastructure development. *Journal of Construction Engineering and Management*, 131(1), 3–14.

16 Lessons from Pakistan's project implementation failures

An appraisal

Iram A. Khan and Asad K. Ghalib

Introduction

Pakistan has come a long way since its independence in 1947. Its intermittent economic growth has not been unimpressive. It has made tremendous improvements in infrastructure, reduced poverty levels, and tripled per capita income. However, according to the data provided in World Development Indicators and more importantly, Human Development Reports, it continues to underperform on most of the social and political indicators for a country of its income level. This is despite the fact that Pakistan was the third highest recipient of official development assistance in the world from 1960 to 1998 (after India and Egypt) (Easterly, 2001; Zaidi, 2011). In addition, it successfully negotiated 22 adjustment loans with the IMF and the World Bank, and also benefited from a lucrative Cold War alliance with the United States (Easterly, 2001).

This foreign funding has been directed at both military and civilian purposes. In case of the latter, this has also contributed towards development of the economic and social sectors through public sector development projects. Pakistan has an intricate and elaborate system for initiating, managing and monitoring development projects, accomplished through the Planning Commission of Pakistan that acts as a secretariat for the whole process (Planning Commission, 2008, 2011).

According to Salihi (1991), growth in development projects is directly proportionate to the increasing role of governments in development. Pakistan also made substantial investments in the social sector through five-year plans[1] due to substantial inflow of foreign development assistance. However, the results show that these investments made through development projects have mostly been unsuccessful (Khan, 1999). This gap in investment and project outcomes needs to be properly investigated to draw lessons of experience for the future.

The public sector projects are different and unique from private sector projects as they are altruistic in nature and ensure a level of service to the community; they cost more, may take more time to execute, and involve an array of stakeholders spread across a socio-economic continuum in society. This chapter focuses on public sector development projects only.

There is a tendency to look at development projects with a mechanistic approach, with the chief objective being achieving results within cost and time constraints and achieving specified quality (McCollum and Sherman, 1991). They are managed as 'technical systems instead of behavioural systems' (Belout and Gauvreau, 2004: 2). However, despite this focus on targets and objects, projects fail (Matta and Ashkenas, 2003). Project failures can take different forms: its failure to meet performance targets, or its termination before completion. There are also instances when a project is completed but is still considered a failure or becomes controversial due to exorbitant costs and little benefits to stakeholders.

A project is considered a success when it achieves its objectives within time, cost and scope of activities with efficient and effective use of resources at a desired technical performance level and final acceptance by its customers and clients (Matta and Ashkenas, 2003). In other words, the success or failure of a project is predicated on the identification, quantification, assessment, and hedging of different risk factors.

The rest of the chapter is as follows. The next section reviews literature on the subject, which also helps in framing research questions. The third section brings different theoretical perspectives together and develops a model that collates different factors that contribute towards the success/failure of development projects. The penultimate section undertakes analysis of data. The chapter concludes with summing up of discussion and makes suggestions for enhancing the efficiency and effectiveness of public sector development projects in the country.

Review of literature

The analysis of reasons for the failure of development projects has been a popular subject for study and research. Different authors (Belassi and Tukel, 1996; Ke et al., 2011; Taylor and Ford, 2006; Tukel and Rom, 1998) have outlined different reasons/risks for failure in development projects. However, most of the literature published in international journals refers to projects in the context of private sector firms implementing them for public/private sector clients. However, the current study focuses on development projects being executed in the public sector only. The following paragraphs provide a brief review of literature on the subject.

Fortune and White (2006) state that the three most-often cited critical success factors (CSF) for a project are support from senior management, having clear and realistic objectives and producing an efficient plan. However, the authors find this approach deficient from two perspectives. First of all, the inter-relationships between factors are at least as important as the factors themselves. However, the CSF approach does not take the former into account. Secondly, this approach takes project implementation as static which actually which is not in reality. The dynamic and evolving nature of the projects gives different levels of importance to different factors at different stages of the implementation process.

Salihi (1991) focuses on the essential aspects of development planning, implementation and evaluation processes. He defines four categories of factors that determine the success or failure of a project. These are (1) technological, (2) sociocultural, (3) environmental and (4) institutional. These factors influence the outcome of a project individually as well as dynamically by interacting with each other. The author collected data from six sub-Saharan countries with the help of interviews and survey questionnaires that used a Likert scale of 1–4. He used simple cross-tabulations and bivariate comparison between the frequency distributions of variables making each of the factors and project outcomes.

Mastroianni (2011) investigates risk management methodologies applied to R&D projects. The author proposes a risk management framework in which Project Risk Failure Mode and Effects Analysis principles are applied to development projects. The model is tested in four case studies, and this proves the validity and value of the model.

Belassi and Tukel (1996) suggest a new scheme of classification for critical success factors. An important contribution made by the authors is to highlight the interaction between different individual factors and group them in accordance with their relationship with each other. They have also conducted an empirical analysis to test the practicality of their new scheme. The statistical tools used in their study identify many critical factors such as those related to project managers' performance, team members and environmental conditions.

Based on the review of literature, the following research questions have been framed and will be answered with the help of primary data collected through a survey questionnaire:

1   What are the critical factors that are important for the success/failure of development projects?
2   What are the factors related to a project manager and his/her team that are important for the success/failure of development projects?
3   What are the factors in external environment that are important for the success/failure of development projects?
4   What type of project organizational structure is important for the success/failure of development projects?
5   Is there any difference in the monitoring of local and foreign funded projects that makes them run differently?

Conceptual framework

Based on the review of literature, a conceptual framework has been developed which is based on the four principal factors that determine the success or failure of a development project. These are:

- Factors related to a project.
- Factors related to the project manager and his team management.
- Factors related to the external environment.
- Role of organizational structure.

The role of foreign donors in projects is surveyed separately. These factors have been graphically presented in Figure 16.1.

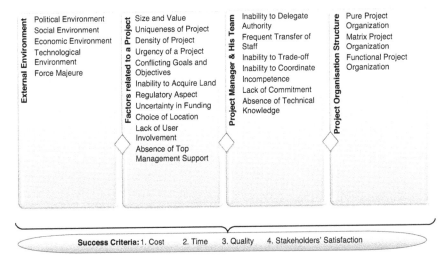

Figure 16.1 Conceptual model with respect to success and/or failure in a development project

Figure 16.1 indicates that all the variables are interrelated with each other and contribute towards the success/failure of a project individually as well as collectively. Grouping different variables under different broad categorization allows us to determine whether a project failure was due to external circumstances or project management team or project organization structure.

The model given in Figure 16.1 is based on the work of Belassi and Tukel (1996) but has also benefited from different other research papers (Belout and Gauvreau, 2004; Dvir, Raz and Shenhar, 2003; White and Fortune, 2002; Yu, Flett and Bowers, 2005; Yu and Kwon, 2011).

Ranking of success criteria

The four criteria have been selected for ascertaining the success or failure of a project. These are cost, time, quality, and stakeholders' satisfaction. It is quite possible that one criterion, say cost, is not achieved though the project is completed within the time limit. Quality and stakeholders' satisfaction are also not necessarily interrelated. If a project has the requisite quality but has not been located at an appropriate site, it will not lead to stakeholders' satisfaction. It is also possible that the stakeholders are satisfied, but the project lacks good quality, which leads to stakeholders' satisfaction in the short run only.

Factors related to a project

Characteristics inherent in a project are not generally given sufficient importance. However, they carry a lot of weight and play a pivotal role in its success or failure.

Some of the factors listed in Figure 16.1 are size and value, urgency, uniqueness, density and conflicting goals and objectives, amongst others. Density is about project complexity: the number of activities that need to be completed to begin a new one. Urgency in initiating a project gains significance for example in case of natural disasters, when there is little time available for planning. This absence of planning adversely affects a project. Uniqueness refers to a characteristic of a project which makes it different and unique from other current or previous projects. Uniqueness makes the selection of a competent project team difficult; and in the absence of a qualified and competent project team, the probability of project failure becomes high. Conflicting goals and objectives highlight the contradictions (such as equity vs. efficiency) that are many times inherent in public sector development projects.

Factors related to project manager and his team

Human resources play an extremely important role in determining the success/ failure of a project. While a competent, committed and qualified project team manages difficult situations and goes a long way in ensuring project success, this will not be the case for a project team that lacks these characteristics.

External environment

The external environment is usually given a lot of importance. It not only has significance for every stage in the project cycle but also in the overall success or failure of a project. This includes political, social, economic and technological factors.

Factors related to project organization

The project organization type or institutional factor is not given particular consideration in the literature, though the World Bank mentions its significance in the outcome of development projects (World Bank, 1984). Three types of project organizations currently in Pakistan were considered for this study. First, there is pure project organization, for which a separate and independent project office exists; second, there is matrix project organization for which there is a separate project office but the Project Director and one or two senior project members are appointed on an additional charge basis from a Ministry. If the organizational form is a pure project form overlaid on the functional divisions of the parent firm, it is called a matrix form (Meredith and Mantel, 1995). Finally, there is also a functional project organization type for which no separate project office is established. The existing staff from the Ministry/departments manages a project in addition to their routine responsibilities.

Research methods

Based on the review of literature, factors instrumental in the success/failure of a development project were identified. A questionnaire was developed keeping in view the conceptual framework, and was distributed to the participants of the

Senior Management Course in the National School of Public Policy. They filled in the questionnaire and returned them to the researchers. Fifty-nine questionnaires were received in total, which were used for analysis and discussion.

The first section of the questionnaire introduced the authors, and had information about area of specialization in education and years of work experience. It also promised the confidentiality of data and the anonymity of each respondent. The second section had four questions about a respondent's knowledge about and experience of working in development projects, while the third section with three questions asked for a respondent's perception about a locally and foreign funded project. The fourth section asked respondents to rank the four criteria (cost, time, quality and stakeholders' satisfaction) to measure the success/failure of development projects, while the last section, in which respondents ranked the success/failure of development projects based on different factors, had four sub-sections. They were (1) general success factors related to a project (10 questions), (2) factors related to a project manager and team members (8 questions), (3) factors related to external environment (4 questions), and (4) role of organizational structure (4 questions).

All the questions, except the last one which required any further comments if desired, were compulsory and the respondent was not allowed to submit the online questionnaire unless he/she had answered all the compulsory questions. This eliminated the problem of incomplete answers to questionnaires, which is common in such studies. A Likert-type scale was used and the respondents were requested to rank a criterion on a scale of 1–6. The least important rating was 1, while 6 being the most important one.

The data compiled through the online survey was analysed with the help of frequency analysis for the top two answers (ranked 5 and 6). The reason for choosing 5 and 6 is that these two indicate an above-average score on the Likert scale of 1–6. Answers for each factor were summed up and then sorted in descending order. This method allowed the author to find out in which order the respondents had prioritized different factors.

Analysis and discussion

Out of 59 respondents, 54 were male, while 5 were females. Thirty-six paticipants held Master's Degrees, 13 had completed MS/MPhil programmes and five had finished their Doctorates. Only 4 respondents had specialization in Project Management, while 24 had degrees in General Management. All the respondents were experienced public sector managers. Officers normally come for the Senior Management Course after they have put in at least 15 years of service. Forty per cent of officers had served for 20–30 years.

Knowledge and experience of development projects

Different respondents had different sorts of experience in a public sector development project. Figure 16.2 shows that most of the respondents had worked in a development project and even a greater number had been associated with it. Sixty-three per cent of the respondents had prepared a PC-I,[2] while 66 per cent

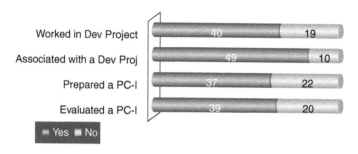

Figure 16.2 Knowledge and experience of development projects

had evaluated it. Preparing and evaluating a PC-I is a technical job, which requires technical and analytical skills.

Ranking the success criteria

With the help of literature review, four criteria were identified to measure the success or failure of a public sector development project. Figure 16.3 ranks the four criteria in terms of importance given to them by the respondents. It can be seen that cost was ranked the lowest, while time, quality and stakeholders' satisfaction were ranked the highest, respondents ranking them on the combined Likert scale of 5 and 6. Quality and stakeholders' satisfaction are closely related concepts and the respondents gave equal rating to these.

Factors related to a development project failure

The section aims to assess the impact of general factors that lead to success or failure in a public sector development project. These have been given in Figure 16.4 and have been calculated by adding scores on scales of 5 and 6 on the Likert scale. Their analysis shows that size and value of a development project, its uniqueness (combines newness and being different from others), urgency (lack of planning, e.g. due to natural calamity), density (number of activities to be completed to begin a new activity) and conflicting goals and targets are not rated highly by the respondents. Conflicting goals and targets in the context of a public sector development project arise in a number of ways. One obvious example is that of predatory elites who try to extract their pound of flesh by forcing project managers to hire workers from their constituencies. The other example is that of a school or hospital being built by public money for the welfare of the poor, but also with a mandate that it should generate its own funds, thus putting it outside the reach of the poor. Though the public sector development project has been initiated in the name of equity, its results may lead to inequity and further socio-economic imbalance in society. However, conflicting goals and targets is not considered important by the respondents, which signifies a positive dimension of public sector development projects in the country.

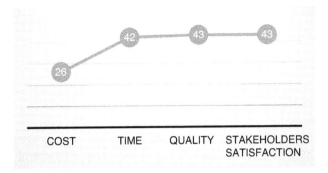

COST   TIME   QUALITY   STAKEHOLDERS
                                         SATISFACTION

Figure 16.3 Ranking of criteria

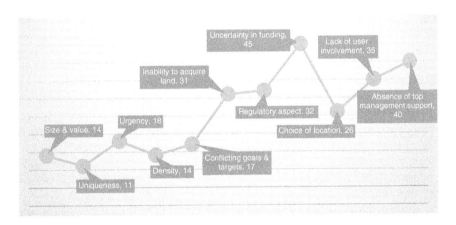

Figure 16.4 Factors related to development project failure

There are, however, some factors which have been ranked highly by the respondents. They find them important and significant for ensuring the success or failure of a public sector development project. Inability to acquire land figures highly on the scale. Though the Planning Commission of Pakistan has made it mandatory that no project (especially pertaining to infrastructure) will be approved unless land required for the project has been earmarked and acquired, this continues to be a major factor for the failure of development projects. Regulatory aspects (compliance with different laws, rules and regulations), choice of location for establishing a development project and lack of user involvement (absence of local participation in project formulation and execution, especially in social sector projects) are rated as important factors for its success or failure. Location has been given a high rating because the selection of location is based on political expediency rather than the real needs of a project or its beneficiaries. The result is that the public sector development projects, despite their completion, fail to benefit the intended population.

The most important factor is uncertainty in funding for public sector development project. Twenty-five respondents gave it a ranking of 6, while another 20 rated it at 5. Thus 45 out of the 59 respondents ranked uncertainty in obtaining funds for a development project as the biggest hurdle in its success. This aspect has acquired greater significance with the passage of time. As the number of public sector development of projects has increased over the years, the requirement for funding has also increased proportionately. However, the development funding has not kept the same pace. The result is that funding for a project not only gets delayed but also becomes uncertain.

Another factor is absence of top management support. The respondents rated this as one of the most crucial factors for the success of a public sector development project. Forty out of 59 respondents ranked it at 5 and 6 on the Likert scale.

Factors related to project manager and his team

Factors related to project manager and his/her team (Figure 16.5) reflect their attributes that can contribute towards the success or failure of a public sector development project. Their importance has been calculated based on the number of respondents rating them 5 or 6 on the Likert scale. Inability to delegate by a project manager is the first attribute respondents were requested to comment on. Their aggregate response comes to 25. However, frequent transfer of project staff was given a very high rating, with 13 and 27 respondents ranking it at 5 and 6, respectively. This shows that this factor was given greater importance when it comes to the success or failure of a project. Inability to trade-off, defined as 'sacrifice something in an exchange', is rated low, while inability to coordinate with other individuals and offices for furthering the objectives of a development project is rated as an important factor (aggregate rating of 37).

Incompetence and lack of commitment on the part of project staff were the next two questions asked from respondents. Forty-four and 43 are the two highest ranking scores given to them in this category. This shows that both the incompetence

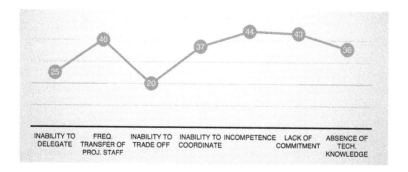

Figure 16.5 Factors related to project manager and his team

of project management and lack of commitment on their part are two major reasons for the failure of a development project. Absence of technical background is another factor that has been rated relatively highly by the respondents. It can be inferred that project management has been found to be a technical and professional subject for which special expertise is required. Therefore, this aspect has also been rated highly by the respondents.

Factors related to external environment

The external environment includes five dimensions. These are political, social, economic and technological factors as well as force majeure. Of these, the factor considered most important by the respondents is political. Despite having a low aggregate score of 26 in the top two rankings of 5 and 6, the political economy aspects of a development project are rated the highest (Figure 16.6). The force majeure is given the least importance in the external environment category. Technological factors also figure low in priority, suggesting that most of the public sector development projects are not greatly affected by technological advancements outside in society. Intriguingly enough, though stakeholders' satisfaction was given high priority by the respondents, the social factors figure low. This contradiction can be attributed to the fact that the involvement of stakeholders in the project cycle is generally very low.

Factors relating to project structure organization

This aspect covers three types of project organizational structures which are prevalent in Pakistan. These have been graphically presented in Figure 16.7.

There is once again no clear pattern emerging from the frequency distribution of responses. Though the Planning Commission of Pakistan has clearly stipulated that all the projects above a certain limit should have an independent project office headed by a Project Director, this has not been reflected

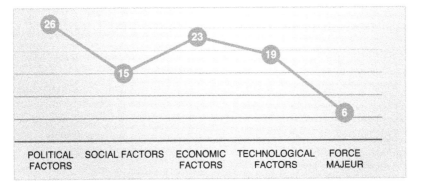

Figure 16.6 Factors related to external environment

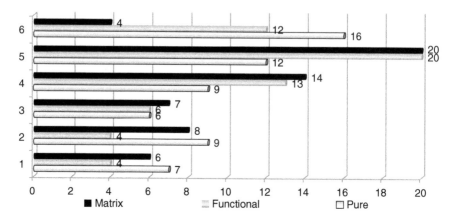

Figure 16.7 Factors related to project structure organization

in the responses. The recommended organizational structure of the Planning Commission is closer to the pure project structure, but we can see that the responses stagger across the 6 scales, which reflects a large variance. Compared with that is the functional project structure, in which there is no separate project office and officers posted in the Ministry/department manage the project in addition to their routine responsibilities. This enables them to get hefty project allowances from the projects. This has been pointed out by the respondents as the most important reason for the failure of development projects in Pakistan. Matrix project organization, which is a mix of pure and functional forms, has been considered as the third most important reason for the failure of development projects. The frequency of responses show that 20 respondents rate it at 5 (the same number as for functional structure); however, only 4 respondents rate it at 6 compared with 12 for the functional structure.

Distinguishing between local and foreign funded projects

The respondents were requested to differentiate between local and foreign funded projects. According to 95 per cent of respondents (56), it was possible to draw different lessons of experience from foreign funded projects (Figure 16.8). Sixty-three per cent (37) found that the foreign funded projects were more likely to achieve their goals and objectives. The reason for this was the supervisory missions of donor agencies to review the progress made in foreign funded projects (Figure 16.9). 75 per cent of respondents (44) found this to be a reason for such projects to achieve their goals and targets.

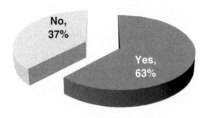

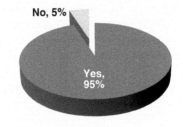

Figure 16.8 Perception about local and foreign funded projects

Figure 16.9 Effectiveness of supervisory missions

Conclusion and recommendations

Analysis in the previous section shows that all the five research questions have been answered. Different factors related to a project and project management have been identified that are important in explaining the success/failure of a public sector development project. Similarly, factors in the external environment and type of project organizational structure also impact the success/failure of a project. The role of supervisory missions in foreign funded projects was also found positive.

We can conclude from the study that the success or failure of a development project depends on stakeholders' satisfaction and quality followed by its completion in time which is a close second. Cost is the least important criterion.

There are a number of reasons for the failure of public sector development projects in Pakistan. The online survey form asked for the respondents' opinion regarding eleven different factors responsible for the success/failure of public development projects. 'Uncertainty in funding' was rated as the most important factor followed by the absence of top management support. Uniqueness was given the lowest rating by the respondents. This shows that public sector development projects are generally routine in nature.

For a project manager and his team, incompetence was the topmost reason for the success/failure followed by lack of commitment (a close second) and frequent transfer of project staff. Inability to trade off and delegate were considered the least important by respondents. There has been a general deterioration in the quality of civil servants, who normally act as project directors. This factor is supplemented by their frequent transfers, which severely affects continuity in a project. These aspects are also closely linked with lack of top management support. All these factors complement each other with the result that the project scope and objectives lose their meaning and purpose.

As for external factors, political factors topped the list closely followed by economic and technological factors, respectively. However, these were not given a very high rating by the respondents, which is evident from the low scores for each factor. As for factors related to project organization, the pattern is not clear, as matrix, functional and pure project structures were given scores of 24, 32 and 28, which provides a mixed picture. This shows that the results for this factor are ambiguous for the success/failure of public sector development projects.

The respondents differentiated between local and foreign funded projects. They found the latter to be better managed, and one of the reasons for this is the supervisory role of donor agencies through their regular review missions. Compared with local funded projects, they were more likely to achieve their goals and targets. This also shows that the project monitoring and review functions at the Planning Commission of Pakistan are weak and need reinforcement.

Notes

1   Except for 1973–77, which is known as the non-plan period.
2   PC-I is a feasibility report on a template designed and developed by the Planning Commission of Pakistan.

References

Belassi, W. and Tukel, O. I. (1996). A new framework for determining critical success/failure factors in projects. *International Journal of Project Management*, 14(3), 141–151.

Belout, A. and Gauvreau, C. (2004). Factors influencing project success: the impact of human resource management. *International Journal of Project Management*, 22(1), 1–11.

Dvir, D., Raz, T. and Shenhar, A. J. (2003). An empirical analysis of the relationship between project planning and project success. *International Journal of Project Management*, 21, 89–95.

Easterly, W. R. (2001). *The Political Economy of Growth Without Development: A Case Study of Pakistan*. Cambridge, MA: John F. Kennedy School of Government, Harvard University.

Fortune, J. and White, D. (2006). Framing of project critical success factors by a systems model. *International Journal of Project Management*, 24(1), 53–65. doi: doi:10.1016/j.ijproman.2005.07.004.

Ke, Y., Wang, S., Chan, A. P. C. and Cheung, E. (2011). Understanding the risks in China's PPP projects: ranking of their probability and consequence. *Engineering, Construction and Architectural Management*, 18(5), 481–496.

Khan, S. R. (1999). An assessment of basic education under the social action plan in Pakistan. *The Lahore Journal of Economics*, 4(2), 35–51.

Mastroianni, S. A. (2011). *Risk Management among Research and Development Projects* (MSc.). Lehigh University, Bethlehem, PA.

Matta, N. F. and Ashkenas, R. N. (2003). Why good projects fail anyway. *Harvard Business Review*, 81(9), 109–116.

McCollum, J. K. and Sherman, J. D. (1991). The effects of matrix organization size and number of project assignments on performance. *IEEE Transactions on Engineering Management*, 38(1), 75–78.

Meredith, J. R. and Mantel, S. J. (1995). *Project Management: A Managerial Approach* (3rd ed.). Canada: Wiley.

Planning Commission (2008). Guidelines for Project Management. Islamabad: Planning Commission, Government of Pakistan.

Planning Commission (2011). Analytical review of the PSDP project – Public Sector Development Project. Islamabad: Planning Commission, Government of Pakistan.

Salihi, D. O. (1991). Factors Influencing the Success of Donor Funded Pastoral Projects in the Sahel (PhD). University of Arizona, Phoenix.

Taylor, T.. and Ford, D. N. (2006). Tipping point failure and robustness in single development projects. *System Dynamics Review*, 22(1), 51–71. doi: DOI: 10.1002/sdr.330.

Tukel, O. I., and Rom, W. O. (1998). Analysis of the characteristics of projects in diverse industries. *Journal of Operations Management*, 16(1), 43–61.

White, D., and Fortune, J. (2002). Current practice in project management – an empirical study. *International Journal of Project Management*, 20, 1–11.

World Bank. (1984). Toward sustainable development in sub-Saharan Africa: a joint program of action. Washington: World Bank.

Yu, A. G., Flett, P. D. and Bowers, J. A. (2005). Developing a value-centred proposal for assessing project success. *International Journal of Project Management*, 23, 428–436.

Yu, J. -H. and Kwon, H. -R. (2011). Critical success factors for urban regeneration projects in Korea. *International Journal of Project Management*, 29, 889–899.

Zaidi, S. A. (2011, October 2). Friends with benefits: who gains from US aid to Pakistan? – a critical analysis of the aid dynamics, *The News on Sunday*, p. II.

17 Development management and practice

Concluding remarks and lessons learnt

Justice Nyigmah Bawole, Farhad Hossain,
Asad K. Ghalib, Christopher J. Rees and
Aminu Mamman

Developing countries continue to experiment with various forms of interventions as part of efforts to break free from the shackles of poverty, malnutrition, inadequate infrastructure, exclusion and general forms of underdevelopment. In the last several decades, development management has been one of the most fashionable means of ensuring development effectiveness (Turner, Hulme and McCourt, 2015; Hirschmann, 1999). Whilst various countries have implemented different interventions from a development management perspective, the results are rather mixed. A critical analysis of the chapters in this book and an assessment of country-specific interventions provide some useful lessons both from and for development management and practice.

Based on the developing country experiences reported in this book and from our backgrounds as practitioners and academics in the field, we have identified a number of ideas which could be regarded as central to development management. We propose to discuss these ideas and the lessons they provide along the following, sometimes overlapping, themes: conceptual or theoretical ambiguity and its effects, capacity (human and material), the conflicting and complementary role of the state (bureaucracy) and the private sector, actor pluralism, accountability and participation, political incentives and ethical values.

First, we acknowledge that even though the objectives of development initiatives are often similar, their conceptualizations often vary. This is largely due to the ideological orientations of development actors often grounded in the theoretical ambiguities that have characterized the development discourse throughout history. In effect, developing countries are hardly able to optimize the synergistic roles played by various development management actors, including donors and NGOs, in ways that ensure a more coordinated and concerted approach to development. Similarly, within even the same political space in developing countries, orientations loom so large that sometimes there is little continuity in change in development policy implementation. For example, even though Ghana was hailed as having successfully implemented the First Compact of the Millennium Challenge Account, thereby enhancing agricultural production, export and infrastructural development, there were attempts by a subsequent government to change the lead actors in implementation before the commencement of the Millennium Challenge Account II. Similar examples of divergent, often uncoordinated and unsustainable approaches to managing development could be found across other developing countries across the world. However, as some authors sought to point out in one of the chapters, rather than competing for supremacy of theoretical or conceptual orientations, it would be more useful to appreciate the strengths and weaknesses of various positions. The next step then would be to explore ways of leveraging the interventions and success stories of various actors in ways that emphasize a common goal in and a shared approach to managing development.

Another useful lesson in the practice of development management is the need to address capacity concerns. Some countries have resorted to developing small and micro-enterprises (SMEs) or the application of public–private partnerships (PPPs) as viable means of employment generation or local economic development and service delivery, respectively (Mamman et al., 2015; Cunningham, 2011; Hodge and Greve, 2007). However, as the South African experience has shown, these approaches can only provide visible development outcomes if personnel are imbibed with the skills relevant to operate. Besides, governments must of necessity design policies with the collaboration of the private sector to create the enabling environment for the pursuit of development management objects. Additionally, for interventions to be successful, agents of development management should have reliable access to material and financial resources for their work. In relation to the capacity building lessons identified in the practice of development management, it has been found out that some application of nationalization policies inject a sense of patriotism which is crucial in development management. This point is evidenced in the gains realized among the Gulf Co-operation Council Countries. In the case of Ghana, there is evidence from the mining sector that whilst developing national managers has greater prospects of ensuring effective development management, it is equally significant to adopt indigenous training mechanisms. This will remove a possible sense of alienation in capacity building and skill application.

Development analysts have often assumed rather binary approaches with regard to state and private sector involvement in the development management space. Whilst some have called for the state to be the fulcrum of development, others believe that the state should recline and allow the market a free rein. However, in practice, development management provides some useful evidence that neither the state nor the private sector could be left out in the ever widening and globalizing development management space. So, far from relegating public sector bureaucracies, for example, as being inimical to development reforms, we are presented with evidence to the effect that the role of the state in creating the enabling environment for the pursuit of development aspirations is crucial (Hirschmann, 1999). Once this is done, the state would see the private sector as not a competitor, but rather a partner in the provision of development needs to the larger citizenry. The increasing adoption of public–private partnerships, though inevitably fraught with challenges (Boase, 2000), attests to the veracity of this argument.

In addition to the above point, despite differences in the approaches to development management, it is generally recognized that it involves a multiplicity of actors. For example, the immense role of non-governmental organizations in the provision of health, education and business support services has been emphasized. NGOs have also played leading roles in the advocacy for better service delivery across the developing world. The lesson here is that governments and other stakeholders can no longer stand aloof from the operational dynamics of NGOs since the activities of the latter are inescapably linked to broader development interventions. This recognition explains the increasing interest among researchers and practitioners in understanding the internal workings of NGOs. In one of the chapters in this book for instance, the governance structures of INGOs in Kenya were examined in ways that provide useful lessons both for INGOs within that country and other developing countries. Elsewhere in this book, it has also been pointed out that local governments and traditional institutions play important roles in development management. For instance, following the MDG implementation experience and other interventions, there is much to be said for the district assemblies and their ability to mobilize the support of the central government, community and non-state actors for development. This is also evidenced in the changing roles of chiefs from being mere custodians of land and tradition, to being the initiators or supporters of development interventions. Through their powers and influence, chiefs are also able to exact accountability from state and non-state actors in order to ensure judicious and equitable use of resources.

Development management experiences further provide some lessons for rethinking the design of development interventions. It has emerged that where potential change agents feel threatened by development management reforms, they are likely to resist such reforms or create impediments in implementation (Hirschmann, 1999). Also, there are cases where programmes and projects do not align with the felt needs of potential beneficiaries. This often detracts from the gains envisaged by development management advocates and practitioners. We find that a better and more viable means of realizing development effectiveness is to involve potential beneficiaries in the design and implementation of development initiatives. Whilst the bottom-up approach is therefore recommended, we concede that there are isolated cases where capacity concerns require that some modicum of centralization or top-down approach is adopted (Brett, 2003).

The wave of democratic reforms and the accompanying competitive clientelist politics found in developing countries (Khan, 2010) also have implications for development management. It is now evident that ruling coalitions or political elites in developing countries are often motivated by electoral calculus instead of better development outcomes (Abdulai and Hulme, 2014). The implication is that developing country governments largely allocate resources not based on equity concerns or value for money but rather what kinds of investments could inure to their political fortunes (Hirvi and Whitfield, 2015). These considerations are so overwhelming that they tend to serve as impediments in the way of development interventions or objectives across developing countries. This, therefore, provides useful lessons to donors and other stakeholders, to critically assess the competitive political regime in a manner that could address possible impediments to interventions.

Another important lesson worth noting is the primacy of ethical values in the development management process. Indeed, apart from capacity concerns, it is generally felt the absence of, or the relegation of, ethical values and civic consciousness underlie most of the development challenges facing development countries. Cases of bribery and corruption, nepotism, and moonlighting, among others, have been variously cited as characteristic of both the private and public sector organizations in third-world countries (Ryvkin and Serra, 2012; Dwivedi et al., 2007). There is therefore the need to re-awaken the ethical consciousness of development actors in order to make them positive agents of change. Here, the call is to borrow from best practice whilst emphasizing the tried and tested indigenous ethical practices. The significance of this point lays in the fact that previous development management initiatives tended to disregard all traditional forms of ethical conduct as archaic, inimical or ineffective. As a result, most actors, especially in the public sector, felt alienated since they saw foreign ethical values as nothing more than impositions or platitudes which had no meaningful bearing on shaping society.

In conclusion, there is no doubt that some reasonable gains have been made in the developing world through the application of development management tools. However, some useful lessons have emerged in practice which could contribute to shaping future interventions for better and more visible outcomes.

References

Abdulai, A.-G. and Hulme, D. (2014). The politics of regional inequality in Ghana: state elites, donors and PRSPS. *Development Policy Review*, 33(5), 529–553.

Boase, J. P. (2000). Beyond government? The appeal of public private partnerships. *Canadian Public Administration*, 43(1), 73–92

Brett, E. A. (2003). Participation and accountability in development management. *The Journal of Development Studies*, 40(2), 1–29.

Cunningham, L. X. (2011). SMEs as motor of growth: a review of China's SMEs development in thirty years (1978–2008). *Human Systems Management*, 30(1), 39–54.

Dwivedi, O. P., Khator, R. and Nef, J. (2007). *Managing Development in a Global Context*. Basingstoke: Palgrave Macmillan.

Hirschmann, D. (1999). Development management versus third world bureaucracies: a brief history of conflicting interests. *Development and Change*, 30(2), 287–305.

Hirvi, M. and Whitfield, L. (2015). Public-service provision in clientelist political settlements: lessons from Ghana's urban water sector. *Development Policy Review*, 33(2), 135–158.

Hodge, G. and Greve, C. (2007). Public–private partnerships: an international performance review. *Public Administration Review*, 67 (3), 545–558.

Khan, M. (2010). *Political Settlements and the Governance of Growth-Enhancing Institutions*. London: SOAS.

Mamman, A., Kanu, M. A., Alharbi, A. and Baydoun, N. (2015). *Small and Medium-Sized Enterprises (SMEs) and Poverty Reduction in Africa*. Newcastle: Cambridge Scholar Publishing.

Ryvkin, D. and Serra, D. (2012). How corruptible are you? Bribery under uncertainty. *Journal of Economic Behavior & Organization*, 81(2), 466–477.

Turner, M., Hulme, D. and McCourt, W. (2015). *Governance, Management and Development: Making the State Work*. Basingstoke: Palgrave Macmillan.

Index

For Product Safety Concerns and Information please contact our EU
representative GPSR@taylorandfrancis.com
Taylor & Francis Verlag GmbH, Kaufingerstraße 24, 80331 München, Germany